3000 B.C. Babylonians invent dust abacus	**1455** Johannes Gutenberg prints the 42-line Bible	**1876** Alexander Graham Bell invents the telephone
2600 B.C. Egyptians employ scribes for writing	**1469** Arches Papermill is founded in France	**1886** Ottmar Mergenthaler invents the Linotype machine
2200 B.C. Date of oldest existing document written on papyrus	**1495** A paper mill is established in England	**1888** William S. Burroughs patents a printing adding machine
1800 B.C. Babylonian mathematician develops algorithms to resolve numerical problems	**1500** The quadrant, an astronomical/ calculational tool, becomes popular in Europe	**1890** Dr. Herman Hollerith introduces an electromechanical punched-card data processing machine, which is used to compile information from the 1890 U.S. census
Egyptians produce the Book of the Dead	Approximately 35,000 books have been printed	
1500 B.C. Phoenicians develop alphabet	Europeans use the arithmetic symbols + and -	**1899** NEC incorporates in Japan as Nippon Electric Company Ltd.
1270 B.C. Syrian scholar compiles an encyclopedia	**1517** Martin Luther begins his fight against Roman Catholic church	**1900** Thomas Edison produces Enchanted Drawing, the first movie with animation
775 B.C. Greeks develop a phonetic alphabet, written from left to right	**1521** Cambridge University Press is founded	**1904** Germans transmit a photograph by wire
650 B.C. The first rolls of papyrus arrive in Greece	**1522** Luther prints the first edition of his translation of the New Testament	**1906** William DeForest invents the vacuum tube
600 B.C. Mediterranean cultures develop left-to-right writing and reading	**1545** Garamond designs his typeface	**1917** Aberdeen Proving Grounds begins computing ballistics tables
530 B.C. Greece builds its first library	**1609** The first regularly published newspaper appears in Germany	**1919** Eccles and Jordan invent the flip-flop circuit necessary for high-speed electronic calculating
500 B.C. Egyptians invent a bead and wire abacus	**1622** William Oughtred invents the slide rule	People can now dial their own telephone numbers
Chinese scholars use reeds dipped in pigment to write on bamboo	**1639** American colonies have their first printing press	Vladimir Zworykin invents the cathode ray tube (CRT)
200 B.C. The Wax Tablet Codex is made	**1642** Blaise Pascal invents an adding machine he calls the Pascaline	**1920** Sound is recorded electrically
196 B.C. The Rosetta Stone is cut	**1799** Nicholas Robert in France invents a paper-making machine	**1921** Radio Shack opens its first store in Boston
150 B.C. Work on Dead Sea Scrolls begins (to A.D.40)	**1800** Paper is made from vegetable fibers instead of rags	**1923** A picture, broken into dots, is sent by wire
39 B.C. Romans build the first public library	**1804** Joseph-Marie Jacquard invents a loom automated by punch cards to reproduce patterns	

3000 B. C.	**A.D. 1**	**1800**	**1900**

28 B.C. Romans establish Palatine and Octavian library	**1822** Charles Babbage begins work on the Difference Engine	**1924** New owners rename Hollerith's Tabulating Machine Company as International Business Machines Corporation (IBM)
A.D.195 Ts'ai Lun, a Chinese court official, invents paper	**1829** William Austin Burt patents the first typewriter	**1927** Technicolor is invented
391 Alexandrian Library is destroyed	**1831** Samuel F. B. Morse invents the telegraph	Bell Telephone Laboratories demonstrates television to the public
450 Chinese invent ink block printing	**1833** Charles Babbage completes portion of the Difference Engine	**1928** Walt Disney produces a Mickey Mouse Steamboat Willie cartoon with sound
600 Chinese print the first books	**1834** Babbage begins work on the Analytical Engine	IBM adopts an 80-column punched card that will be used for the next 50 years
751 Chinese captured in war manufacture first paper outside of China	**1839** Nicophoe Niepce followed by Henry Fox Talbot announces photography to the world	**1930** Vannevar Bush introduces his differential analyzer
800 Book of Kells is written	**1840** Lord Byron's daughter, Ada, Countess of Lovelace, suggests binary system to Babbage and writes programs for his Analytical Engine, becoming the world's first programmer	**1931** Konrad Zuse builds the Z1, the first calculator
People start to use the number zero		Commercial teletype service becomes available
868 Chinese block print the first dated book The Diamond Sutra	**1844** Samuel Morse sends the first telegraphic message from Washington to Baltimore	**1932** Walt Disney adopts a three-color Technicolor process for cartoons
950 Paper use spreads west to Spain	**1850** George Boole begins to develop Boolean Logic, the basis for computer logic	"Times" of London uses its new Times Roman typeface
1049 Pi Sheng fabricates movable clay type	**1865** American type designer Frederic W. Goudy is born	**1934** Associated Press starts wirephoto service
1116 Chinese make stitched books by sewing pages together	**1866** The first successful transatlantic cable is laid	Half of homes in the United States have radios
1151 First paper mill appears on Spanish mainland	**1868** Christopher Latham Sholes invents the first practical typewriter in the United States	
1298 Marco Polo describes use of paper money in China		
1338 French monks begin producing paper for holy texts		
1392 Koreans have a type foundry to produce bronze text characters		
1423 Europeans begin to use Chinese method of block printing		
1452 Printers use metal plates		

GRAPHIC DESIGN/PAGE LAYOUT   ILLUSTRATION   COMMUNICATION

1935	IBM introduces the electric typewriter
1936	Alan Turing publishes *On Computable Numbers,* setting the theoretical groundwork for computer principles
1937	Disney produces *Snow White,* the first feature-length cartoon
	George Stibitz of Bell Labs invents the electrical digital calculator
	Pulse Code Modulation points the way to digital transmission
1938	John Logie Baird demonstrates live TV in color
	William Hewlett and David Packard found Hewlett-Packard
1939	The New York World's Fair shows television to public
	Regular TV broadcasts begin
1940	TV broadcasts in color for the first time
1941	Konrad Zuse finishes Z3, a fully operational automatic calculating machine
	Turing, Newman, and Flowers complete work on Colossus, the first programmable computer, in England
	Microwaves are transmitted
1943	The University of Pennsylvania begins work on ENIAC
	Colossus breaks German code
1944	Harvard puts Mark I, first digital computer, in service

1953	IBM releases its 700 series of computers with tape storage systems and ships its first stored-program vacuum tube computer
1954	Union of Soviet Socialist Republics launches Sputnik
	Regular color TV broadcasts begin
	Transistor radios are sold
1955	Tests begin on fiber optics communication
	Music is recorded on tape in stereo
	SAGE air defense system first uses vector graphics through a light pen on radar screens
1956	Ampex builds a practical videotape recorder
1957	John Backus's team at IBM create FORTRAN programming
	First book to be entirely phototypeset is offset printed
	Stereo recording is introduced
	The first rotating drum scanners are developed
1958	Data moves over regular phone circuits
	Bell Labs develops the modem
	Jack Kilby of Texas Instruments makes the first integrated circuit
1959	Xerox introduces first commercial copy machine
	The microchip is invented

	The Howard Wise Gallery in New York City is first to exhibit computer graphics in the United States
	Ted Nelson coins the term hypertext
1966	Ivan Sutherland creates a headmounted display (the Sword of Damocles)
	Ralph Baer of Sanders Associates develops Odyssey, the first consumer computer game
	Robert Rauschenberg and Kluver found Experiments in Art and Technology (EAT)
	Linotron typesetters can produce 1,000 characters per second
	Xerox sells the Telecopier, a fax machine
1967	Movie studios sell prerecorded movies on videotape for home TV sets
	IBM develops the first floppy disk
1968	Jasis Reichardt exhibits Cybernetic Serendipity at the London Institute of Contemporary Art
	Intel Corporation begins to manufacture memory chips
	Evans & Sutherland founded to create custom hardware for digital mainframes; their Picture System includes a graphics tablet
	The RAM microchip reaches the market
1969	CompuServe establishes the first commercial online service
	AT&T Bell Laboratories develops UNIX

1940   1950   1960   1970

1945	Grace Hopper finds the first computer "bug" (a moth) in Harvard's Mark I
	ENIAC heralds the modern electronic computer
1947	Transistors invented at Bell Labs begin to replace vacuum tubes
	Holography is invented
1948	LP records are invented
	The United States establishes network TV
1949	MIT's Whirlwind is the first mainframe to display graphics with a monitor (vectorscope) and the first real-time computer
	Magnetic core computer memory is invented
1950	Typewriters use changeable typefaces
1951	University of Pennsylvania develops EDVAC, which is smaller and faster than ENIAC
	U.S. homes have 1.5 million TV sets
1952	Grace Hopper creates COBOL programming
	Univac I accurately predicts the U.S. presidential election on CBS
	EDVAC takes computer technology a giant leap forward

1960	IBM mass-produces transistors
	The laser is invented
	William Fetter, Boeing engineer, coins the term "computer graphics"
1961	IBM introduces the Selectric typewriter
	Fairchild releases the first commercial integrated circuit
	Edward Zajak at Bell Labs creates first computer-animated film
	Steve Russell at MIT creates the first video game Spacewars (to run on a DEC mainframe)
1962	H. Ross Perot starts Electronic Data Systems, a computer service bureau
	Ivan Sutherland creates Sketchpad (in which a pen draws on a cathode ray tube) as his MIT doctoral thesis
1963	ASCII is developed to standardize data exchange among computers
	Doug Englebart invents and patents first computer mouse
1964	M. R. Davis and T. D. Ellis develop a graphic tablet at Rand Corporation
	Videotape recorders for home use arrive from Japan
1965	Gordon Moore formulates "Moore's law"
	The Technische Hochschule sponsors the first exhibit of computer graphics at a gallery in Stuttgart, Germany

	U.S. Department of Defense sets up the ARPANet
	Gary Starkweather uses a laser with xerography to create a laser printer
1970	The daisywheel printer is introduced
	Bell Labs introduces UNIX
	Xerox establishes the Palo Alto Research Center (PARC); Alan Kay develops the Graphical User Interface (GUI) there
	The computer floppy disk is an instant success
	Pierre Bezier creates smooth curves
1971	Henri Gouraud creates Gouraud shading
	Wang releases the first word processor
	National Radio Institute releases the first computer kit
	Intel designs the first microprocessor, the Intel 4004
1972	Hand-held calculators make slide rules obsolete
	Liquid-crystal displays are introduced
	Kay introduces the Alto Computer
	Atari releases Pong
1973	IBM introduces the Winchester hard disk
	Xerox introduces its Parc Alto that uses a mouse and a GUI

Digital Media
An Introduction

Richard Lewis
Marist College

James Luciana
Marist College

Upper Saddle River, New Jersey 07458

Library of Congress Cataloging-in-Publication Data

Lewis, Richard (Richard L.),
  Digital media / Richard Lewis, James Luciana.—1st ed.
    p. cm.
  ISBN 0-13-087390-X
    1. Multimedia systems. 2. Digital media. I. Luciana, James. II. Title.

QA76.575 .L49 2002
006.7—dc21

2002033328

Senior Vice President/Publisher: Natalie E. Anderson
Executive Editor: Steven Elliot
Project Manager: Laura Burgess
Senior Media Project Manager: Joan Waxman
Director of Marketing: Sarah Loomis
Marketing Assistant: Barrie Reinhold
Managing Editor: John Roberts
Production Editor: Suzanne Grappi
Production Assistant: Joe DeProspero
Manufacturing Buyer: Diane Peirano
Associate Director, Manufacturing: Vincent Scelta
Design Manager: Maria Lange
Interior Design/Cover Design: Jill Little
Photo Researcher: Valerie Munei and Mary Reeg
Manager, Print Production: Christy Mahon
Composition/Full-Service Project Management: Carlisle Communications
Printer/Binder: R.R. Donnelly–Willard

Credits and acknowledgments borrowed from other sources and reproduced, with permission, in this textbook appear on appropriate page within text (or on page 351).

Microsoft® and Windows® are registered trademarks of the Microsoft Corporation in the U.S.A. and other countries. Screen shots and icons reprinted with permission from the Microsoft Corporation. This book is not sponsored or endorsed by or affiliated with the Microsoft Corporation.

Pearson Education LTD.
Pearson Education Singapore, Pte. Ltd
Pearson Education, Canada, Ltd
Pearson Education–Japan

Pearson Education Australia PTY, Limited
Pearson Education North Asia Ltd
Pearson Educación de Mexico, S.A. de C.V.
Pearson Education Malaysia, Pte. Ltd

10 9 8 7 6 5 4 3 2 1
0-13-087390-X

For Susan and Robbie,
with love, gratitude, and admiration

Richard Lewis

For my mother Lillian, my wife Kathryn,
and in memory of my father Dominick—
with love and appreciation

James Luciana

Contents

Preface

Today, as in the Renaissance, art and technology have joined together to inspire new visions. New ways of working—indeed, a new culture—for artists is being born with its own vocabulary, tales, history, and lifestyle. Our goal has been to write a book that captures the energy and enthusiasm that artists and designers, both young and old, feel as they explore digital media.

Digital media is an ever-widening and exciting field. Unfortunately, most of the books one finds next to the keyboards of artists and designers are guides to specific software, whose soul is more technical and mathematical than inspiring. After teaching digital media courses for more than ten years, we wrote *Digital Media: An Introduction* because we believe there is a need for a broader view, one that introduces students to a range of different media and approaches. This book is designed to support an introductory course, a gateway to more focused study in the various media that constitute this new field. Written with the perspectives of artists and designers in mind, it limits the jargon and focuses more on the possibilities inherent in the new media. We hope it will be useful for students just entering the field, as well as the many self-taught artists who want to broaden their experience beyond the one or two digital media programs they know well.

All artists, designers, and teachers are painfully aware that software changes quickly and hardware is always improving. Just about any guide in print is outdated the day it is published. The challenge for teachers (and authors) is to find subjects that remain important in the midst of constant change. In this book, we have focused on the constants that face any artist, designer, and student. The ultimate goal remains, no matter what the media, to create successful and sophisticated works of art and design.

Therefore, students need to be introduced to more than new tools and special techniques. As exciting as these tools are, there is more than software code behind each of them. In the digital realm, a new medium cannot be truly understood without understanding the concepts and history of the traditional medium that it mirrors. In addition, students should learn the historical background of the new medium itself–how it has evolved over time. In our book, whenever possible, we connect the new ways of working to the concepts behind their traditional forerunners.

In short, beyond the keyboard shortcuts for a layer mask, there is a great deal to know—not the least of which are the exciting possibilities in every new tool. Readers will find clear, coherent descriptions of common tools and techniques are in every chapter, along with the theories behind their use.

In the last decade, the individual digital media have begun to differentiate themselves, and the organization of *Digital Media: An Introduction* reflects this. For example, earlier books looked at the creation of bitmapped images as a distinct category. Today, while both digital painting and image editing may result in bitmapped images, each media has its own distinct approach to the creation of images and deserves to be looked at separately. Each medium has also generated new and exciting career paths for artists. These are discussed in the final chapter, which focuses on the careers of active practitioners. In addition, special boxes throughout the text include biographies of leading figures in digital media, notable events, as well as ones devoted to clarifying technical issues for each medium with charts and clear explanations.

Finally, we hope *Digital Media: An Introduction* will be a book that readers enjoy learning from and teachers enjoy teaching with. It is meant to open the doors to a new and exciting realm for artists and designers, one with extraordinary potential. It is not meant to provide mastery in any one medium, but to provide a sense of the whole range of new media and how they interrelate. Our goal has been to write a clear text, organized in a logical fashion, with a sense of history that helps bridge the gap between the technical manual and artistic inspiration. We hope that students, designers, and artists will see that we are truly at the beginning of a new era in art. Whatever is ahead will be part of a long, marvelous tradition that began thousands of years ago with carving soft stone into rounded forms and scraping charcoal onto the walls of caves. Just as stone and charcoal were for the inhabitants of caves, and oil paint and chalk were for the artists of the Renaissance, the digital media are the media of our age.

Acknowledgments

This book is the product of years of teaching and working in digital media. Anyone who works in this field knows that no one can do this alone. Many individuals have helped support us and contributed to our understanding of this ever-challenging new realm for artists and designers. This book could never have been written without the assistance of many friends, family members, colleagues, and students, only some of whom are listed below.

We have had the pleasure of working with two teams of talented individuals at Prentice Hall during the writing of this book. We want to express our gratitude to the original team of Acquisitions Editor, Elizabeth Sugg, and Development Editor, Judy Casillo, whose initial enthusiasm was essential to the development of this book. We are, of course, especially appreciative of the team that helped make this project a reality. We want to thank the following for their diligence, thoroughness, and support: our ever-patient and professional Executive Editor Steven Elliot; Managing Editor, John Roberts; Production Editor, Suzanne Grappi; and Designer, Jill Little. We also want to thank our resourceful picture researchers Val Munei and Mary Reeg, who we provided with many difficult challenges. In addition, we want to acknowledge the team put together by Carlisle Communications, especially the always pleasant and conscientious Project Editor, Ann Imhof (and her predecessor Amy Hackett), Norine Strang, Liz Ney, Paula Keck, Craig White, Michelle Sutton-Kerchner, and Jessica Stasinos.

During the development of the manuscript, many readers offered perceptive comments that helped a great deal. We especially appreciate the contribution of the following reviewers: David J. Bennett, Columbus College of Art and Design; Elaine Cunfer, Kutztown University; Chad Dresbach, Winthrop University; Danny Gross, The Art Institute of Los Angeles—Orange County; Brad Justice, Carroll Community College; Jill West Tolbert, Bessemer State Technical College; and Don Shields, Z-Animation.

We are honored by the talented artists who were willing to contribute examples of their work to illustrate this book. In particular, we would like to thank the following artists whose work is featured in the final chapter: Peter Baustaedter, Simon Bosch, John Crane, Robert Lazzarini, Boyd Ostroff, and Maggie Taylor.

The following colleagues at Marist College have helped support our work over the years and deserve our thanks: Artin Arslanian, Justin Butwell, Tom Daly, Donise English, Kamran Khan, Guy Lometti, Roy Merolli, Anita Morrison, Dennis Murray, John Ritschdorff, and Elaine Shelah. As the basis for this book is new technologies, we must thank the very patient and diligent information technology and media support staffs at Marist College, especially Christine Mulvey, Jeanne DeLongis, Dave Brangaitis, JoAnn DePue, Rich Recchia, Jesse Mercado, Bob Smith, Ian Becker, Joan Syler, Joey Wall, Lee Wallis, and their many student workers.

Finally, we must thank our students whose excitement, enthusiasm, and general good humor helped us go on during days when data became corrupted, monitors died, and hard drives crashed. The love for these new media of Nicholas Aronne, Mike Bagnato, Nicholas Baisch, Nick Balestrino, Matt Braun, Andy Buchanan, Matthew Cassella, Dan Cerasale, Linda Cioce, Stefanie DiCarrado, Bridget Garrity, Craig Giattino, Brian Goldsborough, Ben Hecht, Tricia Hohenstein, Jason Hutton, James Johnson, Ron Jones, Kathleen Kelly, Michael Milano, Caitlin O'Hare, Colleen Mulrenan, Nick Ross, Greg Salamone, Raymond Simpson, Jeremy Smith, and many more students like them continues to be an inspiration for us.

Richard Lewis
James Luciana

PART 1

Introduction

CHAPTER

1

The Artist
and the Computer

Introduction

We are at the beginning of a new age for art. While only a few generations of artists have been given the opportunity to pioneer a new medium, this generation has been blessed with many. The arrival of digital media, the art forms created with computer technology, offers a wealth of new possibilities which are just beginning to impact the art world.

New Media, New Freedom, New Realms

For many artists and designers, entering the world of digital art and design is liberating and exciting. Their biggest challenge is choosing which of the digital media to investigate first (see Figure 1.1). From still images to animations to websites to immersive environments, the range of forms and experiences appears limitless. The tools for digital artists are unlike any before them. Rather than starting a collage by cutting out a picture from a magazine, they can simply copy an element with a click of a mouse and then paste hundreds of them into a pattern. Instead of erasing and redrawing a line, they can reshape it with a drag of the mouse. The color of a structure can be changed instantly and the palette of choices runs into the millions

2

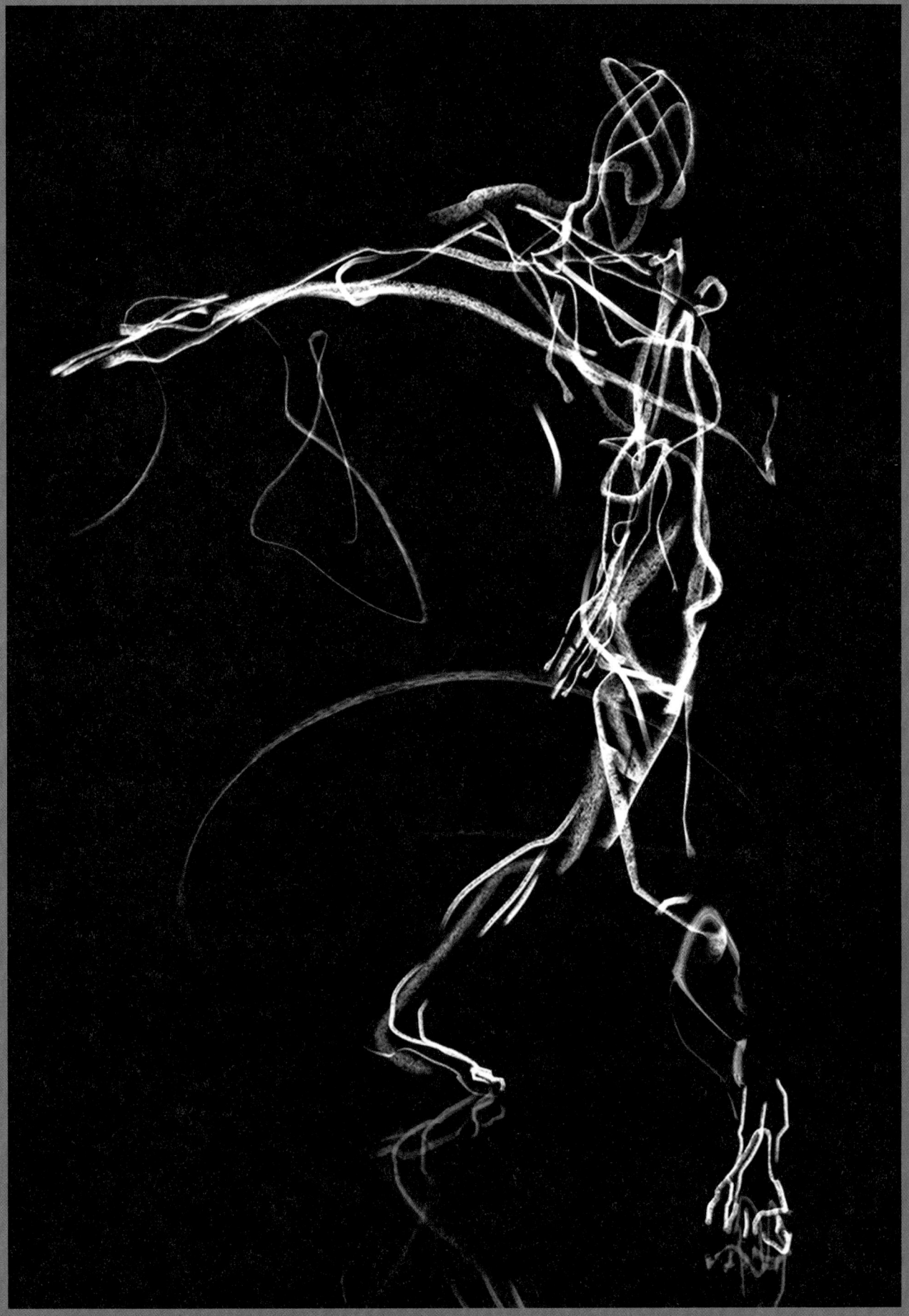

(see Figure 1.2). Unlike an oil painter anxious, yet hesitating, in front of a canvas before making the next stroke, the digital painter "works with a net." When you can undo any experimental action instantly, disaster simply doesn't lurk in quite the same way. Even the foundation of the art world—its gallery and museum system—can be bypassed entirely when artists choose to distribute their art electronically around the globe on the World Wide Web.

Not surprisingly, the new media have not been greeted with universal enthusiasm by the art world. For some artists and critics, it is difficult to imagine that what has been created so far with this new technology could be called art. They feel there is something mechanical—too clean and antiseptic, too distant and nontactile—about art made on a computer. They suggest that the programs for digital art control what is made more than the artist does.

Artists and Technology in the Past

Ours is not the first era where artists have embraced new media and technologies in the face of resistance. It is worth remembering that all of what is currently called traditional once did not exist. Many of the artist's materials we take for granted are surprisingly recent. Even the most basic of art's tools had to be invented or discovered. On some morning in prehistory, *someone* had to reach into the cooling embers of a fire and make some marks on a cave's wall with a piece of charcoal for the first time. (Human nature being what it is and has always been, this new method was probably dismissed by traditionalists from the "stick traced in dirt" school of art.)

A discovery for which we have a bit more documentation was that of graphite in the Cumberland mines of England in the late sixteenth century. This material would transform the nature of drawing and lead to the replacement of metalpoint as the most important artist's drawing tool. Just like today, a new medium—in this case, the pencil—offered artists new freedom. Lines were now easily erased. They could vary in thickness from light scratches to bold, dramatic gestures based on the tilt of a hand and the pressure brought to bear. Two centuries later, the importance of pencils to artists was illustrated during a war between France and England. Because graphite shipments to France had been halted by the war, army sentries had to be posted around the Cumberland mines because of rumors of a planned raid by desperate French draughtsmen.

Time after time, a technology or new medium emerged that sent art in new directions. For centuries, oil paint was considered unsuitable for art because of its slow drying time. It took the vision of artists like da Vinci to see that this once-despised paint's "worst" characteristic was actually its best.

The success of a painting like his *Mona Lisa* is based on being able to rework a picture in oils for hours at a time. Layers could be added weeks, months, and even years later.

Many other technical innovations have helped change the history of art. The arrival of the printing press ushered in the first age of mechanical reproduction. The invention of metal tubes to hold paint liberated artists from having to mix their paint in studios. This allowed them to go outdoors and paint directly from nature—leading to the *plein-air* techniques of the French Impressionists like Claude Monet (whose work was called "an assault on beauty" and "wretched daubs in oil" by critics). The invention of brighter and more intense pigments led to the wildly colorful pictures of the Fauves and the Expressionists in the early twentieth century.

The assimilation of new materials into art is not only a Western phenomenon. The invention of paper in China around A.D. 100 was a catalyst for the lyrical brush-and-ink painting there and later in Japan. By the 1200s, skill in the "arts of the brush"—calligraphy and brush painting—marked one's membership in the cultivated, elite class. Even emperors labored to become experts in the application of ink to paper.

When European colonists brought nails, screws, and machine parts to the African Kongo lands, artists and *nganga* (ritual leaders) stuck them, along with bits of mirrors and glass, in ceremonial figure sculptures designed to hold magical ingredients (see Figure 1.3). Far from rejecting these alien materials, African artists believed it was the act of hammering these bits and pieces into the wood sculptures that activated their power.

■ **Figure 1.3**
Kongo ceremonial figure.

In the twentieth century, artists discovered industrial paint made of plastic polymers in the 1950s and rechristened it *acrylic* paint. Fast drying, water-soluble, cheap, and available in buckets, it became a favorite material of abstract expressionists like Jackson Pollock and Helen Frankenthaler. Pollock loved to drip long lines of airplane paint with a stick across his revolutionary paintings. Frankenthaler was fascinated by how when diluted and applied to raw canvas acrylic paint would soak into cloth and run—a technique now known as "soak and stain" (see Figure 1.4).

Probably the closest analogy to the arrival and reception of the digital media in our time is the invention of photography in the nineteenth century, which would eventually change how images were perceived and even how time and history were recorded. It also met with great resistance in the art world and was not generally accepted as a medium for fine art until well into the twentieth century (see Box 1.1).

Like the photographer in a darkroom, the digital artist works in an environment unlike the studios of the painter and sculptor. The Renaissance workshops and the Impressionist's dusty, crowded attic garrets have been exchanged for rooms with desks, metal cases, and cables, serenaded with the hum of machinery and MP3 files. Replacing the artist's finely ground pigments and secret recipes for modeling paste are now special techniques for using software and a series of keystrokes. Yet, the digital studio remains a magical space. Within the virtual world seen through a monitor, new visions emerge.

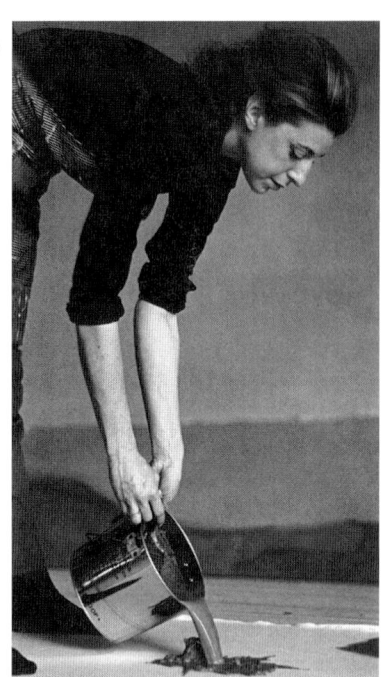

■ **Figure 1.4**
Helen Frankenthaler pouring paint onto canvas.

BOX 1.1

The art world versus photography

Figure 1.5
Mid-nineteenth century portrait photograph by the Matthew Brady studio. The apparently angry subject is George Peter Alexander Healey, a prominent portrait painter.

Like the impact of digital media today, the invention of photography (see Figure 1.5) in the 1800s was a troubling development to the art world of its time. While the new technology didn't make every artist change his or her occupation, it was a new force needed to be contended with. The detailed realism that dominated Western art at the time clearly had an upstart competitor.

Many of the foremost artists, like the French Impressionist Edgar Degas, the American Realist Thomas Eakins, and the French Romantic Eugene Delacroix, were excited by this new technology, taking their own photographs and using them like sketches as references for their pictures. For other artists and critics, however, the new medium was perceived as a threat. Some painters, particularly portraitists, saw it as endangering their way to earn a living. For engravers and lithographers whose income depended on reproducing art works, it was a realistic fear. But the most vehement voices came from art critics who felt obliged to defend art against this mechanical threat.

In an attitude we would find familiar today, photography's "purely scientific" approach to image-making was said to have "ruined" the fine arts. Rather than promoting progress, it was seen as contributing to its "degener-

acy." The great French poet and critic Charles Baudelaire, normally a voice for the avant-garde, wrote, ". . . the disaster is verifiable . . . [photography is] the refuge of every would-be painter, every painter too ill-endowed or too lazy to complete his studies."

Yet almost from its inception the vision of the photographer changed our perspective of the world (see Figure 1.6). Because of the camera's ability to record an instant, we gained a new understanding of movement. Composition changed forever after artists saw the way photographs crop off subjects arbitrarily at the edges of the frame. The beauty of the normally unnoticed alleyway or torn poster, the view from high above a city, the once undocumented atrocities of war and other tragedies have all affected what might be the proper subjects for artists. Photomontage, the combination of photographic elements, sometimes with more traditional art materials, gave artists a new way to play with reality and a better way to picture the rapidly changing nature of modern life.

It was decades before photography was accepted as a unique fine art medium. It may be the same for digital media. As in photography's early days, however, we can expect that the effects on art are already being felt, if not completely understood. ■

Figure 1.6
A new way of looking at the world: Los Angeles in the nineteenth century from a balloon.

The Digital Studio

In reality, the digital studios of most artists and designers are rarely as antiseptic as one might imagine. Just as in the past, their walls are covered with sketches of ideas and reproductions of works they admire. In addition to postcards and photos, they might have their personal collection of artist websites and images as "wallpaper" on their computer's desktop. Still prized are the old sculptor's books of anatomy and Eadweard Muybridge's photographs of figures in motion, particularly for reference by 3-D animators. However, now the bookcases and objects that have always lined the walls of artists and designers have been joined by the clutter of printouts, assorted disks, and CD cases (see Figure 1.7).

Still, while many consistent elements remain between the studios of the digital artist or designer and their traditional counterparts in the past, their tools *are* different.

Hardware

What is needed to make digital art and graphics? At first glance, the desk of today's studio appears to be outfitted in a manner similar to a clerk in an accounting office. On it, you'll see the basic elements of a typical computer: a box or case with slots and buttons (too often, despite the influence of computers like the iMac, an innocuous beige), a monitor (usually separate but occasionally built into the box), a keyboard, a mouse, speakers, and a printer. Looking at the back of the box is even less impressive—it's just a gaggle of wires plugged into connectors. It is hard to imagine that these are the instruments of visual magic.

What separates a business computer from one designed for graphics is the quality of the components. Understanding these elements, explained in detail in Chapters 3 and 4, is critical for any digital artist. (These chapters also will help unravel the mysteries of computer advertisements.)

The first apparent difference is the size of the monitor, the *display* or gallery wall for digital imagery. Digital artists and designers prefer to have large *high-resolution* monitors, ones that can display fine detail and millions of colors on as big a screen as possible. Some artists use two monitors at once: one just for tool bars and windows, the other devoted to displaying a large, crisp image.

The majority of the most critical differences, however, can only be seen when you look inside the box (see Figure 1.8) at what we might call the digital easel. The foundation of every computer is the *motherboard,* a long, flat card that looks much like all electronic boards but is the center of all internal communication in the computer. At its heart is the *central processing unit* or *CPU*—the true computer, the brain of the whole system. Digital art and design makes intense computational demands and

Figure 1.7

Artists at work: a nineteenth century artist's studio and a twenty-first century animator's workplace.

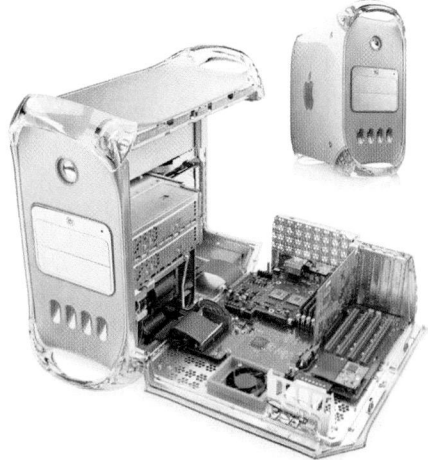

Figure 1.8

More than meets the eye: outside and inside a computer system.

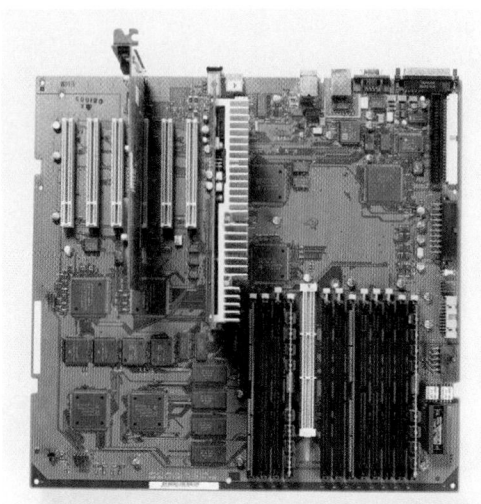

Figure 1.9
A standard motherboard.

requires the most powerful and fast processor an artist or designer can afford. Processing speed is measured in megahertz (MHz) or gigahertz (GHz); thus, a computer will be advertised having a "PowerPC G5 Processor at 2GHz" or "Intel Pentium 4 at 3.0GHz." A CPU is a miracle of miniaturization, not more than an inch wide, a few millimeters high, and containing millions of transistors (see Figure 1.9).

Also attached to the motherboard are thin strips of *random-access memory*, or *RAM*. These memory chips temporarily store programs and information while the computer is running. While this may sound inconsequential, the amount of RAM has a huge impact on how fast your computer will operate. Information bursts quickly while in RAM and slows down when the storage capacity of the RAM is exhausted. For procedures that require complex processing, like applying filters to images or rendering animations, a click of the mouse on a computer without enough RAM can lead to a screen slowly remaking (or *redrawing*) an image, stalling for minutes or hours, or, even worse, crashing. Digital artists and designers will buy as much RAM as they can to avoid these troubles and work smoothly in "real-time."

Inside the computer's case, you'll also see wide, flat cables sprouting off the motherboard and connecting it to other cards and components. One of these is the *video card,* which transforms the digital information generated by the processor into a format that can be displayed on your monitor. Today's high-end video or *graphics cards* have their own memory and processors to speed up these calculations and share the workload of image processing. Graphic artists and animators require the most memory and fastest processing video cards available.

Sound cards function similarly, converting input from the computer itself or from CDs into the analog format understood by speakers. They can also operate in reverse and digitize input (from a microphone, for example) so the sound can be edited in the computer. If your work will involve sound recording and editing, the quality of a sound card is very important.

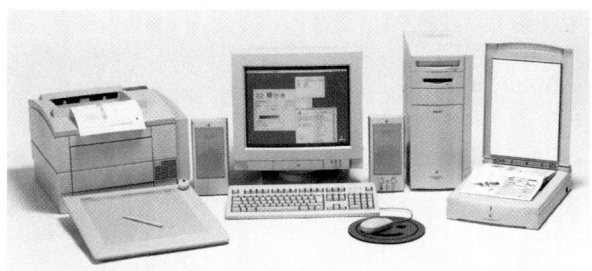

Figure 1.10
A computer system with four input devices: keyboard, mouse, digitizing tablet, and flatbed scanner.

Input, the information sent into the computer, is typically accomplished through the keyboard and mouse (see Figure 1.10). While the invention of the mouse was a big step forward in making the computer an artist's tool (see Chapter 5), many artists and designers demand a subtler tool to create their work. A flat pad with a pen, called a *digitizing tablet,* allows you to draw freely and directly into the computer (see Chapter 8 for a more comprehensive explanation). The sensors on the tablet are sensitive to the slightest movements of the pen (including its tilt and downward pressure).

Scanners are designed to *digitize*, convert to a form that a computer can understand, all kinds of materials used by artists. The most common is the *flatbed scanner,* discussed in Chapter 7, which digitizes flat images, like photographs, prints, and drawings. Slide scanners are used to digitize transparent images. *Digital cameras* are another way to introduce digital images into the computer. Along with digital video cameras, they can be easily connected via cables, and their images and sounds downloaded for editing.

Your carefully edited sounds, images, or other digital information will disappear forever when the computer is turned off unless you store them.

Portable media, like floppy disks, Zip disks, or CD-ROMs, have continued to evolve and increase in storage capacity since the first personal computers were manufactured. The disc drives where you insert these media can be *internal* (built into the case) or *external* (attached by cables to the back of it).

Hard disks are the computer's permanent storage. Once measured in megabytes (MB) or a million bytes of data, today's hard drives have grown by an order of ten into gigabytes (GB). In an age of ever-increasing complexity in software, the growth of computer storage has been both fortunate and essential since the hard drive stores all of a computer's programs.

Software

The best hardware in the world is useless without the computer's programs or *software*. A huge monitor and a computer loaded with RAM, the most powerful processor, and the finest video card cannot display one marvelous graphic without the programs to do so. Software is what makes a computer work, and each kind of software determines what you can do with a computer. The most important software is the *operating system*. This is what first appears when you turn on a computer. It runs the programs and controls all the components of a computer (see Chapter 3 for a full discussion). For PC users, the operating system will be either Microsoft® Windows or Linux. Macintosh owners use one of the versions of Mac OS.

Operating systems have become increasingly easier to work with since the first personal computers. Important developments in their history, like the *graphical user interface* (GUI), are discussed in Chapters 2 and 5. Programs must be written to work with particular operating systems in order to function. For example, a multimedia game written for a Macintosh computer will not work in a PC that runs Windows.

Originally, the domain of the computer scientist, the new field of digital media, really began when graphics programs became both easier to work with and more sophisticated (see Chapter 5 for the evolution of digital art software). Over the last twenty years, computer graphics programs have differentiated themselves into several types. Today, the software they regularly work with can loosely categorize the specialties of digital artists and designers. While most artists use a collection of software, usually one or two programs will be their primary tools and the focus of their imaginations.

For example, *digital layout and design* software (once known as "desktop publishing") is the primary tool for graphic designers. This graphics software transformed an industry, replacing the old methods of cut and paste for laying out text and pictures in ads, magazines, newspapers, and books. Chapter 6 focuses on how designers accomplish their work with this kind of software (see Figure 1.11).

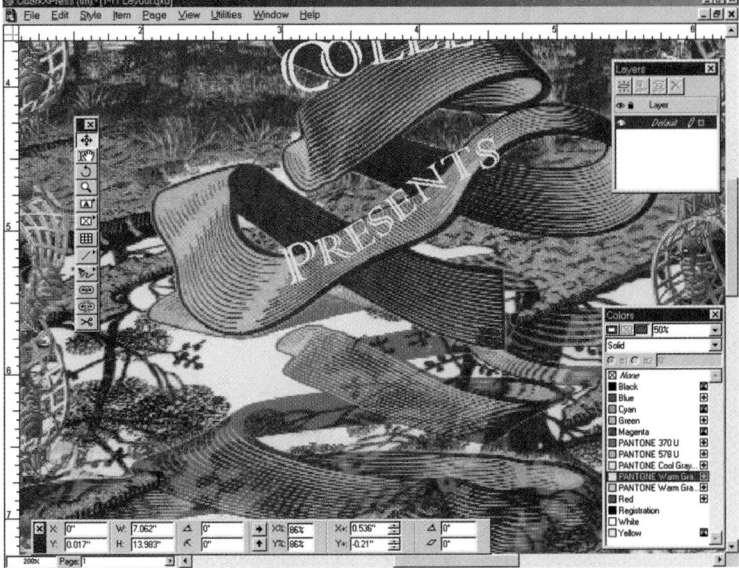

■ **Figure 1.11**

Digital layout and design software has transformed the graphic design profession.

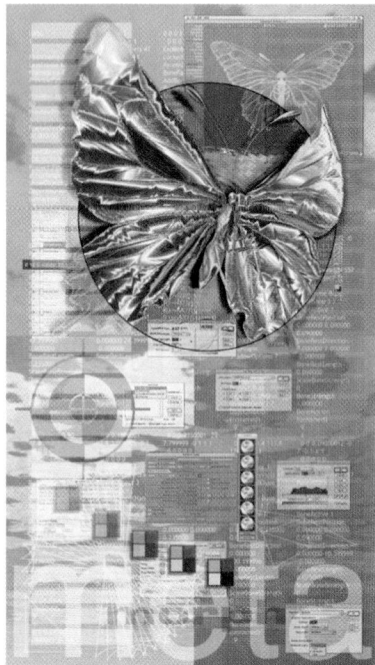

■ **Figure 1.12**

Image editing software has expanded the range of collage techniques.

■ **Figure 1.13**

A digital painting by Chet Phillips, from his series "The Life of An Imaginary Friend."

Photographers use *image-editing* programs that create the computer equivalents of many darkroom techniques, such as dodging and burning. The traditional filters a photographer screws onto a lens for special effects, like warming up the colors of a scene, can now be added digitally, with more flexibility and control. More importantly, image-editing programs have expanded the photographer's tools far beyond traditional ones. Many effects and techniques that never existed before have become the staples of the new field of digital photography (see Figure 1.12). The digital darkroom is the subject of Chapter 7.

Digital painting software was consciously designed to recreate a traditional painter's tools and palette and, therefore, are also known as *natural media* programs. The digital painter can build up surfaces with virtual layers of oil paint, mix colors by dragging a palette knife across the surface, or combine media that normally couldn't be—for instance, mixing markers, oil paint, and watercolors (see Figure 1.13). Digital painting is the subject of Chapter 8.

Illustration software, a unique creation of the computer age, was the first of the digital art software. Its approach to line and shape creation is mathematical and precise, closer to what was once known as mechanical or technical drawing. Yet, in the hands of creative graphic artists, it has become a tool for lively, imaginative illustrations (see Figure 1.14). Chapter 9 focuses on the special flexibility and clarity of illustration programs.

Animation has experienced a rebirth with the new digital techniques (see Figure 1.15). The old methods of *cel animation*, the time-consuming work of drawing every individual frame, has been streamlined by 2-D animation software (see Chapter 10). Artists can create remarkable animations or cartoons in the manner of Chuck Jones on their desktop. Most software packages even include methods of integrating and *synching* soundtracks to the animated action.

The tedious techniques of clay animation, once the territory of teams of animators, have been transformed into the uniquely digital techniques of 3-D modeling and animation (see Figure 1.16). Because of the

■ **Figure 1.14**

A digital illustration by John Kanzler.

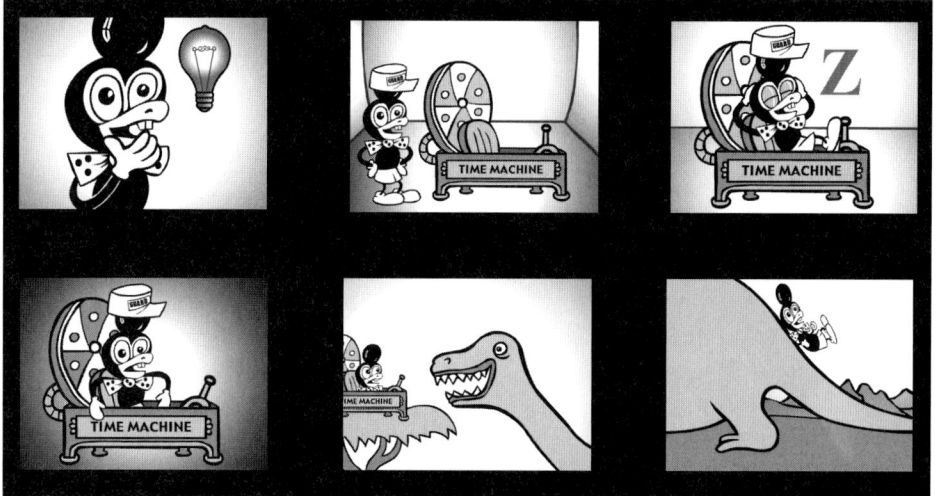

Figure 1.15
Scenes from a popular web animation series by Xeth Feinberg.

Figure 1.16
3-D modeling and animation software makes it possible to construct and populate imaginary worlds.

labors of 3-D modelers and animators, game players and moviegoers around the world have traveled to imaginary realms populated by strange, dreamlike creatures (see Box 1.2). This fascinating but challenging new medium is the subject of Chapter 11.

BOX 1.2

Jim Ludtke's
Freak Show

Like many artists working in digital media, Jim Ludtke began his career as a traditional artist. In the early 1980s, after attending the Chicago Academy of Fine Art, he was doing graphic design, airbrush illustration, and animation. The arrival of the Macintosh in 1984 introduced him to digital art and he has been hooked ever since.

His collaboration with the San Francisco artist band *The Residents* has resulted in two landmark, award-winning CD-ROMs: *Freak Show* and *Bad*

Day on the Midway. While they seem at first like games, they are really bizarre explorations of carnival life, filled with the surreal and seedy characters that Ludtke has become known for. He utilizes multimedia and digital tools to provide strange, unpredictable experiences. For example, as you "click around" and slip behind the sideshow tent in *Freak Show*, you discover the private wagons of the carnival people. Inside, you might find someone sleeping off an alcoholic binge.

(Continued on next page)

BOX 1.2

Jim Ludtke's
Freak Show
continued

As you wander silently, you can look through their private items and learn more about the characters (like Wanda the Worm Woman and Harry the Head) and their generally disreputable past.

Despite the darkness of his imagination, Ludtke has also been very successful in mainstream illustration, publishing, advertising, and television. His computer illustrations have been published in the *New York Times,* *MacUser, PC World,* and *Wired* magazine and as a cover for one of R. L. Stine's horror books for children (see Figure 1.17). His longer animations have been featured on Nickelodeon and ABC, and he has also created animated spots for Nintendo, Nabisco, and MTV. He joined the ranks of well-known, successful artists when he designed "Absolut Ludtke" for a vodka distiller's ad.

■ **Figure 1.17**

Jim Ludtke's cover illustration for R. L. Stine's *Curse of the Blue Monkey.*

Ludtke uses many types of digital media software, the specific combinations depending on the needs of his projects. For a recent website on mummies for the Discovery Channel, he worked with image-editing, video effects, 3-D modeling, and animation software. All contributed to a rich, interactive website designed for broadband Web users (see Figure 1.18). Ludtke created a visit to an Egyptian tomb, whose dark, dusty passages you can explore with a flashlight. Mysterious sweet music plays in the background as you go from chamber to chamber. Once you discover the sarcophagus, it begins to open before your eyes. Step by step, the mummy is revealed. After the wraps around the body are finally unraveled, the process begins in reverse and you learn the rituals of mummification. Finally, you can tour the tomb and learn the purpose for the many artifacts placed in the tomb—essential items for the final journey.

As diverse as Ludtke's projects have been, the themes of "journey" and "discovery" remain constants— both his work and his life. For those just beginning their own exploration of digital media, it would be hard to find a better model for a career. ■

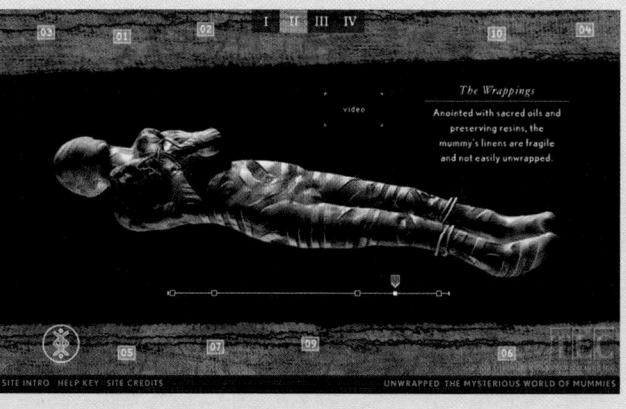

■ **Figure 1.18**

A Web page from Jim Ludtke's "Unwrapped: The Mysterious World of Mummies."

The arrival of the World Wide Web has opened up even more possibilities for the digital artist and designer. It has become a global gallery for the many creations of digital illustrators, photographers, painters, and animators. However, designing Web pages (see Chapter 13) is an art in itself, requiring both the skills of the traditional designer, along with an understanding of how

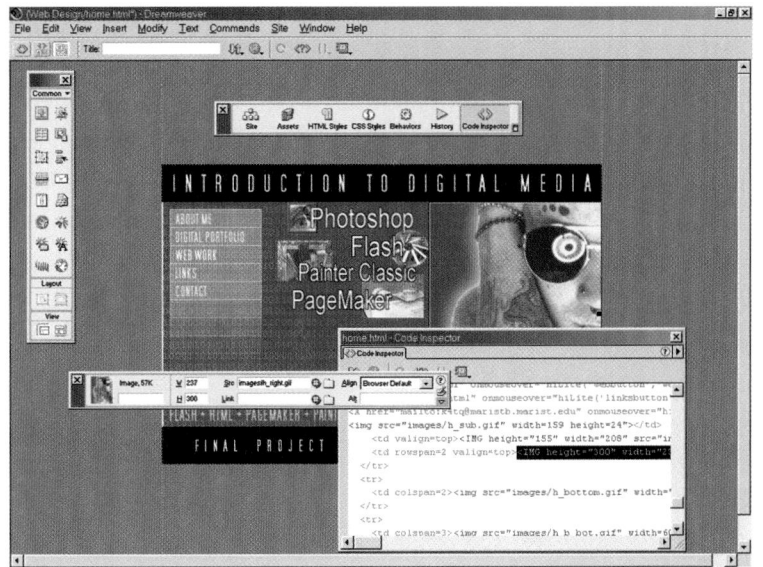

■ **Figure 1.19**
With Web design software, artists and designers can make the Web their world-wide gallery.

people interact with this new medium. Specialized programs for Web designers have moved the field from the realm of pure programming to one for the visually sophisticated graphic designer (see Figure 1.19). A truly successful series of Web pages, however, is rarely the work of one person. Like all multimedia, it requires the efforts of a team (see Box 1.3).

BOX 1.3

The multimedia team

The process of creating interactive media requires a variety of very different skills. Whether the product will be a CD-ROM encyclopedia, a game, or a Web page, a multimedia team typically includes a minimum of three to five people. Larger teams have the general tasks broken up into subgroups with individual leaders. While the titles for these roles may change from project to project, the roles do not.

The Project Leader's role is similar to a movie director or a producer. Clear goals and tasks for the team must be outlined. An understanding of each member's strengths and weaknesses, even his or her way of thinking, is very important. A cooperative and supportive environment must be established so each member will be encouraged to think creatively. However, the Project

Leader also is responsible for ensuring that the final product fulfills the original vision and goals. Usually, the leader's greatest challenge is to orchestrate the team's activities so that the project is completed on time and within the budget.

The Technical Specialist will have a computer science or information technology background. Whatever programming needs to be done is his or her responsibility. This specialist is also responsible for developing the technical plan. The Technical Specialist must understand the ins and outs of the team's equipment and software, as well as the target audience's (which may include many different computing environments). In the case of a multimedia CD, that means managing the

(Continued on next page)

BOX 1.3

authoring software that integrates the graphics, text, animations, video, and sounds (see Figure 1.20).

The Technical Writer will develop the concept and the scripts for the multimedia production. The writer designs the structure for the flow of information and makes sure it is logical and easily understood. Clear writing and an understanding of the overall vision is critical for this team member.

The Artist/Designer (sometimes called the Creative or Artistic Director) is responsible for anything visual, from individual graphic elements to the style or "look" of the whole project. He or she has to understand what the audience needs to see to enjoy and easily utilize all aspects of the production. In a large company, the Artist/Designer will either oversee a staff or hire freelance photographers, illustrators, and animators to create specific elements for the multimedia. In a small company, however, all these tasks may fall to one person.

Depending on the project, other specialists may be needed, such as a Video Producer. This team member will have the technical knowledge of video and editing. Beyond producing all the video elements, he or she may also be arranging locations, hiring and directing actors, and setting up lighting and props. A Sound Producer will handle all audio recording (like narration) and editing, as well as select the background music and sound effects. A specialist in interface design may be utilized to focus on the logic of the overall design. For example, will the links make sense to a new user?

In the end, the Project Leader must make sure that all the parts integrate. He or she must decide if that Neo-Pop look being pushed by the designer is really right for a demonstration on how a nurse should draw blood. As wonderful as it is, will Beethoven's Ninth Symphony be the right soundtrack for a playground scene in a children's game?

From brainstorming to creating the blueprint, to production, to testing the prototype and the final release, multimedia production is a challenging process for everyone involved. Each member will need to be sensitive to the importance of the contributions of others. Artists who are used to working alone in a studio, where every part is theirs to control, may not find the team environment to their liking. Many compromises have to be made for the sake of the whole project. Nonetheless, after the finish of a successful production, there can be great satisfaction in sharing the excitement with your teammates. That's a pleasure that no solitary artist gets to enjoy. ■

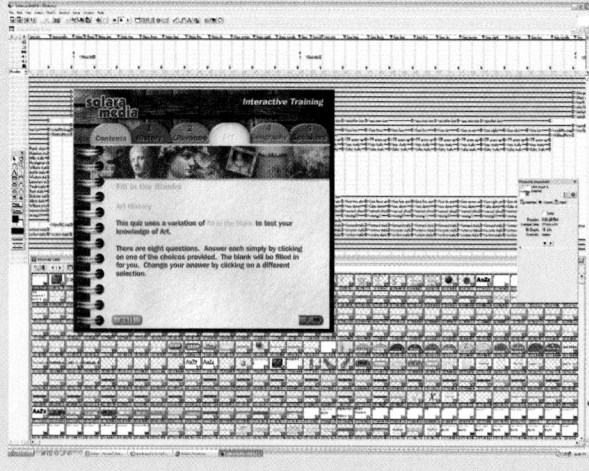

■ **Figure 1.20**
Authoring software is used to weave together interactive CD-ROMs.

CONCLUSION

Whether you will some day be a member of a multimedia team, an animation studio, an advertising firm, or have a career as an independent artist, today you are walking through the first doorway to a whole new way of making art and design. This book will provide you with a solid background for your learning; it will help you understand the potential and strengths of the digital media, and will amplify what you are experiencing as you explore them. We hope you will return to this book time and time again. Some sections may make more sense after you have been working in a particular medium for a while. In every one of the digital media there are years of learning ahead (if not a lifetime or two). The hardware and software will continue to change, as will your skills, interests, and desires.

For some, this exploration of digital media will only reinforce their conviction that they are still most excited about the traditional media. That will not mean that this investigation of new technologies was a waste of time. It is admirable and sensible to try to understand each of the media available to artists and designers, whether one is just beginning or in the midst of a lifetime in the visual arts. And who can tell what change in perception will result from an exploration, no matter how short?

Even if you know you were meant to be a digital artist or designer, don't neglect traditional skills such as drawing and sculpting. Mastering them will only enhance the work you can do on a computer (and lack of such skills is one of the most serious limitations of many young artists, according to digital professionals).

In any case, remember that being a beginner is sometimes an advantage. Beginners try things more experienced practitioners never would, and, therefore, make unexpected discoveries. No baby reads a manual before he or she takes those first steps. Expect many trips and falls. Don't fear them, learn from them. As much as we believe this book will enhance your learning and understanding of the digital media, the most important thing is to begin. There is so much to learn.

Projects: Introducing Digital Media

1 *Using your favorite search engine, look for digital artists who have online portfolios. List the different kinds of work and approaches you have found.*

2 *Using your favorite search engine, look for companies that specialize in design. List the different kinds of projects that digital designers are hired to do.*

3 *Divide a page into three columns. In the first column, make a list of the traditional media that artists and designers have used in the past. In the second column, see if you can find the digital media most comparable to the traditional one. In the third column, list the most common digital media software these artists and designers use to work in these new media. For example, if the traditional media is* photography, *then* image-editing *might be the digital equivalent, and* Adobe PhotoShop *the most common software package.*

PART 2
The Hardware

CHAPTER

2

The History of Computers:
From Calculators to Multimedia

Introduction

Understanding the past has always strengthened the work of artists and designers. Behind all artwork and every design, no matter how new and innovative, are the efforts of past artists. The digital media are fairly unique in the arts because they are not only affected by the practices of artists from past centuries but also the labors of scientists and mathematicians dating back thousands of years. This chapter will help you understand how the primary tool of digital media, the computer, was first conceived, its birth process, and its evolution. The history of computers is much longer than you might expect, as it goes back to nomadic traders roaming the desert.

Important First Steps

The word *computer* has been a part of the English language since the seventeenth century. However, until fairly recently it referred not to a machine but to a clerk in an office who made computations. The word would not get its modern meaning until the twentieth century. Like all technological innovations, today's computer is built on past achievements, most going back no further

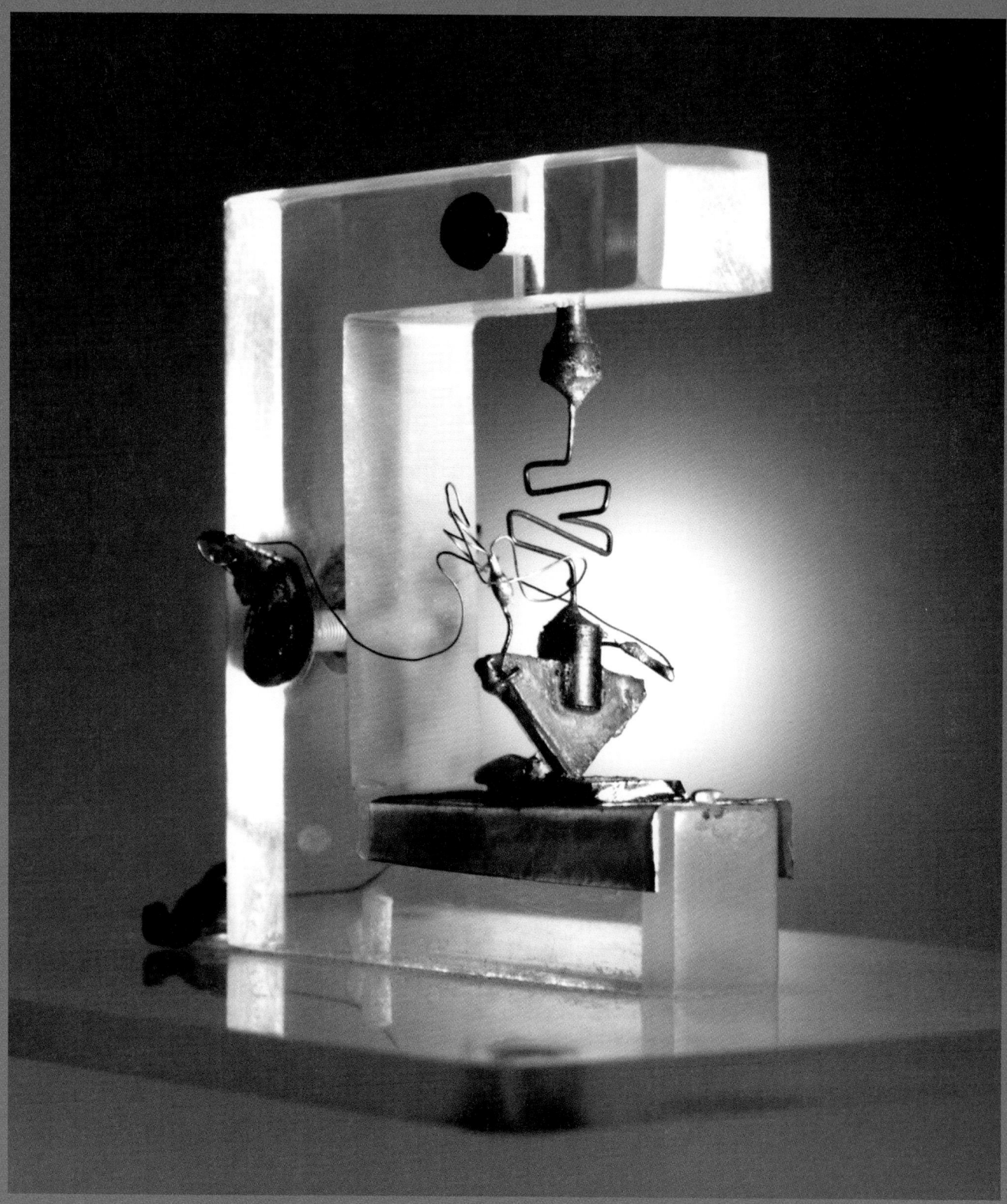

than the nineteenth century. However, if one defines a computer as a machine that performs calculations quickly, it has much older, even ancient, ancestors.

The Abacus: The First Calculator

■ Figure 2.1
The abacus was probably the first computing machine.

Between 3 and 5 thousand years ago, travelling traders in ancient China and Babylonia began to calculate using an *abacus*, originally large, flat stones covered with sand. To use the ancient abacus, the trader would first scratch a series of lines in the sand over the stone, then make his or her computations using smaller stones moved up and down the lines. This early computing machine allowed the trader to add, subtract, multiply, and divide very quickly. Eventually, the abacus developed into a portable system with beads that slid along several strings held in a frame (see Figure 2.1). One string and its beads represented ones, the next tens, the next hundreds, and so on.

Forms of this computer were used throughout the ancient world by the Greeks, Romans, Egyptians, and Chinese. Today, the abacus is still used in the Middle East, Asia, and Russia by merchants, and for teaching children basic arithmetic.

The Pascaline

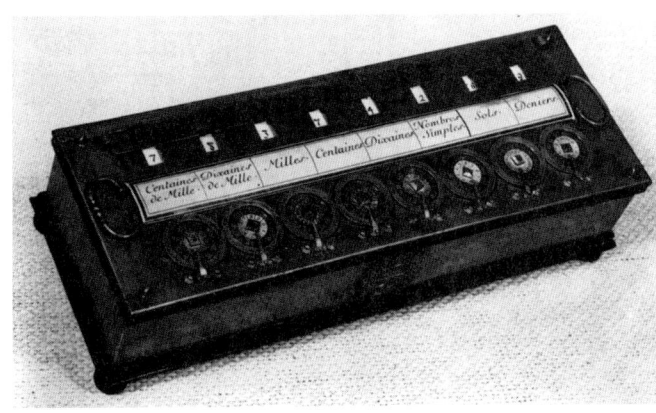

■ Figure 2.2
Blaise Pascal invented the Pascaline to help his father.

Around 1640, a French teenager, Blaise Pascal, decided to help his father in his rounds as tax collector by creating a calculating machine. Pascal's Wheel Calculator or *Pascaline* (see Figure 2.2) added by rotating eight metal dials linked together by gears in a box. Each dial had ten notches. As one dial finished its revolution at the number ten, a gear would move the next dial up one notch. Because there were eight dials, his father was able to add up sums in the tens of millions. While they rarely reach such figures, Pascalines are still in use today—as grocery shopping calculators.

Pascal's Pascaline was an important landmark in the development of mechanical calculators, but much greater fame awaited the ingenious young man. He would later become one of the most important philosophers and mathematicians of the seventeenth century.

The Jacquard Loom

In the early 1800s, Joseph-Marie Jacquard would incur the wrath of silk weavers throughout France by devising a new kind of labor-saving loom. Looms have been in use since ancient times and are used to make cloth and other textiles. In the hands of a skilled weaver, very complicated patterns can be created by interlacing the vertical (*warp*) and horizontal (*weft*) threads. The Jacquard loom (see Figure 2.3), introduced at the 1801 Industrial Exhibition in Paris, controlled the patterns being woven mechanically with a set of boards with punched holes. If a rod on the loom met a hole, it passed through and the thread connected to it would not be added there. If there was no hole, the rod was pushed into action and added its thread.

Prior to the new loom, mass production of intricate patterns was impossible. With the loom, they could be repeated over and over again flawlessly. By varying the color of threads, even cloth with identical patterns but different colors could be offered by merchants.

An unfortunate result of Jacquard's innovation was that weavers had the dubious honor of becoming some of the earliest victims of automation—in the years to come, a worldwide trend for many trades. French silk weavers rioted in protest, smashing the new looms. However, as other skilled workers would learn, automation was a force that could not be stopped. By 1812, there were already 11,000 Jacquard looms used in France. In the next few decades, they would spread throughout Europe and transform the textile industry.

By century's end, Jacquard's innovation of using cards with punch holes to control a machine would prove to be just as significant in the development of modern computers; first, because its cards were one of the first examples of machine memory and, second, because the punch card system permitted only two actions (add the thread or not). This yes or no system is the fundamental language of all computers—what we know today as binary code.

■ **Figure 2.3**
The patterns produced by a Jacquard loom were controlled by a series of wooden cards with punch holes.

Charles Babbage's Difference Engine and Analytical Engine

In the 1800s, producing mathematical tables was the tedious task of office workers known as *computers*. Some of these tables, such as navigational and astronomical ones, were of national importance because they were used for charting the courses of England's fleet of merchant ships. Errors were common and could be catastrophic not only for a ship's crew and the businessman who owned it, but also for the national economy. It was said, at the time, that a table error was like "a sunken rock at sea yet undiscovered, upon which it is impossible to say what wrecks may have taken place." An English mathematician, Charles Babbage, devoted most of his career to creating a machine that could mechanize the very human art of computing and put an end to dangerous human errors. He enlisted his colleagues in the scientific community to gain support for his great project.

He and his friends were able to convince the Parliament that finding a more scientific way to generate accurate tables was in the national interest of England. As a result, Babbage was given large government grants to develop what he called the Difference Engine. According to him, this computer would be capable of doing the calculations for mathematical tables mechanically and flawlessly. Babbage also designed his machine to print automatically because he knew that, in reality, most errors did not come from mistakes in arithmetic but in the process of copying the numbers by hand.

Unfortunately, designing a mechanical computer is not the same as building one. Babbage worked for decades and was regularly advanced more and more government funds for the project (in just one ten-year span, he was given what today would be nearly a million dollars). A small working model of the Difference Engine was actually finished in 1833. However, it did not print and was not quite capable of making a truly functional table.

A model of Charles Babbage's
Analytical Engine.

Babbage was a mathematician with great imagination and was constantly revising and improving his ideas. In 1834, he abandoned his Difference Engine project for a grander one, the Analytical Engine (see Figure 2.4). This computer, a machine powered by steam engines, was designed to perform many more kinds of calculations. Unfortunately, after already experiencing years of investment with no return, this change of direction was the last straw for the British government. They no longer had faith in Babbage's ability to finish any project and stopped funding his research.

Even without government support, Babbage continued to work on the Analytical Engine for the rest of his life, although he never would complete it. In retrospect, this was not surprising—Babbage's plans called for a machine with over 50,000 parts. As an old man, his workrooms were filled with bits and pieces of his various engines, each one abandoned for a new and better approach.

While never realized, the Analytical Engine anticipated much of the conceptual underpinnings of today's computers and, in particular, one technique that would be an essential part of computers through most of the twentieth century. In his effort to create a flexible and universal calculator, Babbage had the brilliant notion of borrowing the punch cards of Jacquard's loom to control it. A carefully organized set of punch cards interacted with pins on metal wheels. By allowing or preventing the pins to pass through a card, a prescribed series of mechanical actions would take place. In essence, the punch cards acted as instructions to create formulas for algebraic operations, what we would today call a "program" but which Babbage named the "mill." These cards could be stored for later use in what he called the "store," or what we would call today "memory." Of course, Babbage used names to describe his machine that were most familiar to his era, thinking the automatic motions of his machine were like the mechanical process of grinding grain.

To sum up Babbage's truly revolutionary and prophetic vision, the Analytical Engine was designed to act universally rather than do only one simple mathematical operation. In his words, "to solve any equation and to perform the most complex operations of mathematical analysis." Today's computers are just such machines—universal calculators whose actions change depending on which programs or software is used.

The case can be made that the machine was even more ahead of its time. The Analytical Engine was a machine controlled by information put on cards. Store the Engine's cards and you could recreate formulas at any later time (as stated before, a very early kind of memory). The Analytical Engine was designed to have a built-in printer that wrote the results numerically or *digitally* (replacing the gauges on early automatic calculators). Thus, in the early 1800s (during the U.S. presidency of John Quincy Adams), Babbage had already envisioned a digital machine that utilized programs to vary actions, with stored memory and a printer.

Across the Atlantic, later in the century, Babbage's concept of using punch cards to transmit instructions to the Analytical Engine would be a crucial element of a successful and more powerful computing machine.

BOX 2.1

Figure 2.5
Augusta Ada King, the
countess of Lovelace.

One of Babbage's colleagues who helped him secure government money for his great project was Augusta Ada King (see Figure 2.5), the only child of the great British Romantic poet, Lord Byron. Abandoned by her father and brought up by her mother, Ada was steered away from poetry and directed toward the sciences, where she became a talented mathematician. After being introduced to Babbage, she was entranced by his ideas and began an extensive correspondence with him.

Ada, later known as Lady Lovelace, understood the Analytical Engine better than anyone other than Babbage. Her *Sketch of the Analytical Engine* explained the inventor's conception to the scientific community. This might have been simply a technical text. However, Ada was blessed not only with a superb analytical mind, she also inherited her father's poetic way with words. For example, her description of Babbage's innovative use of Jacquard's cards was, "We may say aptly that the Analytical Engine weaves algebraic patterns just as the Jacquard loom weaves flowers and leaves." Ada also was a visionary and, in her writings, predicted that an Analytical Engine could be used not only for mathematical and scientific purposes but also to create art and music.

Lady Lovelace is best known for writing a series of instructions that drove the engine, designed to calculate mathematical functions. Because of this, today she is considered the first woman programmer. The programming language ADA, developed by the Department of Defense in 1979, was named in her honor. ∎

The Census of 1890 and Hollerith's Machine

In the United States, the occasion of a national census led to an important leap forward in computing. It also set the nation on a course to ultimately become the world's leader in mainframe computing.

A census is more than simply counting all the citizens of the country. This once-a-decade tabulation has the deepest political ramifications. Census numbers determine how political districts are drawn throughout the country and the number of representatives each area is entitled. Much of the government aid our nation distributes is allocated based on census numbers. An undercounting of any region can limit its political influence and prevent its citizens from getting their fair share of resources.

When Congress first established the national census in 1790, the nation's population was less than 4 million. By 1880, the population had jumped to 50 million, but the census was still primarily being done by hand. The 21-thousand page 1880 census report was tabulated from countless handwritten sheets with many columns and rows. The final report came out in 1887. As the 1890 census drew near, it was feared that the task had grown so great that it might not even be finished before the 1900 census began. A competition was established to come up with a new approach.

Only three people entered the competition, but one of the entrants, a young engineer named Herman Hollerith, would change the history of computing.

Figure 2.6

The Hollerith tabulation system used to tally the 1890 census.

Hollerith proposed replacing the handwritten sheets with a punch-card system that could be tabulated by a machine. The punch-cards were a descendent of Jacquard's and Babbage's innovations and could store eighty variables about each individual on a single card (see Figure 2.6). In a test that used records from the previous census, the Hollerith Electric Tabulating System was ten times as fast as the closest competitor.

The 1890 census would be the largest yet seen in world history. In June, tens of thousands of census workers visited millions of households. Less than two months later, census officials were able to announce the new population of the United States—nearly 63 million, a 25-percent growth in only a decade. Unfortunately, the American public's reaction was not what the officials or Hollerith expected. Rather than being thrilled and amazed by the incredible speed of the mechanical tabulation, there was great anger. Most Americans had assumed the nation had grown to 75 million people (a total that was still another decade away). While Hollerith's punch-card system was a significant scientific achievement, the census count was a blow to national pride.

The Tabulating Machine Company Becomes IBM

In 1896, Hollerith formed the Tabulating Machine Company and was hired to compute the 1900 census as well. However, with the assassination of President McKinley in 1901 and the change to Theodore Roosevelt's administration, the new Census Bureau director decided it was in the government's interest to stop paying Hollerith's fees and, instead, develop its own devices. Once his firm completed the 1900 census, Hollerith was suddenly faced with finding new uses for his tabulating machines.

Hollerith simplified them for general office use and renamed them *automatics*. In the Hollerith system, tabulation became an organized three-step process with three different machines: a keypunch, a tabulator, and a sorter. In the next ten years, Hollerith's automatics could be found in all kinds of businesses, from department stores to insurance companies, textile mills to automobile plants. Because the machines were rented and the keypunch cards needed to be restocked regularly, his company had a steady and dependable stream of revenue. Despite being rejected by the Census Bureau, Hollerith went on to sell his machines to government agencies at all levels. The tabulations generated regular and special reports for sales, manufacturers, and officials efficiently and economically—making monthly reports a normal part of business life.

In 1911, Hollerith, in ill health and on the advice of his doctor, sold the Tabulating Machine Company for $2.3 million. The new owner hired a young, ambitious man to run the company—Thomas J. Watson, a name that would become synonymous with the rising computer industry (see Figure 2.7).

Watson was well equipped to understand the potential of the tabulating machines. He had been a successful salesman and rising star at the National Cash Register Company (NCR). Fired abruptly when on the verge of NCR's presidency, Watson joined the new company with a small

Figure 2.7

IBM's Thomas J. Watson Sr. and Thomas J. Watson, Jr.

salary but a 5 percent commission on all the profits. Two decades later, he was the highest paid individual in America.

Watson applied the successful marketing and sales techniques of NCR to his new company, tripling its income. He opened offices around the world. In 1924, as the company's president, he renamed it the International Business Machines Corporation, or, as the world knows it, IBM.

IBM continued to follow Hollerith's business model, which made it less vulnerable than most companies to business downturns, even catastrophic ones like the Great Depression of 1929. Because most of its machines were rented, there was always a steady income each year, even if a single new machine was not sold. In addition, there continued to be dependable and substantial earnings from selling punch cards. Even during the Great Depression, IBM was selling 3 billion new cards every year.

Throughout this dark period, Watson stayed loyal to his workforce, even though there were very few new contracts. IBM factories continued making new machines to prepare for the return to the better times, which Watson was confident were ahead. As an advisor and friend to Franklin Delano Roosevelt, Watson's IBM found that prosperity *was* just around the corner. FDR's New Deal unleashed a myriad of government programs, which created a great demand for accounting machines, both in the public and private sectors. IBM, with a ready storehouse filled with new machines, became the biggest office-machine producer in the nation. By the end of the Great Depression, IBM had nearly doubled its sales and had more than 12,000 workers.

As the 1940s began and World War II broke out across Europe and Asia, the urgent need for developing more powerful and sophisticated computing machinery would be a catalyst for the creation of the first modern computers.

Big Iron: The First True Computers

Colossus Breaks the Code

The official mathematical tables that so worried Charles Babbage in the early 1800s took on fresh importance during World War II. The navies on the seas, the bombers in the air, and the gunners in the artillery all required the most precise tables to locate and attack the enemy. An inaccurate weather forecast could cripple the best planned of military missions. Computing machines with punch cards were enlisted in the war effort, along with hundreds of civilians to operate them. There was tremendous government support, particularly in the United States and Great Britain, for developing machines that could work faster and make more complex calculations.

The effort to develop calculating machines that could break Nazi codes was the focus of a secret team of somewhat eccentric academics from a variety of fields in Bletchley Park, outside of London. Among them was D. W. Babbage, a relation of Charles Babbage; Ian Fleming, the author of the James Bond novels; and Lewis Powell, a future U.S. Supreme Court Justice. The most brilliant was a mathematician, Alan Turing (see Figure 2.8).

Turing was a visionary genius. He designed a machine that he called the *universal automaton* but became known as a *Turing machine*. It was the twentieth-century version of what Charles Babbage had worked so hard to

■ **Figure 2.8**
Alan Turing.

create almost a century earlier. Hypothetically, this machine could solve any mathematical problem, if given the proper information. In reality, the Bletchley team created a machine specifically designed to work on code ciphers. It was fed information via a tape marked in binary code. While much of the work at Bletchley remains a secret, Turing's first functional machine, code named "Bombe," was able to decipher the German *Enigma* code (of course, the capture of an Enigma machine also helped). The Allies could translate intercepted German messages almost immediately.

Unfortunately, the Germans soon replaced Enigma with a much more complicated cipher, which the British called the *Fish*. To conquer this code, Turing and his colleagues devised a much larger machine, called *Colossus*. It was the first truly programmable computer. Rather than the electronic relays used by other computing machines, it was filled with over 1,800 vacuum tubes. Hot, expensive, and ravenous devourers of energy, vacuum tubes were much faster and quieter than relays. Too fast, perhaps, because when run at top speed, the tape fell apart and pieces flew in all directions. Since speed was of the essence in code-breaking, the Bletchley team slowed the processing down but put in five different processors that could work simultaneously, a technique known today as *parallel processing*. Colossus would run until it solved a problem. It would then print out the solution.

Like Babbage before him, Turing felt it was essential to remove the human element from computing to eliminate errors. In order to achieve this, he conceived one of the most important ideas in the development of the computer—the *stored-program concept*. Instead of a machine depending on instructions fed to it with tapes or punch cards, the program was stored in the computer itself and only the data was fed in.

The influence of Colossus as a tool of war was considerable. The Germans never learned of its existence or knew that their new code was regularly being broken. (It was said that Churchill read Hitler's messages before Hitler.) Many Allied lives were saved by the work at Bletchley Park.

However, Colossus's influence on the history of computers was limited. The Colossus computers were destroyed at the end of the war and the details of their existence were kept secret long after the war had ended. Only during the last twenty-five years has the visionary work of Alan Turing and his colleagues at Bletchley Park begun to be understood.

Though only thirty-three when Germany surrendered, Turing would not live to see the birth of the Information Age he helped conceive. After World War II was over, he devoted himself to realizing his dreams of a universal machine controlled by programming. Unfortunately, before he finished his work, he was arrested on charges of homosexuality (then a crime in Great Britain). Despite the testimony of his Bletchley colleagues about Turing's important contribution to the survival of Great Britain, he was convicted and later committed suicide at the age of forty-two.

The Mark 1—Harvard/IBM

In the 1930s, Howard Aiken, a physics graduate student at Harvard, had tired of doing lengthy, complex calculations for his dissertation (the subject of which, by coincidence, was vacuum tubes) and thought it would be better to make a machine that could do them quickly. He tried to draw some colleagues into participating in such a project, but none were interested. However, a lab technician, after overhearing Aiken's futile attempts, told him they "already had such a machine and nobody ever used it." Aiken was then shown a dusty old relic—Babbage's calculating engine—one of the few working models he ever created. It had been donated to Harvard by Babbage's son in the late 1800s and promptly forgotten.

Aiken had never heard of Babbage, but found his autobiography in the Harvard library. While reading it, he sensed that "Babbage was addressing him personally from the past" and calling on him to continue his work.

Disappointed with his colleagues, Aiken began approaching business machine companies with his idea. He found an enthusiastic audience at IBM. By 1939, Aiken was working with some of the best IBM engineers on developing the machine of his dreams.

In 1943, the Automatic Sequence Controlled Calculator was completed. A gift to Harvard from IBM, the project's cost had grown from the initial planned $15,000

to $100,000. The machine itself, which became known as the Mark 1 (see Figure 2.9), had also grown to the size of a room. It weighed five tons, was fifty-one-feet long and eight-feet tall, and looked like a huge manufacturing machine. With almost a million parts and hundreds of miles of wire, it could add, subtract, multiply, and divide. Fed information with rolls of paper tape, it was the first truly automatic machine. Once started, it could run for days doing calculations. Unlike the Colossus, it did not use vacuum tubes, but the older electronic relays. The sound of the Mark 1 working was described as "a roomful of ladies knitting."

The public dedication of the Mark 1 in 1944 at Harvard was a huge event. IBM's Thomas Watson commissioned one of the top industrial designers, Norman Bel Geddes, to enclose the machine in a sleek, modern, luminous design of steel and glass. Headlines celebrated the robot brain and, for the first time in the century, the public became fascinated with computers. What the public didn't realize was that the Mark 1 was remarkably slow in its calculations and limited in its true accomplishments.

Aiken, now in the Navy, put the Mark 1 to work on computing mathematical tables for ship navigation. Twenty-five volumes of tables were ultimately created but little more. Despite its limited achievements, the development of the Mark 1 was an important milestone that ushered in the era of the giant computers. It also was an important training ground for the first generation of computer scientists (see Box 2.2).

ENIAC and EDVAC

At the University of Pennsylvania, another team of engineers under contract with the Army was developing a massive computer that would work much faster than the Mark 1. Called the Electronic Numerical Integrator and Computer or ENIAC (see Figure 2.11), its speed was largely due to replacing old-fashioned mechanical relays with vacuum tubes—almost 18,000 of them. Aiken, who had done his thesis on vacuum tubes, had avoided them in the Mark 1 because he knew that their lifespan was very short. With so many tubes, engineers would be

BOX 2.2

Grace Hopper (see Figure 2.10), one of the leading figures in computer programming, was a young Navy lieutenant when she worked on the Mark 1. As its primary programmer, she wrote the first book on digital computing—her manual for the Mark 1. A colorful, quick-thinking, and resourceful scientist, Hopper was able to save the day more than once for her colleagues. For example, during a visit by admirals, the Mark 1 was having many problems—the most obvious being that it shut down every few seconds. Hopper solved the problem by simply leaning on the start button during the whole visit.

Her most famous solution came during the development of the Mark 2. In 1945, on a hot summer day, the Mark 2 shut down suddenly without warning. Hopper went inside the machine, searching for the source of the trouble. She found a dead moth in one of the relays and began to remove it. When asked by Aiken what was going on, she told him she was "debugging" the computer. Since then, "debugging" software has become every programmer's chore. ∎

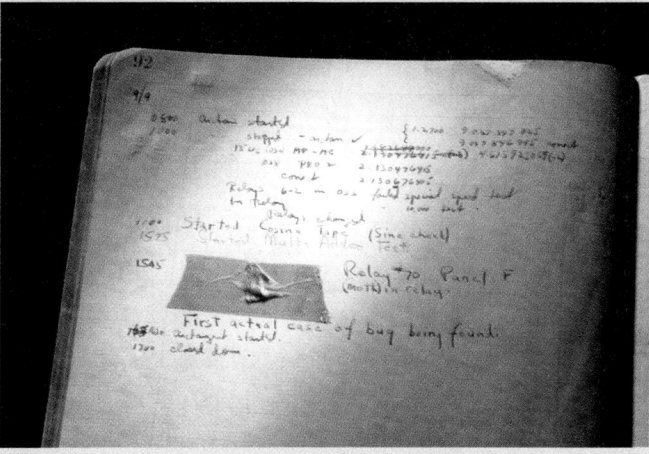

■ **Figure 2.10**
Grace Hopper and "the bug" she discovered.

replacing them constantly. Most knowledgeable engineers agreed with Aiken that tubes were undependable and thought the project was doomed to failure. However, the creators of ENIAC realized that the tubes largely failed during powering up—so they rarely turned it off. This turned out to be a good thing because the ENIAC drew so much power that whenever it was turned on, the lights dimmed across a whole neighborhood in Philadelphia.

When completed in 1945, ENIAC was the fastest calculating machine ever created. It could calculate the trajectory of an artillery shell quicker than one actually fell (less than thirty seconds). One test showed it could do a complex calculation in two days that would take a person with a desk machine forty years. One thousand times faster than the Mark 1, ENIAC replaced the earlier machine in the public's fascination.

However, the fifty-ton ENIAC had some serious problems. Engineers needed more tubes to increase its capabilities. Yet there was little interest in increasing the gigantic computer's complexity, particularly by adding to the number of tubes. More tubes would only increase the frequency of failures, as well as its demand for power. The superior speed of ENIAC was actually another problem, as punch cards and tape could not be fed fast enough to keep up with its 5,000 operations per second.

John von Neumann, a colleague of Albert Einstein at Princeton, devised a solution. Already famous for developing the mathematics of quantum mechanics and his work on the first atom bomb, von Neumann was fascinated by ENIAC, its calculating speed, and its problems. He became a consultant on a new machine: the Electronic Discrete Variable Automatic Computer, or EDVAC.

Von Neumann's design called for a machine with true computer memory: one that would store not only the program but the data, too. The engineers of EDVAC responded to von Neumann's challenge by creating a new type of storage, which replaced vacuum tubes with mercury delay storage lines (devices already in use in radar equipment). One of these lines could replace more than twenty tubes. When completed in 1951, the much faster EDVAC contained only 3,500 tubes compared to ENIAC's 18,000. The first significant miniaturization of computer hardware had been accomplished, initiating a trend that continues today. "Smaller" and "faster" would be watchwords for future computer innovations.

Figure 2.11

Whenever the initiator panel for the ENIAC turned on the huge mainframe, it would dim the lights of a nearby Philadelphia neighborhood.

Perhaps even more important, von Neumann's concept of stored programs, manifested in EDVAC, would be fundamental in all future computers. Because the computer's electronic memory now stored programs along with all numbers, the computers could operate with much greater speed. EDVAC's additional innovation of a central processing unit, or CPU, with memory that coordinated all operations was also critical to future computers. It enabled swift switching of tasks back and forth where previously, for each change, a person would need to feed in new instructions with cumbersome rolls of paper tapes.

UNIVAC—Remington-Rand

After World War II, the development of new, huge computers switched from military to peacetime applications. Two key engineers on the ENIAC project at the University of Pennsylvania, J. Presper Eckert and John Mauchly, decided to go into business together and design the next generation of huge computers.

Like Herman Hollerith more than a half-century earlier, in 1946 they proposed to build their new machine for the U.S. Census Bureau. They called it the Universal Automatic Computer or UNIVAC (see Figure 2.12). Facing the first stirrings of the post-war baby boom, an anxious Census Bureau gave the men $300,000 to begin the project. Unfortunately, Eckert and Mauchly were better engineers than businessmen and underestimated the cost of building a new machine by more than half. Within two years, the men had nearly exhausted their funds.

Figure 2.12

Illustration from a 1950s advertisement for the UNIVAC.

The Eckert-Mauchly Computer Company was saved by being acquired in 1950 by Remington-Rand (later Sperry-Rand), a typewriter manufacturer that was already expanding into computers. With fresh resources and personnel (including Grace Hopper, the lead programmer of the Mark 1), the team was able to deliver UNIVAC to the Census Bureau in 1951 at a cost to the company of nearly $1 million. Despite the financial losses, the new computer was a success and the most technologically advanced computer of its time. UNIVAC was much faster than Eckert and Mauchly's ENIAC and, at 352 square feet, less than a fifth of the old mammoth's size. UNIVAC's internally stored memory could hold up to one thousand words, and data was stored not on the old paper tapes but on new magnetic ones. Magnetic tape could be read a hundred times faster than punch cards or paper tape and wasn't as fragile.

Luckily, during the height of Eckert and Mauchly's troubles, the government had ignored the advice of Howard Aiken, whose Mark 1 had begun the era of large computing in America. In a famous false estimate of the need for new technology, he argued that the project should be cancelled because the United States simply did not have "enough work for more than just one or two of these computers."

In 1952, the government ordered five more UNIVACs. By 1955, more than fifteen had been built, and huge firms like General Electric began placing orders for their own UNIVAC computers (see Box 2.3).

BOX 2.3

UNIVAC gets a national audience

The commercial success of UNIVAC was confirmed by the presidential election of 1952. In an inspired piece of public relations, Sperry-Rand convinced CBS News to allow UNIVAC to be part of their election night coverage (see Figure 2.13). The company announced that their electronic brain would be able to predict the outcome. On election night, even though CBS stationed a reporter near the real computer in Philadelphia, viewers actually never saw it. Instead, a mock wooden one with blinking Christmas lights inside was shown all night behind the anchormen in the New York studios.

As the coverage began, CBS newsmen announced that the contest between Dwight D. Eisenhower and Adlai Stevenson was too close to call. Viewers were told that even UNIVAC was "stumped." This was disappointing but not a surprise since all polls had predicted a close race. What the viewers didn't know was that they were being misled. UNIVAC was far from stumped. In fact, early in the evening it had predicted an Eisenhower landslide. Because the computer's prediction was so far from conventional wisdom, the newscasters decided to ignore it. Even UNIVAC's engineers were convinced that something was wrong with their computer and began reworking its programming.

Hours later, however, it became clear that there really was an Eisenhower landslide, and UNIVAC's original prediction was finally broadcast. It had been astonishingly accurate, off by only four electoral votes from the final results. The public was enthralled by a machine that appeared smarter than all the experts and commentators. UNIVAC was "seen" by millions on television and became the symbol of a new era. Today, one of the original UNIVACs is housed in the Smithsonian Institution as a landmark of the computer age. ■

■ **Figure 2.13** CBS News' Walter Cronkite at a demonstration of UNIVAC.

IBM Responds to the Challenge

Under Thomas Watson, IBM continued focusing on government contracts and did not see the potential in the work of Eckert and Mauchly. It was Watson's belief that IBM's dependable punch card accounting machines were a separate and distinct market from the inefficient and expensive colossal computers. However, his son, Thomas J. Watson, Jr., a veteran of World War II who shared control of the company in the 1950s, understood the threat UNIVAC posed to IBM's dominance of computing. The popularity of UNIVAC among big commercial accounts was growing and IBM had no competing product to offer. Just as threatening was UNIVAC's use of magnetic tape for data storage. Suddenly, the revenue from millions of punch cards was no longer assured. Probably even more upsetting to Watson, Jr. was that Eckert and Mauchly had offered their company to his father before selling it to Remington-Rand and the elder Watson had turned them down.

After years of trying, Watson, Jr. was finally able to convince his father that IBM was being left behind. The company responded by doubling the budget for research and development and hiring hundreds of new engineers. IBM moved into what was internally called the "panic mode," and the result was the IBM 700 series of computers (see Figure 2.14). While a typical system did include a cardpunch and reader, it also stored information on magnetic tapes—beginning the end of the punch-card systems, just as Watson, Sr. had feared. Designed for business and accounting, each system rented for $20,000 a month. Capitalizing on a superior salesforce, smart modular design (for the first time each component was made small enough to fit into an elevator), and its reputation for customer service, the rental of IBM 700s exceeded UNIVACs by 1956. Ultimately, IBM would control 75 percent of the market worldwide.

■ **Figure 2.14**

The IBM 700 series of computers was the first to be designed with modular components.

The First Programming Languages

By the late 1950s, the use of large computers in business, government, and universities was becoming routine. Besides IBM, large computer makers included Sperry-Rand, Honeywell, Control Data, and Burroughs. Each computer company had its own proprietary machine codes, making it difficult for companies to change systems or even hire computer programmers trained in other systems. If a company dared to switch computer systems, all its programs had to be rewritten. The need for standard programming languages was becoming more and more apparent.

In 1957, a team led by John Backus at IBM created the first programming language that was hardware-independent. They called it *FORTRAN,* which stood for "formula translation." Upgraded versions of FORTRAN are still in use in today, primarily in the scientific community.

The U.S. government, meanwhile, had directed Grace Hopper, programmer for both the Mark 1 and UNIVAC (see Box 2.2), to lead the movement for a standard language for government and business. In 1959, she developed the *Common Business Oriented Language* (COBOL) for programmers. Unlike FORTRAN, it was a language that used words rather than numbers. As Hopper described it, "I felt that more people should be able to use the computer and that they should be able to talk to it in plain English." While computer makers resisted giving up their control over profitable proprietary languages like UNIVAC's *Flow-Matic* (which Hopper had designed), in 1960 the government announced it would not use any system that couldn't be programmed with COBOL. That promptly ended the era of proprietary languages, opening the door to future hardware-independent languages like BASIC, Pascal, C, and C++.

The Transistor, Silicon, and Software

Transistor Invented at Bell Labs

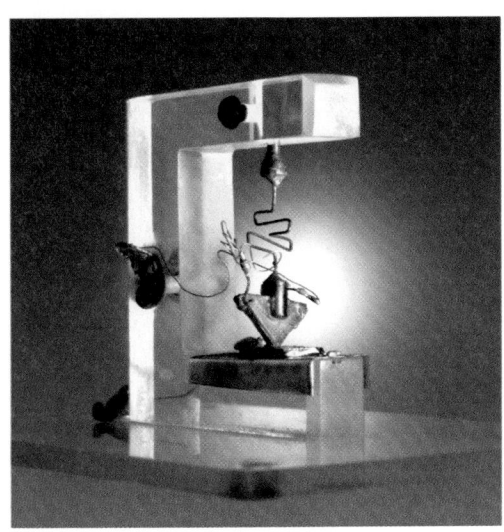

■ **Figure 2.15**
The first transistor.

In 1947, while the UNIVAC was under development, an important invention took place at Bell Telephone Laboratories that would eventually transform not only the young computer industry but also most consumer appliances. The *transistor* (see Figure 2.15), invented by John Bardeen, Walter Brittain, and William Shockley, had many advantages over the vacuum tube it ultimately replaced. It was much smaller, did not need to warm up, required very little electricity to operate, created much less heat, and was much longer lasting. It was called a *solid-state* device because all its working parts were solid, unlike a vacuum tubes.

Initially, there was little interest in the invention; the vacuum tube was well proven and cost less than a dollar. But a small Japanese company, Tokyo Tsushin Kogyo, took the lead by developing *portable* radios in the mid-1950s. The first portables were a quarter of the size of the smallest vacuum tube radios. As attractive as the new radios were, the company realized that in order to enter the U.S. market, they would need to find a name that was easier for Americans to pronounce. Based on the Latin word for sound, "sonus," they called their company *Sony*. The Sony Corporation became the world's leader in utilizing transistors in a broad array of consumer appliances, such as record players, tape recorders, and television sets. Perhaps more importantly, the company's success was critical to the recovery of the Japanese economy after the devastating effects of World War II.

The Birth of Silicon Valley

William Shockley, leader of the transistor team at Bell Labs, left in 1955 and went across the country to start his own company in the Palo Alto section of California. His Shockley Semiconductor Laboratory (transistors are known as *semiconductors* because they conduct electricity only under special conditions) was the first of many labs to settle in the area around Stanford University.

One of these labs, Fairchild Semiconductor (ironically, formed by defectors from Shockley's own company), would devise a new manufacturing method for transistors, which would lead to the next generation of computers and the region's nickname, *Silicon Valley.*

Initially, transistors were wired into circuit boards by hand, limiting both the quantity that could be manufactured and the size of any circuit board to the number of transistors that could be installed with tweezers. Fairchild engineers realized that all parts of a circuit could be made of silicon, not just the transistor itself. By imbedding transistors directly into silicon sandwiches or *chips* with printed metal connections, machines could mass-produce the circuit boards, and the size of transistors could shrink to no more than the size of a flea. This was called an *integrated circuit.*

Intel and Moore's Law

In 1968, two of the founders of Fairchild Semiconductor, Robert Noyce (who had co-invented the integrated circuit) and Gordon Moore, along with their colleague Andrew Grove (who had discovered the best form of silicon for circuits), (see Figure 2.16) did not approve of the way Fairchild was going. Together they founded a new company that focused on building special silicon chips designed strictly for storing computer memory. They called their company Integrated Electronics, or *Intel.*

Moore was a brilliant scientist, but his greatest fame came from a graph he drew in 1965 that showed the capacity of memory chips would double roughly every eighteen months while the cost of producing them would be cut in half. *Moore's Law,* as it became known, has stood the test of time and explains why a computer you bought today becomes obsolete in a very short time.

Three years after its founding, Moore's law was more than proven by Intel's ability to build a chip with more than four thousand transistors on it. Intel engineer Ted Hoff utilized this new technology to create the first *microprocessor* (see Figure 2.17). Originally designed for calculators, Hoff's microprocessor combined on one chip all the arithmetic and logic circuits necessary to do calculations—a "computer on a chip" as the company's advertising described it. When Hoff's team connected this new chip to Intel's memory chips, they created the processing power of the landmark ENIAC of 1945 in a package less than an inch wide.

The microprocessor's first impact was in the production of low-cost handheld calculators that spread worldwide and immediately made the slide rules of engineers obsolete. Today, microprocessors that would have astounded the pioneers of computing can be found in all kinds of electronic devices and appliances, from microwaves to electronic fuel injection. For example, the microprocessor in a typical VCR has more computing power than Eckert and Mauchly's early colossal fifty-ton computer. But unlike ENIAC, which drained enough power to dim a Philadelphia neighborhood, the VCR's chip requires less energy than a lightbulb.

The Sovereignty of the Giant Mainframes Comes to an End

The first microprocessor was called the Intel 4004 (the number referring to the number of transistors). While some manufacturers put the chip in toys, its limited

■ **Figure 2.16**

The founders of Intel, Andrew Grove, Robert Noyce, and Gordon Moore, in 1975.

■ **Figure 2.17**

The Intel 4004, the first microprocessor (seen 4 times its actual size).

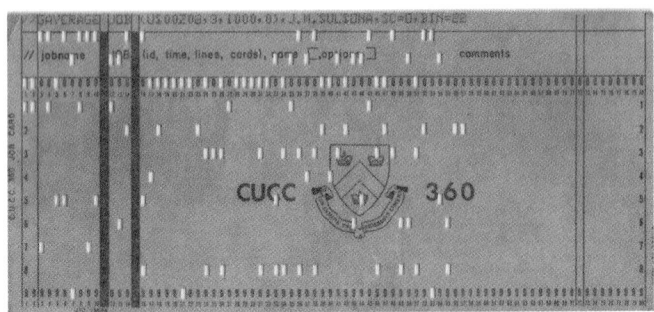

Figure 2.18

The bane of 1970s computer science students: one of a stack of punch cards to run programs on the university mainframe.

computing power restricted its use to fairly simple operations, like those used by handheld calculators.

Meanwhile, IBM became the dominant force in the mainframe world with its System/360 computers. This was a family of computers that all shared accessories and used the same language—a concept called *scalable architecture*. If customers needed to increase the size of their computers, they could easily do so without purchasing new software and retraining the entire staff. By the 1970s, the dominance of IBM was so complete that competing mainframe companies could only survive if their system ran IBM software.

The lure of computers began attracting a new generation of students to the industry in the 1960s and 1970s. Computer science became one of the fastest growing majors at colleges and universities across the country (see Figure 2.18). Programming homework required each student to sign up for valuable computer time, when a large package of computer cards they had carefully punched would be fed into readers wired into the campus mainframe. A successful program would result in long, wide sheets of green paper pouring out of the printer. However, bent punch cards and programming errors were much more common. Phrases like "do not fold, spindle, or mutilate" and "garbage in/garbage out" were born from the frustrations of young student programmers.

If those frustrated students could have only known what was ahead; however, few could see that the little processor in their handheld calculators was opening a door to a whole new approach to computing and the beginning of the next revolution in computers. From the 1940s to the 1970s, computing meant mainframe computing. However, like the stone David hurled at Goliath, the tiny chip in the hands of some young visionaries was going to change the world and leave the old giants behind.

The Personal Computer

Figure 2.19

Inspiration for the revolution: the Altair 8800.

Two events mark the beginning of this next era of computing: Intel's release of the 8080 chip in 1974 and the printing of an article in *Popular Electronics* magazine at the beginning of 1975. Twenty times more powerful than the 4004, the 8080 had enough capacity to handle about 4,000 characters of memory, more than enough to store not just numbers and letters, but even some simple programming. The chip cost less than $200.

The cover of the January 1975 issue of *Popular Electronics* announced "World's First Minicomputer Kit to Rival Commercial Models," accompanied by a picture of a small box with diodes called the *Altair 8800* (see Figure 2.19). The kit cost less than $400 and used the 8080 chip as its brain. It was the machine that inspired a revolution. Young hobbyists swamped the manufacturer, MITS, with orders, and began writing their own programs.

■ **Figure 2.20**

Paul Allen and Bill Gates, the founders of Microsoft, working on a computer.

■ **Figure 2.21**

The first Apple computer. Hobbyists had to build their own cases because it didn't come with one.

In the state of Washington, two imaginative young friends spent five weeks adapting a simple programming language, BASIC (Beginners All-purpose Symbolic Instruction Code), for the Altair. They were so excited about the future of small, cheap computers that they decided to start their own software company. One, Paul Allen, quit his programming job at Honeywell, and the other, Bill Gates, dropped out of Harvard. They moved to New Mexico where MITS was located. Their company would later move to Seattle and take the name *Microsoft* (see Figure 2.20).

When the Altair was released, two young men from California were already in business selling "blue boxes," illegal machines that let users make free long-distance telephone calls. Steve Wozniak, a Hewlett-Packard programmer, and Steve Jobs, who later dropped out of Reed College, became members of a group of hobbyists called the "Home-brew Computer Club." In Jobs' parents' garage, they built their own microcomputer, which they called the Apple I (see Figure 2.21). Jobs thought he could sell it to the same hobbyists who were so excited about the Altair. He soon had his first order of twenty-five. To raise the money to build their machines, Wozniak and Jobs sold their most prize possessions: a Volkswagen minibus and a programmable calculator. With the $1,300 they raised, they formed a company called *Apple* and designed their famous logo—an apple with a bite out of it (a pun on the word *byte*). The Apple I cost $666; they would eventually sell 600 of them.

It was their Apple II in 1977 that truly launched the minicomputer revolution. Not a kit, but an already assembled machine, the Apple II had graphics, sound, and a color monitor. It even had a computer game designed by Wozniak that bounced a ball around the screen with paddles. Jobs recruited programmers to design other applications. One, VisiCalc, was the minicomputer's first budget spreadsheet program. It was this program that transformed the market for minicomputers beyond the hobbyists to the business world. The Apple II would eventually generate over $100 million in sales. Also contributing to their success was the introduction in 1978 of the first floppy disk drives for consumers, which replaced the cassette tapes that had been used to store information.

While the Apple II would be the top-selling microcomputer for five straight years, as the microcomputer explosion continued, other companies began selling them. Among the competitors were Radio Shack, Atari, Texas Instruments, and Commodore.

The IBM PC

In 1980, while they controlled 80 percent of the mainframe market, executives at IBM became concerned that they were not participating in what was becoming a significant, fast-growing market in small computers. Never known for quick product development cycles, IBM, acting out of character, authorized an innovative lab director named William Lowe to put together a team of engineers to quickly develop a prototype minicomputer which could be on the market in one year.

Figure 2.22
The original IBM PC.

The development of what would be called the IBM Personal Computer or PC would have lasting effects on the development of the PC industry (see Figure 2.22). Breaking with past practices, IBM decided to sell the PC in retail stores and buy components, rather than manufacture them themselves. Even the PC's operating system and software would be outsourced. This was the beginning of the concept of *open architecture*. The processor selected was the Intel 8088.

In Seattle, Bill Gates and Paul Allen had a growing business selling versions of BASIC for the various microcomputers being developed. When IBM approached Microsoft for a version to be used in their new computer, Gates proposed that his company design the PC's operating system, too. Microsoft quietly bought the rights to an operating system called QDOS (or "quick and dirty operating system") from another company, hired its chief engineer, redesigned it, and called it *PC-DOS*. Microsoft offered it to IBM for a low, one-time fee that allowed IBM to use it on as many computers as it wanted. In return, IBM agreed to let Microsoft retain the licensing rights, allowing the small company to sell it to other companies (under the name *MS-DOS*).

In August 1981, almost exactly a year after the project began, IBM began selling the IBM PC at retail outlets (among them, Sears). It cost $2,800 (not including the monitor) and was a huge hit. In four months, 35,000 had been sold. Small microcomputer companies soon found it difficult, if not impossible, to compete with the huge IBM sales and marketing teams. Primitive by today's standards, the IBM PC had only 64K of RAM and one floppy disk drive. A color graphics card was optional.

With the success of the PC came many innovative software packages. While the original PC came with its own version of VisiCalc, Mitch Kapor designed a spreadsheet called *Lotus 1-2-3*, which would become the PC's *killer-app*. Word-processing packages like *WordStar* and *WordPerfect* not only helped make the IBM PC a success but also Microsoft's DOS, which was necessary to run them. Within three years, no competing minicomputer company, other than Apple, would use any other operating system. The majority of those that had unique software systems and hardware simply went out of business. A few survivors, like Commodore and Atari, would migrate their businesses into computer game machines (see Chapter 5).

By 1984, an IBM-compatible or *clone* industry developed, led by Compaq, Texas Instruments, and Toshiba. A college student, Michael Dell, took the innovative approach of selling mail-order computers from his dorm room.

IBM kept ahead of its rivals by releasing new machines that would later be cloned. In 1983, it released the PC-XT with a 10MB hard-drive. Its AT with an

80286 (or "286") processor was three times faster than the original PC and would lead to IBM's controlling 70 percent of PC sales in 1985.

Still, all these systems were text- and code-dependent. Users constantly had to refer to thick manuals to make the programs work. To simply copy a file from one drive to another, one had to type, "COPY A:\BOOK.TXT B:\BACKUP\BOOK.TXT." If a letter or space was wrong, one had to type the whole line over. In addition, while they all worked with DOS, each program had its own interface and codes for users to remember. Although artists had begun exploring the computer as a new medium in the early 1980s, PC graphics were remarkably simple and limited to 256 colors.

The Graphical Age Begins

A revolution in personal computers was announced in one of the most famous commercials of the 1980s. Shown only once, during the 1984 Super Bowl, viewers saw a runner in full color run past crowds of gray, bland workers. She then hurled a heavy hammer at a giant screen showing Big Brother, an image from George Orwell's *1984*. As the screen shattered, the voice-over said simply, "On January 24, Apple Computer will introduce the Macintosh. And you'll see why 1984 won't be like *1984*" (see Figure 2.23).

Figure 2.23

The first Macintosh was introduced by this commercial during the 1984 SuperBowl.

The design of the Apple Macintosh computer (see Figure 2.24) was part of what made it extraordinary. It was simple with clean, curved lines and a monitor built into the same box as the CPU. However, what made it stand out from the PC and its clones was what its users saw on the screen. All of its software, including the operating system, was *graphical,* or picture-based rather than text-based. Microsoft collaborated with Apple in designing the first graphical word-processing program (*Word*) and spreadsheet (*Excel*). A graphical user interface (or GUI—pronounced "gooey") had been on earlier machines, but it was the widely marketed Macintosh that was the first to be known as "user friendly" (see Chapter 5).

The Mac's GUI (see Figure 2.25) could be understood and used with a little experimentation and without a manual. It had windows, icons, and pull-down menus that were controlled, not by a keyboard, but by moving and clicking a mouse. Using the desktop as a metaphor, files could be dropped into folders that were easy to label. A file could be copied into another drive by simply clicking and dragging it to the icon for the drive.

Most business users never embraced the Macintosh, due to IBM's established reputation in the business community and the wider array of business software on the PC platform. But because it was a graphics-based machine, the Mac was immediately accepted as *the* computer for artists. It offered a wide array of digital art programs, as well as fun *MacDraw* and *MacPaint* software. The Macintosh's ease of

Figure 2.24

Apple's Macintosh computer became immediately famous for being user-friendly.

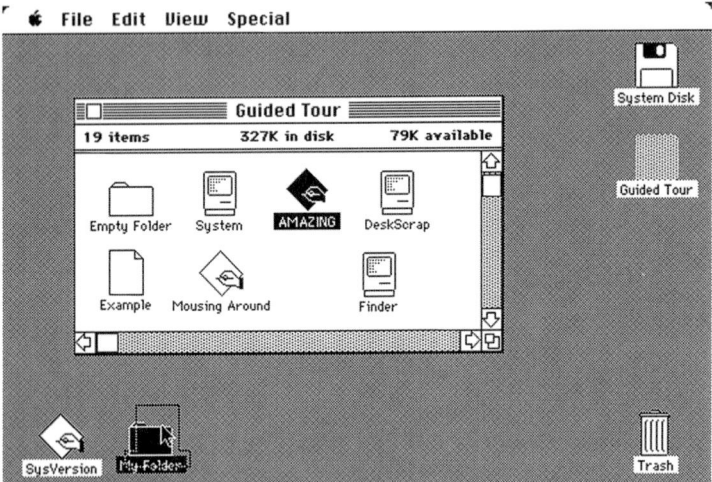

Figure 2.25

Folders, windows, and the ability to drag and drop files were all features of the first Macintosh's GUI.

use made it popular in homes and in schools, too. In addition, combined with the Apple LaserWriter printer and new design software by Adobe, the Macintosh became the favorite of the design and publishing industries. It introduced *desktop publishing* (see Chapter 6) and a world of variety in typefaces and styles. A creative person could write, edit, design, illustrate, and layout a whole book—all on one small computer.

The arrival of the Mac solidified the divide between PC and Apple computing: PC users were seen as straight-laced, serious, and old-fashioned, while Mac users were creative, spontaneous, and youthful.

Windows Comes to the PC

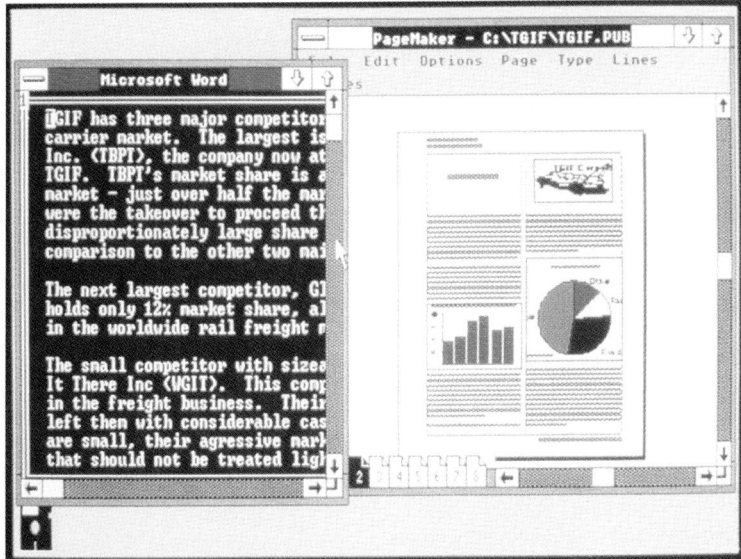

Figure 2.26

An early version of Microsoft Windows.

A year later, GUI came to the PC in Microsoft *Windows*. Bill Gates had begun its design back in 1981 when he first saw what Apple was working on. Despite imitating the Macintosh interface, Windows was far from popular in this first version due to two significant handicaps. First, the market required that DOS remain the main operating system so old DOS software could still be used. This made Windows, in essence, a second operating system sitting on top of another. Second, it ran very slowly, frustrating users and comparing badly with the Apple Macintosh (see Figure 2.26).

It wasn't until five years later, with the release of Windows 3.0 in 1990, that Microsoft really created a GUI environment that worked as well as the first Apple Macintosh. Its windows could be resized, and several software packages could be open at the same time. PC users finally embraced Windows as the standard design for all PC software.

Microsoft's software designers rewrote their other software to complement the new environment, creating its *Office* suite of *Word*, *Excel*, and *PowerPoint*. The once-dominant competing products, like WordPerfect and Lotus 1-2-3, now found themselves turned into secondary players. Even before the release of Windows 3.0, Microsoft had become the largest software company in the world. In the early 1990s, it seemed that by the end of the decade, Microsoft was going to have few competitors other than Apple.

The Attack of the Clones

One factor that made Windows 3.0 successful was the arrival of faster processors. Since the beginning of the 1980s, Intel had steadily released faster and cheaper microprocessors, proving the law of their founder, Gordon Moore. With 386 and 486 chips that could run not only the new, more demanding Windows type but also earlier software faster than ever before, Intel dominated the chip industry much as Microsoft dominated software.

By the time the first Pentium (in essence, 586) chips were released in 1993, PC-clone manufacturers were beating IBM in the race to release the first machines with the latest chips. New industry leaders whose focus was on mail-order sales, like Gateway and Dell, took the lead in developing the fastest, most sophisticated PCs. With lower prices than the older manufacturers, they began to dominate the market.

A shocked IBM and Apple began to lose ground in the personal computer market. With the success of Microsoft's Windows 95 and the proliferation of low-cost, powerful PCs, many experts predicted that Apple would not survive to the end of the decade. While loyalty to Apple among graphics and multimedia users remained strong, by the mid-1990s, it was not unusual to see some PCs next to Apple computers in former strongholds of Mac computing.

The Birth of the Internet

In the 1990s, another revolution was brewing that caught almost all the technology experts by surprise and, once again, created a change in direction for the entire computer industry. The first signs for most computer users was the growth in the use of e-mail at their offices and schools. This was the first popular application of the *Internet*.

The Internet had been born nearly thirty years earlier as the ARPANET, begun by the U.S. Defense Department in 1969. It was designed to network powerful computer systems together to store information, share computing power, and help researchers at their many military sites around the world communicate with each other. When research scientists at universities began to use this system, the Internet's use expanded rapidly (see Chapter 12 for a fuller discussion of the development of the Internet).

Today, the Internet consists of tens of thousands of computer networks around the world communicating together. It connects networks over telephone wire, fiber optic lines, cable, radio, and satellite. Its success can be traced to the fact that its content is *distributed*. The Internet is a huge database of information, a worldwide shared database, containing far more information than can be stored on any single computer.

The World Wide Web: The Internet Goes GUI

The original Internet was purely text-based, with screens displaying black or green backgrounds and white or yellow characters. The World Wide Web is a relatively recent development of the Internet. It began in 1989 at CERN (Conseil Europeen pour la Recherche Nucleaire) in Geneva, Switzerland, as an effort to ease collaborations between physicists and engineers working on different systems. Its goal was "universal readership." Like the Internet, the Web's development and impact has expanded far beyond what the originators first envisioned (see Box 2.4).

In 1990, the British engineer, Tim Berners-Lee, was a researcher at CERN (see Figure 2.27). On his own initiative, he wrote a program initially designed to store and link documents by the many CERN scientists across their computer network. He soon saw that it had a far wider application as a way to help organize information on the Internet. His program assigned addresses to all the documents on the Internet, which allowed users to quickly travel from one computer in the system to another.

The proposal was circulated around the scientific community. Berners-Lee's vision of a global Web of linked information became known as the World Wide Web. In 1992, Berners-Lee designed the first World Wide Web *browser* and distributed it for free. However, at that time, there were less than thirty Web servers in the world. The experience was quite different, too. It was a completely text-based environment—there were no pictures and no buttons. Still, you could easily link from one page to another.

However, it was Berners-Lee's vision of documents linked across the globe utilizing hypertext that transformed the world of computing today. ■

It required the imagination of a group of computer science students at the University of Illinois, whose leader was Marc Andreessen, to change the Web from a tool for elite computer scientists to one that captured the imagination of people around the world. They devised *Mosaic*, the first true Web browser, in 1993, and made it available to the public for free. Mosaic changed the Internet from a text-based environment to an interactive one with colors and images much like the change from the command-driven DOS to the GUI of the first Macintosh a decade earlier.

Web browsing has several features that have led to its immense popularity. First, it is *interactive* and utilizes *hypertext* and multimedia. Instead of getting information in a linear way (like a book or magazine), you can click on a topic and go directly to more information on it. A series of links can lead to "deeper" information or related topics. Documents are not limited to text but can contain colors, images, sounds, animations, and video.

The Web's information is both *searchable* and *dynamic*. Websites with *search engines* scan millions of websites to locate ones that appear appropriate for your question. These search engines are critical because information on the Web is constantly being updated. With the advent of streaming audio and sound files, you can even hear events as they are happening.

Most importantly, the Web is *platform independent*. It doesn't matter what kind of computer and operating system you are using, any computer with a browser and Internet connection can access the Web's information.

When Marc Andreessen graduated from the University of Illinois, he was not allowed to take Mosaic with him. In 1994, he formed a new company called *Netscape*. Netscape's *Navigator* was a more sophisticated browser that supported e-mail and plug-ins, which expanded the kinds of media browsers could display. Easy to use and free to the general public, millions of people first experienced the Web through a Netscape browser. Millions of individuals, organizations, and businesses also began developing their own websites. By 1996, there were more than 16 million different websites.

Today, the World Wide Web is managed by the World Wide Web Consortium based in the United States and Europe (CERN turned authority over to it in 1994). Led by Tim Berners-Lee, the Consortium's 500 members are responsible for establishing the standards for all Web applications, such as those for addresses and updates to the language of the Web, *HTML* (see Chapter 13). Its mission is to maintain universal access and promote the evolution of the Web.

CONCLUSION

When Charles Babbage imagined a universal calculator, able "to solve any equation and to perform the most complex operations of mathematical analysis" more than a century and a half ago, he was truly a visionary. Yet, the results of this vision are far more universal than anyone could have imagined. They continue to unfold. His colleague, Lady Lovelace, was the first to perceive that artists might see this universal calculator as a new medium for creativity. We are still at the pioneering edge of this vision.

As discussed in the first chapter, technology has long been an important catalyst for artistic innovation. In the nineteenth century, the invention of tubes for oil paint liberated painters from their studios and led to Impressionism. The discovery of new pigments by German chemists at the beginning of the twentieth century led to the wild, imaginative colors of Modern Art. By the end of that century, computers that were hundreds of times more powerful and fit in a briefcase easily surpassed huge computers that once filled a room.

It is a cliché but nonetheless true that in our time the only constant is change. How today's artists and designers will respond to rapid changes and utilize the new tools that have been put in their hands is unfolding before our eyes. It is both a blessing and a challenge to live in a time when an important chapter in the history of the collaboration between art and technology is being written.

Projects: the History of Computers

1   *Interview your family members about their first encounters with computers. Find out when they first heard about them and what they were like then. Ask when they first purchased a computer and to describe it.*

2   *Visit the websites of two major computer manufacturers (for example, Apple and IBM) and write a report on their histories, comparing them.*

3   *Write an essay on the impact of computing in your life. Consider how pervasive computing is today. Try to identify how many appliances you own that have computer chips in them. Then, consider how the manufacturing processes of other items you own require computer technology.*

4   *Which five major events in the history of computing do you consider most important? Explain and defend your choices. If you could extend the list to ten, which five would you add? Why?*

Inside the Box:
The Computer

Introduction

Never before, not even during the Renaissance, have artists and scientists been so closely allied as they are in the new field of digital media. Because technology is the medium, it is important that artists and designers understand not only how their new tools evolved (as described in this chapter and Chapter 5) but also how their new tools are constructed and operate. This is not entirely unprecedented. For centuries, artists needed to be able to construct their brushes and understand the chemistry of pigments and binders in order to grind good paint. Designers who didn't understand the technologies behind the production process were doomed to failure.

This chapter takes us on a tour of the inner workings of the computer itself. We will learn its various parts, how they operate, and why they are important. Unlike a brush that begins to misbehave or a tube of paint that leaks, computers are a major investment and cannot be discarded with little thought. Part of the challenge of being a digital artist or designer is handling the numerous malfunctions—some minor, some major—during the process of creating art. A better understanding of the interaction of the various parts of a computer will help us overcome the occasional roadblock and even promote better use of this incredible new medium for artists and designers.

A computer, while it can be stylish, isn't much to look at—even when you open it up and look inside. Nothing moves except for a fan. Only one or two lights can be seen blinking; nothing buzzes or whirs. Unlike the marvelous and massive computing machines described in the last chapter, our current-day computers do their job effectively but quietly and rather uneventfully to the human eye. Computers simply translate information from one medium to another—from analog to digital. They accomplish this task by converting information into a series of on–off, yes–no commands that are then interpreted and translated into what you see on the computer screen. When you type a command into the computer, you are actually using an interpreter—a program—which then tells the computer what you want to do in a language that it can understand.

When we think of a computer, we think of a box, a monitor, a keyboard, and a mouse. Most of us understand a keyboard through its analog, the typewriter. We also understand the monitor as a kind of television. The mouse, as unique as it is, has the feeling of moving a pen or pointer around a page. The box and its contents, which we know is really the true computer, is somewhat more mysterious.

The Box

The box, or *case,* that houses most of the parts of what we refer to as "the computer" is an important element in and of itself. In addition to protecting various internal mechanisms, it provides the frame for the pieces that make up a computer: the motherboard, central processing unit (CPU), hard drives for long-term storage, random-access memory (RAM), the video and sound cards, CD- or DVD-ROM drives, and, of course, the floppy drive. Each of these will be more fully described in this chapter.

The power supply, an indispensable part of the computer incorporated into each and every case, adapts regular household electricity to a form of power the computer can use. It also contains a fan for cooling computer components and directing airflow in and around the various cards and cables. Without the power supply, the computer could not function.

Computer cases come in many forms and sizes, from the ubiquitous desktop to the mini-tower, to large full-tower models (see Figure 3.1). The larger the size of the case, the more internal and external bays are available for housing hard drives, CD-ROMs, and a variety of other peripherals.

A good case will not only provide reliable power and a stable working environment, but also will allow easy access to the inner workings and adequate space for any optional additional components. An inferior case will be made of flimsy materials and often is not well organized in terms of component placement and airflow (which is important in order to keep the internal workings from overheating).

■ **Figure 3.1**

This photograph of a MAC G4 computer shows the easy-to-open and service design of newer MACS. PCs usually offer a design that allows the entire case or a side panel to be removed for ease of service.

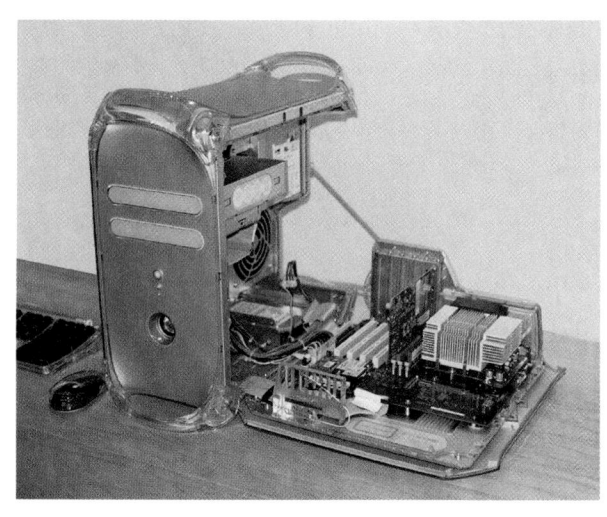

The Motherboard

The *motherboard,* or primary circuit board, is the nerve center of the machine, connecting to the power supply and distributing electricity to all the other parts of the computer (see Figure 3.2). It is also where many of the most critical elements of a computer are located. The motherboard contains several openings or *sockets* where computer chips are installed. Among the chips housed on the motherboard is the most important one, the CPU, and the computer's memory. There are also *expansion slots* for attaching a variety of special circuit boards or *cards* (like a video card, sound card, and an internal modem) directly into the motherboard. At the portion of the motherboard available to the user at the rear of the case are ports; places to plug in peripheral devices (see Figure 3.3). Most computers have at least one port each for a keyboard and mouse, serial ports, a parallel port, USB ports—

even ethernet and game ports. Motherboards that contain built in sound will also have connections for microphones, speakers, and input from other sources. These can be seen at the back of the case, along with other ports from the ends of expansion cards.

The Brain on the Motherboard: Central Processing Unit

The brain that runs everything inside your computer is a microprocessor called the *central processing unit* or *CPU*. Everything a computer does, whether word processing or digital imaging, is executed by this microprocessor. While other components can be very important to the overall performance of your system, the CPU is without a doubt the single most important one. Among the common names for CPUs are the Intel Pentium series, the AMD Athlon, and the Motorola PowerPC microprocessors.

When we look at the microprocessor, what we are really seeing is the housing for the CPU chip. Actually, what we often see on the motherboard is the heat-dissipating *sink*, which is often capped with a fan to keep the CPU cool while it is working. The CPU itself is less than 1 mm thick and only one-third of an inch square in size. Contained in this fragile wafer are millions of embedded transistors created by a photolithographic process in which the physical map of the CPU design is layered onto the chip (see Figure 3.4). When the chip is complete, hundreds of connections are made to the larger housing, which is what is inserted into the motherboard (see Figure 3.5).

A key element of the microprocessor is the *control unit*. The control unit interprets a program's instruction and then launches the action that will carry it out. It does this in four steps: first, it gets the instruction; second, it decodes the instruction; third, it executes the instruction; and fourth, it writes the result to temporary memory. The time it takes to get the instruction and execute the instruction is referred to as a *machine cycle*.

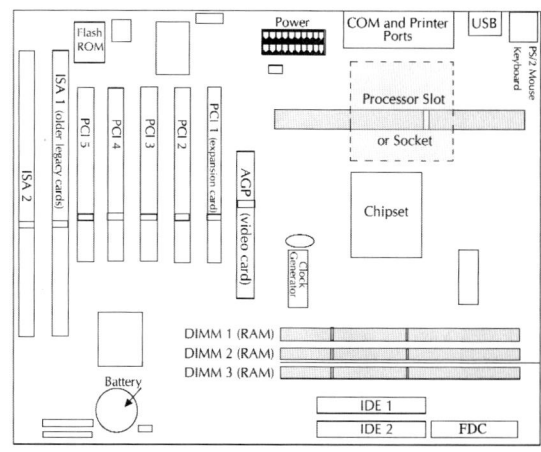

■ Figure 3.2

A basic motherboard usually contains PCI slots for expansion cards (and in older boards ISA slots for legacy expansion cards), DIMM slots for RAM, a processor slot or socket, and IDE and floppy drive connectors for hard and floppy drives.

■ Figure 3.3

a. While most contemporary designs offer a sleek profile to the viewer, both MAC and PC computers connect to external devices through a series of ports. **b.** Even the newly styled IMAC connects through its ports visible in the rear of the computer.

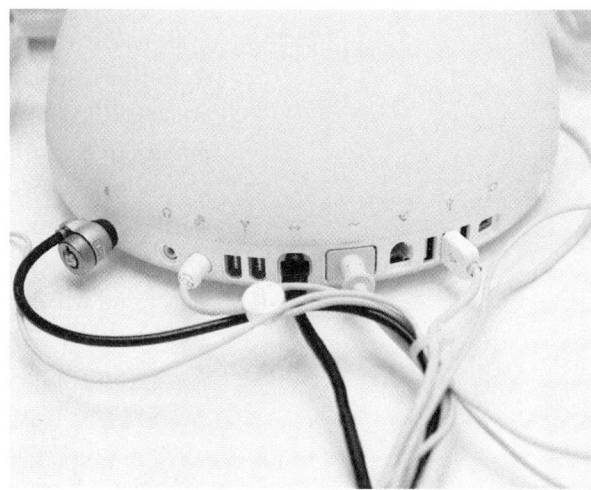

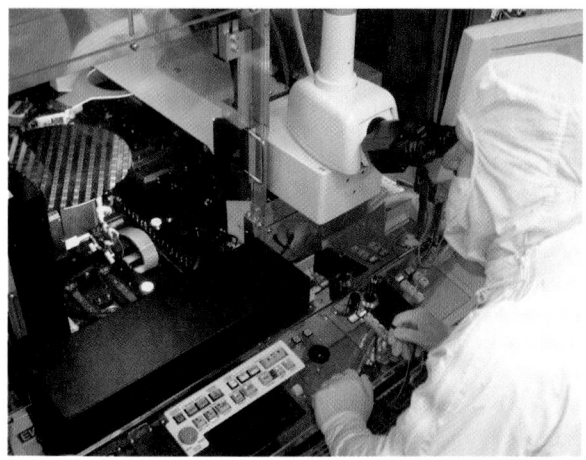

■ **Figure 3.4**

An IBM worker monitors the production of a wafer containing many potential individual chips.

The CPU depends on the *system clock* to coordinate a computer's operations. The system clock times the activities of the chips on the motherboard and makes sure that all processing activities are discharged according to the *clock tick* (the speed with which the CPU can execute instructions) of the system. The more clock ticks per second, the faster the CPU is able to execute instructions.

A CPU's speed is normally measured in *megahertz* (MHz). One megahertz is equal to 1,000,000 clock ticks (cycles) per second. The early 8088 processor used in the IBM XT computer of the 1980s ran at 4.77 MHz or 4,770,000 ticks per second. One *gigahertz* (GHz) equals 1,000 megahertz, or a billion clock ticks per second. A 2.2 gigahertz processor can process 2,200,000,000 clock ticks per second. Generally, the CPU's hertz rating is the most important indication of how fast the processor is. However, other factors, like extra instructions written into the code of the chip, can affect its speed. For example, to speed up the handling of multimedia data, a special instruction set called MMX (multimedia extensions) has become standard in all Intel Pentium 2, Pentium 3, and Pentium 4 processors. Equivalent instruction sets have also become standard in the chips of Intel's competitors.

Earlier CPUs executed instructions one at a time. Current processors have the advantage of *pipelining* instructions, which allows them to start a second cycle before the first one is finished. Without having to wait for an entire cycle to finish, three additional cycles can be started before the first one is done. Some CPUs, known as *superscalar,* can run two or more pipelines that rapidly process many instructions at the same time.

As processors become faster and faster, and smaller and smaller, there is the danger of heat buildup due to the densely packaged transistors. Chip manufacturers have addressed this problem by shrinking the actual circuit size. This trend will continue; smaller and smaller dye sizes will allow for faster and cooler running processors. Researchers are currently working on chips whose size is at the molecular level.

As various processors or CPUs often require different ways of attaching to the motherboard, a motherboard is usually chosen based on the processor you wish to use and the *chipset* it requires. The system chipset is the most important element that determines the functionality of the motherboard. Controlling the flow of information from one part of the computer to another, the chipset determines the way in which the processor will access memory, communicate with peripheral devices, and much more. It even determines the type of RAM memory that can be used, as well as its speed.

Memory on the Motherboard

ROM Memory

There are several different types of memory used in computers, and they differ in significant ways. *Read-only memory,* or *ROM,* is relatively slow and can only be read, not written to (changed). However, ROM memory is relatively permanent and far more secure for certain types of small programs. A good example of this is the BIOS ROM, which begins the start-up or *boot* process for the computer. The BIOS ROM is a permanent part of the system. BIOS ROM can even be removed from a computer and later returned without losing the information inside.

Electrically erasable programmable ROM, or *EEPROM,* is the type of ROM that is used most often in motherboards today. It allows the user to "flash" or upgrade the BIOS to take advantage of processor improvements or bugs found in earlier releases of the BIOS ROM.

RAM Memory

Random-access memory, or *RAM,* is what most users think of when discussing computer memory. This short-term kind of memory is used by a computer for holding data and programs while working on the computer. It sends information to the computer's CPU at high speed so there is a minimum of time the processor must wait for it. Unlike ROM, RAM can be read and written to.

However, the reason you lose work when your computer suddenly crashes is RAM, unlike ROM, is a temporary storage medium. It only stores information while the computer is running. When RAM stops receiving power, everything contained in the RAM is lost. Therefore, unless the data is written to a more permanent storage medium, or *saved* (for example, to a hard or floppy drive), whatever was contained in the RAM will vanish when the power is turned off.

The type of RAM most often referred to is actually *dynamic random-access memory (DRAM).* While the underlying technology of DRAM is fundamentally the same, the small circuit boards they are installed on come in a variety of types and sizes. A *single inline memory module* or *SIMM* (housing 4, 8, 16, 32, 64, or 128 megabytes of RAM or even higher) must be installed in matching pairs in order to work. Motherboards designed for SIMMs come equipped with multiple memory expansion slots for SIMMs. A more recent development in DRAM technology called *dual inline memory modules,* or *DIMMs,* use the same RAM found on SIMMs but are designed to allow a single DIMM board to work alone (see Figure 3.6).

■ Figure 3.5

The CPU is very small and housed in a casing with external pins for connection to the motherboard.

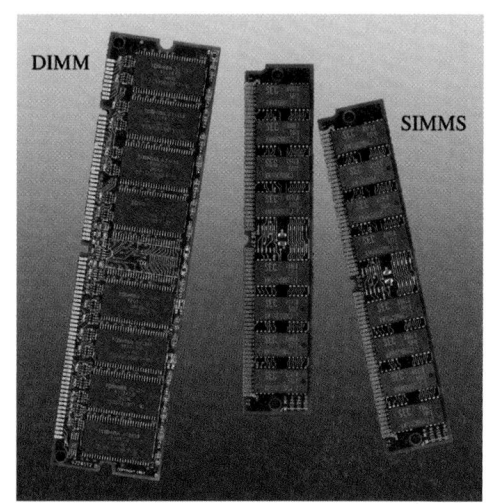

DIMM

SIMMS

■ **Figure 3.6**
While RAM is fundamentally similar, it must be compatible with the other parts of your system. Older SIMM must be used in pairs while DIMM (dual inline memory modules) are used individually.

As computers became faster and faster, new processors required RAM that could keep up with the faster bus speeds. SDRAM, for example, has two banks of internal memory rather than one. This allows SDRAM to prepare data in one bank while the second bank transfers data. In addition, SDRAM has a "burst mode" capability, which allows it to keep up with faster bus speeds (see Box 3.1).

BOX 3.1

Basic RAM

Although there are seemingly many different types of DRAM available today, all DRAM is fundamentally the same. Each DRAM unit uses one capacitor and one transistor. When powered, the capacitor will hold an electrical charge, which will signify a "one." No charge will signify a "zero." The transistor reads the contents of the capacitor. Due to the fact that the minute capacitors in DRAM will only hold a charge for a very short time, they need to be read row by row, which also serves the purpose of refreshing and recharging the capacitor.

There is a major difference between static RAM or SRAM and DRAM, however. Static RAM can hold information as long as it receives power, while DRAM must be refreshed periodically due to the use of capacitors as the memory cells that are used to hold data. SRAM is faster, larger, and more expensive than DRAM, which makes it too unwieldy to use in place of DRAM, which is smaller and far less expensive. SRAM is traditionally used for level 1 and level 2 cache memory (a temporary storage area for recent or commonly used information), which needs to be very fast. Cache memory is usually connected directly to the CPU on the motherboard. Since cache memory is faster, and connected directly to the CPU, time is saved in processing this information. Because there is not as much cache memory as there is DRAM memory, the size of the chip is not an issue here. ■

Take the Bus

The motherboard contains several slots called *expansion slots* that are used for different kinds of cards that control peripherals. Buses are essentially a series of pathways that connect components of a computer and transfer data between the CPU and peripherals. Just as conventional passenger buses can travel at different speeds depending upon their agreed upon route, how wide and easy the road is to travel, and the number of stops they must make, computer buses also convey data at different speeds depending upon the width of their path and the distance the information must travel. Wider pathways can accommodate more information, and the result is faster processing.

The history of bus development has been a search for wider and faster data paths as hardware performance has increased. Interestingly, one can see the whole history of bus development on the motherboards in many of today's computers. That is because, even as computers rapidly increase their speed, many consumers want to be able to use earlier or *legacy* components. As a result, many motherboards still have an industry standard architecture (ISA) bus developed by IBM for their first PCs, or NUBUS developed by Apple for their Macintosh II, along with other faster and more contemporary bus offerings. Some sound cards and mice continue to use slower buses. The relatively slow eight bit (one-byte) bus soon gave way to a thirty-two bit data-path bus capable of transferring information four bytes at a time. These faster or "wider" bus paths allowed information to travel more quickly through the computer, which increased performance. New motherboards for both MAC and PC now use a high-speed, *local* bus called the peripheral component interconnect (PCI). The PCI bus can transfer data at speeds of up to 132MB per second and has the ability to perform certain tasks independently of the CPU.

The trend of retaining the complete history of buses on the motherboard is ending. Many of the newest motherboards now offer only PCI expansion slots or, at most, one or two of the earlier bus slots to accommodate older expansion cards that users may still want to use.

One of the newest buses available on current motherboards is the AGP bus. The AGP bus is dedicated specifically to video cards, and provides a faster and more direct interface between the video card and memory. This works especially well for 3-D graphics and video.

The *universal serial bus* (USB) provides an excellent system for installing devices outside the computer. External devices such as keyboards, CD-ROMs, scanners, printers, and other peripherals can be plugged directly into the USB port on the back of the computer. The USB port connects to the universal serial bus, which then connects to the PCI bus on the motherboard.

Small computer systems interface (SCSI, pronounced "scuzzy") is another bus standard used to connect peripheral devices, including hard drives, to computers. A SCSI interface provides faster data transmission rates than other buses (up to 320 megabytes per second for the fastest standard today) and allows multiple devices to be connected to one another on the same bus.

While SCSI buses are often included in Apple Macintosh computers and some PCs, most systems usually require the installation of a SCSI card to add this bus. Most SCSI cards allow devices to be added both internally (hard drives, for example) and externally (usually scanners and portable storage like Zip and Jaz drives).

Bus Ports

Ports are plugs that permit external devices to be attached to the computer. The ports where the devices are plugged in connect to the buses that transfer information inside the computer. Along with the standard keyboard and mouse ports, one of the earliest and certainly one of the slowest is the serial port. A serial port is only capable of transferring data one bit at a time. While this can easily handle the fastest of conventional modems, for newer devices like digital cameras, it is excruciatingly slow.

Developed as a faster alternative to the slower serial bus, a parallel port is capable of transferring information eight bits at a time. Usually reserved for printers, parallel ports are also used for external storage devices such as Zip drives and scanners. Two newer types of parallel ports include the enhanced parallel port (EPP) and extended capabilities port (ECP). While they use the same connector as a regular parallel port, they are ten times faster.

The original serial bus (and the external port that connects to it) is being replaced with the newer, more versatile, and faster universal serial bus. Most new computers provide two USB port connections to allow devices to be connected to this bus, and with the addition of an adapter or *hub*, many more can be added. Often used for digital cameras, scanners, and keyboards, this port can transfer information at speeds approaching 12Mbps. This is over fifty times the speed of older serial port connections. Another advantage to connecting devices to the USB port is that it is *hot swappable*, which means you can plug and unplug devices from this port without having to first turn the computer off. The most apparent limitation to USB is that older operating systems like Windows 95 or NT and MAC operating systems before OS8 do not support it. PC users must use Windows 98 or later and MAC users must use at least OS8. In addition, USB2 is now available and is approximately forty times faster than USB1.

Other types of ports include musical instrument digital interface (MIDI) ports for attaching a digital musical instrument such as a piano keyboard to the computer, and infrared data association (IrDA) ports for wireless infrared devices such as keyboards, mice, and printers.

Permanent Storage

Unlike RAM, whose contents are temporary and are lost when the computer is turned off, permanent or *secondary* storage holds information even after the power to the computer has been turned off. It is this ability to retain information, move information from one computer to another, and archive data for future use that makes secondary storage so important to us. Secondary storage functions as both an input and output source, depending upon whether it is being read from or written to.

Floppy Drives

Introduced by IBM in the early 1970s, the original floppy disks were given that name because they were just that—eight-inch disks containing a round, flexible piece of magnetically coated plastic covered by a soft, thin, flexible plastic outer shell. The magnetic plastic was spun at the hub by the disk drive's motor. Read/write heads in the drive (as in a cassette tape machine) were positioned over the correct location on the disk and information on the disk could be read, modified, or added to. These disks first shrank to 5 1/2″ flexible disks and then to the 3 1/2″ disk we use today. The 3 1/2″ disk still contains a round, flat piece of magnetically coated plastic, but it is now covered by a hard plastic outer shell. At one end of the plastic casing is a metal housing on a spring. When placed into a 3 1/2″ disk drive, the metal housing is moved aside, revealing part of the recording surface of the disk (see Figure 3.7).

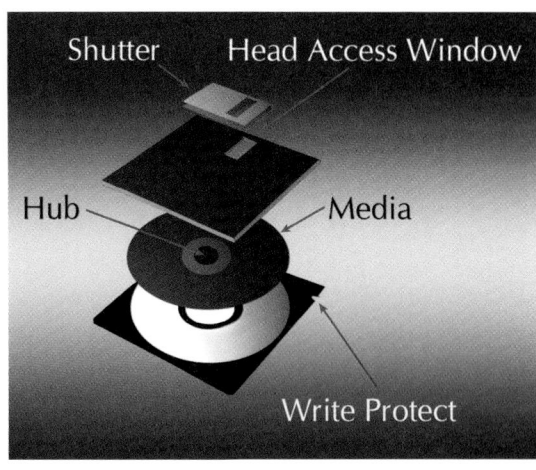

■ **Figure 3.7**

This floppy disk illustration shows media sandwiched in between a hard plastic shell. The shutter moves aside when data is read from or written to the media.

As a magnetically coated media, a floppy disk can be read and written to many times. However, before any information can be written to the disk itself, it must be prepared to accept the information by being *formatted*. While different computer platforms and operating systems format the disk in different ways, formatting organizes the disk into individual storage locations called *tracks* and *sectors*. The "tracks" are essentially thin concentric bands forming a full circle on the disk while sectors are segments of the tracks, each of which can hold 512 bytes of data. A 3 1/2 floppy disk can hold 1.44MB of information, which is 1,440,000 bytes.

Floppy disks also have a write protect notch that can be switched on to prevent you from accidentally writing to a disk. While this doesn't affect your ability to read the disk, it will prevent you from changing in any way the information already contained on the disk.

Hard Drives

In 1956 IBM invented the first computer disk storage system, which was called random-access method of accounting and control (RAMAC). This disk storage system could store a then-astounding five megabytes of data on fifty 24″-diameter disks. Today, hard drives commonly range in size from 20 to 120 gigabytes (a gigabyte is 1,000 megabytes) and larger in capacity and are approximately 4″ × 6″ × 1″ in size. (Twenty gigabytes is the equivalent of nearly 14,000 standard floppy disks.)

Like floppy drives, hard drives store information within a series of tracks and sectors. Unlike floppy drives, however, they are capable of storing information on a series of platters that are stacked together and that spin in unison.

A read/write head for each platter floats with it ready to read a specific area of the disk. This is similar to a conventional phonograph record and playback head. However, the data on a hard drive platter is arranged in concentric circles rather than the spirals of a phonograph record. The density of the platters and the fact that many can be stacked together give the hard drive far greater storage capacity than the floppy disk (see Figure 3.8).

The faster a hard drive spins, the more quickly it can retrieve data. The platters themselves are made from glass or ceramic to avoid the problems cre-

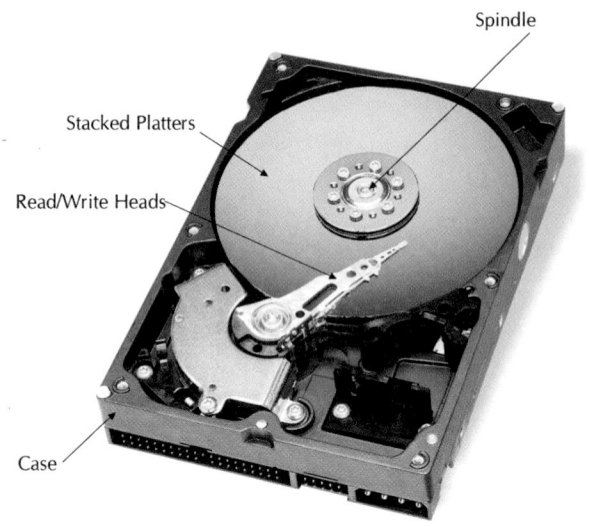

Spindle

Stacked Platters

Read/Write Heads

Case

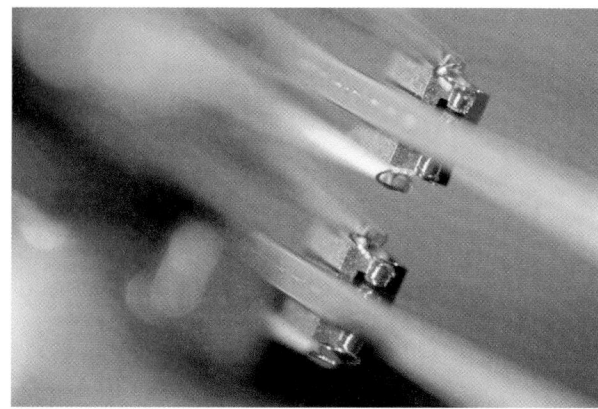

■ Figure 3.8

a. Illustration of hard drive interior. **b.** Close-up of read/write heads on platter.

ated by the heat they generate as they spin. Most current hard disk drives spin at 5,400, 7,200, or 10,000 RPM, with 15,000 RPM drives emerging as technology continues to develop.

With important research underway, hard drive storage size promises to continue to grow quickly. Given the increasing size of programs and the nature of digital media to create file sizes that can often be more than fifty megabytes for a single image, this is a necessary and important development for digital artists (see Figure 3.9).

CD-ROM

Compact disc read-only memory, or *CD-ROM,* devices have all but replaced floppy drives for installing programs. They are not only a lot faster, but contain far more data than a floppy disk—650MB to a floppy disk's 1.44MB. Rather than using concentric tracks and sectors like floppy disks and hard drives, the CD-ROM uses a spiral of equally sized sectors that starts at the center of the disc and winds its way outward. Data is stored on CD-ROMs as pits (recessed surface areas) and lands (raised surface areas). A *land* represents a

■ Figure 3.9

Storage size relationships.

Media	Capacity	Number needed to back up 40 GB hard drive	Estimated cost of single unit of media	Cost to back up 40 GB hard drive	Costs per gigabyte	Costs per megabyte
3 _" floppy	720 KB	—				
3 _" floppy	1.44 MB	2778	.40	1111.2	27.78	.28
Zip	100 MB	400	12.	4800.	120.	.12
Zip	250 MB	160	14.	2240.	56.	.056
Jazz	1 GB	40	90.	3600.	90.	.09
Jazz	2 GB	20	110.	2200.	55.	.055
CD-R	650 MB	62	.75	46.50	1.16	.0012
CD-RW	650 MB	62	1.00	62.	1.55	.0015
DVD-R	4.7 GB	8+	5.50	44.	1.1	.0011
40 GB HD	40 GB	1	65.	65.	1.63	.0016

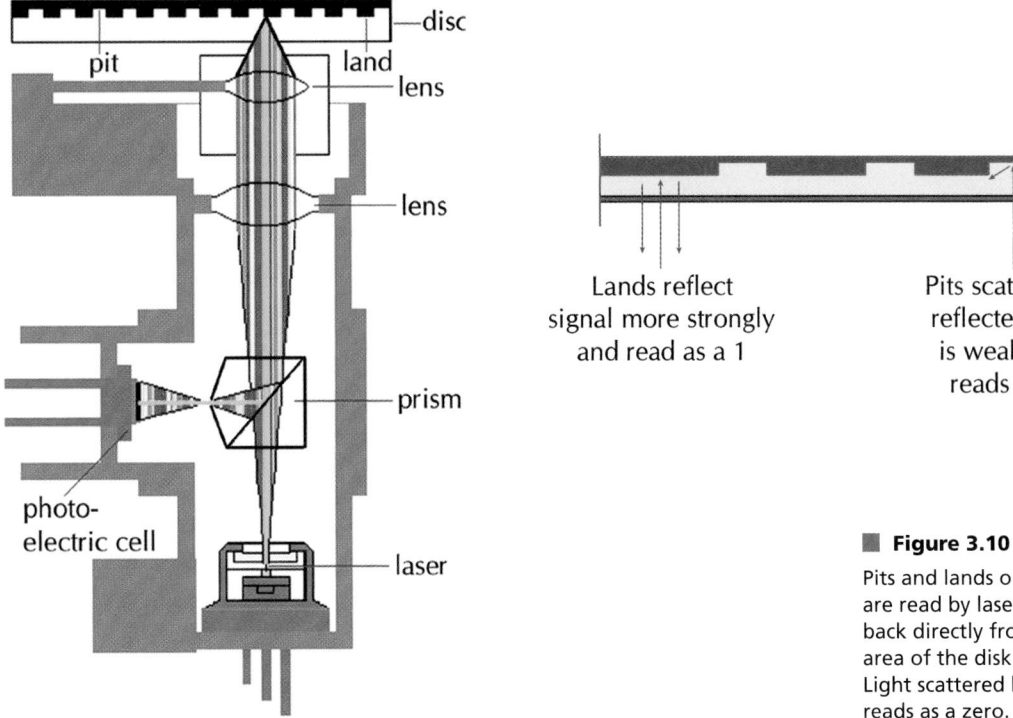

disc
pit land
lens
lens
prism
photo-electric cell
laser

Lands reflect signal more strongly and read as a 1

Pits scatter light, reflected signal is weaker and reads as a 0

Figure 3.10

Pits and lands on a CD-ROM disc are read by laser. Light bouncing back directly from a land or flat area of the disk is read as a one. Light scattered by striking a pit reads as a zero.

"one" and a *pit* represents a "zero". A laser reads the disc by distinguishing a pit and a land by the shift in position of the reflected laser light that occurs when the beam hits the surface (see Figure 3.10).

In order for the CD-ROM to work well, the rotational speed of the disc must be kept precise. Special motors are dedicated to spinning the disc at the correct speed. Another motor, with an arm, moves the laser to the sector of the track to be read.

From the first single speed CD-ROM drives, we have now migrated to forty-eight speed variable drives with faster ones on the horizon. Transfer speeds have jumped from 150 *kilobytes* (KB) per second for single speed drives to over 6MB per second, and *seek* (or searching for information) times have jumped from 150 milliseconds to twenty to thirty milliseconds. Nevertheless, even the fastest CD-ROM drive is slow when compared to a hard drive.

CD recordable, or *CD-R*, drives give you the opportunity of writing information to a blank, recordable, CD-R media. At first glance, a CD-R might seem identical to a CD-ROM but the process of creating a disc is quite different. Instead of creating pits and lands in a disc, the CD-R heats (burns) special chemicals on the disc causing them to reflect less light than areas not burned. The *burned* areas reflecting less light work in a similar fashion as a "pit" on a conventional CD-ROM, with unburned, more highly reflective areas becoming the land. Due to the chemical composition of their coating, CD-R discs can be written to only once.

CD-R media are excellent for archiving large amounts of data. A typical CD-R disc costs nearly the same as a floppy disk. However, one of the key concerns in purchasing any CD-R drive is the software that comes with it. The software should support the full range of CD-R *protocols* so it can be read on many different drives and, most importantly, support multisession writing which allows you to add information to a disc in several writing sessions. Once a disc is full, its information cannot be changed.

Rewritable CD, or *CD-RW,* is similar to CD-R, but it allows you to change or overwrite material on the disc. This is made possible by a different chemical coating on the surface of the disc that allows you to reverse the burned spots so that data can be erased. The major disadvantage with CD-RW disks is they usually require the use of a similar CD-RW device in order to be read, so a conventional CD-ROM often cannot read them. CD-R discs, however, can be made so they can be read in standard CD-ROM drives and are becoming the medium of choice for artists and designers who need to save large amounts of information quickly and inexpensively.

DVD

Digital versatile disc, or *DVD,* is very similar to CD-based media with several notable exceptions. Like a CD, the disc is read with a laser. However, the DVD has two sides instead of one, and each side can have up to two layers. The first layer is similar to a conventional CD-ROM, with the data track spiraling from the inside out, but it can store up to 5.4GB of data. The second layer on the same side starts from the outside and spirals in, and can also hold 5.4GB of data. With two layers to each side, each with two layers holding 5.4GB of data, the DVD has a capacity of about 22GB of data compared with 650MB for a conventional CD-ROM. DVD drives are *backward compatible;* in other words, they can also read older, conventional CDs. However, CD-ROM drives cannot read DVD discs.

CD-ROM, CD-R, CD-RW, and DVD drives can connect to the computer using any one of several interfaces. A drive connected as an internal device will connect on the IDE channel like a hard drive or to a SCSI bus (requiring a SCSI card to be installed in the computer). If the device is an external model, it will most often connect either through the USB or a SCSI bus. Some can even connect through the computer's parallel port, although this slower option is disappearing fast.

The first popular application to take advantage of the substantial increase in the DVD's storage capacity has been full-length digitized movies. For digital artists who create multimedia, DVD represents a new opportunity. The 650MB size of CD-ROMs has been the limit for any multimedia production for many years. As DVD drives begin to replace CD-ROM as the standard in new computers, digital artists will be creating more complex and richly detailed multimedia to take advantage of the new, expanded boundaries.

Removable Hard Disks

Removable hard disks are disk systems with removable media that have much larger capacities than a standard floppy disk. The media can resemble a floppy disk or be in a thicker plastic cartridge. These portable media are particularly useful for digital artists who need to transport images or multimedia of large sizes to printing centers or clients.

The most common removable drives on the market today are the Iomega *Zip* and *Jaz* drives. The Zip comes in two disk sizes—100MB and 250MB—while the Jaz comes in both 1GB and 2GB sizes. Both the Zip and Jaz drives are treated by the computer very much like a regular hard drive. Depending on the model, the Jaz and Zip drives can connect to the computer externally through parallel or USB ports, or as a SCSI device through an external port of a SCSI card. Internally, they can connect directly to the IDE channel or to a SCSI card. While the Zip drive is great for transferring large files from one machine to another, because of its larger capacity, the Jaz performs more like a faster hard drive than a removable media drive. Special drivers for the Zip and Jaz add additional features, including special copy utilities, format commands, backup utilities, and more (see Figure 3.11).

■ Figure 3.11

Portable media have made it possible to easily transport larger files (images and graphics for instance) from one computer to another. The size of transportable disks has continued to increase as file size has grown to accommodate the needs of graphics professionals.

The LS-120 floppy disk uses a drive very much like the traditional 3 1/2″ floppy except that the storage capacity is substantially larger—120MB instead of 1.44MB. This drive can connect externally through the printer or parallel port, or internally through the IDE channel or SCSI bus. Using a higher density magnetic disk, it runs at speeds similar to that of a regular floppy drive.

What You See

Video Adapters

All information sent to a video monitor is broken down into *pixels* or picture elements, an individual point of light on the screen. Video cards and their ability to display color is related directly to how many bits of information they use to compose each pixel. The more bits per pixel, the greater the data on color and shades that can be stored, which is called *color depth*.

Most video cards allow you to choose the color depth by selecting the number of colors you wish to display on screen. Four-bit color results in no more than sixteen colors, while eight-bit color gives you 256 colors. Most digital artists want all the color they can get and so work at twenty-four-bit depth, which provides 16.7 million colors to work with.

While older video cards didn't need built-in memory to do an adequate job, today's requirements of increased resolution and color depth demand dedicated memory on the card itself (see Figure 3.12). In addition, newer 3-D technologies and faster bus speeds have resulted in a need not only for more, but faster memory. The earli-

■ Figure 3.12

As this chart demonstrates, different screen resolutions and bit depth require different amounts of video RAM.

Monitor size	Pixel Count	Colors	Video Memory Required
14 inch	640 x 480	16	512 KB
		256	512 KB
		65536	1 MB
		16777216	1 MB
15 inch	800 x 600	16	512 KB
		256	512 KB
		65536	1 MB
		16777216	2 MB
17 inch	1024 x 768	16	512 KB
		256	1 MB
		65536	2 MB
		16777216	4 MB
19 inch	1280 x 1024	16	1 MB
		256	2 MB
		65536	4 MB
		16777216	4 MB
21 inch	1600 x 1200	16	4 MB
		256	4 MB
		65536	4 MB
		16777216	8 MB

est form of this faster RAM was known as *VideoRAM* or **VRAM**. *Synchronous graphics RAM* or **SGRAM** is much faster and was designed for graphics-intensive applications. It synchronizes with the bus clock of the CPU in order to increase speed.

Today's video cards are more accurately called *graphics accelerators*. In addition to RAM, they have a dedicated processor to boost performance beyond that, of a simple video card. Newer and faster chipsets handle everything from decoding MPEG movies to special features of 3-D graphics and games.

Output: The Monitor

It is difficult for most people to visualize a computer without its primary output device—the *monitor*. This is what we see and often it is what we judge a computer by. It is the face for all the computer's information.

Most computer monitors implement a relatively old technology currently used in television sets, the cathode-ray tube (CRT). CRT technology shoots a beam of electrons from the back of the screen to the front of the picture tube. This beam contains a stream of electrons for each of the three primary colors (red, green, and blue). A coating on the back of the screen, composed of triads of red, green, and blue phosphors, lights up when hit by the electron beam. It is the mix of electrons fired by three color guns—red, green, and blue—hitting the back of the screen, and their relative strength, that determines the colors we see. As the strength of the electron hitting a particular phosphor determines how much light it will emit, the intensity of the electron beams are varied to control how individual colors will appear on screen.

Directed by plates surrounding the tube, the beam of electrons moves at high speeds in an organized fashion; from left to right starting at the top of the screen, one line at a time. This particular technique of scanning one line at a time is what determines whether a display is *interlaced* or *noninterlaced*. Older CRTs had interlaced displays that scanned in two passes, first scanning the even lines and then the odd lines to create a single scan. This is how our home television sets still work today. However, a computer's often static (nonmoving) images on screen appeared fuzzy, so the one line at a time or noninterlaced process evolved. As the scan moves down the screen, a clearer image forms (see Figure 3.13).

The vertical *refresh rate* of the video card and monitor determine how many times each second this scan happens. A refresh rate of at least 72Hz (full screen scans each second) is often recommended to avoid "flicker" and resulting eyestrain. The higher the refresh rate allowed by both the video card and the monitor, the better.

Shadow Mask

Cathode-ray tube monitors utilize either *shadow* or *aperture grill masks* to arrange their colored

■ **Figure 3.13**

Illustration of CRT (monitor interior). This cutaway of a monitor interior shows the guns hitting a phosphor screen to create an image.

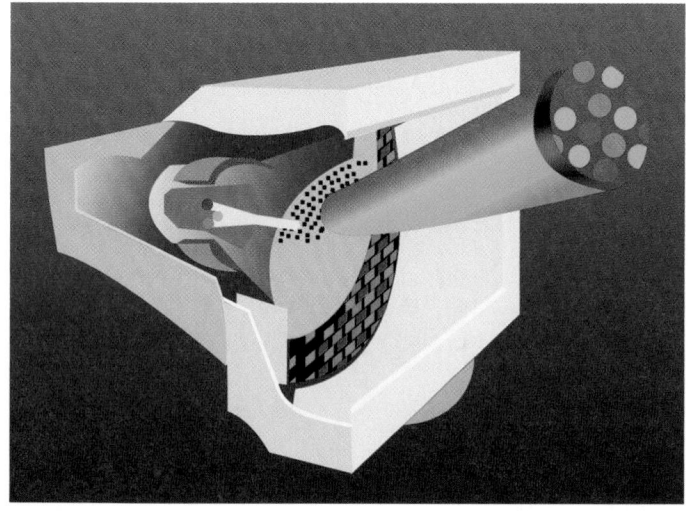

pixels at the front of the screen. Shadow masks are essentially metal screens and are typically made of *Invar,* an alloy that resists expansion and distortion as the shadow mask gets hot. Shadow masks have round holes (dots) punched through them and lie just inside the monitor tube and in front of the phosphor layer. Each perforation in the shadow mask lines up with the triads of phosphor dots and helps to prevent the electron beam from illuminating more than one dot, which would result in a blurring of the image.

Dot pitch is measured by the distance between similar colored phosphors on the inner surface of the CRT. The closer together the phosphors are, the smaller the dot pitch and the finer the screen image will be. For a 17″ monitor, a dot pitch of .26 to .28 millimeters (smaller is better) is considered essential for detailed images (see Figure 3.14).

■ **Figure 3.14**

Dot pitch is measured from the center of one colored phosphor to the center of another of the same color.

Aperture Grill

Sony Trinitron or similar technology tubes have vertical stripes rather than holes and are known as *aperture grill masks.* Instead of placing phosphors in groups of three, Trinitron-type tubes have alternating stripes of colored phosphors that go from the top to the bottom of the screen. Instead of a shadow mask, there is an alloy *aperture grill* that separates the stripes. Because these stripes of phosphors are unbroken from top to bottom and there is less mask to break them up (the electron beam defines the top and bottom of each pixel), colors appear brighter and more saturated. In this case, resolution is measured by *stripe pitch* or the distance between stripes of the same color. This is not directly comparable to dot pitch (see Figure 3.15).

To prevent the narrow and delicate stripes of phosphors from moving due to expansion or vibration, horizontal damping wires hold them in place. These wires reduce the possibility of the aperture grill moving out of alignment. They are also visible to the naked eye and some users find them to be a distraction.

Generally, text seems sharper on shadow mask tubes, while for graphics use, many people prefer an aperture grill mask such as the Sony Trinitron or Mitsubishi Diamondtron because images appear brighter and colors more saturated. Nevertheless, conventional shadow masks, when focused well, often provide exceptional performance.

■ **Figure 3.15**

A *stripe pitch* or T*rinitron tube* monitor uses stripes of color held together by twin bands at the top and bottom of the screen.

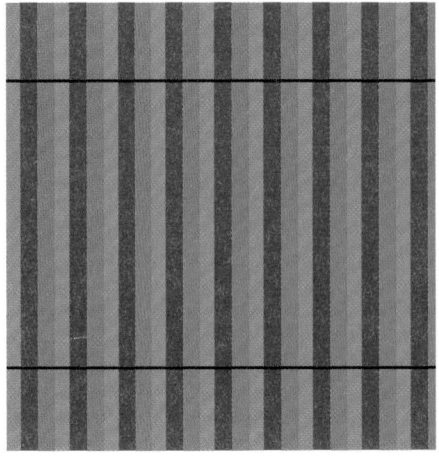

Monitor Size and Resolution

The most common monitor sizes are 14, 15, 17, 19, 20, and 21 inches. However, despite these measurements, a 17-inch monitor might have a screen that only measures 12 1/2″ or so horizontally and perhaps only 15 1/2″ vertically. This is because the screen size is measured on a diagonal and part of the monitor's tube is hidden by the bezel surrounding the screen. Like most computer equipment, the cost of monitors continues to drop. While in the past, a 17-inch monitor was considered an essential part of an excellent digital media system, most

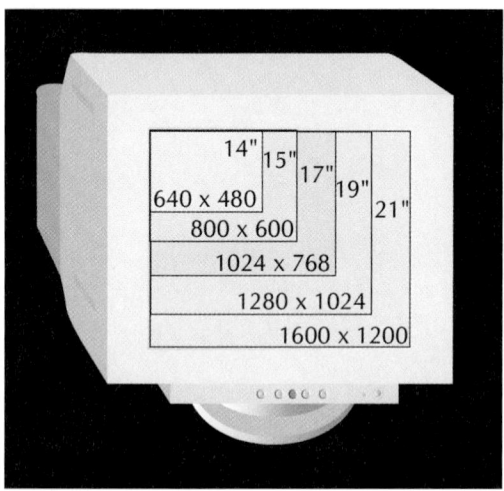

Figure 3.16

Monitor size and standard pixel resolution.

digital artists today consider a 19-inch monitor the minimum size and prefer 21inches.

Screen resolution is important to a comfortable working environment. Screen resolution that is set too low will appear coarse and pixilated while screen resolution that is set too high may make things uncomfortably small on screen. Most video cards today can handle resolutions of 1,280 by 1,024 (and higher) at 16.7 million colors (bit depth) quite easily, so choosing the right screen resolution for your monitor is simply a matter of personal preference. Traditional screen resolutions are 640 pixels wide by 480 pixels high for a 14-inch screen, 800 pixels wide by 600 pixels high for a 15-inch screen, 1,024 pixels wide by 768 pixels high for a 17-inch screen, and 1,280 pixels wide by 1,024 pixels high for a 19-inch screen. However, variations on these settings are dependent upon the individual user (see Figure 3.16).

Liquid Crystal Display

Some newer monitors and notebook computers use a *liquid crystal display,* or *LCD*. These flat panel LCD displays require far less room than conventional CRT displays.

LCD displays are actually composed of liquid crystals between two sheets of glass or similar material. When an electric current passes through the liquid crystals, they twist. Depending on how much they twist, some light waves are passed through while other light waves are blocked. This creates the variety of color that appears on the screen.

Figure 3.17

Color illustration of active matrix screen composition.

The major problem with *passive matrix* LCD screens is their response times. Things that change quickly—video or mouse movements—can cause an afterimage, which interrupts the flow of information on the screen. Stylish and quite modern looking, an up-to-date thin film transistor display screen (or TFT) is also known as *active matrix* because the LCD panel has an extra matrix of transistors, with three transistors assigned to each pixel—one transistor each for red, green, and blue. *Active matrix* technology does not usually have the problems associated with older types of passive LCD screens; problems like *ghosting*, where shadows can be cast on "off" pixels by "on" pixels, and slow response times. Because each pixel is turned on and off by a transistor in active matrix LCDs, refresh rates are no longer relevant, screens are bright and colorful, and they respond quickly to changes (see Figure 3.17).

The price for this newer technology places LCD monitors above that of more conventional CRTs. In addition, the best angle for viewing an LCD monitor is far more limited than that of a conventional CRT monitor. Viewing from the side or with a bright light coming over your shoulder makes LCD screens challenging to read.

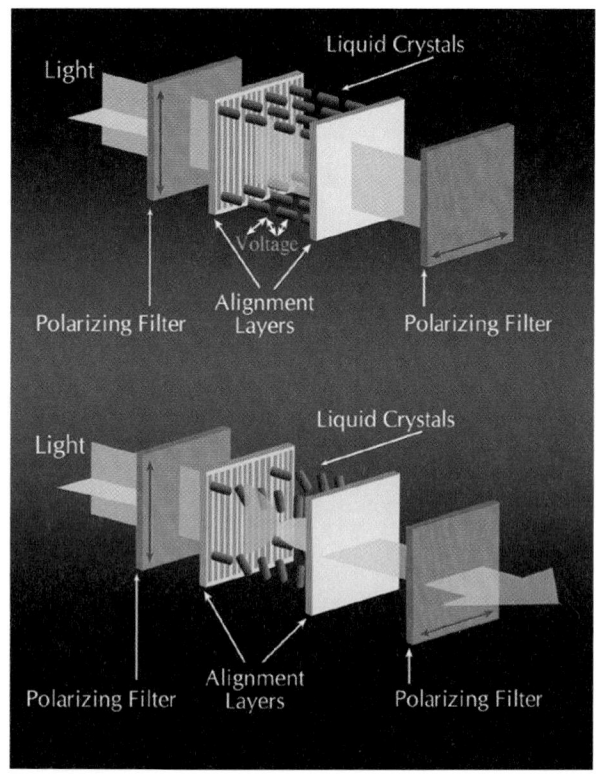

Keyboard/Mouse/Tablet

The computer's keyboard is perhaps the most familiar input device for those of the generation who grew up with typewriters. For all intents and purposes, it serves the same function as a typewriter's keyboard, but with additional keys for specific computer functions. There is a numeric keypad on the right side of the keyboard, which makes entering numerical data quite a bit easier than simply using the top row of numbers. Navigational cursor keys are also available between the typing keys and the numerical keyboard.

Function keys (or F-keys) are usually located along the top or left side of the keyboard and are specially programmed to issue commands. In many cases they can be programmed by the user. The F-keys can also be used in combination with the shift, control, and alt keys for greater flexibility of function.

As technology has evolved, particularly the Internet, keyboards have added features dedicated to additional tasks. Some keyboards have specific controls for sound, while other keyboards contain shortcuts for Web surfing. There are also keyboards that are more ergonomically friendly than others, with a split and angled keypad to ease wrist strain.

Regardless of what type of keyboard you use, it will plug into the keyboard connector at the back of the computer case. Special software is only necessary for those keyboards with enhanced functions.

Mice

The computer mouse is an astonishingly intuitive pointing device that moves a cursor around the computer screen. It is most often used instead of the keyboard navigational keys to position the insertion point in a document. In a graphics-oriented program, however, with just a click, it can take on an extraordinary variety of roles—from an airbrush to a selection tool to a paint can to an eraser.

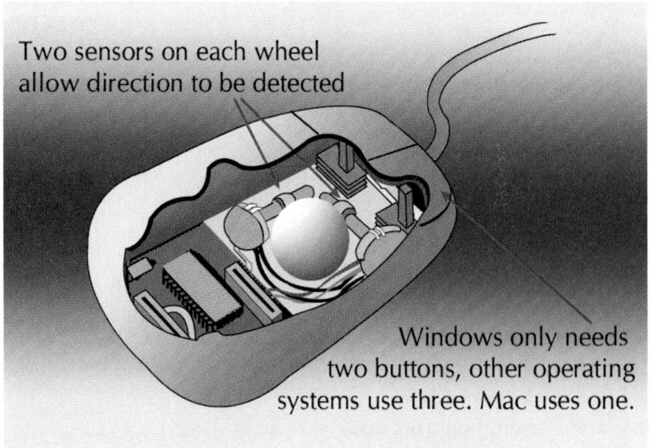

The mechanical mouse most of us are familiar with contains a small ball that moves against sensors as you roll it. The sensors translate the movement of the ball to movement on the screen. Mice also contain one, two, or three buttons (usually at the top front of the mouse) that control various functions within programs. There are many variations of the simple mechanical mouse including optical and infrared mice. A *trackball* device is actually an upside-down mouse with a larger ball that can be rolled between your fingers or under your palm (see Figure 3.18).

Two sensors on each wheel allow direction to be detected

Windows only needs two buttons, other operating systems use three. Mac uses one.

■ Figure 3.18

A traditional mouse senses the action of a ball against turning rods that provide friction feedback for positioning the cursor on screen.

Graphics Tablets

A graphics or digitizing tablet is far more sophisticated than a mouse in terms of function and sensitivity. Ranging in size from a small notepad to as large as a tabletop, artists can draw directly on the tablet with a special stylus (see Figure 3.19) that has a small, spring-loaded, plastic tip. The tablet is extremely sensitive to the movement of the stylus. It can sense not only where a

line has been drawn, but how hard the artist has pressed down, and at what angle the stylus was held. Some styluses can even be turned over to act like a pencil's eraser. Using a graphics or digitizing tablet with image-editing or painting software is probably the closest you'll ever get to drawing directly into a computer. In fact, more advanced tablets are now available with a flat screen built in so users can draw directly on their images. The ability of a graphics tablet, when used with specific software, to mimic natural art media is surprising and rewarding.

■ **Figure 3.19**

Drawing tablets allow the user to use a special pen tool to work in a more natural and traditional manner.

Scanner Overview

Scanners do the important work of converting flat artwork, such as photographs and drawings, into digital information. Once digitized, scanned imagery can be manipulated and developed in various digital media software programs. Photographic films, and the human eye, respond to light quite differently than scanners do. We tend to be more sensitive to shadow detail and variations in color and value when we view an image. Scanners, however, have a linear response to light—essentially a one-to-one ratio between the light they read and the outgoing signal they send. Therefore, a scanner often doesn't differentiate the subtlety of values to the degree that we do when we look at an image. Scanners also vary considerably in their ability to record the full extent of values in an image. Tonal correction is often necessary, even with the best of scans.

There is a wide range of scanners, varying in both quality and cost. The *drum scanner* (see Figure 3.20) is considered to be the zenith of scanning devices, and provides scans of unsurpassed quality and tonal differentiation. Expensive (as much as $50,000) and too difficult to operate for the occasional user, a drum scanner uses a stationary *photomultiplier tube* or *PMT* to read an image vertically, line by line, as the drum containing the image spins past the PMT.

■ **Figure 3.20**

Drum scanners are the epitome of scanning hardware and provide unsurpassed sharpness and tonal separation from both reflective art and transparencies. However, they are expensive and require specialized training to use them properly.

This line-by-line reading gives the drum scanner the ability to scan at extremely high resolutions and capture a wide *dynamic range,* a measure of a scanner's ability to differentiate in tones from light to dark.

Flatbed scanners are the most common form of scanner. Unlike drum scanners, they use a series of *charge-coupled devices,* or *CCDs,* to convert an analog image to digital signals. Flatbeds read an image in a series of horizontal passes. The earliest flatbeds read an image in three passes using a single light source and a series of red, green, and blue filters to create an RGB scan. Most scanners today use a single pass with multiple rows of CCDs to accomplish the same thing. In addition, many flatbed scanners also have attachments that allow transparent materials like slides and negatives to be scanned. Unfortunately, these devices, in all but the most expensive flatbed scanners, don't have the dynamic range (ability to represent a full scale of values from light to dark) to do much more from transparencies than provide scans for Web use or other low-end output (see Figure 3.21).

Dedicated *slide scanners* (see Figure 3.22), however, can provide exceptional scans from slides and negatives. Most of the slide scanners on the market are specifically for 35mm film materials. While their quality is not quite as high as a drum scanner, they can provide excellent quality scans from film materials for nearly any purpose you can imagine. Film scanners for larger format films (2 1/4″ and 4″ × 5″) are also available, but are rather expensive, often costing four to six times as much as 35mm film scanners.

Basic Flatbed Scanner

Scanner Cover

Material to be scanned

Lighting tube — Sensor — Glass top plate

Moving scanner head — Belt drive to move head back and forth

■ **Figure 3.21**
Basic flatbed scanner.

Scanning Considerations

When people purchase scanners, they are often most interested in the scanner's resolution—how many samples per inch or *spi* the scanner takes as it scans. This is directly related to the number and density of the CCDs contained inside the scanner. This number is what determines the *optical,* or true resolution of the scanner. For example, a flatbed scanner might be advertised as having 4,800 dpi (actually a misnomer for spi) resolution. This number is actually not the optical resolution, but the *interpolated resolution.* The interpolated resolution is what the scanner's software can deliver by making up additional pixels beyond those actually scanned optically. While it may seem strange, scanning anything other than line art at higher-than-optical resolution actually *lowers* the quality of the scan because the computer is calculating the values of pixels near each other and then creating new ones based on this calculation. The new information being created is based on mathematical probabilities and can lead to a softening and blurring of the actual image.

Very often, users ignore one of the most important elements of a scanner—the software. Scanners today come with a range of software possibilities. Some have limited controls and very basic choices for the home user, while others have an extended range of scanning controls that might include everything from color correction controls to sharpening algorithms to the ability to *descreen* images in order to remove the dot patterns from printed material. Artists are usually interested in more sophisticated software controls that will allow them to better control the quality of the scan.

■ **Figure 3.22**
As a slide moves slowly over the light source of a transparency scanner, photo-multiplier tubes behind the slide will read information as light comes through the slide and record that information in digital form.

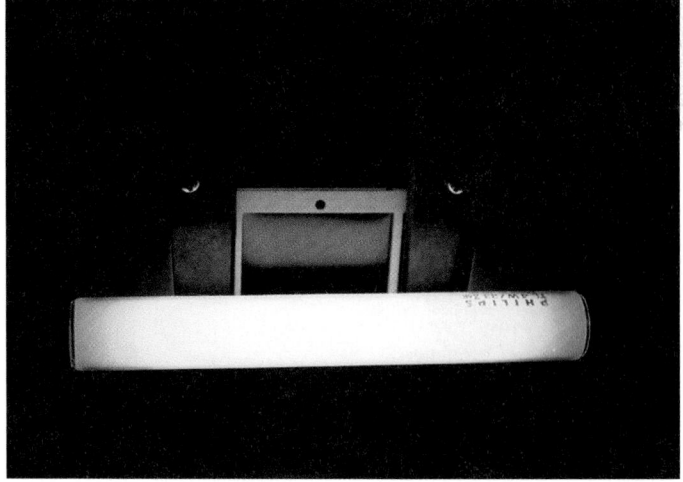

Digital Cameras

As their quality has increased and cost declined, *digital cameras* (see Figure 3.23) are becoming a more popular source of digitized images for artists. There are two kinds of digital cameras, one which is actually an attachment for traditional

■ **Figure 3.23**

Creative view of a digital camera.

■ **Figure 3.24**

Many traditional cameras have been modified to accept digital camera backs and now compete in areas that were once the sole province of film cameras.

professional cameras that can also use film, while the other is a truly integrated digitizing nonfilm camera.

Linear–array digital camera backs (see Figure 3.24) contain a single row of sensors that work much like a flatbed scanner. They are often attached to a large format camera and record directly into the computer. Because they record in a single pass in a scan that can take several minutes, they must be mounted on a tripod so that all vibration can be kept to a minimum. Quality is exceptionally high and in many cases these scanning camera backs have replaced conventional film in applications where speed of capture is not an issue. However, this type of camera back is currently very expensive, normally costing between $10,000 and $50,000.

The quality of *instant–capture digital cameras* is becoming better each year, as they are seen more and more as an alternative to scanning and even conventional film. Like scanners, digital cameras use an array of CCD devices to digitize an image. Depending on the number of these devices, the digitized images may be suitable for everything from Web design to large, high-quality inkjet output. Often rated in the number of pixels they can capture, a two megapixel camera is suitable for printing high-quality output of approximately 5″ × 7″, with three-to-five megapixel cameras offering images 8″ × 10″ and larger for high-quality output. Their ease of use and portability, combined with the ability to see images on a small screen on the camera back immediately, have made digital cameras increasingly important to digital artists.

Sound

Most computer users' first experience of sound on a computer was as a musical score that played when the operating system became active, closed a program, or announced an error. However, as music is downloaded from the Web or played on the computer from CDs, sound has become increasingly important. For digital artists, sound is an integral part of most multimedia productions.

In addition to speaker output, sound cards also have external connectors for a microphone, a joystick/MIDI connector, and even stereo components. The CD-ROM is usually connected internally with an audio wire that plugs into the back of the CD-ROM on one end and a receptacle on the body of the sound card on the other.

Increasingly sophisticated sound cards have been created to respond to the demands of music listeners, game players, and creative artists. Sound recording and playback is one of many features sound cards can offer in addition to simply playing back prerecorded sound. Sound is essentially analog—a rippling flow of sound waves that we continuously encounter. Just as traditional images need to be digitized, analog sound waves must also be converted to digital form in order for a computer to be able to use them. To convert analog to digital sound, the computer must *sample* the original analog sound and convert that information to a format (zeros and ones) it understands. A sound sample is a quick picture of a sound wave. The more samples the computer takes per second, the finer the image of the sound wave, and the higher the quality of the digitized sound. Most computers have the ability to sample sound from 11,000 to 44,000 times each second. Analog sound sampled at 11kHz (hertz equals per second, kilo equals thousand) is only one-fourth of the quality of sound sampled at 44kHz. As one might expect, the higher the quality of the digital sound recording, the larger the file necessary to store that information (see Figure 3.25).

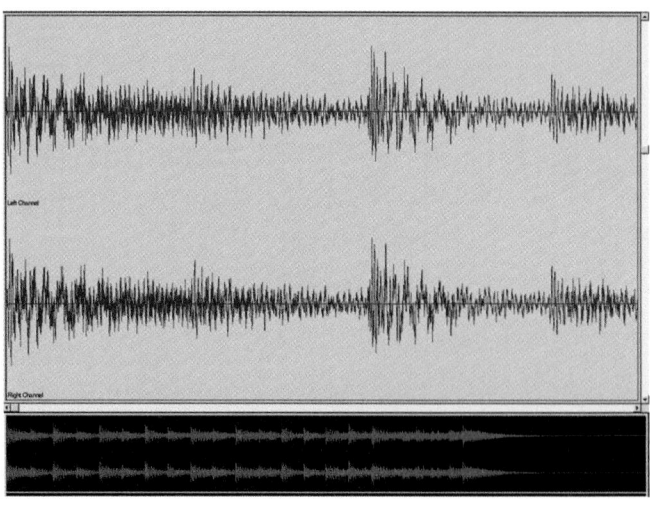

■ **Figure 3.25**
Visual representation of sound ready for editing.

Early sound cards used *frequency modulation* (FM) synthesis to create sound. These cards were noticeably inferior to wavetable sound cards. FM synthesis attempts to recreate the sound an instrument makes by mathematically calculating an approximation of the sound wave an instrument creates when played.

Originally developed in the early 1980s as a standard for electronic music synthesizers, MIDI encodes data for digitally recording and playing musical instruments. Organizing sounds into sixteen families with eight variations in each one, MIDI encoding creates very small files. A MIDI file is actually not digitized sound but a description of music, which your sound card interprets. A MIDI file typically contains header bits and one or more tracks. The header identifies the data, the arrangement of the tracks, and their timing. The track determines the type of instrument or sound to be played and its duration. MIDI files are very small and are often only a few kilobytes in size for a three-minute song. By comparison, a three-minute song on a CD might require thirty megabytes of storage.

Newer cards have *wavetable synthesis* and use samples of actual instruments and sounds to create the music dictated by the application. Many sound cards have several megabytes of sound samples in reserve to recreate sounds as we would naturally hear them. Wavetable cards can differ in quality depending on the caliber of the original recordings (sound samples), the frequency at which the samples were recorded, the number of samples taken to create each sound, and the compression scheme used to store the samples. Sound that is overcompressed will suffer a loss in quality.

Speakers

Regardless of the quality of a sound card and the sampling rate of a sound file, what a listener finally hears is directly affected by the quality of a computer's speakers. As computers have developed and improved, so have the speakers attached to them. Once a cheap addition—lower in quality than a child's tape recorder—today there is a wide range of speakers available for computers.

All speakers connect to the sound card and most have built-in amplifiers. They are different from the speakers in a typical audio system because they must be shielded to protect the monitor from the magnetic fields that are created around conventional speakers. A subwoofer can be added to the computer's speaker system to extend the range and presence of the sound.

Operating Systems

Macintosh

The choice of a computer for digital imaging applications *used* to be a simple one. Adopted early on by designers and the prepress industry, Apple Computer's Macintosh, first released in 1984, offered a graphical interface and an operating system described as "intuitive and user friendly," unlike previous text-based operating systems. In addition, with the Mac operating system controlling every facet of memory, several programs could be started simultaneously and the user could switch back and forth between them. As the Macintosh developed, it revolutionized the personal computer industry. With the advent of PostScript language and the desktop laser printer, *WYSIWYG* (what you see is what you get) was born—and along with it, Apple's now-traditional association with the world of computer graphics.

Like all operating systems, the Mac OS has evolved to support advancements in technology. With more or less complete control of both the operating system and the hardware using it, Apple has been able to closely integrate sound, video, and other multimedia areas. Nevertheless, it wasn't until the Mac OS8 that true multitasking—running several programs at the same time—became possible. Network functions in the Mac have always been a part of the operating system. *AppleTalk* has allowed Macs to communicate with one another and share printers and disk resources. The advantage of controlling the hardware attached to the computer, unlike the open system of PCs, continues to give Apple a real advantage in device implementation and integration. Their systems are "plug and play," so each new component runs more or less effortlessly when plugged in.

Apple's newest operating system, OSX, while maintaining the user friendliness of earlier systems, is a departure in many ways. It is not only aesthetically similar to Unix, but is based on a variation of Unix and Linux designs. This provides greater stability and even greater multitasking capability. New to the Mac operating system is a terminal window that shows the file system tree (with Unix type directories). This will make it easier than previous versions for third-party development. The new Mac operating system also includes many new features including an e-mail client and address book, Internet Explorer, and an FTP server.

The PC

In 1975, when Bill Gates became aware of BASIC and wrote a usable compiler for it, microcomputers were slow by today's standards. Their entire operating system was contained in a small amount of ROM which provided basic input/output or I/O. Realizing the lack of what he considered to be a real operating system, Gates purchased and modified a disk operating system, later named MS-DOS, that was soon adopted by IBM as PC-DOS for their first commercially available microcomputers (see Chapter 2).

Providing only basic functions for input and output, DOS underwent continued upgrade revisions to accommodate and control developing technology—the addition of hard drives, for example—as they developed.

DOS was a resounding success, even with its difficult-to-remember text commands. MS-DOS also left it to software developers to fully implement printing capability and other enhancements. In fact, outside of the most basic device support, it depended on *drivers* developed by individual hardware manufacturers to implement the devices they manufactured.

Microsoft's early attempts to develop a GUI like the Apple Macintosh's were not successful. It wasn't until Windows version 3.1 that their system became truly functional. Since Windows 3.1 ran on top of DOS, it was limited by many of DOS's shortcomings. It still required third-party device drivers for most peripherals connected to it and had only a primitive form of task switching—*cooperative multitasking*—that allowed the user to change from one program to another. *Windows for Workgroups* added peer-to-peer networking capabilities and updated drivers, but the operating system itself was still running on top of DOS and was restricted by many of DOS's limitations. For example, file names could have no more than eight characters and a three-character suffix.

Despite the primitive workability of Windows 3.1 and Windows for Workgroups, developing technology was driving operating systems toward true thirty-two-bit code in order to take full advantage of the new *Pentium* processor architecture. Windows 95 was like a breath of fresh air for PCs. Working from a combination of sixteen- and thirty-two-bit code, Windows 95 offered many of the same elements as the MAC operating system—even a trashcan. For the first time "drag and drop" became available on a PC. No longer running on top of DOS, it still maintained a backward compatibility for using many of DOS's power functions. Long file names were now possible (longer actually than the MAC) and plug and play compatibility with a true desktop was now a reality. With the introduction of Windows 98 and Windows 2000, the choice between operating systems for the digital artist had narrowed considerably.

Microsoft followed the introduction of their new Windows 2000 operating system with Windows ME (Millennium) for the individual home user. It includes, among other enhancements, many new multimedia features including an automated video editor, automated scanner and video camera installation, simplified home networking and broadband access, and system protection features. While earlier DOS programs can still be run in DOS windows, the Windows 95/98 restart features have been changed. Windows ME has borrowed some features from Windows 2000, which helps Windows ME run faster on the Web. However, it is still an upgrade to Windows 98 and doesn't offer the robust networking, security, and stability that Windows 2000 does.

Microsoft's newest operating system, XP, has several new versions, including XP Home Edition, XP Professional for business, and XP 64 Bit Edition for developers. Based solidly on the Windows 2000 core, XP offers a new user interface, better connectivity and security features, and stronger multitasking capability.

Unix

Unix was developed in 1969 by AT&T labs as an improvement on a still earlier operating system, Multics (multiplexed information and computing service), in an attempt to create an operating system that could accommodate up to a thousand simultaneous users. Ken Thompson, working at UC Berkeley, and Dennis Ritchie, working at Harvard, collaborated as one of the development teams for Multics. When the project disbanded, they rewrote the operating system in order to play space travel (a game) on another, smaller machine. Their new system was called UNICS (uniplexed information and computing service), as compared to Multics.

By the late 1970s and early 1980s, Unix systems were fairly widespread, although they were usually customized for specific computer architectures and software packages. While the Unix name appeared on many products, those products were often incompatible with one another.

To eliminate compatibility problems, in the mid 1980s Unix developers agreed on the concept of *open architecture* and certain specifications and standards. This concept has faced many challenges. In 1987, for example, AT&T entered into an agreement with Sun Microsystems, a leading proponent of one form of Unix. Viewing this event with concern, the rest of the industry banded together to create their own open-operating system. This new organization was called the *Open Software Foundation* (OSF). In response, AT&T and Sun Microsystems formed *UNIX International*. These two Unix system technologies formed the basis for system development during the coming years. During this time, X/Open Company continued standardizing the technologies necessary for an open-operating system specification and published their work in a regular series of *X/Open Portability Guides,* which detailed information on database connectivity, networking, and other similar features. Through their releases of information, the X/Open Company became the major definer of Unix open specifications.

The strength of Unix lies in its multitasking capability, which allows the computer to do several things at the same time. Users can start a new task while a previous one is finishing. By the late 1980s, Unix users could print a document while simultaneously editing a file and formatting a floppy disk. In addition, this same design allows the computer to be used by more than one person at a time. It even allows multiple users to access the same files.

Another of Unix's many strengths is its portability. It can move from one type or brand of computer to another with minimal difficulty. Always backward compatible, Unix can be easily upgraded to newer versions, and Unix is organized so that new tools or programs can be easily added.

Linux

In 1991, Linus Torvolds was interested in running Unix on his home computer but found it cost over $5,000 and was designed to run on workstations costing $10,000. In order to bring the power of Unix to his PC, Torvolds began to develop his own operating system based on Unix. After creating the heart of the operating system—the kernel—he called it "Freax" (free Unix). However, when he tried to post it on the Web, the site manager, not liking its seeming reference to "freaks," changed the name to "Linux" after a site label Torvolds had included.

By October 1991, Torvolds announced the first fully operational Linux system and distributed it, along with the source code, over the Internet. Before long, programmers all over the world were modifying it to run on a variety of systems, including PCs. Soon, improvements to the code led to numerous applications.

With a "development team" spread throughout the world, working on a variety of implementations, Linux has developed into a powerful market force. Estimates place Linux on over 8 million computers throughout the world. Today there are numerous companies selling their version of Linux, including support and upgrades as they become available. One of the earliest (1994) and best known is Red Hat, a company that markets a packaged version of Linux complete with full documentation and a host of software—games included. Linux already has a following among those proficient in computer use. However, it is growing in popularity as new ways of customizing its *shell* (user interface) makes it easier for the novice to take advantage of its powerful features.

CONCLUSION

During this chapter, we have examined the basic nature of hardware components, related software, and operating systems. With new plans for chipsets projecting even smaller and faster speeds; connectivity increasing in both speed and breadth of service; and *virtual reality* being used more and more in science and medicine, training, and, of course, gaming, the integration of computers in our lives is expanding at breakneck speed. Knowing the individual components that make up a computer is one important element in knowing what to look for when purchasing a new computer, upgrading or troubleshooting an existing one.

Projects: Inside the Box

1 *Make a list of the components (type of video card, RAM, hard drive, modem, and so on) in your computer, either by looking at the documentation that came with the computer, researching your computer on the Internet, or by contacting the manufacturer.*

2 *Making sure the computer is turned off and unplugged, open the case of your computer. Make a sketch of the interior and identify as many parts as you can.*

3 *Compare the major operating systems for personnel computers. Visit the websites of Microsoft, Apple, and review sites featuring Linux. Make a list of their similarities and differences.*

Outside the Box: Hard and Soft Copy

Introduction

As the computer has become a consumer appliance for everything from information processing to game playing to use as an artist's creative tool, it has redefined the world in which we live and has opened new visions of what that world can become. It has crept into our cars, home appliances, and communication systems, and has become a transparent and accepted force in our lives. At the beginning of the computer revolution, analysts predicted that users would soon communicate directly with others exclusively through the computer. This would lead to a "paperless society." Yet, as computers have become more powerful and printers more sophisticated, the promise of a paperless society has met the reality of a world where the quantity of printed documents to cross the world's desks has grown astronomically, creating small mountains on desks everywhere.

■ **Figure 4.1**
Illustration of an early typewriter.

This phenomenon began long before personal computers. It was the typewriter that was the world's first desktop mechanical printer. It eliminated the difficulty of reading someone's handwriting and created a document that conveyed a sense of formality suitable for business (see Figure 4.1). Even through the beginning stages of computer development, it was the typewriter that produced the letters, memos, reports, and spreadsheets that kept the business, the economy, and the country moving ahead. As the computer industry evolved, the need for *output* or hard copy, became increasingly apparent. In the early years of the computer as a consumer appliance, output was accomplished through impact character printers.

Impact Character Printers

By the early 1980s there were a variety of printers available for home computers. However, most cost over $1,000 for even the most basic printer, which limited the number of people who could afford them. As expensive as they were, the majority of these printers could only print the standard, universal American Standard Code for Information Interchange (ASCII) text set of ninety-six characters. This code read the combination of data bits from the computer and assigned each a letter, number, punctuation mark, and even mechanical functions like carriage return and line feed. A few higher end printers could print *both* upper- and lowercase characters (most only printed uppercase characters) and could even be programmed to change the typeface or font.

■ **Figure 4.2**

This photo of a daisy wheel print assembly shows the individual letters that will print when the head spins to the correct location on the wheel.

Daisy Wheel Letter-Quality Printer

Impact character printers contained an assembly that resembled a conventional typewriter, but unlike the typewriter prongs ending in a type character, it had a spoked *daisy* wheel, with the characters positioned at the end of each spoke (see Figure 4.2). A print hammer would strike the key and push it into an inked ribbon, which would then strike the paper to create a text character. These printers were capable of producing text that was indistinguishable from a conventional typewriter, and they soon became known as *letter-quality* printers. Daisy wheel printers cost up to $2,000 when they were initially introduced and were usually reserved for business use. Unfortunately, they were relatively slow and soon fell from favor as the new, faster, but lower-quality dot-matrix printers grew in popularity.

The Dot-Matrix Printer

The dot-matrix printer was a less expensive alternative to the daisy wheel or letter-quality printer. It was also an impact printer, but instead of using actual type letters like a typewriter, small hammers pushed pins against an ink-coated ribbon, which in turn transferred ink dots onto the paper to form letters (see Figure 4.3). Dot-matrix printers used either nine-pin or twenty-four-pin dot arrangements—*the matrix*—to create the letters used to make up documents. Compared to the clarity of letters created by even a simple typewriter, dot-matrix documents were relatively coarse, with heads containing twenty-four pins capable of improved letter formation. The printers with 24-pin capability were sometimes called *near letter-quality* printers because they placed the dots close enough together to minimize the broken, dot-like nature of the letter form.

■ **Figure 4.3**

Dot matrix print head assemblies drive a pin into an inked ribbon in order to make a dot on the paper underneath. Most pin assemblies were either 9 or 24 pins. More pins meant finer and less obvious dots.

In this era of printers, speed was not measured in the number of pages per minute but the number of characters per second (cps) it could produce. By 1977, dot-matrix printers could average approximately 50 cps cost well over $1,000. As with most technologies, speed and quality rose, even as prices dropped. By the 1980s, cheaper dot-matrix printers could easily produce between 100 to 200 cps (see Box 4.1).

Despite quality that was lower than a conventional typewriter, users found it exciting to use a computer and dot-matrix printer to produce a document that could easily be revised without completely retyping the entire composition. The tradeoff between high-quality "typed" output and convenience made

BOX 4.1

Epson-one origin among many

In 1881, in Japan, the Hattori family started a small import-export business dealing primarily with Swiss watch movements. By 1942 they had created the Suwa Seikosha company which originated and manufactured Seiko watches. As the company evolved into today's Seiko company, it distinguished itself by becoming the official timekeeper of the Olympic games. However, for the 1964 Tokyo Games, the Olympic Committee asked Seiko to create a timer that could record athletes' times directly on paper. They responded by creating the EP–101 *(electronic printer–101),* which could not only time speeds to hundredths of a second but also contained a dot-matrix printhead. This printer could create numbers by pushing tiny pins into a ribbon, which in turn transferred ink to paper.

In 1968, a commercial version of the EP-101 was released as a component for printing calculators and by 1975, Epson America was launched. The name Epson was derived from the original EP-101 printer with new products based on the technology termed "son of the electronic printer," or son of EP.

Initially, Epson America sold parts to companies wishing to manufacture desktop calculators and cash registers. While Seiko pioneered the use of dot-matrix technology, others had filed patents as early as 1937 for moving printheads that could punch text onto a piece of paper. Companies were already selling huge, heavy-duty dot-matrix printers for mainframe computers used in the business and academic worlds.

It was in 1978, with the development of the first commercially available personal computers, that companies began to build inexpensive desktop versions of dot-matrix printers. Centronix was the first to market with a printer that cost less than $1,000. Other companies soon followed and, by 1979, Epson had produced a second generation machine that was lighter, less expensive, and more reliable than its competitors. For $800, it filled a niche that the larger and more expensive printers could not. In 1981, it was adopted by IBM as the printer for its new personal computer, thus making it one of the first *original equipment manufacturers* (OEMs) for dot-matrix printers. This became important to the development of new dot-matrix printers. Epson software became an industry standard, which meant that software manufacturers included an Epson driver in all the programs they produced. Other printer companies were forced to emulate the Epson driver so that their printers would also be compatible with the leading software packages. ∎

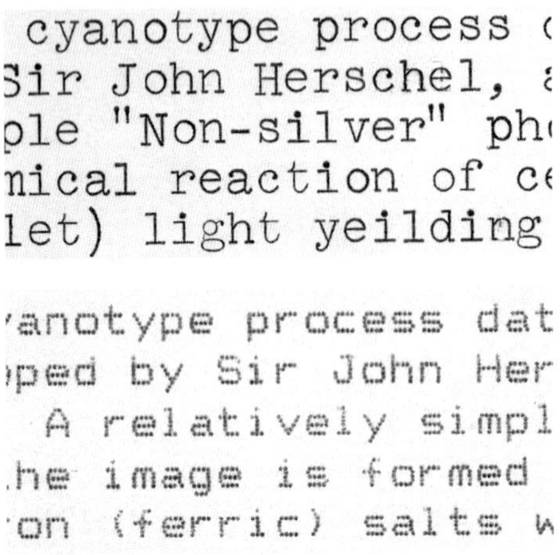

cyanotype process (
Sir John Herschel, a
ple "Non-silver" ph
nical reaction of ce
let) light yeilding

'anotype process dat
>ped by Sir John Her
  A relatively simpl
.he image is formed
'on (ferric) salts w

■ **Figure 4.4**

Typed (top) and dot matrix
(bottom) output.

the less expensive dot-matrix printer a popular addition to any computer system (see Figure 4.4).

With dot-matrix printers clearly established as the printer of choice, other technologies were evolving. One company, Trendcom, created a different kind of dot-matrix-like printer that was originally sold with the Apple II. Rather than use a mechanical device to drive the pins as in conventional dot-matrix printers, they used a thermal technology that used special heat-sensitive paper (much like electronic cash registers today) to create the dots that made up the letters. One advantage of this method was that, unlike the dot-matrix printers, these printers were very quiet. In June of 1979, Apple released a version of this printer under the Apple logo as the *Apple Silentype* for half the cost of a conventional dot-matrix printer. These printers had more control over where each dot would be printed and so were better suited to print the high-resolution graphics associated with the Apple II computer.

Even though the dot-matrix printer remains lower in quality than other forms of printers, it is still used today by older applications for printing forms and reports that require a carbon-like duplicate, which is only possible with impact printers. It can also print connected (*continuous-feed*) sheets of paper. By the late 1980s, even as newer printing technologies emerged, the dot-matrix printer remained the most popular printer for home computer users. It also dropped in price ($200 or less by the late 1980s), and became accepted as an inexpensive and easy-to-maintain printer.

Why would we ever want to change?

The Change

In 1984, while most of the computing world hammered along the impact road of dot-matrix printers, one of the most important computers the world had yet seen was being introduced. The Apple Macintosh, with its thirty-two-bit Motorola 68000 processor, larger random-access memory capability, relatively large hard drive for storage and, most importantly, a graphical user interface complete with a mouse, opened the way for programs that incorporated graphic elements as part of their function. Programmers could now create programs that allowed the user to easily draw images on the screen. With the development of the first desktop *laser* printer by Hewlett-Packard in 1984 (initially costing as much as an average car of that time period), Apple Computer released the *Apple LaserWriter* and ushered in what we now know as the birth of the desktop publishing (digital layout and design) industry (see Chapter 6). Even at its initial price of over $5,000, this new technology gave designers the ability to print an entire page at one time, instead of character by character, and dramatically changed the way in which the world defined quality output for computers.

Xerox: the Father of Laser Printers

Chester F. Carlson completed his Bachelor of Science degree in physics at the California Institute of Technology in 1930. He first worked for Bell Laboratories as a research engineer but was soon laid off, like so many others during the Great Depression. Unable to find a job in his field, he accepted a position at P. R. Mallory, an electronics firm famous for making batteries. At night, he went to law school to become a patent lawyer. As he studied, he found that copies of patents were scarce, and to make a copy of a patent, one had to either laboriously hand copy the original or send it out to be photographed. Either way, it was time-consuming and expensive. He became determined to find a better way.

Carlson spent months studying scientific articles at the New York Public Library. He eliminated photography as an answer, feeling that it had already been studied without result. Eventually he came across the relatively new field of *photoconductivity,* which recognized that the conductivity of certain materials increased when struck by light. He realized that if an image were projected onto a photoconductive surface, current would flow in the areas hit by light. The dark areas, those not hit by light, would have no current flowing over them. He applied for his first patent in 1937 (see Figure 4.5).

■ **Figure 4.5**
Model A Xerox Copier.

Working first in his kitchen and then in the back room of his mother-in-law's beauty salon in Astoria, Queens, Carlson continued his experiments. He hired Otto Kornei, an unemployed German physicist, to help him work more quickly. It was Kornei who first took a zinc plate, covered it with sulfur (which conducts a small amount of electrical energy when exposed to light), rubbed it to give it an electrical charge, and placed a microscope slide on top of it. The slide had the words "10-22-38 Astoria" written on it in India ink and was exposed under a bright light for a few seconds (see Figure 4.6). After the slide was removed, the sulfur surface was covered with lycopodium powder (created from fungus spores). When the excess powder was removed, some remained adhered to the words exposed through the slide. To preserve the image, Carlson heated wax paper over the powder forming the words. It coated the powder, preserving it.

During the next four years, until 1944, Carlson's research was ignored by some of the most prestigious companies in the world, including IBM, Kodak, and General Electric. It wasn't until one of Carlson's business trips for Mallory took him to Battelle Memorial Institute that someone expressed an interest. Battelle was a nonprofit organization that invested in technological research. They signed a royalty agreement with Carlson and began work on the technical areas that needed to be resolved before the process would become commercially feasible. The Battelle staff developed three important improvements: a new photoconductive plate using selenium (a better conductor than sulfur), a *corona* wire to apply a charge to the plate and also transfer powder from the plate to the paper, and better dry ink. Their ink was composed of an iron powder, ammonium chloride salt, and plastic. The plastic melted when it got hot and fused the iron to the paper.

When the process, then called *electrophotography,* was first introduced in 1948, it took fourteen steps and forty-five seconds to make a copy. The process's

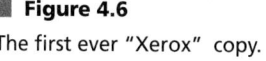

■ **Figure 4.6**
The first ever "Xerox" copy.

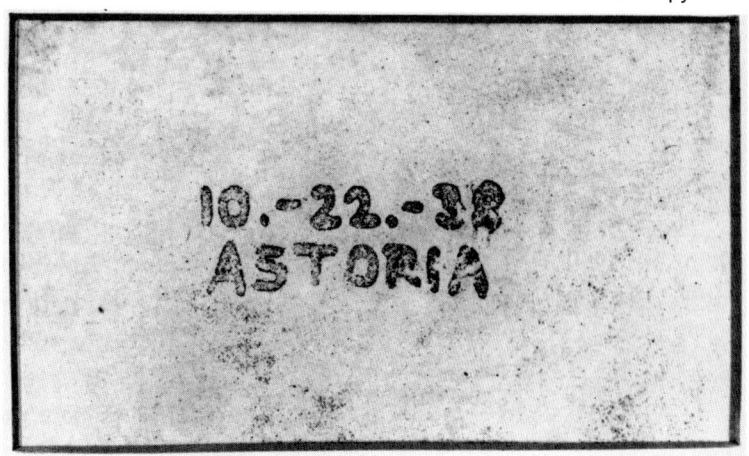

name was later changed to *xerography* (Greek for "dry writing") and then finally to *Xerox*. In 1959, the first easy-to-use machine that could handle 9″ × 14″ legal size paper, known as the Model 914, became a huge success. By 1965, the Xerox Corporation had revenues of over $500 million.

Xerox to Laser

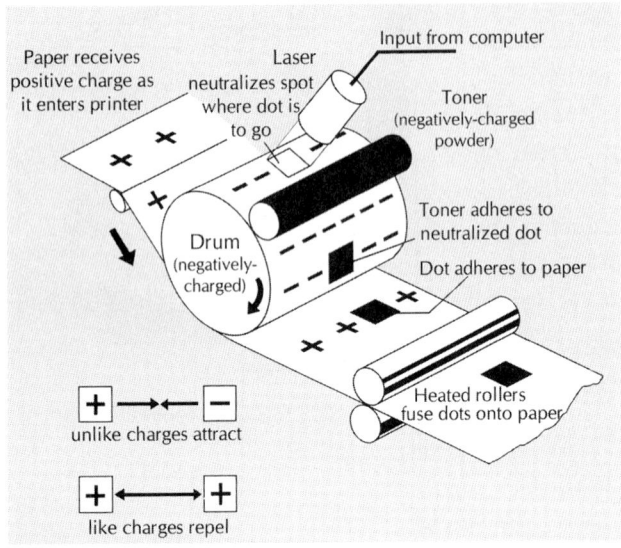

■ Figure 4.7

Inner workings of a desktop laser printer.

The Xerox process itself works its magic in a series of integrated steps (see Figure 4.7). A photoconductive (sensitive) drum receives a positive charge of electrons. An image is then reflected from a piece of paper (by mirror) onto the positively charged photosensitive drum. The white, nonimage areas become more conductive and their charge dissipates. A negatively charged black powder known as *toner* is spread on the drum and is attracted to the drum's positively charged areas (those corresponding to the darker parts of the image). A piece of positively charged paper is then placed on the drum. The paper attracts the negatively charged powder (toner). The charged ink (in the dark areas) is then fused to the paper by heat and pressure. This process has made possible the untold number of copies that have flooded the world since its invention.

In the early 1970s, computers and programs were already becoming capable of doing more than simply creating text. However, printers could not accurately depict images and graphics. Xerox researchers worked to create an image on the drum itself directly from the computer and invented the *laser* printer.

Instead of an image being reflected onto a drum, as in the case of the Xerox machine, a laser printer writes an image onto the drum with a high-intensity laser. Ten thousand times brighter than a reflected image, the laser is spread over the drum by mirrors and lenses that spin at a high rate of speed in order to synchronize with the laser switching on and off to write the information on the drum.

Wherever the light from the laser hits the drum (which has a coating that allows it to hold an electrostatic charge), it places points of positive charge onto the surface. These points represent what will appear as the output image. As the drum rotates it records one line at a time. To build high resolution, the drum must move in smaller rotations. If a drum moves 1/600th of an inch, a 600 dots-per-inch dpi vertical resolution will result. The faster the laser beam switches on and off, the higher the horizontal resolution.

As the drum is exposed, it rolls through a tray of negatively charged toner, which adheres to the positively charged portions of the drum. As this is being done, a piece of paper passes underneath an electrically charged wire and receives a negative charge. When the sheet of paper passes over the drum, the toner is transferred from the drum to the paper and forms the image. Parts of the drum that hold a negative charge do not affect the negatively charged paper and so result in white areas.

Once the toner is transferred to the paper, a fusing system applies heat and pressure and permanently adheres the toner to the paper. It is wax, just as in Carlson's first attempts, rather than the plastic placed in the original toner developed for the Xerox machine by Battelle engineers, that makes it easier to fuse the image to the paper.

Resolution

Perhaps the most important defining characteristic of a laser printer is the resolution it is capable of achieving, defined by how many dots per inch the printer is capable of placing on the paper. Early laser printers were limited to 300 dpi by the *print engine,* which controls the action of the drum and laser. As print engines have become more sophisticated, this has increased to 600 dpi and, most recently, 1,200 dpi. Some lasers also include special resolution enhancement techniques that can vary the size of the dots in order to make the appearance of curved edges smoother. The advantage of more dots per inch is a reduction in the jagged quality of curved lines.

Fonts

While laser printers are capable of printing whatever fonts one chooses to use, many laser printers also have a basic font set stored internally. These resident or internal fonts are built into the hardware of the printer and reduce the time it takes to print documents containing these fonts. In some cases, cartridges containing additional "hard" fonts can be inserted into the printer to extend the printer's font storage capacity. Resident fonts will print quickly and cleanly.

Printers also have the ability to download "soft" fonts from a computer's hard drive into the printer's RAM memory. However, this causes a delay in print time, and also uses more of a printer's memory to make a print. Today, this rarely creates a problem in printing documents. However, if it does, the RAM memory of most laser printers can be increased to handle additional fonts and graphics.

Controlling Laser Printer Output

Because laser printers are "page printers" that must process an entire page of information before that page can be printed, *page description languages* (PDLs) are important. The document to be printed usually includes more than appears on the computer screen. Standard 8.5″ × 11″ letter stock paper can hold over 8 million dots at 300 dpi. At 600 dpi this can increase to over 33 million dots. A laser printer's ability to interpret information about the page being printed is critically important to the speed at which it prints and the ultimate quality of the finished document. There are two standard languages that most printers adhere to in order to accomplish this.

The first commonly used standard was Hewlett-Packard's PCL. Originally intended for dot-matrix printers, the HP's first PCL language supported only simple printing tasks. In later versions, HP added support for graphics, scalable fonts, vector printing descriptions, and bidirectional printing. HP's most recent PCL offers an object-oriented control language made specifically for graphics and WYSIWYG capability. Unfortunately, it also increases the time it takes the printer to output the first page by about 30 percent.

The second standard is *PostScript* (see Chapter 6), the professional choice for anyone involved with graphic design and typography or those with a need for more sophisticated output. A printer that supports the more expensive PostScript option will also support PCL.

Unlike Hewlett-Packard's early PCL language, PostScript was always a vector or object-oriented language that treats images and fonts as geometric objects that can be made larger or smaller without a loss in quality, rather than *bitmap* images that are created by a series of dots. Bitmap type can lose quality as it is enlarged. Because of this, PostScript fonts are fully scalable, always smooth edged, and can be resized using PostScript commands rather than being recreated as bitmap or *raster* images. PostScript fonts and graphics improve dramatically when printer resolutions increase.

Color Laser

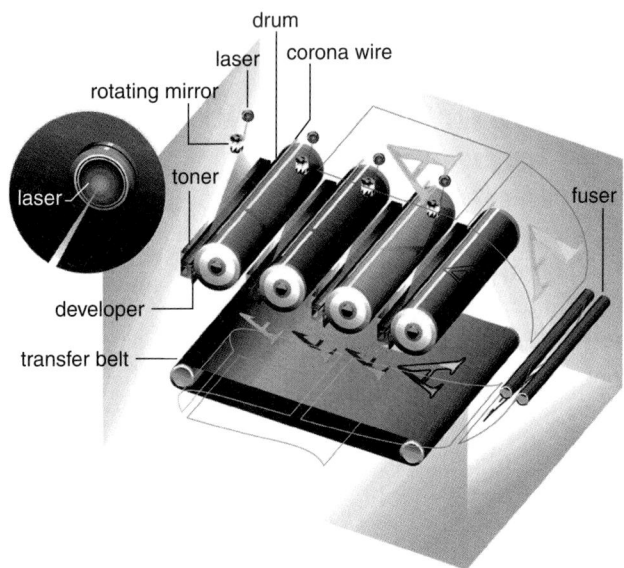

Color laser printers work exactly like their black-and-white counterparts, but make four passes through the process, usually building the four-color image on a transfer drum with cyan, yellow, magenta, and black toners (see Figure 4.8). The toners are then fused to the paper using heat or a combination of heat and pressure. Color laser prints are very durable. The toners are chemically inert and are fused onto the paper's surface instead of being absorbed into the paper's fibers. Because of this, color lasers can print onto almost any paper stock, or even transparent materials.

Color lasers are more expensive to operate than black and white lasers. Not only do they have four separate toner cartridges with a limited life expectancy, but the surface of the print drum can wear out, needing to be replaced periodically. In addition, the developer unit and fuser units also have to be replaced as the printer reaches certain page counts. This all contributes to the cost of running the printer.

■ **Figure 4.8**

Color laser printers print with four separate toner cartridges (cyan, magenta, yellow and black) in order to create the illusion of a full color print.

Inkjet

Inkjet printers are far less expensive color printers. Available in the mid-1980s first as a low-cost monochrome alternative to the laser printer, today's inkjet printers have made rapid improvements in quality, based on improvements in technology, starting with the move from three-color to four-color printing. Early inkjet printers required the user to choose between a black or color ink cartridge. In order to print in monochrome, the black ink cartridge was installed. To print in color, the black cartridge had to first be removed and then replaced with the CMY (cyan, magenta, yellow) cartridge. Today's inkjet printers allow the use of both cartridges at the same time and use black even when printing in color in order to improve the depth and crispness of shadow areas and extend the range of tonal values. Not only have inkjets become more popular, they have continued to improve in quality as they drop in price.

Inkjets are not impact printers like the dot-matrix printer, nor are they page printers like the laser. Instead they spray ink from nozzles as the nozzles pass over the paper. Mechanically, a motor assembly moves the printhead containing the ink nozzles back and forth over the paper in a series of horizontal bands. In coordination with this, another motor moves the paper in vertical increments as the inkjet nozzles drop the ink that builds the letters or images being printed. The page is printed one strip at a time as the printhead drops a row of pixels every time it passes over the paper.

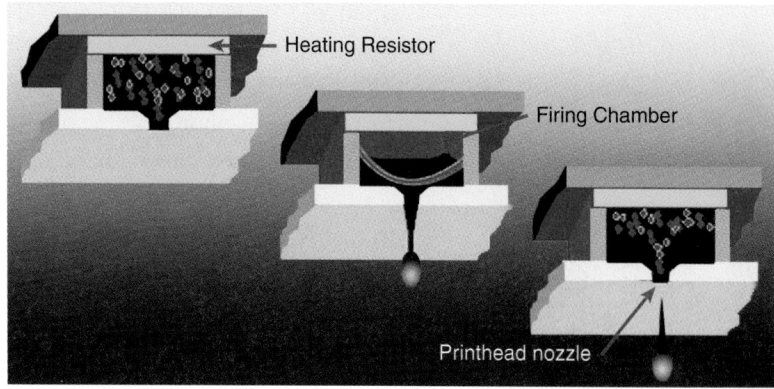

■ **Figure 4.9**

Thermal inkjet nozzles depend on heat expansion to drive ink from the ink cartridge.

Thermal Inkjet Technology

Invented in 1979 by John Vaught while at Hewlett-Packard, *thermal inkjet technology* (TIJ) is a *drop on demand* (DOD) technology in which small drops of ink, triggered by heat, squirt onto the paper through hair-thin nozzles controlled by a printer's software. The software determines how much ink should be dropped, where it should be dropped, and when it should be dropped. The heat applied to the ink creates a tiny bubble, which is forced to burst under pressure onto the paper (see Figure 4.9). As the heating element cools, it creates a vacuum that pulls ink from the ink reservoir to replace the ink that has been discharged. The average thermal inkjet has between 300 and 600 nozzles. Each hair-thin nozzle delivers an almost-microscopic ink dot with a diameter of only fifty microns. Variable dot sizes can be created by combining several color ink drops to create larger dots and additional colors. Black ink requires a larger inkjet nozzle and is kept in a separate cartridge.

Piezo-electric Inkjet Technology

Known for their ability to produce stunning color reproduction of photographs and complex graphics, Epson's *piezo-electric* inkjet printers are the strongest competitor to Hewlett-Packard's approach to inkjet printing. Their special technology uses a *piezo* crystal (a thin section of a crystal which oscillates when voltage is applied) behind the ink reservoir. Instead of heat being applied when an ink droplet is needed, electrical current is applied to the piezo crystal, which then flexes, forcing ink out of the nozzle (see Figure 4.10).

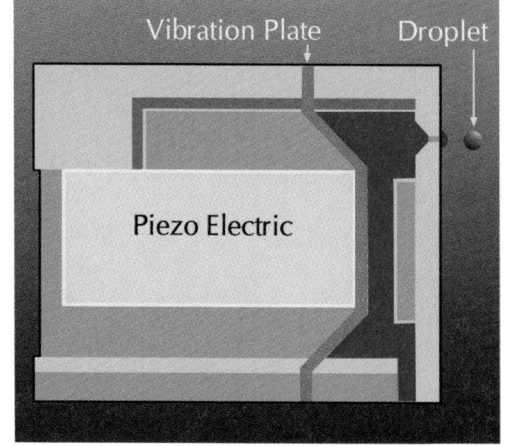

■ **Figure 4.10**

Piezo inkjet print head assemblies use an electrical current to flex a plate to drive ink from the ink cartridge.

Piezo technology allows for more precise control over the size and shape of the ink drop and, as a result, more nozzles can be used to drop the ink onto the paper. This increases control of the ink drop size and placement. Unlike thermal technology, the ink does not need to withstand heat and so can be formulated in ways unavailable to thermal inkjet printers. Epson inks are solvent based and dry very quickly. Therefore, rather than hitting the paper and spreading out into the paper fibers, they maintain their shape and individuality, creating sharp, highly detailed prints without bleeding into one another.

For artists, the increasing level of detail in inkjet printing, along with a corresponding decrease in the visibility of the dots of ink as they become smaller, has been very important. However, the issue of permanence has been of equal concern. Third-party vendors have been able to formulate inks for Epson printers that are more stabile and have greater archival characteristics. This has opened a fine art printing market for Epson inkjet printers, and their current line of photographic quality ink jet printers offer specially formulated ink with strong archival characteristics.

Inkjet Resolution and Photographic Quality

When discussing inkjet printer resolution, whether it be generated by thermal or piezo means, quality is determined by a combination of two elements. The more dots per inch the printer can deliver, the more potential for a crisper image. This is especially important when printing hard-edged items like text and business graphics. However, it is the number of levels of gradations per dot that determines how close to photographic-image quality the printer can achieve.

The ability of a printer to create a grid of *halftone* cels—groups of dots positioned closer together or further apart to create what appears to be a continuous tone—is one of the things that determines its ability to mimic photographic quality (see Figure 4.11). By mixing halftone patterns of color dots, the *process colors* of cyan, yellow, magenta, and black can be intermixed to create the illusion of many more colors as the human eye mixes them together. The greater the number of dots that can be overlapped, the better the illusion of continuous tone. Recently, six-color inkjet printers have been developed, which add a light cyan and light magenta in order to produce more overlap and subsequently an even better representation of color tonal values.

■ **Figure 4.11**

Although color laser and inkjet prints appear to be continuous tone, they are composed of tiny overlapping spots of four colors (six in the case of some inkjet printers).

Many printer manufacturers have opted for increasing the number of colors that can be overlapped on an individual dot rather than increasing the number of dots in an inch. In 1996 the Hewlett-Packard Deskjet 850C could print four drops of ink on a single dot. More recently, by decreasing the size of the dot, that number increased to twenty-nine drops of ink per dot.

An important element of inkjet printing is the choice of which paper to use. Unfortunately, inkjet printers do not print equally well on all types of paper. Some brands are better at printing on conventional papers than others. Others are superior when using special coated paper stocks or even heavily glossy photographic-type paper. For the artist, experimentation with various papers is necessary to achieve the best possible printing quality for a given printer. Recent developments of archival inks and papers have opened new vistas for photographers and other artists seeking permanent (or at least more archival) digital prints of their images. In the past, this could only be achieved through specially equipped and very expensive high-end inkjet printers like the IRIS. Today, this possibility is being realized on each artist's desktop.

Inkjet Costs

Generally, inkjet printers are more than ten times more expensive to operate than a laser printer. Not only do special inkjet papers cost more than regular paper, the ink cartridges used in many printers are not economical. While most inkjet printers have now separated the black ink from the color ink into two separate cartridges, most printers still maintain a single shared *tri-color* cartridge for the cyan, yellow, and magenta inks. When one of the color inks runs out, the entire cartridge must be replaced, even if the other ink reservoirs are not empty (see Figure 4.12). High-end inkjet printers have addressed this by separating each of the color inks into their own separate cartridges. Nevertheless, the small size of the ink reservoirs is not able to support more than several hundred pages that incorporate color. If full-scale photographic images are printed, the number of pages drops dramatically. Some

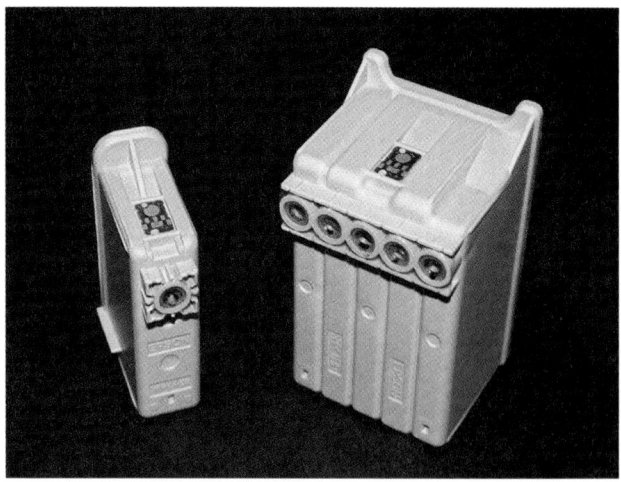

■ Figure 4.12

Many inkjet printers have one cartridge for black ink and another, separate cartridge for the individual color inks.

newer, high-end printers have solved this problem by incorporating larger separate ink reservoirs. Ink manufacturers have also marketed systems that use larger bottles of ink connected directly to the printer's ink delivery system in order to continuously replenish the primary ink supply. In both cases the cost of running the printer has decreased while quality and ease of use has increased.

IRIS Printers

IRIS printers are, without a doubt, the most sophisticated inkjet printers in use today. IRIS printers are sometimes referred to as Giclée (pronounced, zhee-clay) printers when they have been modified to produce prints of archival quality. Capable of producing prints on any smooth material up to 35″ × 47″, the IRIS printer sprays ink through each of its four nozzles at the rate of 4 million drops of ink per second. For fine arts printing, an acid-free fine arts paper is wrapped around a drum on the printer, which rapidly spins the paper. A computer controls the jet-like spraying of the tiny drops of ink, which are no larger than a red blood cell, with pinpoint precision. The computer can overlap from zero to thirty-one of these miniscule droplets per pixel to create true continuous tone images without the dot patterns usually associated with other inkjet technologies (see Figure 4.13).

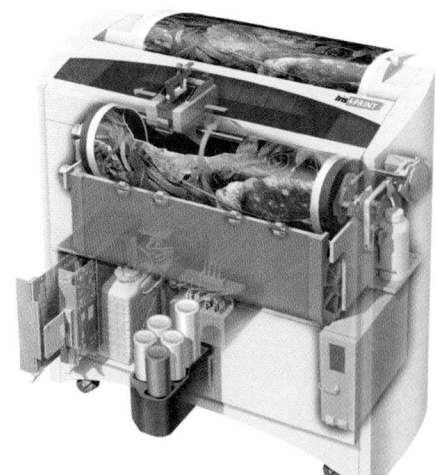

■ Figure 4.13

Considered the Rolls Royce of inkjet printers, IRIS printers create large format inkjet prints of unsurpassed quality in the inkjet arena.

Many artists and photographers producing their work as IRIS prints do so not only for the beautiful, rich prints, but also because an edition can be produced one at a time as the print sells, rather than all at once as is required by lithography and other print technologies. Artists have also found that IRIS prints are sharper, have truer color, and are superior in overall quality to lithographic prints. Most major museums and galleries now accept IRIS prints as a fine art medium, especially for photographs. Unfortunately, at this point, IRIS printers are not for home use. Costing upward of $50,000, these printers are clearly for the professional market.

Phase-Change Printers

Solid Ink Printers

At first glance, solid ink printers appear to be a synthesis of a laser and an inkjet printer. Like laser printers they are page printers, but they use color in

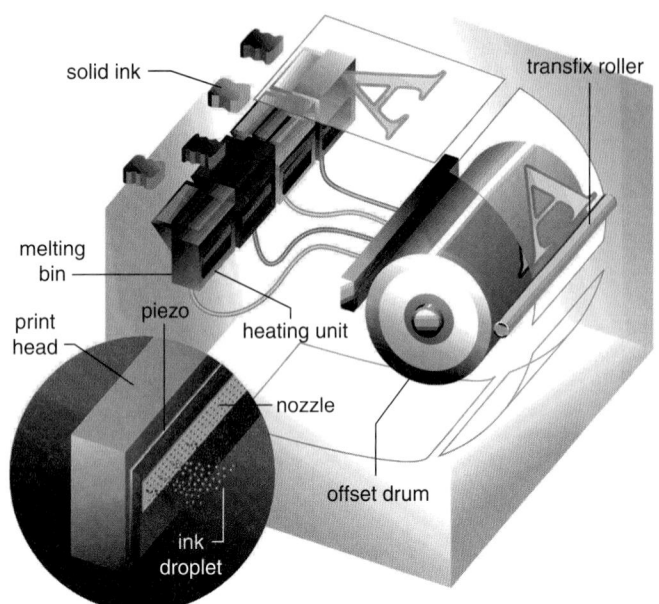

solid ink

transfix roller

melting bin

print head

piezo

heating unit

nozzle

offset drum

ink droplet

◼ Figure 4.14

Tektronix, now part of Xerox, produced printers that print from sticks of solid wax. They are easy to maintain, and designed to compete with color laser printers.

much the same way an inkjet printer does. Unlike either, they liquefy solid cyan, magenta, yellow, and black wax ink sticks and store the melted colors in separate reservoirs. The ink is then squirted onto a transfer drum that has been coated with a special transfer agent. When the drum image is complete, it is *cold fused* (bonded under pressure between two rollers) onto a piece of preheated paper (see Figure 4.14).

These printers are relatively economical. They print extremely vivid and solid colors, and are very well suited for graphics work. In addition, they can print on any paper stock without a loss in quality, making them particularly useful for printing on unusual surfaces or special materials. However, they are not as good as color lasers for text or color inkjet printers for photographic-quality reproduction.

Thermal Wax Transfer

Thermal wax transfer printing uses a plastic ribbon that is coated with cyan, magenta, yellow, and black wax-based ink in panels the same size as the paper on which it will print. A roll of transfer ribbon contains many sets of page-size four-color panels. Heating elements on the printhead melt the wax and cause it to adhere to a special receiver paper or transparency film (see Figure 4.15).

When a page is printed, the ribbon mechanism brings the first color panel (cyan) in contact with the paper and, through heat, applies every dot in the image that contains this color. After the cyan panel is printed, the yellow panel is placed onto the paper and the process is repeated. Next the magenta panel is printed, and finally the black. If examined closely, the final image can be seen to contain minute dots of colored wax.

The positive side of this process is the pure, strong, light-fast, and waterproof color. The downside is the potential for waste. Regardless of how much or how little of a particular color is printed, the entire panel of each color is employed. Because of this, costs for this process are determined only by the number of pages printed, not the coverage of the color on the page.

◼ Figure 4.15

Some printers were designed to create images from wax transfer ribbons. An image would print, in register, from a series of cyan, magenta, and yellow sections of a ribbon in order to create a full color image.

Dye-Sublimation Printers

Dye-sublimation printers are capable of producing prints indistinguishable from those produced in a traditional photographic darkroom. They do this by vaporizing inks, turning solid colors into a gas, which then solidifies or *sublimates* on the paper.

Instead of reservoirs of ink, *dye-sub* printers use a plastic transfer ribbon (similar to the thermal wax printer previously described), that holds a series of panels with cyan, magenta, yellow, and black colors in sequence. A single roll can hold many sets of colors (see Figure 4.16). As an image is printed, a thermal printhead with thousands of heating elements moves across the transfer ribbon, vaporizing the appropriate portions of the ribbon and allowing the color to diffuse onto specially coated paper. The hotter the heating element in a particular location, the more dye is vaporized and diffused onto the paper's surface. Varying color densities can be achieved through precise temperature variations. This provides a true continuous tone, photographic-quality image without visible dots or halftone screens of any kind.

The dye-sublimation process, while producing truly photographic-quality images, is the most expensive printing technology used by artists. Like the thermal wax printer, an entire set of color panels is used for each print, regardless of color coverage. Costs per print can range from four dollars and up, depending on the size of the print and the individual machine being used.

■ **Figure 4.16**

Dye sublimation printers also print in register from a special ribbon. However, unlike wax transfer, this printer vaporizes parts of the ribbon in relationship to the density and color values of the image. This material then settles onto the paper receiver sheet to create images without visible dots of any kind. This type of print is the most "photographic" of any from the printers available today.

Soft Copy

The CD-ROM

In addition to conventional printing or hard copy, data is often output to digital storage media. For example, hardware and software manuals are often not printed but, instead, issued on a CD-ROM. Commercially prepared CDs are plastic with an aluminum storage surface (see Figure 4.17). An *analog-to-digital converter* (ADC) converts analog information to either a one or a zero (binary form), which is burned by a laser onto the disc. When the laser is switched on, it burns a *pit*, representing a zero. When it is off, the surface is not damaged and is read as a *land,* which represents a one (see Chapter 3). After a master disc is prepared by this process, it is pressed onto blank discs in much the same way old vinyl records used to be produced.

Once a disc has been "burned," a CD-ROM reader uses a laser to decode the digital information. The read laser is not powerful enough to disturb the information written by the more powerful laser that "burns" the disc. Using a digital-to-analog converter (DAC), the weaker laser reads the pits and lands, and converts the digital information either to sound (by comparing the bit patterns to voltages and then the corresponding sound) or data (by using binary forms or turning the binary forms to ASCII characters). In this way, digital information can be stored and read without physical damage to the disc.

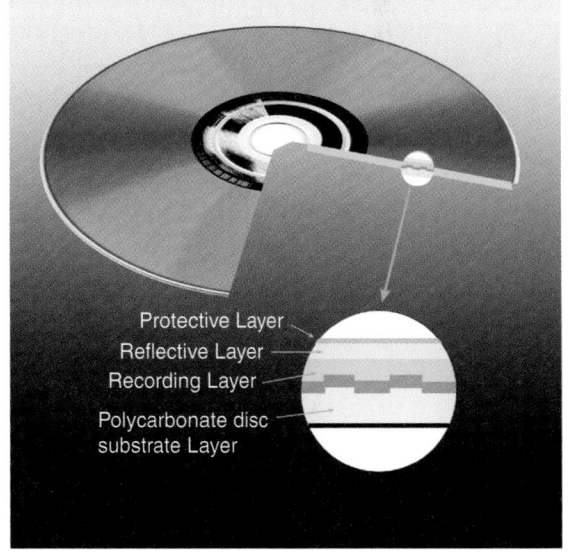

Protective Layer
Reflective Layer
Recording Layer
Polycarbonate disc substrate Layer

■ **Figure 4.17**

Construction of layers on a traditional CD-R disk.

From a Love of Music

This method of data storage was originally conceived by James T. Russell in the late 1960s. An inventor from early childhood, Russell was a physicist for General Electric. He worked on many experimental projects and was one of the first people to use a color TV screen and keyboard to interface with a computer. In 1965, he joined the Battelle Memorial Institute (see section on Xerox/Laser Printing) as a senior scientist. However, it was his interest in music that led to his work in digital recording.

When a vinyl record is played over and over, the needle inevitably damages the vinyl and the sound quality diminishes. Russell hit upon the idea of using light to record and play music instead of the physical methods then employed. Already familiar with digital data and the methods in which it was recorded (punch card and magnetic tape), he knew that if he could represent the binary code of zero and one with dark and light representations, enormous amounts of information, including sound, could be recorded and played without ever wearing out.

At Battelle, Russell invented the first digital-to-optical recording and playback system, which was patented in 1970. Originally, Russell had conceived of the actual recording surface as a 3″ × 5″ rectangle analogous to an early computer's punch card. The final form, however, was a disc much like the phonograph records that had inspired him.

Initially, there was very little interest in the invention; however, by 1985 Sony, Philips, and other companies that manufactured sound systems began to purchase licenses. Within ten years, the CD-ROM all but replaced vinyl records as the medium of choice.

WORM: CD Recording for Everyone

The equipment required for the production of a commercial CD master is complex, expensive, and not appropriate for the home user. However, a write once, read many (WORM) system allows a user to purchase a blank disc and create a CD using a related system (see Chapter 3). Discs used in this system are not mastered and pressed as previously described, but have a chemical coating that allows areas of that coating to be rendered either reflective or non-reflective by a laser, mimicking the lands and pits of commercial CD discs.

While the original WORM drives wrote the entire disc at once, that is no longer true. Today, as long as parts of the disc remain unwritten, a user can go back and write additional data at a later time. This *multisession* capability allows the CD-ROM to be used as one would use a hard drive or other storage device. However, information written to these discs cannot be removed, which can be seen as either an advantage or disadvantage. For those who see it as a disadvantage, rewriteable CDs (or CD-RWs) provide a newer option, where old information can be overwritten with new information (See Box 4.2).

CD-DA (compact disc-digital audio) The CD-DA is a standard music CD pressed from a master disc and readable in all CD-ROM drives. These discs are usually intended for a home CD player.

CD-ROM (compact disc read-only memory) Commercial CD-ROM discs are mastered (burned into pits and lands) and then duplicated (pressed) as many times as necessary for the marketplace. There are also CD-R (writeable) and CD-RW (rewriteable) discs that can be written to by the home user.

CD-1 (compact disc-interactive) The CD-1 format requires a special stand-alone player. It is not meant for a computer but, instead, is meant for the home entertainment market. It can deliver music, animation, text, video—essentially a multimedia experience through the television/stereo system. It also provides an interactive interface that allows the user to control the sequence of activities. If a CD-1 disc is played on a conventional CD-CA player, the music portion of the disc will play, but the other components will not.

CD-ROM/XA (extended architecture) Newer computer CD-ROM readers also contain some of the audio capabilities normally found in CD-1 players. They are capable of using a space-saving adaptive differential pulse code modulation ADPCM waveform code to create more realistic sound. As a result, an XA drive can interleaf audio and other data so that sound and images can be displayed at the same time.

Photo CD Kodak and Philips developed the standard for Photo CDs by combining two different forms of CD technology together. Because each disc had to contain different information, WORM technology was of critical importance. Because new data had to be added to the disc as the customer added new images, it had to be multisession. Photo CD discs also must play on a computer CD-ROM reader and on a home DVD player for viewing on a television. A hybrid disc, capable of being read by both CD-ROM/XA and CD-1 drives, was the answer. The CD-1 bridge disc format solved this problem and created a disc that could be read on both devices. In addition, these discs and their readers support the addition of new data during different "writing sessions," and so are considered "multisession" discs. This is one of the key reasons most conventional CD-ROM drives today support multisession discs.

Video CD is another recent bridge format that allows MPEG-based video to be placed on a regular compact disc for linear playback.

Beyond the CD: New Possibilities

DVDs were originally produced for the home entertainment industry. Their greater capacity, compared to a CD, allowed for full-length motion pictures to be encoded and then decoded by home players connected to a television set. Unlike regular CD-ROMs, a DVD is written on both sides of the disc. Because of its greater capacity, it is likely that most companies will eventually switch to this format to carry software and other information to home computer users. In fact, it has already been renamed *digital versatile disc* to convey its new potential. Rewriteable versions (DVD-RW) are now available for consumers.

As new technologies develop, we can expect to not only see the storage capabilities of compact discs increase, but their performance capabilities as well. The high-definition CD (HDCD), patented by Pacific Microsonics, uses a higher frequency to read bit patterns from the disc, which results in the full detail and resolution of the master recording. It has long been felt that, while technically accurate, CDs often do not capture the fidelity of sound that vinyl records once did. HDCD technology is encoded on a compact disc during the mastering stage and renders a greater dynamic range and more natural musical sound. HDCDs are also completely compatible with earlier CD players and will sound better when played on them. In turn, HDCD players will also make conventional CDs sound even better. When a HDCD disc is played on a HDCD player, the sound is beyond anything previously available.

Internet Publishing

Modems: Modulator/DEModulator

In the era of Web publishing, a significant proportion of artists' creations are not meant for hard copy or even distribution on CD-ROMs but, instead, for an online audience. Transmission of this work is through the Internet or World Wide Web, which for most users is accessed by a modem.

Modems were initially used to send telegrams. Simply put, they change computer information into sound waves that can travel over existing phone lines. These sound waves are analog, not digital. The earliest modems would *modulate* or alternate between two different tones to represent the zeroes and ones of computer language. By modulating at the transmission end of the connection and then demodulating at the receiving end, information was first encoded and then decoded by the modem. Today's modems use far more than the simple modulation early modems used and they now encode data through a series of sounds to convey more complex information.

In the 1970s, modems were not used very often by the general public. However, you might recall seeing films from that era (usually spy thrillers) where someone wants to send something "over the wire," and then places the phone in a special cradle—like a holder with rubber cups—in order to accomplish this goal. These *acoustic couplers* (see Figure 4.18) were in fact very slow, ten-character per second modems—equivalent to a 300 bps (bits per second) modem. They required no electrical connection between the computer and the phone system, but relied solely on audio tones.

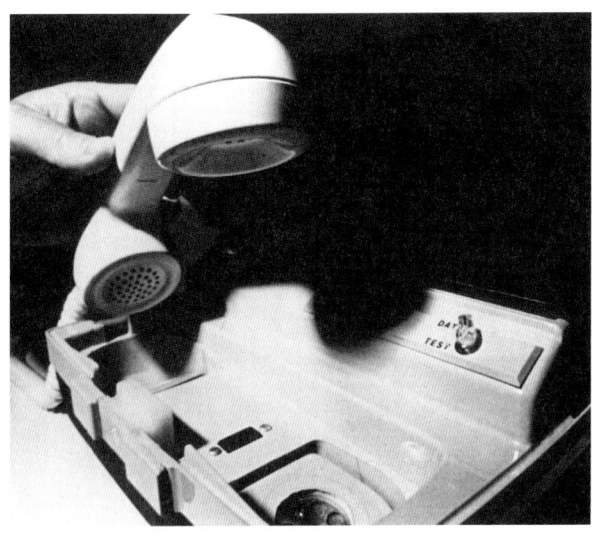

Figure 4.18

Acoustic couplers were the earliest form of modem. Running at approximately 300 baud, they were slow and unwieldy by today's standards.

During the late 1970s, Hayes became one of the leading manufacturers of modems and invented the *AT* (attention) command that still begins each modem command. This modem command language controls everything from commanding the modem to dial a number to how many times the phone should ring before being answered by the modem. Most manufacturers use the Hayes commands and are referred to as *Hayes compatible*.

As modems evolved, a series of standards were established that determined the kinds of modulation that were used and guaranteed compatibility with existing phone line capability (see Box 4.3). The International Telecommunications Union (ITU) was created by the United Nations. It is responsible for coordinating and standardizing international telecommunications standards, such as those that control the speed of communication through a modem.

The newest standard established by the ITU is an improved 56K modem standard called V.92. This new standard does not change the top download speed. It does, however, reduce the time needed to establish a connection by about one-half. It also will disconnect the modem long enough to let the user know that someone is trying to call in—a kind of call-waiting feature. Upload speed for 56.5K modems has also been increased from 33.6K to 48K, which will improve two-way communications.

BOX 4.3   MODEM STANDARDS

The following list, while not exhaustive, provides the major ITU standards and the corresponding change in the speed of modems incorporating those standards. Each of the changes involves a series of complex technical issues primarily related to the type of modulation being used. In addition, a second set of standards that affect fax transmissions through modems is also included. Because all modems are backward compatible, if line conditions do not allow a modem to maintain the speed of connection designated by the standard it is using, it will fall back to an earlier, although slower, protocol.

MODEM COMMUNICATION STANDARDS

1979	V.21 standard—modem capable of sending and receiving data at 300 bps.
1980	V.22 standard—1,200 bps modem.
1984	V.22bis standard—2,400 bps modem. (Bis is French/Latin for "duo" or "twice," meaning full duplex capability for faster modem speed.)
1987	V.32 standard—9,600 bps modem.
1992	V.32bis standard—14,400 bps modem.
1995	V.34 standard—28,800 bps modem.
1996	V.34bis standard—33,600 bps modem.
1997	X2 standard—57,300 bps modem (standard used by U.S. Robotics).
1997	K56Flex standard—57,300 bps modem (standard used by Rockwell).
1998	V.90 standard—57,300 bps modem (a combination of competing X2 and K56Flex variations).
2001	V.92 standard—reduces connection time.

FAX TRANSMISSION STANDARDS

V.29 standard—fax at 4,800, 9,600 bps.
V.33 standard—fax at 14,400 bps; V42—automatic error correction.
V.42bis standard data compression.

POTS: Analog to Digital, Digital to Analog

Despite the improvements in modems, there remains good reason for the WWW to be jokingly referred to as the "World Wide Wait." Physically, there is a speed limit on *uploading* information that is sent from a home computer to an Internet Service Provider (ISP) over conventional phone lines. In most cases, this limit is between 35,000 and 40,000 bps. However, *downloaded* data (when an ISP sends information back to the home computer) is not limited in the same way. This is why 56.6 bps V.90 modems seem so much faster than earlier versions.

Still, maximum speeds are rarely, if ever, reached over a POTS (plain old telephone system) modem. Often, this is due to noise (interference) on the line or heavy traffic by others using the line for their own transmissions or conversations. Most telephone lines are incapable of sustaining the maximum speeds of which today's modems are often capable. In addition, for a V.90 modem to work the way it should, there must be a digital connection at one end of the transmission and the V.90 protocol must be in use both at the home computer and at the remote location to which it is connected. More than one analog to digital conversion in the network path of the transmission will cause serious problems with the speed of the connection.

The modem sending the data is another limiting factor that determines a modem's receiving or download speed. If the modem sending the data is limited to a speed of 28.8 bps, then you will receive it at that rate no matter how fast your modem is. Similarly, if the modem sending the information is capable of fast transmission speeds and performs data compression techniques to speed the transfer, the modem receiving the information must have the ability to decompress the data, using the same compression scheme, in order to benefit (see Figure 4.19).

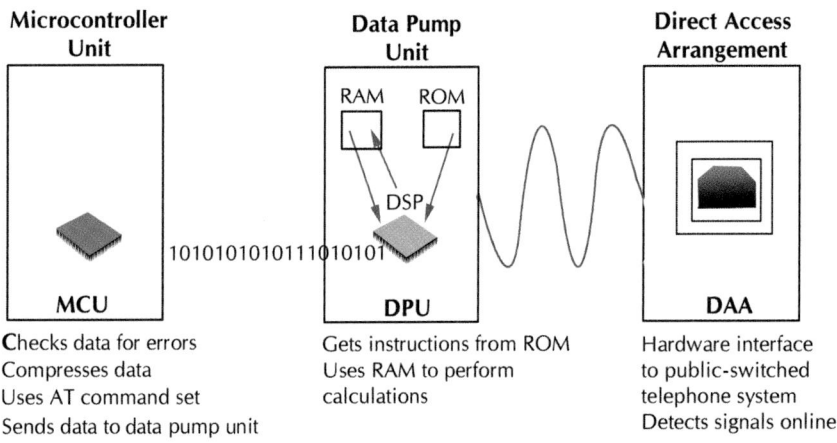

Microcontroller Unit

MCU

Checks data for errors
Compresses data
Uses AT command set
Sends data to data pump unit

Data Pump Unit

RAM   ROM

DSP

1010101010111010101

DPU

Gets instructions from ROM
Uses RAM to perform
calculations

Direct Access Arrangement

DAA

Hardware interface
to public-switched
telephone system
Detects signals online

■ **Figure 4.19**
Modems modulate and demodulate information.

Voice and Data

Many of today's modems will allow you to toggle back and forth between data and voice modes. In voice mode, the modem will react as though it were a regular telephone; in data mode, it will behave like a conventional modem. These modems will almost always have a speaker and microphone built into them. They have the ability to distinguish between a regular phone call and a fax message, and automatically respond to the call in an appropriate manner. When it detects a conventional call, it routes that call to its answering routine. A fax call is answered and the data recorded as a fax for later review.

As with many digital devices today, fax modems come equipped with flash memory rather than regular ROM (see Chapter 3) and can be upgraded easily to accommodate new communications protocols. This feature can extend the life of your modem as new features become available.

Beyond the POTS

ISDN Terminal Adapters: Digital to Digital

Integrated services digital networking (ISDN) is standard for a service that has the ability to deliver two simultaneous connections that allow voice, data, and video to be transmitted digitally through a single conventional phone line. Modems, telephones, and fax machines all can be hooked up to an ISDN line to receive faster, fully digital communication. This is only possible when a telephone company's switches can support digital connections. Unlike a conventional POTS modem in which the ISP converts a digital signal to analog before sending it from the local switching station to your home or office, with ISDN there is no analog conversion. An ISDN line transmits fully digital data with none of the noise or static usually associated with analog transmission, even though it uses the same wiring that POTS systems do.

ISDN connections provide four times the top speed of the fastest POTS modem, and additional speed can be obtained through the use of various data compression schemes. The usual problems associated with obtaining ISDN service are proximity and cost. This service is more expensive than a conventional POTS connection. In addition, to receive ISDN service, you must not only subscribe to an ISDN phone line but must be within 18,000 feet of the telephone company's central office. If you are further away than that, you must have expensive repeater devices in order to connect, if connection is possible at all. You will also need relatively expensive ISDN terminal adapters and ISDN routers.

Broadband: DSL and Cable

In the past, high-speed Internet service has been in the form of T1 lines capable of handling 1.5Mbps (megabytes per second) and even faster T3 lines capable of 45Mbps. These lines were typically leased at a cost of $1,500 per month or more and could serve many individual users. Because of the expense, use was limited to businesses, universities, and other large organizations. Very few home users have a T1 connection.

Recently, more affordable broadband access has become available for home users. Digital subscriber line (DSL) technology allows carriers to use already installed copper telephone wires to provide high-speed throughput. Although it can be confusing, the term digital subscriber line does not signify an actual line. A pair of DSL modems—one at the consumer's computer and one at the service provider's station—connected by a regular telephone line are the only things required for a digital subscriber line. DSL service carries data up to twenty times faster than conventional 56K POTS modems. It does this by using the high-frequency part of the same phone lines that voice is transmitted over. A DSL line is always open and on, which is one advantage over dial-up modems. Another advantage: you can surf

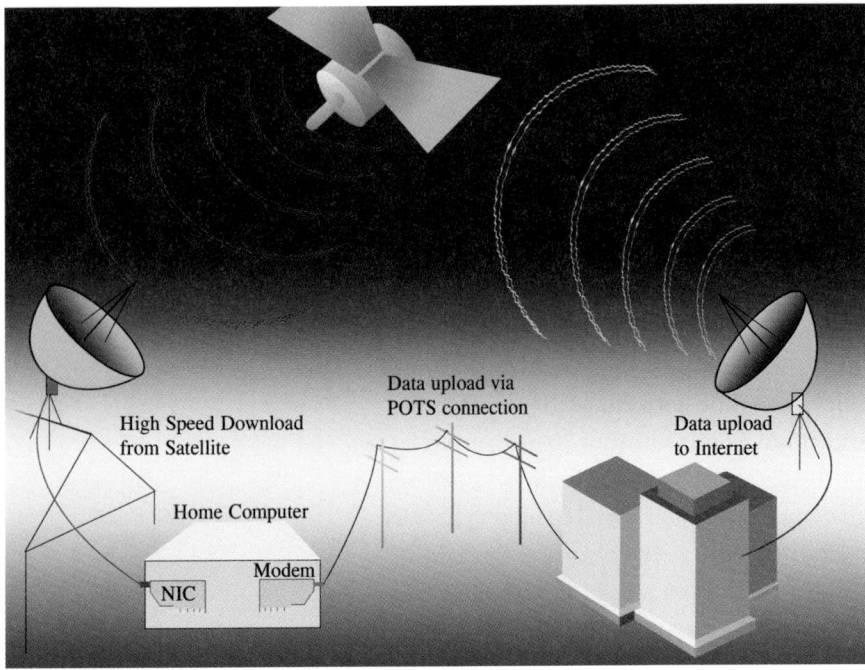

Figure 4.20

Basic satellite modem system.

the Web while simultaneously talking on the phone or sending a fax (see Figure 4.20).

Like an ISDN line, proximity and cost are also factors when considering a DSL service. In order for DSL service to be available, you must be within 17,500 feet of a central office for the most commonly used DSL service. In addition, that central office must have DSL equipment in use.

Cable Modems

DSL service was made possible, in part, by the realization that the copper phone lines that carry voice messages do so at a very low frequency and use only a small part of the phone line's capacity. This was coupled with the discovery that the same lines could carry data at very high frequencies without interfering with voice transmissions on the same line. Similarly, cable companies realized that the same cables that carry television transmissions to a viewer's home can, at the same time, carry data to that viewer's computer.

However, cable systems were designed to send information downstream only—and very quickly. While information can be sent upstream through a cable system, it is slower, although still far faster than a conventional 56.6K POTS dial-up modem, and every bit as fast as the most common DSL systems.

In order for a cable modem to be installed, a splitter is used to separate the cable coming into your house into two separate lines. One line continues to be used for your television and the second line is run from the splitter to the cable modem.

In most cases, cable modems connect to computers through a standard *Ethernet* (network) card. Data between the cable modem and the computer is transmitted at 100Mbps. An alternative to the modem/Ethernet card installation is a USB cable modem that plugs directly into a computer's port (USB port). With this type of modem, the computer's case doesn't have to be opened for installation.

Satellite Systems

Satellite systems are connected to computers by coaxial cable to a satellite dish mounted outside the home. These systems require a traditional dial-up modem to connect to an ISP. A request for URLs is sent through the modem and then routed to the identified Web server and to the satellite system provider. The requested information is beamed to an orbiting satellite, and then sent directly to your home computer. The digital satellite signal is used only for downloading. All uploads (sending e-mail, attachments, and so

BOX 4.4 MODEM DOWNLOAD SPEEDS COMPARED

Usually, the first thing we want to know about a modem is its speed. We tend to feel the speed crunch most when downloading files or attempting to view a large image in our Web browser. As a comparison of potential speed, below are the average downloading times for a ten-megabyte file using a series of different modems.

TEN MEGABYTE DOWNLOAD

Analog Dial-Up Modem (56K V.90)	approximately 28 minutes—often longer depending on line conditions and traffic
ISDN	approximately 11 minutes
Satellite	approximately 3½ minutes
DSL	approximately 2 minutes
Cable	approximately 1½ minutes

As you can see, cable modems, while usually costing about twice as much per month as a conventional dial-up service, offer great speed and convenience. However, they also tend to slow down as more users are added to the system. Nevertheless, even at their slowest they are often at least ten times faster than a 56.6 V.90 modem. In addition, they are "on" all the time without the need to dial up and log on to an ISP.

In determining the best modem for your needs, consider the extent of your usage, the nature (size) of the files you most often download, and of course price. If purchasing a dial-up modem, consider features and pricing. As long as a modem conforms to the latest ITU standards, it will perform very similarly to others in the same class with only slight variations in speed. 56.6 dial-up modems are limited to a 53K maximum speed by phone lines, with actual speeds much lower unless you have your phone company certify a clean line for your connection. Usually the maximum they will actually guarantee is much lower than this. If your phone company has older multiplexed lines then 56.6 V.90 modems won't work at all. However, this is quite rare today.

on) are completed with a conventional POTS dial-up modem. For this reason, you must have both types of modems active on your system.

If you already have an ISP, most satellite system providers will allow you to maintain that ISP or, as an option, provide a new one for you. Currently, proprietary services like AOL cannot be chosen as the primary ISP.

The advantage of a satellite system is primarily in the speed of information conveyed downstream (to the user's computer). Digital data is modulated and placed on a bandwidth allocated by the satellite service provider. This downstream flow of information can be up to 52Mbps. The upstream flow of information uses a conventional telephone modem. This modem must be active in order to receive the faster download stream (see Box 4.4).

Security

Unlike conventional dial-up modems, DSL and cable modems are always online. Unfortunately, this makes your computer more assessible to those who may wish to "hack" (illegally enter) your system or even harm it. When you use a conventional modem, your ISP provides a *dynamic* (temporary) IP address, which changes each time you log on. This makes it difficult for someone to track your actions or illegally enter your system. Most DSL and cable modem connections, however, have *static* (permanent) IP addresses. This means that your computer is sitting at the same spot on the Internet for as long as you leave the system connected. This makes it easy for someone to find you and enter your system if they choose.

If you have a cable or DSL modem, one of the recommended steps to protect your system, is to install *firewall* software. This software examines incoming and outgoing information and stops any transmissions that don't meet pre-set standards. In addition, you can turn off all file-sharing options so that an outside user who gains assess to your system will be limited as to what he or she might find.

Cable modems have even more problems with security than DSL modems. In addition to the issues previously raised, cable systems have a shared-wire design. Unfortunately, this means that the information that leaves your computer is open and available to others that share your cable line. It is conceivable that someone on your cable line could monitor your connection and find out what Internet sites you visit, as well as read your e-mail. However, if this is a concern, then data encryption software is available. Cable companies are working on improving security. Most cable modem companies already encrypt all traffic from the cable modem termination system (CMTS), located at the local cable operator's network hub, to the home or business cable modem.

CONCLUSION

As we have seen, when artists first began to create computer graphics, the publishing choices were limited and crude. Today, there is a wealth of possibilities from photographic quality prints, to CD-ROMs, to online experiences. It is often the way in which artists and designers approach things, and the questions they ask, that push the boundaries of the technologies they encounter, and inspire scientists and engineers to create new ones.

Projects: Outside the Box

1 *Scan a color photograph at resolutions of 75, 150, and 300 spi. Open them in your image-editing program and view them at 100, 200, and 400 percent on screen. What happens as your magnification increases?*

2 *Make an inkjet print of each of the scans completed in Problem 1 above. Compare the prints. Where does the largest increase in quality take place?*

3 *Find a website that tests modem bandwidth (bandwidthplace.com, for example). Test your own Internet connection for speed. What factors other than speed might affect your Web-viewing experience?*

5

The Pioneers of Digital Art

Introduction

The story of digital media is just beginning. This chapter focuses on the period from the 1950s to the end of the 1980s when the tools for the new art medium were being established. Progress in the early years was largely the work of exceptional engineers and researchers who had a fascination with art. In spite of Andy Warhol's statement in the 1960s, "I want to be a machine," artists with an interest in technology in this period were quite rare. Nevertheless, the uneasy alliance of these two groups was necessary to give birth to the field as we know it today.

Marriage on a World Stage

At Expo '70 in Osaka, Japan, the collaboration of artists and engineers was given its first world stage. Two years earlier, Pepsi-Cola commissioned a unique organization, EAT (Experiments in Art and Technology), to design and build its pavilion at the fair as a demonstration of how contemporary art and science were opening new frontiers. EAT had been founded in 1966 by the artist Robert Rauschenberg and the Bell Laboratories scientist Billy Kluver, an

expert in laser light and sound. Their goal was to bring together artists, choreographers, musicians, scientists, and engineers to imagine new forms of art, which combined performance art with technology.

Visitors approaching the Pepsi-Cola pavilion saw a deeply angled, geometric dome veiled in a fog of mist created by sprayers and lit by huge spotlights—a cloud sculpture (see Figure 5.1). Surrounding the building were slow-moving, six-foot-tall pod-shaped sculptures that made sounds, such as a whale singing or a truck's engine. The pods changed direction whenever they bumped into an obstacle.

Viewers were ushered into the pavilion through a dark tunnel. Once inside, they saw the EAT-designed interior—a large dome whose surface was covered with a huge, spherical mirror (at that time, the largest ever created). This was the elaborate backdrop for interactive performance pieces that used programmed multicolored laser lights. Artists and dancers moved freely among lights of all colors and sizes, the mirrored walls reflecting in many directions, creating new shapes and forms (see Figure 5.2). In many performance pieces, viewers were invited to participate. Speakers hidden behind the dome's mirror created imaginative and changing sound experiences. Visitors also carried handsets that picked up different sounds depending on where they were walking, and transmitted from the floor. Each performance became a unique experience that combined artists, scientists, and the public.

The optimism and ambition of EAT had been enormous, but unfortunately so was the cost of their project, much to the distress of the corporate sponsors. Disputes also broke out over who would control the building's events. Pepsi-Cola wanted to use the building for rock bands, while EAT had already arranged for artists, music, and poetry readings. In the end, the building was finished but EAT was removed from control over the programming.

High ambitions and high expenses marked the early days of digital media. Because of the extraordinary costs of computer machinery before the arrival of personal computers in the 1980s, the beginning of the history of digital media could not be written by artists. It required imaginative engineers with access to big, expensive hardware.

Swords into Brushes: The Role of Military Research

Military research and the Cold War played an essential part in the development of digital media, just as it later would for the Internet (see Chapter 12). For example, the semi-automatic ground environment (SAGE) air-defense system of the mid-1950s was designed to visually track Soviet aircraft near

U.S. airspace (see Figure 5.3). Huge computers were combined with radar systems and their displays. The result was not only an early warning system but also the first interactive computer system with vector graphics. Military personnel used a light pen (really more of a gun) on radar screens to follow the blips of enemy aircraft.

An even earlier project called *Whirlwind* at the Massachusetts Institute of Technology (MIT) marked the first time a computer monitor or *vectorscope* was attached to a mainframe computer. As a demonstration of the promise of "computer-assisted graphics" to illustrate scientific and mathematical data, researchers created a sequence showing a ball bouncing up and down, while slowly losing altitude. (Coincidentally, this is now a standard exercise in introductory computer animation classes.) They also created the first digital music when their million-dollar mainframe was programmed to play "Jingle Bells." This performance was so impressive that it was featured before a nationwide television audience on Edward R. Murrow's *See It Now* in 1951.

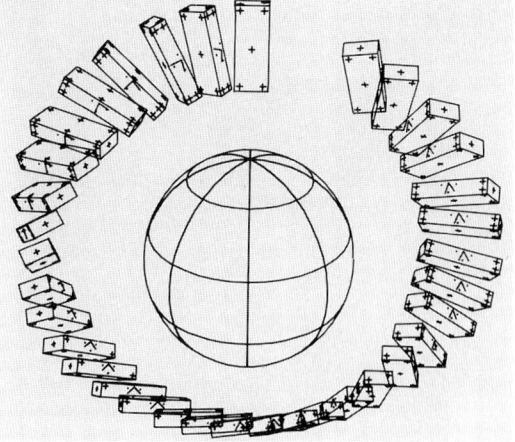

■ **Figure 5.3**
The SAGE air-defense system of the 1950s.

The words *computer graphics* were first used in 1960 by William Fetter, a Boeing engineer. Fetter was a pioneer in the development of computer-aided design

■ **Figure 5.4**
William Fetter's 3-D wireframe drawings for Boeing in the early 1960s were aids for designing cockpits.

(CAD) for manufacturing. Using algorithms, he was able to create 3-D wireframe drawings of a cockpit, and even a digital model of a person, to help design it ergonomically (see Figure 5.4). By 1963, he had created short animations of take-off and landing studies with wireframe aircraft.

Two years earlier, Edward Zajac at Bell Labs created the first computer-animated film, a four-minute black-and-white study of a satellite (represented by a simple 3-D box) orbiting the Earth (a simple wireframe sphere). To accomplish this feat, Zajac first wrote a program, which was fed into the computer with punch cards. The program was transferred by the computer onto magnetic tape, which communicated commands to the computer to create a series of pictures on the screen. It also coordinated the arrival of each picture with the motorized film advance of a movie camera (see Figure 5.5).

Art or Science?

The complexity of Zajac's task should help illustrate why few artists at this time were interested in computer graphics as a medium for art and why it remained largely the domain of scientists. In the 1960s, there were only a few ways to make "computer art." The results were always limited to linear, geometric forms, though often in quite

■ **Figure 5.5**
The first computer-animated film by Edward Zajac in 1961.

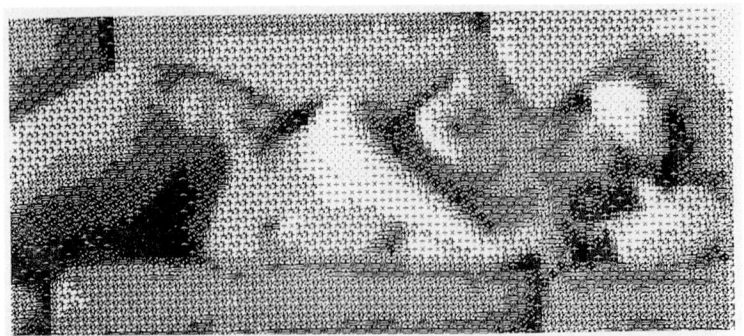

Figure 5.6

Ken Knowlton's *Mural* from 1966, one of the earliest examples of ASCII art.

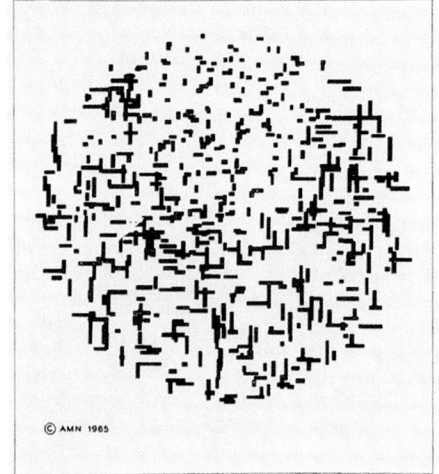

Figure 5.7

A. Michael Noll's *Computer Composition with Lines* from 1965 was based on a Mondrian painting.

Figure 5.8

Ivan Sutherland drawing with his Sketchpad, the first computer-graphics system.

intricate patterns. One way around this limitation was what became known as *ASCII art,* images composed of letters and symbols. After analyzing the tonal levels of a photograph, patterns of predetermined letters and symbols would be used to recreate the image. Much like the dots in a newspaper photo, an image could emerge (see Figure 5.6) like the nude in Ken Knowlton's *Mural* from 1966.

Still, most of what was called computer art consisted of ink drawings printed by *plotters* (large printers with rolls of paper, the marks being made by moving pens). Programmer-artists defined the parameters of a design using mathematical formulas. These were fed into the computers with tape or punch cards. The computers would then draw variations based on the formulas. The creative part of the process involved naming the variables and coordinates, which would determine the results. By allowing for random variables, entire suites of prints could be created.

Creating computer graphics in the 1960s was a very time-consuming process. The program itself might have to run for an hour before the printing process could even begin. Once started, one image might take hours to print. Despite these handicaps and the mathematical and arbitrary nature of these graphics programs, surprisingly sophisticated-looking results were often achieved.

For example, A. Michael Noll, an engineer at Bell Laboratories, created a program based on his analysis of an early twentieth-century black-and-white painting by the Dutch artist, Piet Mondrian. The program created a new "Mondrian," which was actually preferred by nearly sixty percent of the viewers who saw the two together. Two-thirds of those viewers even thought the one made by a computer was the real Mondrian painting (see Figure 5.7).

Sketchpad

In 1962, Ivan Sutherland, a graduate student at MIT, created *Sketchpad* (see Figure 5.8) as his doctoral thesis, which he called "a man-machine graphical communication system." Many historians and researchers mark this development as the true beginning of computer graphics, because for the first time images were created by the hand of an artist, not by mathematical programs, and could be seen as the artist was working on them (not only in a print made hours later). Using a light pen combined with his own software for drawing, Sutherland could draw directly on a nine-inch monitor (or cathode-ray tube, as it was more commonly known at the time). Simple patterns of lines and curves could be created on the screen and manipulated. Keyboard commands could change the patterns, for example, into a series of parallel lines, or could erase lines. There were dials below the screen for zooming in or out.

Sutherland is one of the founding fathers of digital media, and the remarkable features of his drawing program would influence the development of many later computer-graphics programs. Sketchpad utilized a vector system where points are placed on the screen and the software creates the lines between them, the basis of all future vector drawing programs. In addition, an image could be made of parts, which could then be moved into a variety of positions. Each part could also be individually resized independently from the rest of the image. Shapes could be shrunk to the size of a dot, copied over and over again to make a pattern, then enlarged again, so you could see a field of the same shapes clearly defined. The software also was able to save the images created on the screen for later use. Many of the pioneers of digital media technology were inspired by Sutherland's Sketchpad, particularly by the concept that a computer could be designed for the use of ordinary people, rather than remain the domain of a select group of technology experts.

The Mouse Is Born

In 1963, Douglas Englebart, an engineer at the Stanford Research Institute, was looking for ways for people to use computers to solve complex problems. Frustrated with the available methods to interact with information displayed on a screen, he began to think about ways to point and create input more quickly and efficiently. He felt one way to cut down on wasted motion was to eliminate the need to lift the input device off the desk. With a fellow engineer, Bill English, he designed a small black box with a cord in the front and two perpendicular disks on the bottom that tracked its motion. The "X-Y Position Indicator," as it was called (see Figure 5.9), was first used only to draw straight lines but testing showed it outperformed keyboards, light pens, and joysticks in a variety of tasks. When the cord was moved to the back end, it wasn't long before someone in Englebart's lab noticed it looked like a mouse with a tail—gaining the name it has to this day.

Englebart went on to become one of the key visionaries in the history of computing. At a computer conference in 1968, he presented what has become known as "the mother of all demos." In it, the mouse was unveiled, but only as one part of a much larger "online system," or NLS. Englebart's NLS would be a networked environment which supported collaboration between people using computers over long distances (see Chapter 12). The goal of this Internet-like vision was to "find much better ways for people to work together to make this world a better place." Remarkably, in the same presentation, he also introduced several other key concepts that would prove to be essential in the development of computers and the communication industry: computers with a windows-like interface, hypertext, e-mail, word processing, and videoconferencing.

■ **Figure 5.9**

The first mouse built by Douglas Englebart and Bill English in 1963.

Mandelbrot, the father of fractals

Benoit Mandelbrot is a mathematician whose uniquely visual approach to geometry had a profound impact on the development of digital media. Born in Poland and educated in France, he has been a researcher in the United States at IBM for over forty years. His research has been on *fractals,* unusual geometric shapes whose smallest parts resemble the larger shape. In other words, all parts look like the whole fractal when you zoom in on them at various magnifications. These patterns (see Figures 5.10 and 5.11) have been described as geometrical curiosities, but to many they are forms of great beauty and interest.

As Mandelbrot and other researchers explored these truly digital forms, they discovered they were much less abstract and more connected to nature than anyone had imagined. They seemed to be everywhere, from snowflakes to galaxies to the head of a piece of broccoli. Mandelbrot's research has affected not only mathematics but physics, astronomy, biology, and art and design, as well.

In digital media, there have been three main applications for fractal geometry. First, it makes possible the creation of abstract images of unique beauty. Second, it has provided the mathematics behind methods of image compression, allowing for complex images with small file sizes. Finally, because the structure of fractal geometric forms resembles the organizing principle behind natural ones, fractals can be used to create digital landscapes of extraordinary realism, including impressive clouds and mountains, whole forests, and sandy shores (see Figure 11.13).

Fractals have truly bridged the worlds of the scientist, mathematician, and artist. Today, on the Web, one can see the work of fractal artists all around the world creating their own versions of these remarkable patterns. ■

■ Figure 5.10
The Mandelbrot set.

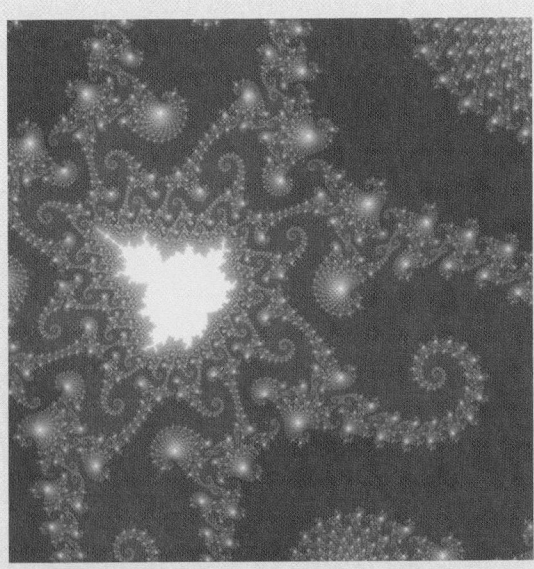

■ Figure 5.11
The same Mandelbrot set seen in figure 5.10 but magnified approximately 15,000 times.

Artists and Engineers (Finally) Unite

In 1965, the first fruit of the exploration of computer graphics was exhibited in galleries (to a mixed reception). The very first exhibition of computer graphics was held at a gallery in Stuttgart, Germany (Technische Hochschule), and displayed the work of three mathematicians. Later that year, the work of A. Michael Noll (see page 94) was among the programmer art shown at New York City's Howard Wise Gallery, the first exhibition in the United States. Most artists, along with the other members of the art world, turned a cold shoulder to the work. One reviewer compared the art to "the notch patterns on IBM [punch] cards."

Despite this reception, exhibitions continued during the 1960s, eventually appearing at major museums. In 1968, *Cybernetic Serendipity,* curated by Jasia Reichardt, opened at the Institute of Contemporary Art in London. This was an important retrospective of the state of computer graphics at the time and expanded the medium beyond plotter pictures. In addition to Michael Noll's Mondrian project, one could see many examples of art and design inspired, not just created, by computers. Spanning the wide variety of visual and performing arts, the exhibition mixed paintings and sculptures about computers with choreography and music designed with computers, poems generated by computer, computer films, and robots. Reichardt acknowledged that the show largely dealt "with possibilities, rather than achievements" and was "prematurely optimistic." However, she also wrote, "Seen with all the prejudices of tradition and time, one cannot deny that the computer demonstrates a radical extension in art media and techniques."

Despite the negative reactions of most in the art world, there was a growing number of artists intrigued by the possibilities of new technologies. As mentioned at the beginning of this chapter, in 1966, the artist Robert Rauschenberg and the electronic engineer Billy Kluver founded EAT. Kluver already had experience collaborating with artists. His most famous partnership before EAT was helping Jean Tinguely fabricate *Homage to New York* in 1960 (see Figure 5.12). This kinetic sculpture was a machine designed to destroy itself. At a private evening event (whose guests included the governor of New York) in the Museum of Modern Art's (MOMA) sculpture garden, the huge sculpture was turned on and slowly blew itself apart (with the added attractions of paint bombs and noxious odors) over the course of a half hour, finishing as a smoking heap of junk.

Kluver and Rauschenberg shared the belief that since technology was now part of life, it should be part of art, too. In 1967, EAT collaborated with a MOMA curator for a portion of the museum's upcoming exhibition, *The Machine as Seen at the End of the Mechanical Age.* EAT sponsored a contest for artists combining art and science, which generated a huge response. When the museum only selected ten of the entries, EAT arranged for a simultaneous exhibition at the Brooklyn Museum of over a hundred of the remaining entries called *Some More Beginnings: Experiments in Art and Technology.*

Lillian Schwartz was one of the ten artists selected for the MOMA exhibition. A traditional artist, she had been disappointed in most early computer graphics because she never saw the hand of the artist in them. She was one of

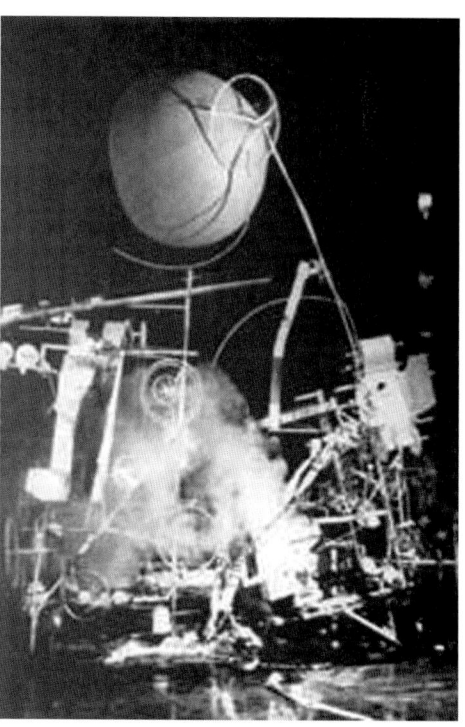

■ **Figure 5.12**

Tinguely, *Homage to New York,* being performed at the Museum of Modern Art in New York in1960.

■ **Figure 5.13**

Lillian Schwartz, one of the pioneers of digital collage, shook up art historians with her MonaLeo.

the first to transcend the typical geometric art of the time by digitizing her realistic portrait and figure drawings with the help of Bell Lab researchers.

In 1983, she designed a poster for MOMA, and became one of the first artists to make a digital collage with digitized images. In a method that has since become very common, she scanned images from the museum's collection, resized them, then varied their transparency as she overlapped them. While today one could use image-editing software on a personal computer to achieve the same result, the poster required the services of technical experts and a large mainframe at an IBM research center.

In the 1980s, a digital collage by Schwartz started a controversy among art historians that ultimately received national attention. In it, she combined two pictures by Leonardo da Vinci, one the *Mona Lisa*, the other a self-portrait drawing. The striking similarity between the two faces led some to speculate that the *Mona Lisa* was actually a self-portrait by Leonardo. Ironically, Schwartz's use of a computer to create the collage appeared to persuade the media that the artwork was "scientific" (see Figure 5.13).

Myron Krueger was most interested in the interaction between people and computers, and created or "composed" spaces for such encounters to take place. His 1970 *Videoplace* was a room where a computer could respond to the actions of visitors. In this "responsive environment," digitized images of visitors appeared on a projection screen. Fun-loving characters, created by Krueger, would move toward visitors' silhouettes and respond to their movements (see Figure 5.14).

■ **Figure 5.14**

Viewer and electronic creature in Myron Krueger's interactive video environment: *Videoplace*, 1970.

Nam June Paik, the video-art pioneer, had always been enthusiastic about exploring art through technology, once claiming that "the cathode ray tube will replace canvas." One of the first artists to use portable videocams, he later integrated video and other technologies into sculptures, installations, happenings, and even a bra. Therefore, it is not surprising that, with the arrival of digital technologies, he began integrating them in his work as well. The Paik/Abe Synthesizer was able to interfere with and manipulate video images on a monitor, creating unusual forms, colors, and patterns (much like how his earlier work with a large magnet affected images on a television screen) (see Figure 5.15).

Despite the works of these and many other artists at the time, the collaboration of artists and engineers continued to face much hostility. The 1971 exhibition at the Los Angeles County Museum, Art and Technology, curated by Maurice Tuchman, opened to the almost unanimous disapproval of critics. It was a huge, expensive project, five years in development. Twenty-two artists were contracted with corporations who promised to finance the substantial costs of technical assistance, fabrication, and maintenance. Even though many of the artists, like Rauschenberg, Andy Warhol, Richard Serra, and Roy Lichtenstein, were already well known and respected, this approach was seen as nefarious by the critics and gave birth to a new term of derision—*corporate art*.

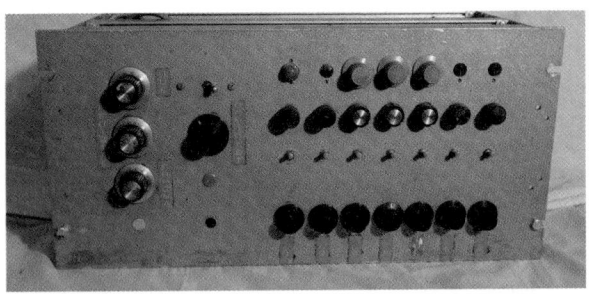

■ **Figure 5.15**

The Paik/Abe Synthesizer.

Research Centers: Heavy Iron on Campus

Unfortunately, because of the high costs involved, few artists before the 1980s could afford to produce computer graphics without such "unholy" alliances. This need flew in the face of a widespread sense during the 1960s and 1970s that many of the ills of contemporary society were due to the destructiveness of money and technology. Ultimately, this would mean that very few artists participated in the development of the tools of digital media during a crucial period.

Access to the giant computer systems and funds necessary for research would remain located in three locations: the military, industry, and research universities. Among those universities, the University of Utah and Ohio State University would emerge as the most influential and significant in the history of computer graphics.

University of Utah

In 1965, Dr. David Evans founded the University of Utah's Computer Science department, and focused its energy on the new field of graphics. A native of Utah, Evans had previously led the team at the University of California at Berkeley that worked for the Defense Department's Advanced Research Project Agency (ARPA). Evans was not just a successful researcher but also a superb recruiter of faculty and an influential teacher. In 1968, he convinced Ivan Sutherland to join the department. After his work on Sketchpad at MIT, Sutherland headed ARPA, then went to Harvard where he created a head-mounted display screen. By projecting a separate wireframe image for each eye, it was able to create a 3-D effect. Called the "Sword of Damocles" because of its great weight, it was the first virtual reality simulation (see Figure 5.16).

In addition to their work together at Utah, Evans and Sutherland also founded the first computer-graphics company in 1968. Bearing their names, it would create powerful custom graphics hardware and software, first for the military, then commercial animation companies.

The list of David Evans and Ivan Sutherland's students at the University of Utah is a Who's Who of computer pioneers. Among them are Alan Kay, a leading researcher at Xerox PARC (see page 101) who is responsible for many of the key concepts behind personal computers; Jim Clark, the founder of Silicon Graphics and co-founder of Netscape; John Warnock, a co-founder of Adobe; Alan Ashton, co-founder of WordPerfect; Nolan Bushnell, the founder of Atari (page 109); and Ed Catmull (pages 106 and 107), co-founder of Pixar.

Talented graduate students at the University of Utah created most of today's methods for realistically shading 3-D objects (for a fuller discussion of these methods, see Chapter 11). Ed Catmull's Ph.D. dissertation developed the concept of *texture mapping*, which wraps a photorealistic image of a texture around a wireframe form. In 1971, Henri Gouraud conceived *Gouraud shading* where, by blurring the facets of a polygon, an object can appear to be smoothly shaded. In 1974, Phong Bui-Toung created

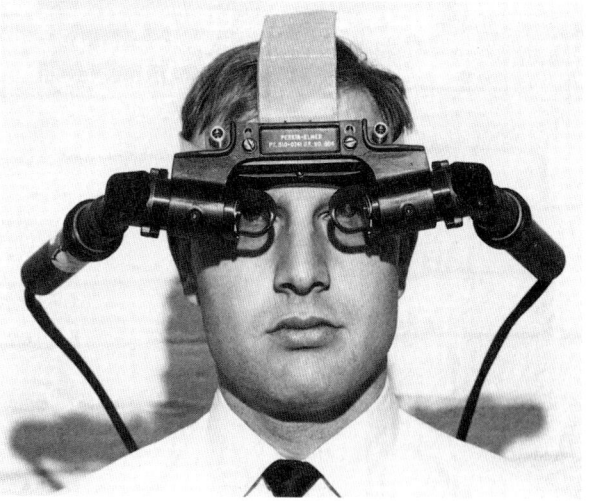

■ **Figure 5.16**

Ivan Sutherland was already exploring virtual reality in the 1960s.

Phong shading, creating realistic highlights on shaded objects. In 1976, Martin Newell worked with his teaching assistant, Jim Blinn, to help him develop *reflection mapping,* where objects are shaded with reflections from their environment. While at Utah, Blinn also developed the technique of *bump mapping,* allowing shading of irregular surfaces. More than a quarter of a century later, these methods still dominate the rendering of 3-D images in animations and computer games.

Ohio State University

A rarity in the early history of computer graphics, Charles Csuri was an art professor at Ohio State University in the early 1960s who played an important role in the development of the new field. A renaissance man trained as both a traditional painter and as an engineer, as well as an All-American football player, Csuri was one of the few early computer artists who created representational images with the new technology. His first works were based on his pencil drawings. Working with programmers, he would scan the drawings and then transform them on the computer. One of his most famous artworks was a series of drawings that showed a young woman slowly changing into an old one.

This precursor of the concept of morphing led Csuri to animated films. In 1967, he created *Hummingbird,* a playful transformation of a hummingbird in flight. Using scanned drawings, Csuri was able to make a film of over 14,000 frames, which broke the bird into floating geometric forms and then reconstituted it again (see Figure 5.17). Today, this landmark film is in the permanent collection of the Museum of Modern Art in New York.

In 1969, Csuri founded the Computer Graphics Research Group (CGRG) at Ohio State, which combined the talents of faculty and students from a wide range of disciplines. With grants from government, the military, and industry, one of their first projects was to develop a real-time animation system. Later, in a public display at IBM's showroom in Manhattan, Csuri showed how he could pull up images from the computer's memory and animate them on the screen with a light pen. Salvador Dali was among the many impressed visitors.

The CGRG's focus was on advancing research in computer animation. New and important animation languages, modeling, motion, and character animation systems were developed there, as well as award-winning animated short films. In 1987, the group was renamed the Advanced Computing Center for Arts and Design (ACCAD).

Xerox PARC

The founding of Xerox Corporation's Palo Alto Research Center (PARC) in 1970 would not only prove to be one of the most important developments in the history of digital media, but of computing itself. The young, talented scientists assembled there were given the mission of developing "the architecture of information"

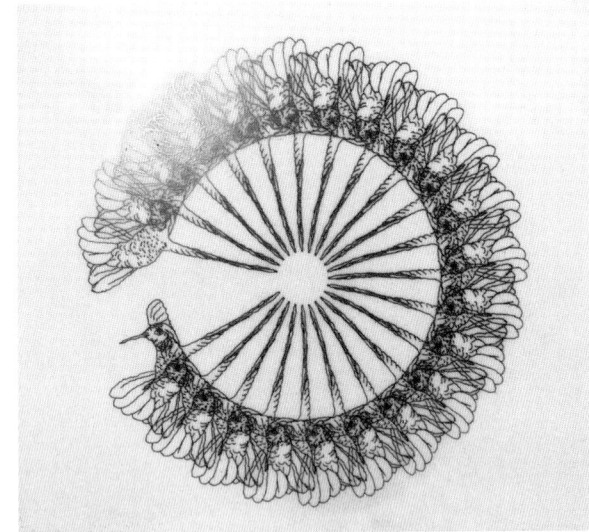

■ **Figure 5.17**

An early computer-animated film: Charles Csuri, *Hummingbird,* 1967.

in ten years—and they would succeed beyond anyone's imagination. More than any one group, they pioneered the foundation of computing today. Their slogan was, "The easiest way to predict the future is to invent it."

Alan Kay was one of those researchers and is credited with the slogan. As a graduate student at the University of Utah, he studied with Ivan Sutherland and experimented with Sutherland's Sketchpad program. On a visit to the MIT Artificial Laboratory, he was amazed to see researchers teaching children how to program. It changed his idea of what computing was about: Rather than a world of huge computers run by experts, he imagined computers that could be used by anyone, even children. Inspired, he visualized a computer as small as a book that was easy to use, which he called *KiddieKomp*.

In 1972, Kay arrived at PARC. He observed and analyzed how children worked with a new kind of programming language he had devised that was object oriented (rather than text based) and called "Smalltalk." He learned that children worked best with images and sounds, rather than words. Inspired by this success, Kay led a team of PARC researchers to develop an experimental system that predominantly used graphics and animation, rather than text. He believed that using graphics to represent computing actions would stimulate learning and creativity.

That same year, he also proposed *Dynabook*, a notebook-sized computer which he said would be so easy to use that his mother could take it shopping. It would be a true multimedia computer, integrating images, animation, sound, and text. While this project never received funding from Xerox, Kay was part of a team that developed a computer that shared many of these ideas. It was called *Alto*—and it revolutionized computing.

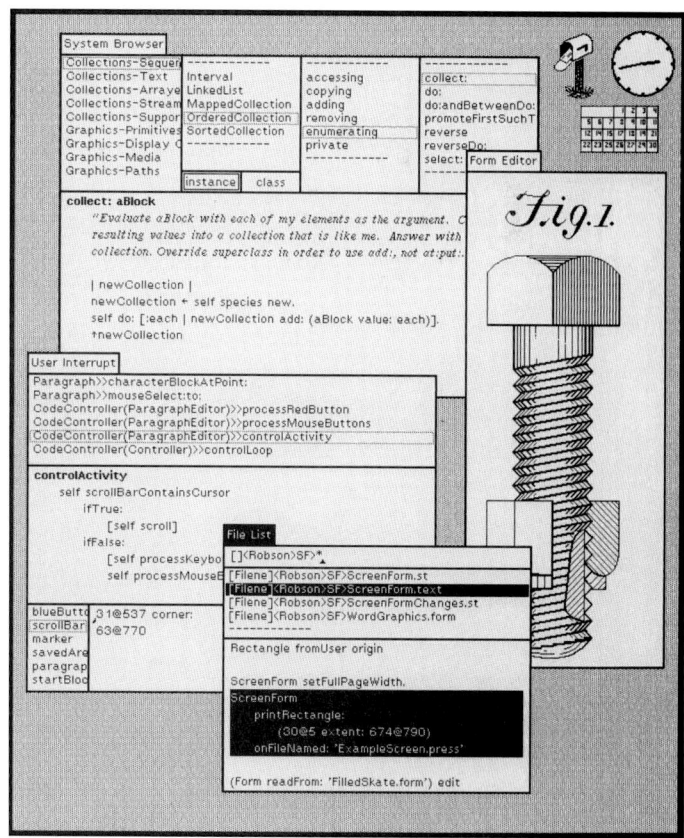

Until the Alto, a computer was always a huge, expensive machine housed in a central facility. Users were programmers or researchers who competed for time and were given printouts of results later in the day. Alto, however, was a small computer that sat on a desk and was designed for one user—in essence, the first personal computer. It had its own keyboard and used Douglas Englebart's mouse for input. Its monitor was the size of a typical page. It even had removable disks for storage.

Equally revolutionary was the Alto's utilization of Kay's concept of a graphically designed system of interacting with the computer—the first of what would become known as a *graphical user interface* (GUI) (see Figure 5.18). Kay's approach should be quite familiar to today's computer users. Each element on the screen was a picture, or *icon*. The icons were designed with an office metaphor; so information was put into files, and files put into folders. Clicking the mouse while over an icon could start a program. The interface even allowed for multiple windows and pop-up menus.

■ **Figure 5.18**

The landmark graphical interface designed for the Alto computer by Alan Kay at Xerox PARC.

By using bitmapping (where every pixel can be used to describe forms) rather than text or shapes composed of vectors, what one saw on the screen was quite close to what one saw when a document was printed. This new approach became known as "what you see is what you get" or WYSIWYG (pronounced "wizzy-wig").

Despite the visionary innovations of the Alto, it was never marketed successfully by Xerox. In time, the shortsightedness of Xerox management in the 1970s became legendary in the history of computing. They mismanaged a tremendous lead in technology on a variety of fronts. Among other PARC innovations that would be developed more successfully elsewhere are Ethernet, laser printing, and the first page-description language. All of the key researchers who created these and many other breakthroughs would eventually leave PARC, forming their own successful companies or working elsewhere. With the failure of the more advanced version of the Alto, called the Star System, in the early 1980s, Xerox decided to step away from computers and concentrate on its successful copying business.

In December 1979, the company made its most legendary blunder. Despite the protests of their own researchers, management ordered them to show the Alto and its GUI interface to a young computer maker, Steve Jobs, in return for an opportunity to buy $1 million of his company's stock.

Apple and the Arrival of the Macintosh

Jobs' small computer company was Apple. Following up on the success of their Apple I and II, the company was in the process of designing the new *Lisa* at the time Jobs visited the Xerox facility. Jobs was amazed by what he saw at PARC and had his engineers integrate the mouse and GUI interface into the Lisa, adding some important innovations. On the Lisa, for the first time, files could be clicked and dragged, pop-up windows overlapped rather than tiled with scroll bars at the sides, and there was a menu bar with pull-down menus. Apple engineers also simplified the PARC three-button mouse to one button and made it smaller, to fit more comfortably in one's hand. Lisa's software included concepts familiar today: cut, copy, and paste, as well as the clipboard and wastebasket. It also included a simple page layout program. However, the cost of the Lisa—$10,000—and its slowness hurt its acceptance by the public. Luckily for Apple, they already had another computer in development.

Possibly the most important milestone in the history of digital media was the release of the Apple Macintosh computer in 1984 (see Figure 5.19). Its impact on the history of computer technology has been compared to the first flight of the Wright brothers in aviation or Edison's lightbulb in the electric industry.

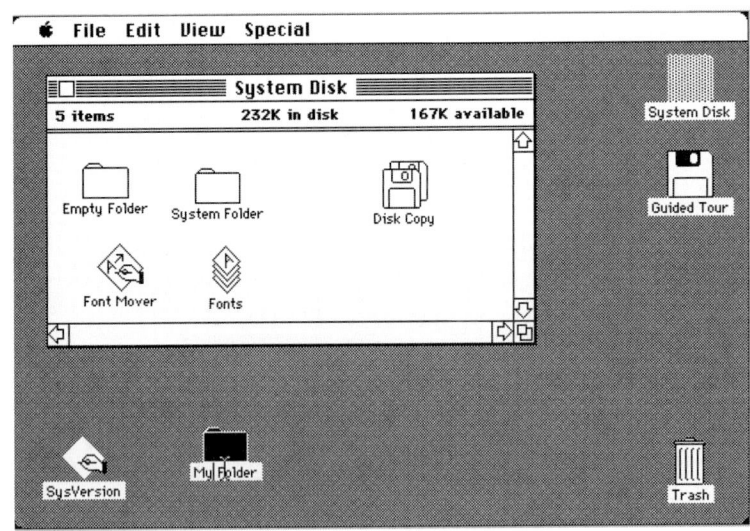

■ **Figure 5.19**
User interface from the first Apple Macintosh, 1984.

Faster than the Lisa and designed to be small, simple, and affordable for not just thousands but hundreds of thousands of people, the Mac was a tremendous success. The Mac came with the first 3 1/2″ floppy disk drives, storing twenty-five percent more than the then common 5 1/4″ floppy while being smaller and sturdier. Most importantly, ease of use was the overriding philosophy in the Macintosh's design. Even the packaging of the computer was done simply and clearly, with easy to read manuals that made unpacking and setting up a Mac a pleasure. Within two years, 500,000 Macintoshes had been sold.

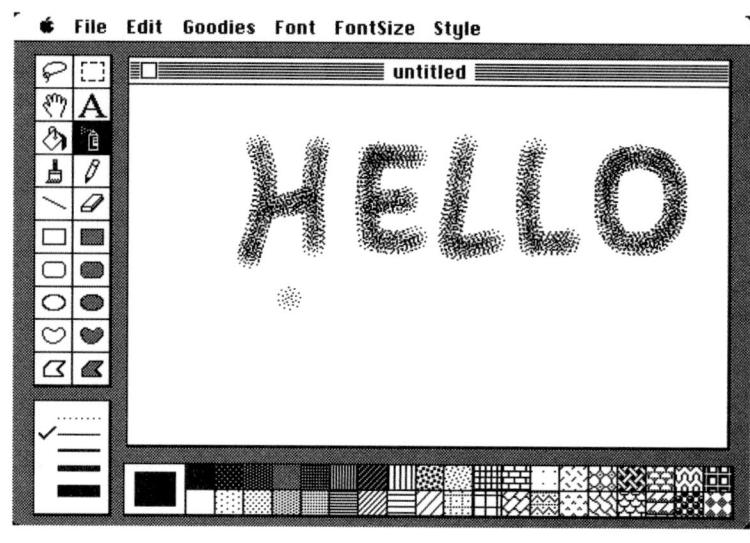

■ Figure 5.20

MacPaint, the Macintosh's painting program for consumers.

Part of the reason for the success of the Macintosh was that it was a graphics-based machine from the beginning. Its makers assumed that users wanted to do more than type or program. Painting software, called *MacPaint* (see Figure 5.20), came with the machine, as well as *Hypercard*, so users could create interactive multimedia. Compared to Lisa's GUI interface, the Mac workspace was clearer and cleaner. Especially unique about the Mac was that, unlike previous small computers, the Mac abandoned the old approach of character generation for text and replaced it with typefaces that were bitmapped. This gave users much more flexibility for varying fonts, styles, and sizes—and would play a crucial role in ushering in a new era in layout and design.

The Beginning of Electronic Printing

As with many other revolutionary technologies, it was not just the release of the Macintosh but the simultaneous arrival of several breakthroughs that would lead to what became known as the "desktop publishing revolution." The first step toward the new world of electronic printing was made with the arrival of a new light. In 1960, Theodore Maimon, a research scientist for Hughes Research in Malibu, California, invented the first practical way to generate laser beams. This technology would, of course, have many ramifications beyond the world of art and design, but it was an important first step in developing laser printing (for a detailed discussion, see Chapter 4). Laser light could be used to expose very fine dots, permitting both crisp type and the detailed reproduction of images in halftones. The first applications of laser printers, however, would not arrive until the early 1970s and, even then, only in the form of large commercial machines dedicated to typesetting.

What would first become known as desktop publishing didn't truly emerge until the 1980s. To the surprise of most professional designers and printers who treated the new technology with contempt (calling it more appropriate for a church newsletter than a professional publication), electronic publishing became the industry's standard before the decade was finished.

What was needed for this to occur was the arrival of relatively inexpensive and easy to use computers and methods of printing, along with digital methods of defining typefaces and pages. These seemingly monumental challenges were overcome in just a few years.

In the early 1980s, *Bitstream* was founded, the first company dedicated to developing digital typefaces. In 1983, a new company called *Adobe*, founded by

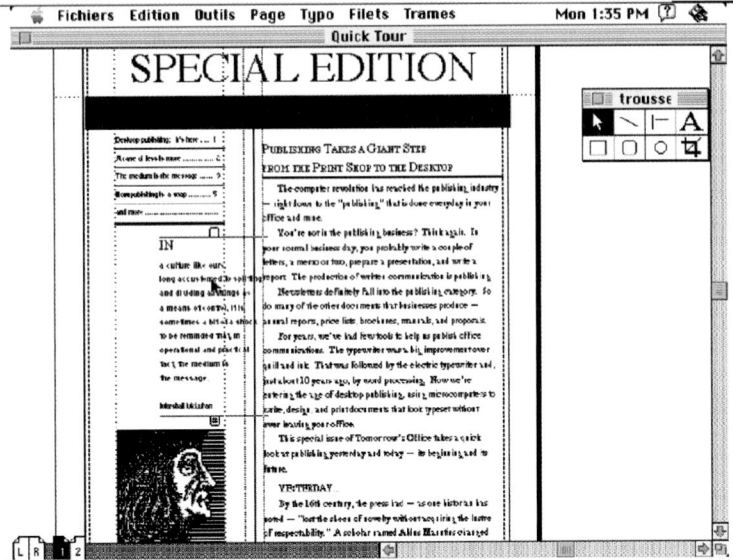

Figure 5.21

Aldus Pagemaker, the pioneer desktop publishing program, 1985.

John Warnock of the University of Utah and Charles Geshchke, developed a language for describing page layout called PostScript. Adobe PostScript makes the printed page an image where every pixel has been arranged to form the graphics and text clearly. The same year, Canon developed a laser printing engine that could print cheaply at 300 dpi. Together they would be the foundation for the Apple LaserWriter, the first laser printer for the general public.

The final piece in the puzzle was released in 1985—Aldus Corporation's *Pagemaker* page layout software (see Figure 5.21). Designed for the new Apple Macintosh, it allowed users to easily combine and manipulate text and graphics. Users could choose from hundreds of typefaces, in a variety of styles and sizes. Suddenly, an electronic publishing system (see Chapter 6) that cost less than $10,000 was available to designers at both large and small firms. An individual could control design, fonts, and printing from his or her desktop.

The days of cutting and pasting waxed pieces of paper galleys onto boards to make mechanicals were ending, and a new way of understanding the words *cut* and *paste* had begun. For many designers and typesetters, the effect was like that on actors in silent films after the arrival of sound for motion pictures.

For other designers and many artists, it was as if one small computer opened up a whole new world. The result was a continuing loyalty among artists and designers to Apple computers that transcends mere technology or software. Well into the 1990s, Macintoshes dominated the worlds of graphic design, multimedia, and education.

Pioneers of Computer Graphics and Animation

As sophisticated as it was, the original Macintosh was only available with a black-and-white display. It took three years, with the arrival of the Mac II, before Apple users could work in color graphics in digital imaging. However, pioneer work had already begun a decade earlier.

As in personal computing, Xerox PARC was a leader in the development of digital painting software. In the early 1970s, researchers Richard Shoup and Alvy Ray Smith worked on a painting program that would allow artists to paint on a computer the way they painted on a canvas. It was called "SuperPaint," the prototype for all future bitmap painting software. It included a palette where one could select up to 256 colors from 16.7 million choices. Brush sizes could be varied and a user could apply colors and shapes with a tablet and stylus. As with the Alto, Xerox management failed to capitalize on their advanced technology. Soon after SuperPaint's release, Xerox decided to focus on black-and-white projects, rather than color. Shoup and Smith soon left PARC.

The Jet Propulsion Laboratories

As Xerox's imagination and funding began to dwindle, its top researchers began to search for institutions with greater resources. One new home was the Jet Propulsion Laboratories (JPL) in Pasadena, California, part of a U.S. space program at the height of its funding.

David Em's motives were quite unambiguous—he wanted access to huge computers to create his art. In 1975, he left Xerox PARC and joined the JPL as artist in residence. There, using software created to show trajectories of space-craft exploring the universe, Em created beautiful abstract visions and surrealistic landscapes (see Figure 5.22).

Much of the advanced software Em used was developed by Jim Blinn. After finishing his dissertation at the University of Utah on reflection and bump mapping, Blinn was hired by the JPL to continue his 3-D animation research. His first important project was to create simulations of the planned Jupiter and Saturn planetary flybys. Unlike previous simulations, they would be not just for planning purposes, but also to interest the public in the mission. In order to accomplish this, Blinn had to create new techniques and software, but the result was well worth the effort.

Due to Blinn's groundbreaking work, viewers were able to follow Voyager I in its travels (see Figure 5.23) as it approached the huge planets. Distributed to the media, the animations received worldwide attention from both the computer-graphics community and the general public. While only two to three minutes each, they had a degree of realism never seen before (in fact some television stations described them as actual footage of the mission). While scientifically accurate and great technical achievements, it is a sense of drama that makes these truly remarkable. The planets come toward the viewer at an angle, growing larger and larger as the gravitational pull draws in the space probes. We then appear to whip past the planets and out into space. Blinn has explained that his study of traditional animation techniques, including those of the Disney animators (see Chapter 10), were an important part of how he designed his movies. Blinn's cinematography, as well as his animation software, shaped the appearance of most subsequent space sequences in television and films.

■ **Figure 5.22**

David Em, *Tranjovian Pipeline*, 1979 (left). The artist in his studio (right).

■ **Figure 5.23**

Scenes from Jim Blinn's animated simulation of the Voyager I flyby for the Jet Propulsion Laboratories.

New York Institute of Technology

After he left PARC, Alvy Ray Smith joined a new research center in New York, the New York Institute of Technology (NYIT). Alexander Schure, a wealthy entrepreneur, had decided to fund a computer graphics laboratory there and outfit it with the best hardware, software, and scientists. Smith described it as a place with "plenty of money" where researchers would get "whatever was needed." In 1977, he developed the first 24-bit painting software, *Paint3,* which made 16.7 million colors available to the artist. It also introduced many of the tools digital artists use today: digital airbrushing, compositing images, selecting colors from any part of an image, and making paintbrushes of any shape or size.

Smith had been recruited by Ed Catmull, the head of the computer graphics laboratory at NYIT, whose Ph.D. dissertation at the University of Utah developed the concept of texture mapping. One of the important early applications of *Paint3* was creating richly detailed textures to map on 3-D forms. NYIT's lab became a center of research in 3-D modeling and animation, attracting scientists who would be leaders in computer animation for decades to come. Among the firsts developed there were video editing with a computer, the alpha channel, tweening (which creates the in-between frames from one drawing to another in an animation), a complete 2-D animation system (SoftCel), and morphing software.

Toys and Monsters: The Computer Graphics Industry

In 1979, when director George Lucas convinced Ed Catmull and Alvy Ray Smith to leave NYIT and start a computer-graphics unit at his Lucasfilm complex, it began a new era in the development of graphics and animation tools. High-end applications were now less likely to be created in university research centers than as proprietary systems at commercial computer-graphics studios for use in mainstream films, commercials, and especially television.

Digital media went on view for the first time by the general public in the late 1970s when computer graphics began appearing on television news and sports broadcasts in the form of backgrounds, charts, and flying logos. Not long after, commercials featured 3-D animations of dancing candy and gyrating fuel pumps (see Figure 5.24). In 1978, computer graphics received worldwide attention when the artist Leroy Neiman drew his trademark sport scenes with a digital paint system during the Super Bowl.

New companies were being formed, like Digital Effects, R/Greenberg (later R/GA), and Pacific Data Images, as special-effects firms housed in small apartments. In just a few years, they would grow to fill entire buildings, producing commercials, television graphics, and, occasionally, astonishing sequences in full-length films like *The Last Starfighter, Futureworld,* and *Tron.*

■ **Figure 5.24**
"Rock 'n Roll" was a landmark 3-D animated Shell Oil commercial by R/GA in 1994.

Initially, however, commercial computer graphics were primarily produced for television because they required lower-resolution effects compared to movies. Filmmakers were not open to including what they saw as expensive, low-quality imagery in their motion pictures. However, in 1982, the computer-graphics division of Lucasfilm created one of the landmark sequences in 3-D animation history—the Genesis effect for *Star Trek II: The Wrath of Khan.*

The original screenplay had called for a small special effect—a rock would turn green and glow after being shot by the Genesis machine. It was Alvy Ray Smith who suggested the idea of demonstrating the Genesis effect with computer simulation, showing a dead planet coming to life. To accomplish this, new software was specially developed, including some of the first commercial applications of fractals (depicting realistic mountains) and particle systems (for flames and explosions) (see Chapter 11). While it lasted for only a minute, the sequence was so impressive and successful that it was used in the next three *Star Trek* films and continues to be used in commercials.

In addition to particle systems, the computer-graphics unit at Lucasfilm created important tools for 3-D animation, such as advanced ray tracing and motion-blur effects. Despite their successes, the staff remained frustrated. Even at a visionary company like Lucasfilm, there remained little support for going beyond short special-effect sequences and developing independent computer animation projects.

In 1985, George Lucas decided to let the unit become independent and allowed his employees to look for investors. The next year, with their purchase by Steve Jobs (who had left Apple), it became an independent company led by Catmull, Smith, Bill Reeves, and John Lasseter (see Chapter 11). The new company was named *Pixar,* while the special-effects part of Lucasfilm that remained became *Industrial Light and Magic.*

Together and separately, these companies would help define the range and promise of commercial 3-D animation and special effects in such films as *The Abyss, Terminator 2, Jurassic Park,* and *Toy Story.* By the 1990s, the venerable traditional animation company, Disney, began integrating more and more computer-animated sequences into its films—with a system devised by Pixar. Even traditional films like *Forrest Gump* routinely had computer-animated sequences (hint—the floating feather). At the end of the decade, following *Star Wars Episode I*'s successful inclusion of over sixty digital characters, George Lucas would decide to film Episode II as a completely digital production.

BOX 5.2

Commodore: a computer for the masses

In the 1970s, Commodore led the push to create a very affordable computer for consumers. Its *PET* of 1977, with a built-in monitor, cost less than $1,000. The *VIC-20* of 1981 cost less than $300. The next year, they released the *Commodore 64,* one of the most successful computers in history, selling about 20 million computers (see Figure 5.25). Besides word processing, the Commodore 64 introduced computer painting to the general public. With a simple wax printer attached, artists could make their first affordable color prints. With a machine that cost only a few hundred dollars, consumers could not only make pictures but also music with the first built-in synthesizer chip.

In 1985, Commodore leapt far beyond the rest of the young industry with their introduction of the *Amiga.* Designed from the start as a graphics machine and costing only $1,200, this was the first truly affordable multimedia computer. It integrated graphics, sound, and even video and animation. While other personal computer makers were proudly announcing machines that could display sixteen colors, the Amiga displayed more than 4,000.

Combined with the *Video Toaster,* a video editing board designed by Tim Jenison's NewTek, the Amiga became a machine that is still astounding. With this $1,600 board, users could input video from camcorders, VCRs, or directly from a TV and add special effects, characters, and animation. Also included with the board was a paint program with a palette of 16.8 million colors and a 3-D modeling program. In the early 1990s, Amigas with Video Toasters were used for special effects on television shows like *Star Trek: The Next Generation* and by musicians like Todd Rundgren, as well as many early digital animation and video artists. Even Andy Warhol (just before his death) had an Amiga in his studio, with which he colorized photographs of celebrities as he had on canvas in the 1960s and 1970s.

Commodore and NewTek shared a dream of multimedia computers being a democratizing force, allowing creative people to produce professional-quality art, animation, and video in their homes and broadcasting their work for free on public-access television stations. Unfortunately, a series of poor financial decisions by Commodore led to their bankruptcy and the end of Amiga production (though there remains a loyal underground of Amiga users). Ironically, only a few years later, their dream would be revived in a format they had not imagined—the World Wide Web. ■

■ **Figure 5.25**
In 1982, the Commodore 64 cost only $595 and became the best-selling computer in history.

The Games: From the Arcade to Your Home

An argument can be made that after the military, the single most important driving force behind the development of computers has been video games. Many of the essential elements of digital media, high-end graphics, 3-D modeling and animation, and interactivity can be traced back to the ever-increasing demands of gamers.

Today's multibillion-dollar industry began with the simplest of forms bouncing across a screen. In 1961, Steve Russell, a computer programming student at MIT, secretly created the first video game. He called it *Spacewar* and it ran on the institute's huge $120,000 DEC mainframe. With a crude joystick, one could maneuver a spacecraft (a rotating triangle) and fire space torpedoes (white dots) at an enemy ship (another triangle). The long tradition of underground gaming began. Enthusiastic programmers around the country secretly circulated copies with others who worked at the large universities or at companies who rented DEC mainframes. Surprisingly, when DEC management finally discovered the game, rather than blocking it, they recognized its popularity and embraced it. *Spacewar* was used to test new mainframes and the DEC sales staff used the game as an impressive demo for prospective customers.

Five years later, Ralph Baer of Sanders Associates designed *Odyssey,* a simple computer game where players moved lights around the screen. With a licensing agreement with Magnavox, it became the first consumer computer game. However, it was Nolan Kay Bushnell, a University of Utah graduate, who truly created the computer game industry. In 1969, he designed the first video arcade game—*Computer Space.* In 1972, he founded a company whose sole focus was video games—Atari. That same year they released Bushnell's *Pong,* a simple black-and-white form of table tennis that captured the enthusiasm of young programmers around the world (see Figure 5.26). Among the classic Atari games released in the next few years were *Asteroids, Breakout, Centipede,* and *Missile Command.* In 1977, Atari unveiled a home video-game console, the Atari 2600. When they included a home version of the hot arcade game *Space Invaders,* demand for the consoles overwhelmed the company, capturing the attention of the news media, and a new industry was created. Five years later, in 1982, the first Nintendo game console was released. Over 30 million machines would eventually be sold.

It was about this same time that the first personal computers came on the market. The first computer games for personal computers were no match for the game consoles. They were completely text based with no images. A popular game called *Zork* began with these words on a black screen, "You are standing in an open field west of a white house" and the user would type on the keyboard, "walk east." But over the next decade, images, animation, and video would be integrated into increasingly powerful personal computers with the arrival of new storage media and multimedia peripherals like CD-ROMs, sound and video cards, and new formats like MIDI and Quicktime.

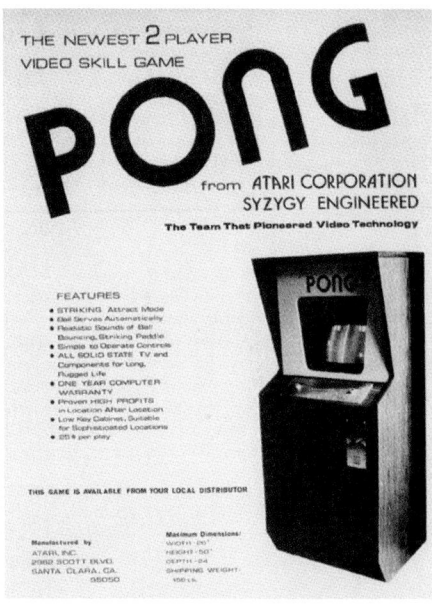

Figure 5.26

Ad for one of the earliest video arcade games from Atari—Pong.

Figure 5.27

A scene from Myst.

During the early 1990s, games on the PC finally became the equal of those on dedicated game machines. Living Book's *Just Grandma and Me,* released in 1992, ushered in a new era in children's interactive and educational software. In 1993, the Zork-like exotic adventure puzzle, Rand and Robyn Miller's *Myst* (see Figure 5.27), became the most successful CD-ROM game in history. Its direction, sophisticated textured graphics and sound, and imaginative approach truly took advantage of the potential of the new medium. Id software's *Wolfenstein,* along with the later *Doom* (released in 1994), established a whole new genre which dominates gaming to this day. *Doom* became the second most popular game in terms of sales, but those sales figures do not take into account the millions of players who downloaded the first-person shooter game as shareware from a new outlet for games and artists—the Internet.

The World Wide Web: Another Revolution Born on a Campus

Researchers in computer graphics were among the first to utilize the early stages of the Internet. In addition to information, graphics software and models were shared via downloading from Internet bulletin board systems, newsgroups, and archives. In 1987, CompuServe created the Graphics Interchange Format, or GIF, so images could be shared easily. In 1991, the JPEG was introduced by the Joint Photographic Experts Group.

In 1992, Marc Andreessen and other fellow graduate students at the University of Illinois Champaign-Urbana learned of Tim Berners-Lee's concept of a hyperlinked and graphic Web and decided to see if they could build the first graphical browser (see Chapter 12 for a fuller discussion). They worked for eighteen hours a day, over three months. In the development process, there was some debate over whether to allow large graphics, whose file sizes might threaten to choke computer networks. Andreessen insisted there was no need to limit the size of images, since few would want to include anything larger than small icons to identify links.

The success of their free browser, *Mosaic,* in 1993 was beyond anything they imagined (see Figure 5.28). Andreessen later recalled, "We introduced Mosaic to three people at the beginning of 1993, and by the end there were one million people using it." By transforming the Internet into a visual environment, they had made the Internet easy to use and hugely popular. In the first year after its release, the traffic on the Internet increased by 350,000 percent. As feared, almost immediately, large scale images flooded and overwhelmed the networks. Confronted with this by one of his co-workers, Andreessen is reputed to have laughed and said he knew it would happen all along.

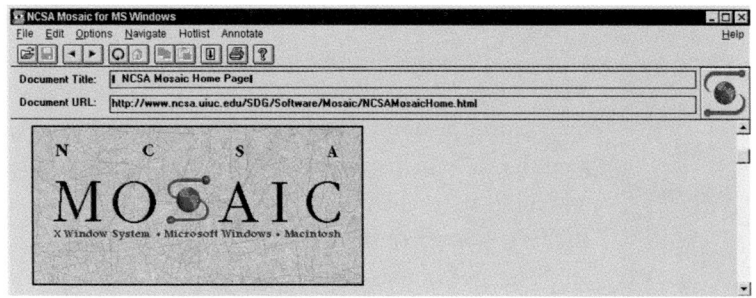

■ **Figure 5.28**
The opening screen of Mosaic.

Recognizing the World Wide Web's potential, many artists were among the first users. In fact, within two years, they accounted for nearly ten percent of all websites. What excited many artists was the way the Web offered an escape from the narrow confines of a commercial gallery system devoted to profit. This concept was in tune with earlier art movements of the 1960s and 1970s, such as happenings and mail and copier art. Now artists, with a small financial investment, could directly reach a worldwide public. For these artists, the notion of a new world where all information and ideas were free should apply to art as well.

Among the early users of the Web as an environment for art was Jenny Holzer, an electronic artist. In 1995, she was among a group of artists who created "ada'web", one of the first sites for Web-specific art, named for the early programmer Ada Byron, the Countess of Lovelace (see Chapter 2). Like her computer-controlled Diamond Vision message boards, *Please Change Beliefs* is an interactive display of Holzer's mottoes on politics, power, religion, and fear designed to communicate directly to the public. Among the truisms are "You are a victim of the rules you live by" and "Lack of charisma can be fatal." Visitors can write their own aphorisms or edit Holzer's, as well as vote for their favorites.

Designed as a place for artists to experiment, ada'web has changed and evolved since its creation, adding new artist projects and new interfaces.

Virtual Reality

When prognosticators look at the Web and attempt to predict its future, many see a 3-D environment. The virtual reality modeling language or VRML was created in 1994 to allow groups of visitors to interact and explore what appears to be 3-D spaces on the Web. Special plug-ins are usually required for today's users to experience this. Despite the enthusiasm for VRML, because of slow speeds and the complexity of the programming, the medium has not gained widespread use. A more modest but popular Quicktime version allows visitors to explore 3-D movies and panoramic scenes. Research continues on truly immersive experiences, including 3-D interfaces, as new ways to navigate the Web.

The concept of virtual reality is far from new, having been explored by researchers long before the arrival of the World Wide Web. The military has been supporting research in this area since the 1960s for its application in flight simulations. In the 1980s, building on Sutherland's "Sword of

Figure 5.29

Jaron Lanier, a pioneer explorer of virtual reality.

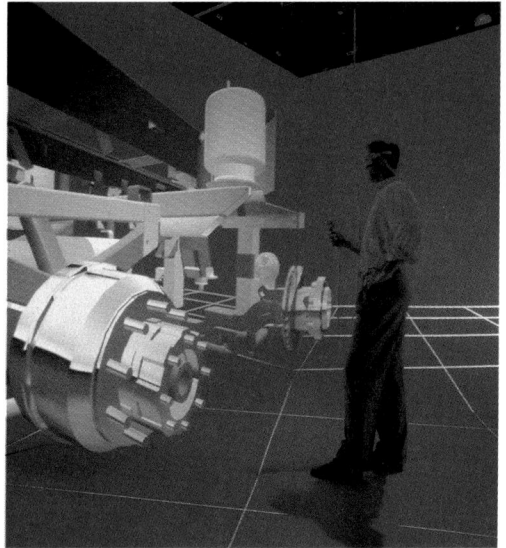

Figure 5.30

Daniel Sandin's CAVE.

Damocles," Scott Fisher of the NASA Ames Research Center in California (who had worked previously with Alan Kay at Atari Research) updated Sutherland's work by creating a stereoscopic headset with headphones for sound and a microphone. Participants wore a *dataglove* which allowed them to touch and manipulate objects in the virtual environment.

The dataglove was developed with the visionary computer scientist, musician, and artist Jaron Lanier (see Figure 5.29), who is also credited with coining the term *virtual reality*. In 1983, Lanier founded VPL (visual programming language) Research, the first company to sell virtual reality products such as headsets, datagloves, and datasuits. He led pioneering research in a wide variety of virtual reality applications, including *avatars*, the representations of visitors in 3-D worlds, and real-time virtual surgery.

In the 1990s, Daniel Sandin at the University of Illinois, Chicago, created the Cave Automatic Virtual Environment or CAVE (see Figure 5.30). This small room projected images on the walls and floor and contained a complex audio system. Once inside, one is thrust into a virtual world that responds to one's movements. Each visitor carries a wand so he or she can interact and change the environment, and wears stereoscopic glasses that allow him or her to see the projections as well as fellow visitors. Perspectives on the glasses are calculated from each visitor's point of view. CAVEs have been installed around the world. Their hardware and software are still in development and continue to be refined to increase the sense of being immersed in a fluid and to have an uninterrupted experience.

CONCLUSION

Over the last fifty years, a group of visionary engineers developed the hardware and software to create digital media in all its myriad forms. Because of their high cost and complexity, few artists or designers participated in the early stages of development. But today, the needs of artists and designers are driving further developments of many of these tools. Digital media hardware and software have become sufficiently mature so that artists and designers rarely require the collaboration of a team of technical advisors. Costs have dropped as well, so digital artists and designers can finally afford their own tools and shift their focus from gaining access to expensive equipment to what they want to create.

We have entered an important moment in the history of digital media because, as necessary as the visionary engineers were, it was just as necessary for digital artists to move out of their shadow. For the digital media to become truly art media, artists needed to become independent of the programmers and engineers to make their art.

However, the need for collaboration is far from over. Multimedia and interactive art, by their very nature, are meant to be produced by teams with a variety of backgrounds. The era of new technologies and media is also far from over. As others emerge and develop, like dynamic immersive virtual environments, the exciting teamwork of technology experts, researchers, and artists and designers will still be necessary. In the years ahead, we are sure to see remarkable new creations born from the marriage of art and science.

Projects: The History of Digital Media

1 *Using images found on the Web, create a visual history that traces the developments of one hardware component found in a typical digitalmedia studio (for example, a mouse or monitor). Below each image, add captions with dates that explain the changes from the hardware's first appearance to today.*

2 *Trace the history of video games from Pong to the present. Explain the technical advances that took place (for example, the arrival of 24-bit color) and their relevance to digital media.*

3 *Using the Web as a resource, write a report on the history of one of the key digital media software manufacturers (for example, Adobe or Macromedia). Explain how their software developed over time and what that has meant to digital artists and designers.*

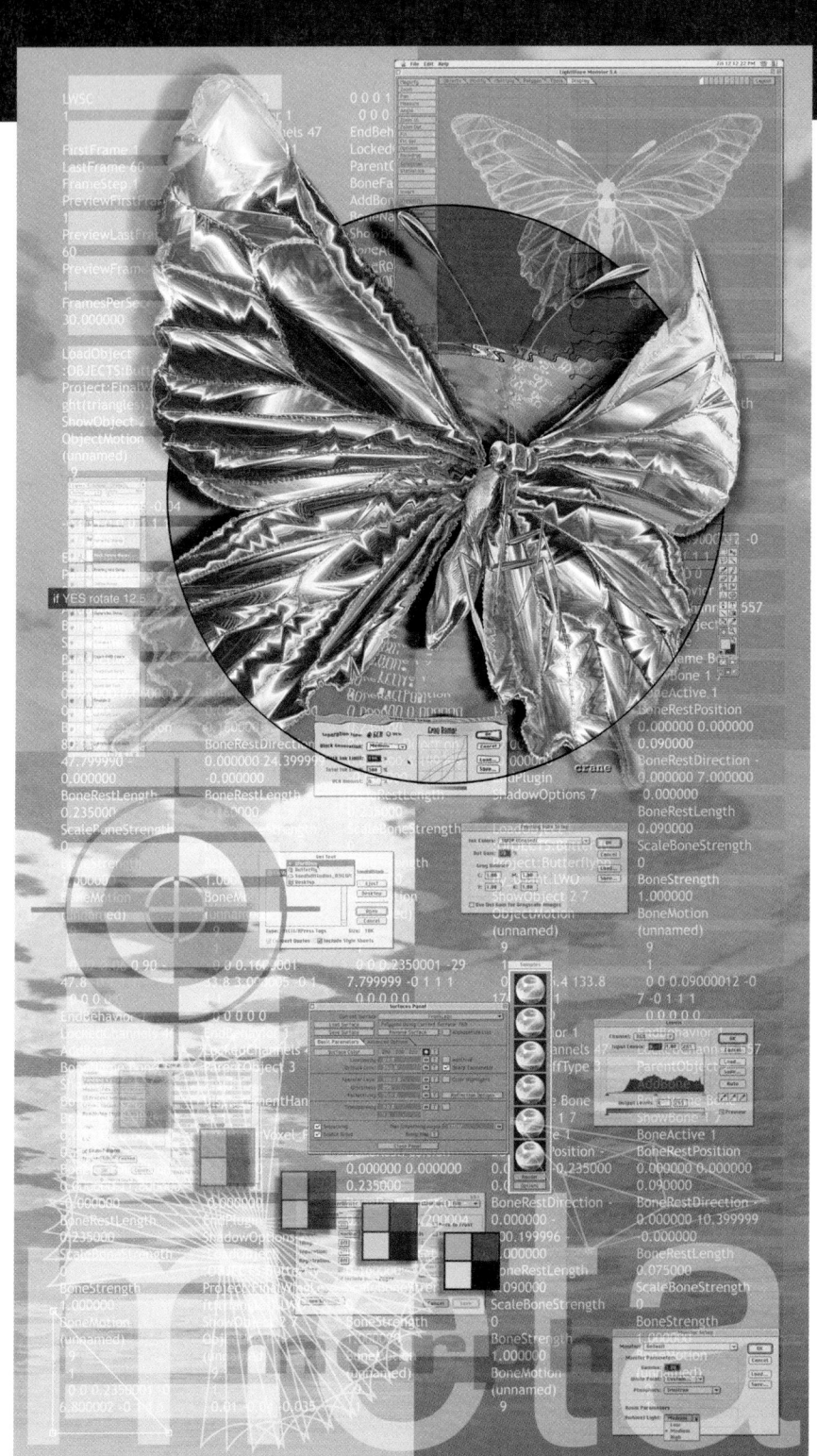

6

Digital Layout and Design

Introduction

Performing digital layout and design on a computer has truly revolutionized the graphic design profession. In its most basic form, page layout programs bring type, graphics, and photographs together in a single document. As long as the information you wish to include is in a file format the program recognizes, it can be used in the design.

The principal element that distinguishes a digital layout and design program from a sophisticated word processing program is the way it handles type. Unlike a word processing program that processes type in rows of letters (much like a typewriter would), digital layout and design programs see type as blocks of information that can be picked up and moved around, much like designers a few decades ago picked up and moved around cut pieces of printed typography and pasted them to boards (hence, the phrase "cut and paste"). Professional digital layout and design programs offer extensive capabilities for type treatment and layout variables. Text can be wrapped around a curved line or shape, distorted, or skewed, and the spaces between lines of text and even the letters themselves can be adjusted.

Graphic design was once the exclusive province of trained professionals. Today, many programs contain templates, including typestyle information and layouts for a variety of standard design functions, like newsletters or business cards. While not appropriate for the design professional, this is especially helpful to the many users of digital layout and design programs who do not have extensive training in design, but who, with these new tools, are able to design serviceable documents on their own.

A Brief History of Publishing

Throughout much of its history, a literate elite has controlled publishing. One can say publishing began with the first form of written, portable communication, the scroll. Scrolls were at first prepared from *papyrus*, a special kind of reed found in Egypt, which was slit, peeled, and soaked in

water. The flattened reeds were laid next to each other, overlapping slightly. A second set of prepared reeds was then laid on top of the first at a ninety-degree angle. Under pressure, the reeds would bond together to form a writing surface. Sections of papyrus were glued together to form the scrolls we are familiar with today (see Figure 6.1). Papyrus has proven to be one of the most durable writing surfaces ever created.

The creation of a smooth writing surface using papyrus matured around 1500 B.C., and revolutionized the process of recording information. Papyrus sheets were the common writing surface for centuries in the Middle East and parts of Europe until being replaced by parchment during the Roman Empire.

Initially papyrus scrolls were used to record religious texts and other important information, although it was not uncommon for more mundane subjects like the sale of a donkey to be duly recorded (see Figure 6.2). Around A.D. 500 the codex (see Figure 6.3), a primitive form of book made of smaller individual sheets of papyrus (and later parchment) became common (see Figure 6.4). This might have happened for several reasons. The codex was not only more economical and convenient to use but also took less space to store. Unlike a scroll, where only one side of the surface could be written upon, the codex was able to use both sides of the writing surface.

In addition to the codex, wax tablets were used well into the Medieval period. To make a wax tablet, a flat piece of wood was carved out on one side, filled with wax, and smoothed into a flat writing surface. Several of these could be joined together to make a form of notebook. Due to the ease upon which they could be written, they were often used for general personal and business correspondence and quick notes (see Figure 6.5). With the use of a stylus, a scribe could write and record information quickly and, if deemed important, that information was copied to a more permanent material—papyrus roll or parchment codex. The wax tablet was then resurfaced and used again. Wax tablets were used through the eleventh and twelfth centuries until finally being replaced with pen and parchment, a smoother and superior writing surface that came from the smoothly scraped hides of butchered lambs.

These various forms of early writing and publishing are in certain ways similar to today's. We may make notes for publications in a notepad (wax tablet) or even a palm-pilot-type device, then enter the information to a desktop computer for a more workable form. For permanence, we might decide to publish the work in "codex" form as hard copy on paper (rather than papyrus or parchment, which tend to jam in laser printers).

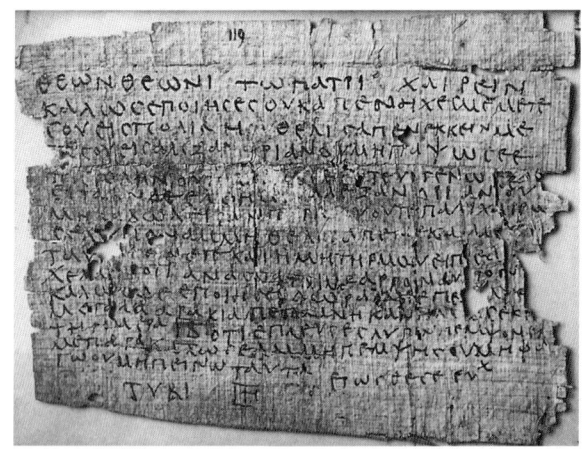

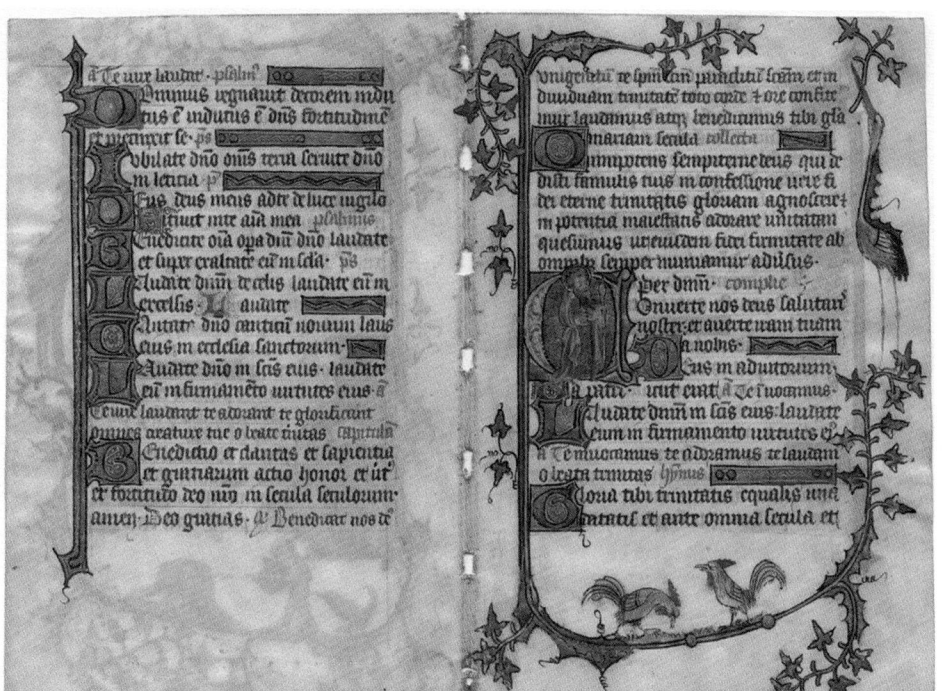

Figure 6.6

Reproduction of early books required a scribe to copy the entire text by hand.

Whatever form early books took, they were, by necessity, one-of-a-kind items. During the Middle Ages, for example, if additional copies were needed, then someone (usually a monk or scribe trained in this discipline) would meticulously and laboriously copy each scroll until another had been completed. Waiting for a new copy of a book might take well over a year (see Figure 6.6). Needless to say, early books produced in this fashion were extremely rare and valuable. Most people never saw, much less owned, a book. Libraries or repositories of books were almost always centered in monasteries or in some cases with the nobility. The personal library of a wealthy and educated nobleman might contain no more than two hundred or so books.

The Paper Revolution

Hundreds of years before those in the West were scraping hides to make parchment and painstakingly copying documents one at a time, the Chinese had discovered that a fibrous material like cotton could be mixed with water and heated until it became soft and pliable. Pouring the mixture over fine bamboo screens allowed the water to escape, leaving the cotton fibers nesting together on the surface. This primitive paper was pliable and held ink well. Traditionally, the invention of paper has been attributed to Cai Lun, who lived in the Eastern Han Dynasty, and presented the new writing surface to Emperor He Di in A.D. 105. However, it is very likely that this primitive form of papermaking was in use several hundred years before that date.

Paper would play a critical role in the history of publishing for two reasons. It was less expensive than silk, an earlier Chinese writing surface, or any of the other materials used around the world. It was also firm enough to stay on the surface of carved, inked, wooden blocks. Long before its invention in the West, the Chinese had discovered that individual blocks of wood or clay could be carved into various symbols, organized together, and used to print copies of documents. As early as A.D. 740, China had its first printed newspaper, and by 1041 the Chinese had developed their own form of movable type.

During the Renaissance, a variety of products, inventions, and technologies began making their way from the East to Europe because of trading. Although the Chinese had been guarding the secret of manufacturing paper, in A.D. 751 when the T'ang army was defeated by the Ottoman Turks, a number of papermakers were captured along with the Chinese soldiers. Consequently, papermaking spread to the Arab world. Four centuries later, as a result of the Crusades, papermaking made its way from the Middle East and Northern Africa to Spain.

The Print Revolution

By the fourteenth century, inexpensive paper was readily available throughout Europe. Fine art printmaking was already in full bloom, but it was not until Johannes Gutenberg's printing press in 1455 that true multiple copies of books

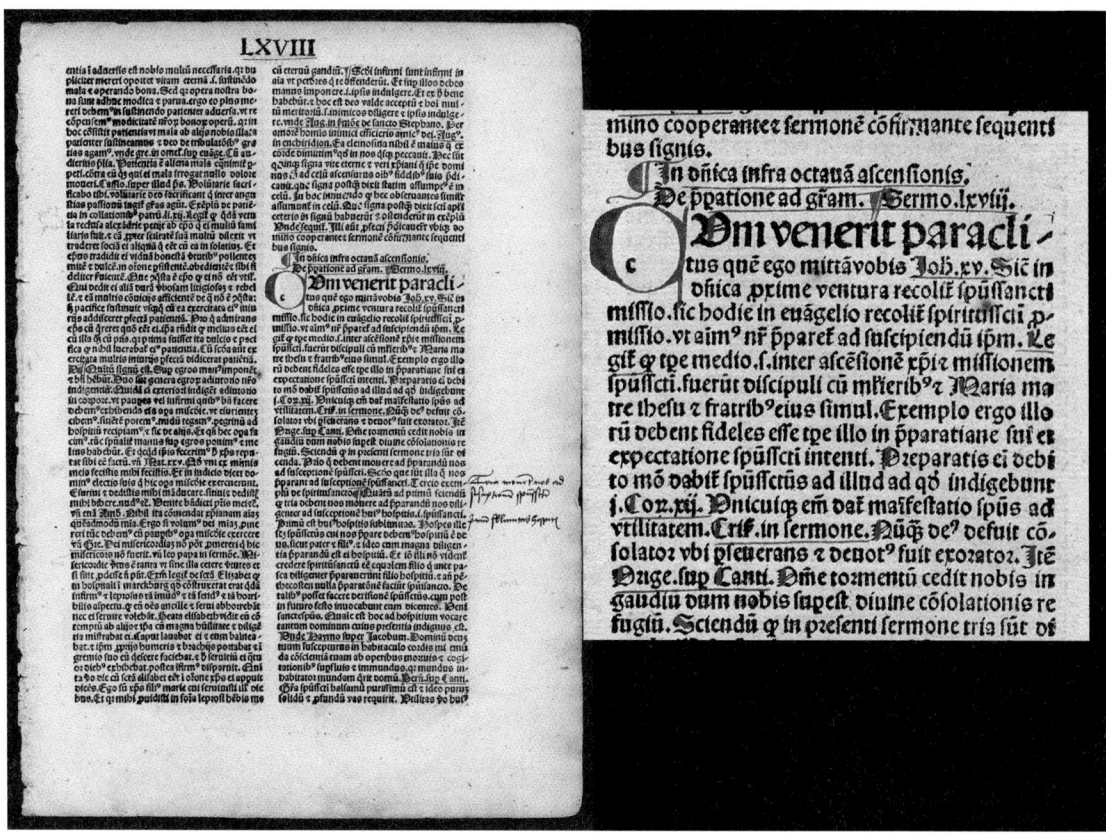

■ Figure 6.7

The term *Incunabula* (Latin for "swaddling clothes") represents the earliest printing technologies from Gutenberg through 1501.

became a reality (see Figure 6.7). Gutenberg's most important contribution to publishing was not, however, the printing press. It was actually *type founding,* the mechanical production of cast type, which made the printing of books possible. By casting the face and body of the type in one operation, Gutenberg was able to cast multiples of the separate types in metal molds. His movable type was designed so that it could be aligned in the manuscript he was printing to form a flow from letter to letter and word to word. This mimicked the hand quality of letterforms used to that point (see Figure 6.8). While movable type was first used in China some 400 years before Gutenberg's printing press, Chinese type was far less durable, being made of clay or wood rather than metal.

Gutenberg's printing press was actually a modified winepress. On it, he assembled rows of type, which were locked into place and inked (see Figure 6.9). Dampened paper was positioned over the inked type and the *platen,* a kind of pressure plate, was screwed down on top of the paper and type. A lever was used in order to further increase pressure, resulting in firm and even contact between the paper and type. After the impression was made, the press was opened and the paper hung to dry. It was in this manner that Gutenberg's forty-two-line Bible was published in Mainz.

This process, while excruciatingly slow by today's standards, dramatically changed the way in which information was disseminated. It was a revolution in every sense of the word, paving the way for sharing culture and knowledge with the general populace instead of limiting it to the ruling classes. It also made spreading

■ Figure 6.8

Example of an illuminated letter form.

Figure 6.9

This shows Gutenberg examining a print in his "press room."

the word about new scientific developments during the Renaissance much easier. By 1499, more than 250 cities around Europe were printing documents using some form of Gutenberg's invention.

As presses became more sophisticated and faster, newspapers were established and published works of fiction were circulated to the world. By the Industrial Revolution, *rotary presses* were developed (see Figure 6.10), capable of making up to 1,000 impressions per hour as compared to Gutenberg's 200–300 impressions per day. In 1886, the *Linotype machine* (see Figure 6.11), a form of automatic typesetter, replaced the tedious job of handsetting type one character at a time, line by line (see Figures 6.12 and 6.13). Using molds of type, it was able to drop a mold of each letter into place using a keyboard to type the letters. The type was then cast line by line instead of character by character (see Figure 6.14).

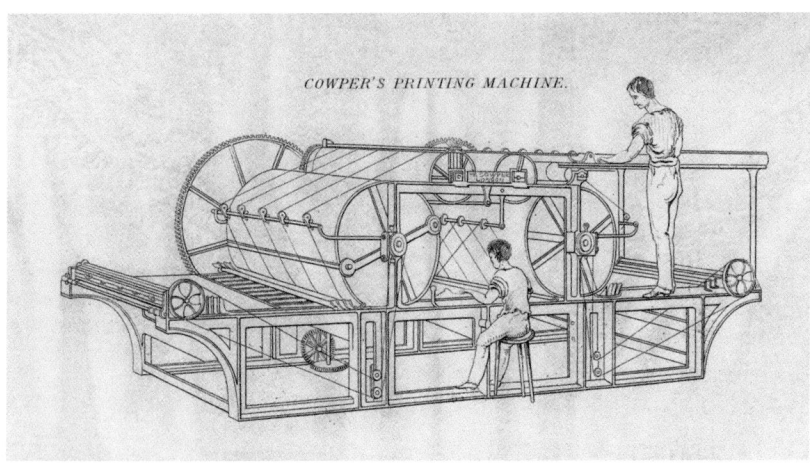

Figure 6.10

Rotary presses made multiple prints at a greatly increased rate.

Figure 6.11

Linotype machines replaced hand-set type and soon became the standard for typesetting.

The evolution of print technology was not only a series of mechanical advances but aesthetic ones as well. Type forms and type foundries developed along with the technology, creating different typefaces as the technology evolved. We still recognize the genius of many of this era's type designers. Names like Garamond (1480–1561), Caslon (1692–1766), Baskerville (1706–1775), Bodoni (1740–1813), and Goudy (1865–1947) live on in the names of the fonts they designed.

The Desktop Revolution

When the first printed books appeared in the middle of the fifteenth century, they were usually print versions of manuscripts like the Bible and prayer books. In the sixteenth and seventeenth centuries, printed books moved beyond religious tracts to include nonsecular subjects like science, poetry, and drama. As a result, they began to have a powerful impact on European society (see Figure 6.15). By the eighteenth century, independent printers like Benjamin Franklin helped foment revolutions in Europe and America.

In the last 200 years, an enormous number of books, periodicals, newspapers, and other forms of publications have been printed on ever-widening subjects. Technology evolved to the point where millions of copies of a particular book or other publication could be printed in a matter of days. Distribution of those books, as well as the change from private subscription to public libraries, guaranteed access to anyone who wished to read. One thing, however, remained constant from the days of ancient imperial China—book publishing remained in the hands of those controlling the technology, or those

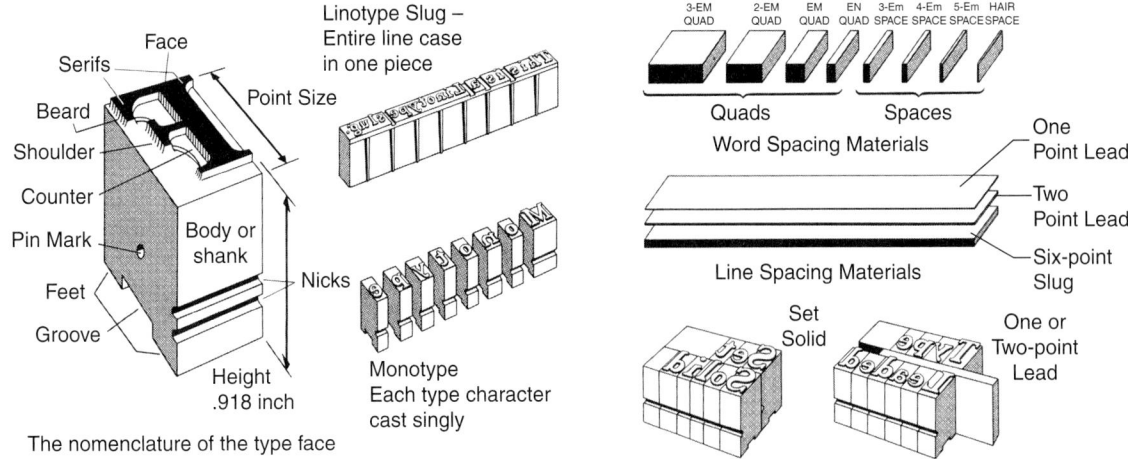

Figure 6.12

Hand-set letterforms required skill and care. Minding your p's and q's was important.

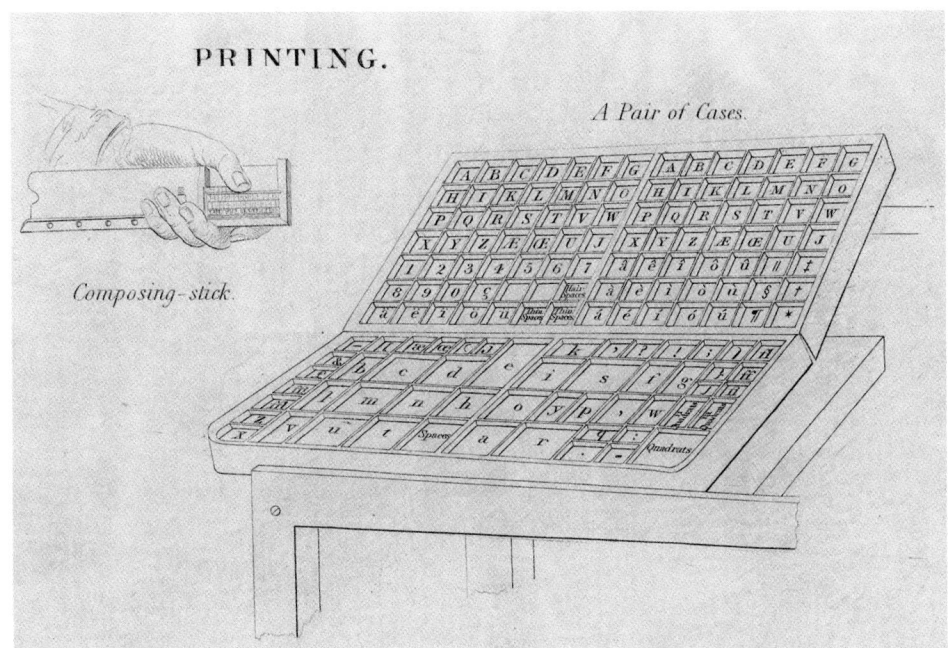

Figure 6.13

Composing stick and type drawer.

Figure 6.15

The Martin Luther bible had a profound impact on German culture and language, which soon spread throughout Europe.

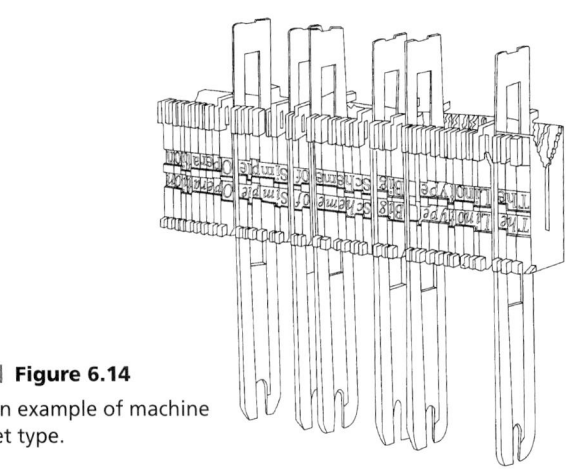

Figure 6.14

An example of machine set type.

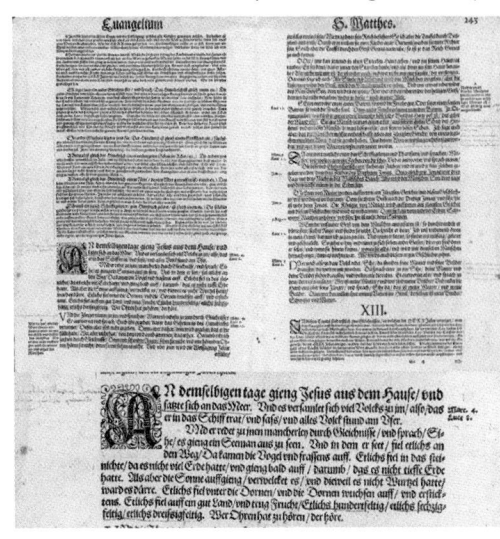

wealthy enough to purchase access to that technology. However, that changed in the 1980s.

Like the development of movable type and the printing press, desktop publishing or digital layout and design—the ability to combine text and image together within a computer in preparation for printing—has brought the power of publishing within the reach of the nonprofessional. In addition, desktop publishing has established itself as a legitimate force in digital imaging today, forever changing the face of the design world and the publishing industry. Available to anyone who wishes to create designs, newsletters, forms, advertisements, catalogs, and similar kinds of printed matter, it has been applauded by many but often scorned by professionals who see the quantity of publications designed by amateurs rising at the expense of design excellence. Learning a computer program is not the same as having the background and art training necessary to create coherent, visually appealing designs.

Designers and Publishing Before the Desktop Revolution

Prior to the advent of today's digital layout and design programs, the training that went into developing someone capable of working in the design/publishing field was far more rigorous in terms of practical, hands-on skill development. The roles for creating a publication were separated into those of graphic/production artists and graphic designers.

Graphic Arts professionals were fundamentally involved with various forms of print production. They used to photograph artwork on a large copy camera in order to make the halftone negatives (necessary to create the illusion of continuous tone) or line art (black and white with no halftone dots) needed to create a printing plate that could run on an offset lithography press. Graphic artists (pressmen) might run the press itself or hold any one of a number of other jobs relating directly to the production of a printed piece. Their training was more vocational in nature and might have included developing copy-camera skills, *stripping film* (positioning and assembling negatives from the copy camera or typesetter in their proper placement, orientation, and registration), identifying paper types and their printing characteristics, inking and running large offset presses, running the bindery, setting type, and much more.

Graphic designers, however, were and are primarily involved with designing the material to be printed. The graphic designer must be familiar with the skills of the graphic artist, but be more concerned with specifying how the material to be printed should look. Beyond that, areas of specialization and a hierarchy of jobs evolved within the design and publishing world itself.

In the past, students entering a college or university to study graphic design or publication design took a series of foundation courses shared by all art majors. Courses in 2- and 3-D design, drawing, painting, and photography were usually taken as the student began his or her art and design training. Courses in lettering were then taken in order to understand the structure and development of the letterform itself—the differences between serif and sans-serif typefaces, why they were different, and how that affected the way in which they would communicate. They created letterforms by hand, drawing them until they could clearly visualize the way in which they would affect the space around them, understanding their rhythm and balance, and appreciating the differences between them (see Figure 6.16).

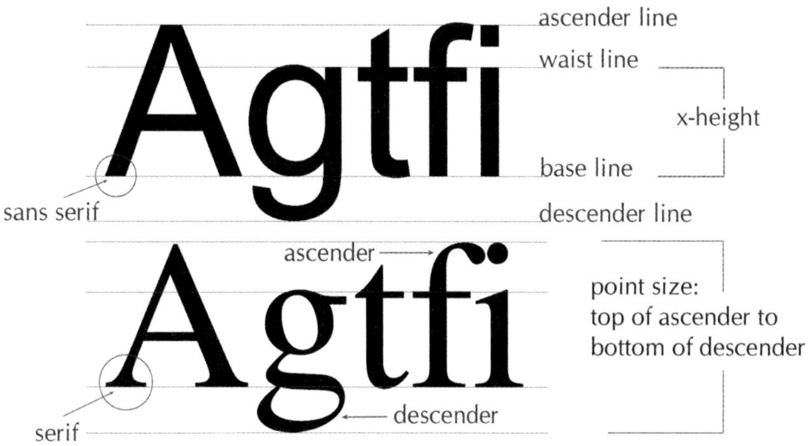

Students were also required to learn what might become the most important skill of all—the ability to specify or *spec* type. After their design was finished, they had to be able to communicate to the typesetter which typeface to use, just how large the type should be, the spacing of the type on the page, and even the spacing between the letters themselves. Without the ability to spec type, their design work would not translate to the printed page.

Before digital layout and design programs, students were also trained to do *paste-ups and mechanicals* (see Figure 6.17) where the various materials used in the design would be cut up and pasted down on a piece of white mounting board that would go to the printer. All of this would evolve into an understanding of how a variety of visual elements could come together to create a coherent and visually appealing publication. This was often considered an entry-level job in a professional design firm.

Today's design students still take foundation courses in a variety of art studio related areas, but much of the work in studying letterforms and typography has been integrated into other courses connected to digital design. Even if still called typography, their study enlists the computer in working through the complexities of type and how it can be used creatively. Their goal is still to gain a more sophisticated understanding of the different typefaces available, how they evolved, and how they are used creatively in design. They still study the color of type, not in terms of hue but in terms of type density and how that affects the aesthetic quality of the document they are designing. Studying the history of type and its development through the ages gives them an appreciation of various typefaces and how type foundries evolved. Differences between classic and contemporary typefaces and their relationship to changing printing technologies are also studied. However, in WYSIWYG (what you see is what you get) digital layout and design programs, designers can make changes directly instead of specifying work to be done by others (typesetters and paste-up artists, for example).

As the description of the training of design students indicates, much of the work in graphic design and publication design prior to 1984 was done by hand—and we may liken this to the type of manual effort that was required prior to the printing press and movable type. The digital revolution in design and publishing has been no less extraordinary than Gutenberg's invention was to publishing in 1455. While much of the training described in this

ascender line
waist line
x-height
base line
descender line
sans serif
ascender
serif
descender
point size:
top of ascender to
bottom of descender

■ **Figure 6.16**
As these examples of sans-serif and serif letter forms show, type is clearly defined by its structure.

■ **Figure 6.17**
Artist working with traditional paste-up and mechanical materials and techniques.

section remains a fundamental part of the training of graphic designers, some skills, like specing type and producing paste-ups and mechanicals, have been relegated to the dust bin of history.

The Birth of Digital Layout and Design

The digital revolution in publishing can be traced to the mid-1980s with the production by Aldus Corporation of a new software program called Pagemaker. It was developed for the recently introduced Apple Macintosh computer (see Chapter 4, p. 70) and fully utilized its GUI to create an extraordinary new tool for designers. The Pagemaker program was able to combine text and graphics in the same document. The combination of the Macintosh and desktop publishing software would allow designers to see pages on the computer screen as they would look when printed. This WYSIWYG capability proved to be of critical importance.

At the same time, computer-printed output took a huge step toward professional quality with the first laser printers. Unlike the then-conventional dot-matrix printers, where text and images were composed of large, quite apparent dots, Apple's LaserWriter printed much sharper and clearer text.

As we have already noted, prior to this development, documents were prepared for publication using traditional and mechanical cut-and-paste techniques. Images were prepared separately, while text was sent out to a professional typesetter using a *Compugraphic* (one of the earliest) or similar typesetting machine that could set and space the text according to the designer's specifications. It would then be sent to an *imagesetter,* a machine that would print the text at high resolution (1,200 dpi to 4,000 dpi, depending on the machine being used) to film or on long sheets of photographic paper that were then developed in special chemicals similar to a regular black-and-white photograph. The typesetting machine itself held a group of internal fonts or typefaces that could be printed at a very high resolution to ensure smooth crisp typography. Generally, 1,200 dpi was considered to be typeset quality. The sheets of printed type, or *galleys,* were cut apart and pasted onto cardboard layout panels along with various graphics or photographs. This *camera-ready art* would be photographed, stripped, made into plates, and then run on an offset lithography press to create the final printed piece.

With the arrival of digital layout and design programs, a new graphic design environment was born. Type and text could be brought together and combined in the computer. Text styles, the text font, size, and spacing could all be seen on the screen and problems corrected or changed. The relationship of the type to graphics or photos could be adjusted almost endlessly. Changes in composition or content could be completed without having to send out new specifications to a printer, eliminating the once-typical loss in time and money.

Digital Layout and Design: Not Just for Amateurs

Due to the accessibility of desktop publishing software and equipment, the term desktop publishing was initially applied to the home user or amateur wanting to save money while doing many of the design tasks that would normally have been the province of the professional designer. As smaller companies and businesses began to handle publishing activities that would normally have been "hired out to professionals," the concept of desktop publishing expanded beyond self-publishing to include professionally prepared and printed documents. Professional tools were suddenly at the disposal of anyone who wished to use them, whether trained as a designer or not, on their desktop computer. While in the past individuals engaged in the design of publishing went through rather rigorous training (as described earlier) in everything from the aesthetic qualities of type to page layout and design, today anyone with a computer and the appropriate software can engage in publication design. This has ushered in much speculation over the current state of design and, according to many design professionals, a deterioration in the quality of many items published today, from company newsletters and advertisements to brochures and even larger and more costly productions.

Today, professionals also use the tools of digital layout and design. The training that the professional has received, coupled with the tools of digital layout and design and its associated programs, give designers the opportunity to produce publications with a variety and flexibility that would have been difficult to imagine just a few decades ago. Even in magazines, newspapers, and advertising agencies, the era of paste-ups and mechanicals is over and digital layout and design, tuned to the requirements of the job, is the order of the day. The offset lithographic presses, with their roots going back to the fifteenth century, are now giving way to fully digital printing methods. Designers have found they can work more quickly and with greater accuracy using digital tools. More variations of a single design can be explored and shown to a client. Changes can be made less expensively and more quickly. So, while desktop publishing has, perhaps for the first time, made the tools of publishing available to the masses, professionals have also benefited and found their work expanding in new ways because of it.

Digital Layout and Design: The Equipment

Although digital layout and design software was originally produced for the Apple Macintosh computer, the PC has long since caught up with this technology. Whatever format you choose to use—Mac or PC—the programs will have a GUI. Other important components include a scanner for digitizing artwork and a printer for output. An image-editing program (Chapter 7) is necessary for correcting or modifying images to be placed in a publication, while some form of word processing software is useful in preparing text for long documents.

Of course, the publishing software itself is of prime importance. Although Pagemaker introduced the world to desktop publishing, other software producers quickly entered the field. QuarkXPress (see Figure 6.18) appears to have become the current program of choice in the professional world. Adobe, the current maker of Pagemaker, has created a new digital layout and design program called InDesign that has many of the same features as Quark. Each program offers its own workspace, interface, and depth of features. Still, all

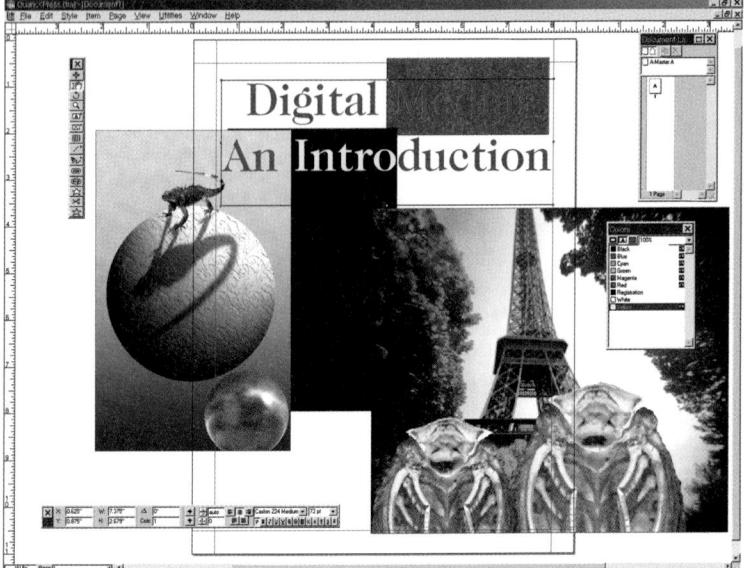

Figure 6.18

Quark XPress screen with a variety of layout information.

digital layout and design software is able to combine text and graphics to create an on-screen display representing a draft of an actual document page complete with both text and graphics.

Input: Scanners

Scanners are often used to digitize photographs or other artwork for use in a desktop publishing program. Scanners can take many forms (additional information about scanners is available in Chapters 3 and 7). The most important element to consider is the scanner's ability to digitize images at the size, resolution, and bit depth you need for the output you intend to use (see Figure 6.19). The resolution of your scan can affect the smoothness of the tonal range of a bitmap image and how clearly detail is depicted. Bit depth can determine the scanner's ability to see subtle variations in similarly colored areas. Depending on your output (laser printer, offset lithography press, direct digital printing), the *spi* or samples per inch of the scan will need to be adjusted for maximum effectiveness.

It may be tempting to scan at the highest optical resolution your scanner can provide in order to include more data for printing a bitmap image, but that would be as significant a mistake as scanning at too low a resolution. If your scan contains more data than an output device needs, it will simply take longer to print (in the case of desktop printers) or output to film for offset printing, and the quality of your output can be degraded. If your scan is at too low a resolution, the overall quality of your output will be degraded (see Box 6.1).

In order to include photographs of high quality in publications, film/slide scanners (see Chapter 3) are becoming increasingly important. While not able to deliver the quality of scans originating from professional drum scanners, they can deliver scans that have a greater dynamic range than those of a flatbed scanner. More importantly, by scanning from the original negative or slide, one

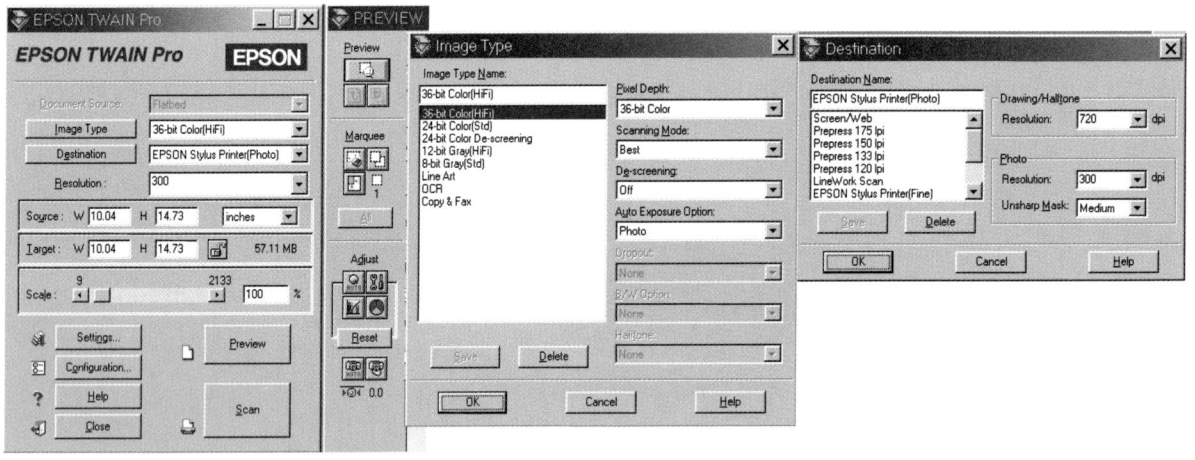

Figure 6.19

Sample of scanning-software variables.

Generally, the formula used for determining the (spi) at which to scan a photographic image is decided by the halftone screen or *screen ruling* the printer intends to use. This, in turn, is determined by the nature of the job to be printed, the absorbency of the paper, the type of press to be used, and even the resolution of the imagesetter.

Screen ruling is measured in *lines per inch* (lpi). The relationship between *dots per inch* (dpi) and lpi is the key factor that will control how a bitmap image will appear when printed. The finer the halftone screen (more lpi), the smaller the halftone cels. As a result, the image will appear smoother with less obvious dots. Coarser halftone screens create images in which the dots or halftone cels that create the image are clearly visible.

As a general rule of thumb, at an image's final printed size, the scan resolution should be one and one-half to two times the line screen to be used (determined by the printer). The following formula can be used to quickly arrive at a scan resolution for images using conventional halftone techniques:

$$\frac{\text{final image height}}{\text{original image height}} \times \frac{\text{Screen ruling} \times 2}{\text{(or 2 1/2)} = \text{scanning resolution}}$$

If a 6″ × 6″ image will be printed at a smaller size of 4″ × 4″ using a 133 line screen, the result would be:

$$\frac{4}{6} \times 133 \times 2 = \text{a scan of the } 6 \times 6 \text{ inch image at 100 percent at 176 spi}$$

When the image is resized to its final 4″ × 4″ printed size, the resolution will be almost exactly twice the line screen of 133. ∎

can avoid the problems that might be associated with scanning from poor, damaged, or out-of-focus prints.

Printers

The exciting thing about desktop publishing is that it can take many forms. Output is determined by need. If simply producing several black-and-white posters for an event is your goal, then a laser or simple inkjet printer (see Figure 6.20) will be sufficient. If color is added to the design, then a higher-quality color inkjet printer or color laser printer is necessary. If more than a few copies are needed, digital files containing your completed design can be delivered to a commercial offset printer. While greater information is available about various kinds of printers in Chapter 4, you will find that most designers use desktop printers to create relatively inexpensive proofs, in order to give clients a clear idea of what the finished piece will look like prior to going to press. High-quality desktop inkjet printers are now available that can print pieces up to 16″ × 20″ so that *full bleed proofs*, showing what a print would look like if an image goes right to the edge of the paper, are possible. Having a printer that can show you the final output can

■ **Figure 6.20**

Oversize print from a large format inkjet printer.

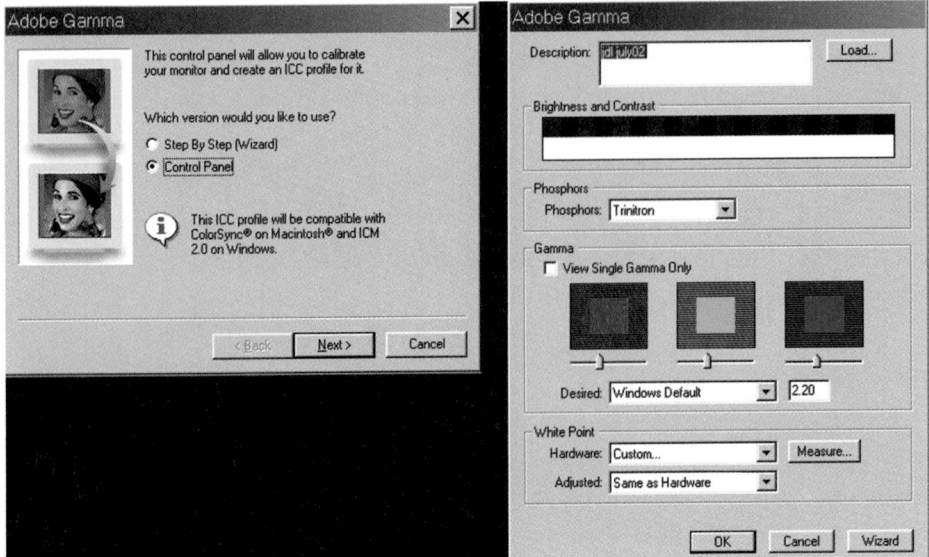

Figure 6.21

Basic monitor calibration can be accomplished through the Adobe color control panel.

help you spot problems that even WYSIWYG on your computer monitor might not make obvious.

Color Calibration

How can you know that the images, colors, and gradations you see on the computer screen are the same as those that will be printed? The answer is accurate color calibration. However, searching for that has often been com-pared to a search for the Holy Grail. Color modes and a description of color gamut will be reviewed in Chapter 7, but an awareness of color calibration is of critical importance to anyone attempting to print from a file composed on a personal computer.

There are a variety of software applications that can help designers cali-brate their system. The most readily available system for both PC and Macintosh is the *Adobe Gamma* control panel (see Figure 6.21). This simple tool makes it easy to adjust gray values on the monitor in order to eliminate color casts that might affect the color balance of your work. Some desktop pro-grams offer their own calibration systems, such as Pagemaker's Kodak Monitor Installer which creates ICC (International Color Consortium) or ICM (which is Windows' version of ICC) profiles for use in color-managed applications that support the Kodak Color Management System.

For very critical work there are also hardware solutions that will physi-cally measure color and density on your monitor and then compare it to printed output and suggest changes in your system to bring the two closer together. While the importance of accurate colors on a screen cannot be over-estimated, neither can the difficulty in achieving them. Even the color temper-ature of the light in the room we are using to view prints can affect our sense of accuracy in determining color fidelity.

Support Programs: More Than an Addendum

Desktop publishing requires the coordination of work in several programs. You will find these programs covered in greater detail elsewhere in this book. However, the brief descriptions given here will serve to illustrate how work completed in other specialized programs can be brought together within a desktop publishing program to create a publication design.

Image-Editing Programs

While many desktop publishing programs can scan an image directly, it will come into the program as an uncorrected raw image. Desktop publishing programs are limited in their ability to adjust and correct images. This is usually left to more powerful image-editing programs, like PhotoShop. Image-editing programs have the ability to do rather sophisticated color correction and can also crop an image to the exact specifications needed. You can find more on these programs in Chapter 7. Image-editing programs also have the ability (along with the scanner) to determine the resolution of the image in terms of file size, print dimensions, and dots per inch. In addition, a good image-editing program can save an image in a variety of formats. While a tagged image file format (TIFF) is often used due to its portability and universal recognition, a professional image-editing program can also create EPS or *encapsulated PostScript* files. The EPS file format can contain both vector and bitmap graphics and is supported by all page-layout programs so that PostScript language artwork can be transferred between applications (see Box 6.2).

Preparing an image for printing before bringing it into a digital layout and design program requires at least a basic understanding of printing technology. When printing on an offset lithographic press, *contone* (continuous tone) images are represented by a series of halftone dots. The smaller the dot, the lighter that portion of the image will be. Shadows have larger dots that are perceived as darker areas. *Dot gain* is the spreading of ink dots as they print on the paper and is determined by the absorptive qualities of the

paper. Primarily affecting the mid-tone areas of images, uncorrected dot gain can make images appear too dark and shift color values. Many things, including the size and shape of the halftone screen dot (see Figure 6.22), the type of paper being used (coated or uncoated stock), and even the printing press itself determine this. If you are using a professional printing firm with offset lithography presses, the printer can help with information that will aid you in matching your desktop system to their printing system. Every professional image-editing program will allow you to compensate for dot gain in contone images, make adjustments for the type of ink being used, and allow you to set the amount of dot gain and ink coverage depending on whether you intend to print on a coated or uncoated stock. ∎

Greyscale   Diffusion Dither   Pattern Dither

Bitmap 50%   Bitmap Halftone   Bitmap Custom
threshold

■ **Figure 6.22**

Halftones can take many forms as defined by your image-editing or digital-layout-and-design program.

Word Processing Programs

While text can certainly be entered directly into a digital-layout-and-design program, this is often awkward for long documents like books or reports that will require multiple pages. Because we are familiar with word processing programs and can work more quickly with them, it makes sense to type and edit most of the information we need directly into a word processing program and then later import the text into the digital layout and design program. This also allows clients to provide editable data, which can save time and streamline workflow.

Vector-Based Illustration Programs

A *vector*-based (resolution independent graphic) illustration program uses mathematically defined shapes made of lines and curves rather than *raster* or bitmap images that use a grid of small squares known as *pixels* to represent images. Vectors, which describe graphics according to their geometric characteristics, are very useful for cleaning up *line scans* (crisp one-bit black-and-white images with no gray values) and especially for converting raster scans of logos and other simple objects to vector images. While the quality of raster or bitmap images will change depending upon the number of pixels in the image, vector images are not dependent upon resolution and can be resized without a loss in quality. Most importantly, vector-based programs can create EPS files of vector-based images for use in digital layout and design programs. (See Chapter 8 for more complete information concerning vector-based illustration programs.)

Inside Digital Layout and Design Programs

When you open a digital layout and design program you will be asked questions about the size of your document, the number of pages you wish to start with, the size of the margins, and other information about your document. After setting those parameters, you will see something that appears to be a sheet of paper on a desktop. Items, whether graphics, photographs, or type, can be placed either in the document or on the desktop for future use. This is referred to as a paste board or layout table, a reference (as in many other parts of the program) to the tools and workplace of a traditional designer (see Figure 6.23). You may have to "zoom out" to make your page appear smaller so you can see the desktop.

You should feel comfortable with the initial view of the program. As in most digital media programs, drop-down menus run along the top of the

Figure 6.23

Different layout and design programs may have differences in the way in which they are designed, but they all share the concept of a desktop with a pasteboard at the center.

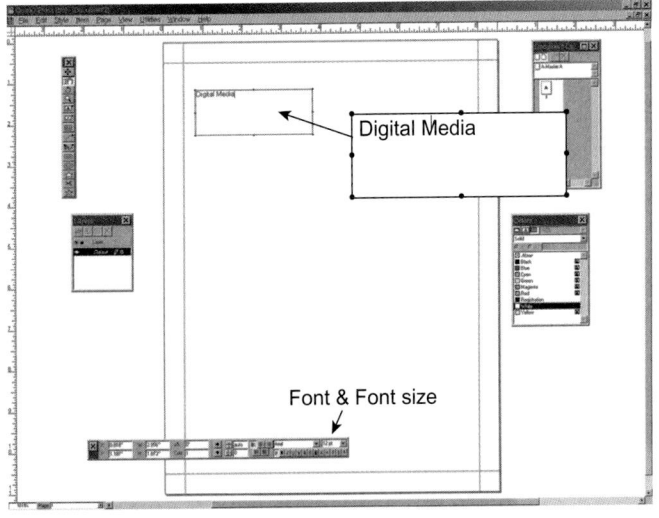

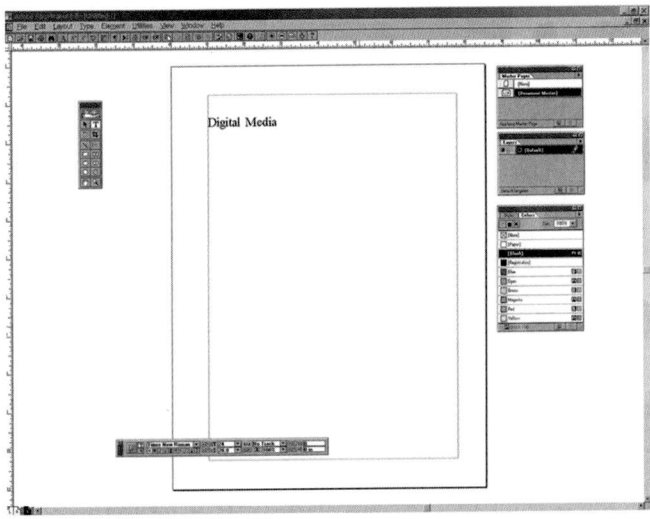

screen, with various program functions nested inside. A floating toolbar will appear on the desktop with the most often used tools for your program, and floating palettes are available for many of the nested functions in the menu bar at the top of the screen. Floating palettes are visual shortcuts for accessing various functions of the program without having to click on a menu item, then click on a function, and perhaps click still again to refine the function you wish to use. Often palettes can be modified to reflect the way in which you work. Palettes can be toggled on or off, usually from the "window" or "view" menu, depending on your program. If all the tools suddenly disappear, they can easily be brought back on screen from one of these menus.

Rulers and Guidelines

Unlike a word processing program, the rulers at the top and left side of the screen do more than give you an idea of the size of your document (see Figure 6.24). By clicking your mouse inside the ruler and then dragging outward while the mouse button is held down, a guideline will be dragged onto the document. This guideline can be easily moved and you can drag as many guidelines as you wish into the document.

Guidelines, while visible on the page, do not print with the document. They are similar to the non-photo "blue pencil" once used to mark guides on a page in traditional cut and paste design to help the artist align different elements. When the design was photographed, the blue pencil marks became invisible. Guidelines can also be made to allow design elements to "snap to" them. When "snap to guides" is selected, an item will automatically align itself with the guide.

The rulers can be set to display the measurement system you wish to use (such as inches or picas) and whether the horizontal ruler should cover a page or spread (two facing pages), depending on the type of document you are working on.

■ **Figure 6.24**

Guidelines can be used to help align information within a composition.

The Basic Tools

The toolbar or box allows you to select the individual tool you want to use (see Figure 6.25). It is necessary to click on a tool in order to activate its function. For example, before you can add text into your document, you must first click on the text tool before typing. If any other tool is selected, you will not be able to add text. Various tools on the toolbar can have other tools nested with them. By clicking and holding down the mouse button on a tool, you can see if additional variations of the tool are available. While actual tools may vary from program to program, the following tools in one form or another should be available.

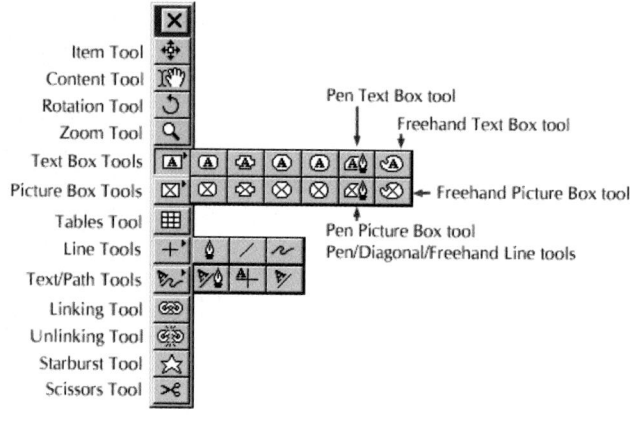

■ **Figure 6.25**

Toolbox with nested tools all revealed (Quark XPress).

The Pointer/Select-Item Tool

The pointer or select-item tool is used to select, then move, an item from one place on the page to another. It can also be used to resize or reshape items, including text boxes, text paths, and wraparound text. By holding down the shift key and clicking on several items to select them, you can temporarily group them together. A menu command will allow you to more permanently group or ungroup the selected items. This is helpful when moving or duplicating large collections of elements.

Text and Text Block Tools

The text or "content" tool is used to enter text directly into a program such as Pagemaker—or, in the case of newer, more sophisticated programs like QuarkXPress and InDesign, a *text block*, which is a space drawn by the user in which text is entered. The text block itself, while most often rectangular, can be any shape at all. Once the text has been entered with the content or text tool, the text block can be moved anywhere in the composition as though it were a graphic element. The text block itself can be pulled or pushed to make it longer or shorter, which changes the length of the typed lines. The flexibility of moving and organizing text as a series of movable units is of crucial importance to digital layout and design programs (see Figure 6.26).

Figure 6.26

Type following a curving path.

Another variation of the text tool, which is a more recent addition to most programs, is the text path tool. This tool allows you to create a *path*, a curved line drawn between connecting points, and then add text, which will flow along the path. A freehand text path tool allows you to draw any line you wish and then type text that will flow along that line. These lines have special anchor points that can be adjusted so that the path can be further corrected or altered using the item tool. There are even options that allow you to choose how the text will behave when it flows along the path.

Rotation Tool

Once an item has been selected with the item tool, switching to the rotation tool allows you to grab and rotate the object in any direction you wish. Unlike numerical rotation tools, this is a visual tool that allows you to see the changes directly on the page.

Zoom Tool

All programs have a zoom tool that allows you to enlarge or reduce the view of the document on the desktop. This can also be accomplished in percentages from the view menu.

Picture Box Tools

Picture boxes create various shapes that act as placeholders for photographs or other art. Whether they are rectangular (with a variety of corner treatments), oval, free form, or drawn with a *Bézier* tool, these boxes contain an X from end to end that signifies their use as placeholders or containers only. A Bézier tool is used to create irregular or curved-shaped boxes by setting a series of anchor points which are then connected with straight lines. Handles at the anchor points can be further adjusted to change the direction and curvature of the lines.

Other Common Tools

The line tool is used for creating straight lines at any angle. The thickness and style of the line (dots, dashes, double, and so on) can be easily set depending on the effect you want. In addition, there is usually a special line tool that draws only perfectly straight horizontal or vertical lines.

There are also a variety of shape tools. These can be used to create elliptical or rectangular shapes. By holding down the shift key when creating them, the shapes become perfect circles or squares. In addition, there are tools to create polygon and star shapes. By using the menu for that specific tool, you can specify the number of sides on a polygon or points on a star.

The grabber hand allows you to literally grab the page and move it around so that you can see the area you wish (see Figure 6.27). This is especially useful when you have the page zoomed in and must move from one part of the page to another. There is usually a shortcut key that allows you to access the grabber from any tool without having to actually select it.

Finally, in QuarkXPress and InDesign there are linking and unlinking tools which allow you to link text boxes together so text can flow from one box to the next. This allows you to create unusual and distinctive text blocks. The unlinking tool breaks those links.

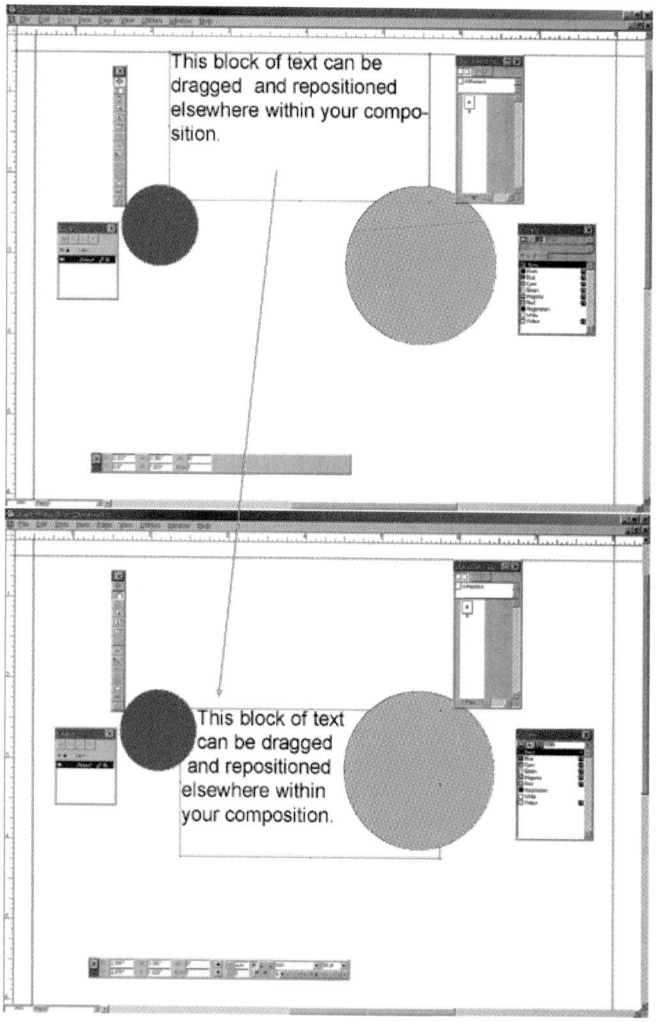

Basic Text Control

The ability to adjust and control the way text looks on a page is what really sets digital layout and design programs apart from word processing programs. While the kind of typeface you use, its size, and its style (bold, italic, and so on) are all tools available in a word processing program, they are only the beginning for digital layout and design programs. The controls that set these programs apart center on their ability to make both global document changes

■ Figure 6.27

One of the key elements that distinguishes digital-layout-and-design programs from word processing programs is the ability to "pick up" and move text around as you would a graphic element.

Figure 6.28

Digital-layout-and-design programs allow you to change the horizontal and vertical scale of your type without changing its font size.

Figure 6.29

Dropping out type or reversing it to white is also easily accomplished in a digital-layout-and-design program.

Figure 6.30

Like traditional word processing programs, text can be aligned in a variety of ways.

and minute adjustments to individual groups of words or even letters. There are a variety of controls to accomplish this.

One should not, however, underestimate the importance of selecting a font, its size, typestyle, or color. Certain typefaces are much easier to read in an extensive body of text while others are better suited for headlines and other display type. The size of the text can also have a profound impact on your document. Digital layout and design programs allow you to adjust the size of your text in much the same way as a word processing program but with much finer control. The typestyle menu allows you to select how the font is to be displayed. Within the typestyle menu are the typical choices of bold, italic, and underline. There is also the option of selecting a word and changing it to all capitals or small capitals, or even striking a line through the word so that it appears as though it were crossed out. In addition, text can also be selected and its color changed. Not only can the color of the text be changed to whatever you wish, the value or *shade* of the text can be changed to a percent value to make it appear lighter or darker on the page. These basic text controls give you enormous creative freedom when it comes to simple text modifications.

Other options for type modification include the ability to change the *horizontal or vertical scale* of selected text, stretching the letters wider and fatter or taller and thinner (see Figure 6.28). *Reversing* text (see Figure 6.29) essentially creates white text on whatever color background you are using. This can be especially useful when working on a dark background color where black or color text is inappropriate.

Finally, text can be aligned with the borders of the page. Again, this is a control offered in many word processing programs. The options are *flush left,* which aligns text with the left side of the text block; *flush right,* which aligns text with the right side of the text block; *centered,* which centers text between the left and right edges of the text block; *justified,* which aligns text with the left and right sides of the text block; and *forced justification,* in which all lines, including the last line (which may be shorter) are aligned with the left and right edges of the text block (see Figure 6.30).

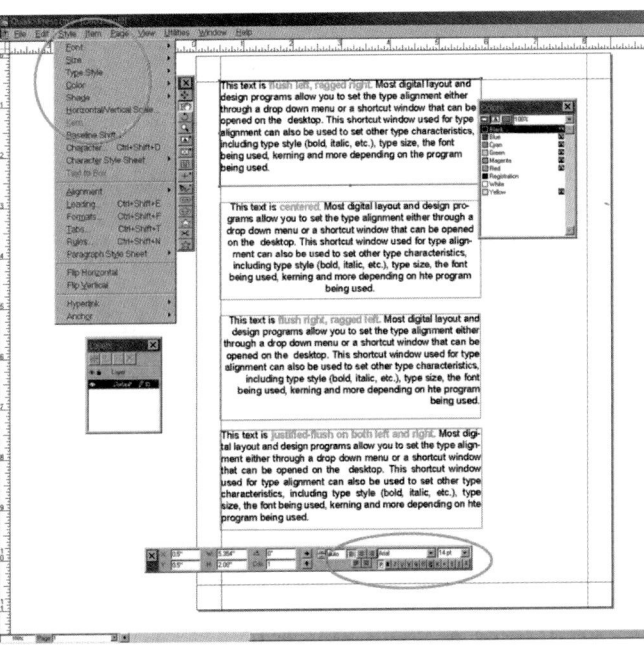

Advanced Text Control

Beyond the relatively simple text controls previously listed, digital-layout-and-design programs also allow you to make fine adjustments to the spacing of letters and lines of text. It is the proper use of these controls that often separates professionals from amateurs. Often with *proportionally spaced text*, where the space each letter occupies is different, spacing needs to be adjusted. Monospaced fonts, like Courier, are designed so that each letter takes up exactly the same amount of space. *Kerning* adjusts the amount of space between two type characters (see Figure 6.31). The kern command displays the character attributes dialog box, which allows a value to be entered in the highlighted kern amount field. Positive values increase the space between characters while negative values decrease the space.

In most programs you can make these adjustments in the menus at the top or use a type palette with many shortcuts. On the type palette, you can click a triangular arrow in the kern amount field to adjust the kerning. This allows you to see the letters getting closer together or further apart so you can make adjustments visually rather than by setting a predetermined amount in a menu's dialog box. The newest option in this arena is optical kerning, which analyzes the shapes of the characters themselves and then applies kerning to properly space the characters automatically.

If an entire word, sentence, or paragraph needs adjusting, the font's *tracking* or letterspacing can be set instead of using kerning. Tracking sets the amount of space between letters and words and can appear to lighten or darken a page as overall tracking or spacing is loosened or tightened (see Figure 6.32). In the tracking menu a specific value can be set (again, positive values expand the spaces between the letters while negative values contract the spaces) to change the spacing between letters. If using the visual shortcuts in the type palette, you have the option of selecting the words or sentences you wish to change. You can then adjust them visually by holding down either the negative (to the left) control or positive (to the right) control. By watching the words expand or contract as you hold down the key, you can stop when you have achieved the spacing needed.

Leading (pronounced "ledding") refers to the space between lines of type (see Figure 6.33). In a word processing program, a simple form of leading might be to choose between single or double spacing. Leading is a relatively archaic term, describing the way in which a typesetter, during the days of hand-set type, would add narrow strips of lead between lines of type in order to maintain the proper spacing. In a digital-layout-and-design program, leading can be adjusted

Digital Media
original text - no letter adjustment

Digital Media
basic kerning to adjust letter spacing

Figure 6.31

Kerning, or the adjustment of letter spacing between adjacent letters, is easily accomplished with a digital-layout-and-design program and is most often applied to pairs of letters to fine-tune character spacing.

The principal element that distinguishes a digital layout and design program from a sophisticated word processing program is the way in which it handles type. Unlike a word processing program that processes type in rows of letters much like a typewriter would, digital layout and design programs see type as blocks of information that can be picked up and moved around much like designers a few decades ago picked up and moved around cut pieces of printed typography and pasted them to boards (hence the phrase "cut and paste"). Professional digital layout and design programs offer extensive capabilities for type treatment and layout variables. Text can be wrapped around a curved line or shape, distorted or skewed and the spaces between lines of text and even the letters themselves can be adjusted.

Graphic Design was once the exclusive province of trained professionals. Today, many programs contain templates including typestyle information and layouts for a variety of standard design functions, like newsletters or business cards. While not appropriate for the design professional, this is especially helpful to the many users of digital layout and design programs who do have not have extensive training in design, but who, with these new tools, are able to design serviceable documents on their own.

-20 tracking

The principal element that distinguishes a digital layout and design program from a sophisticated word processing program is the way in which it handles type. Unlike a word processing program that processes type in rows of letters much like a typewriter would, digital layout and design programs see type as blocks of information that can be picked up and moved around much like designers a few decades ago picked up and moved around cut pieces of printed typography and pasted them to boards (hence the phrase "cut and paste"). Professional digital layout and design programs offer extensive capabilities for type treatment and layout variables. Text can be wrapped around a curved line or shape, distorted or skewed and the spaces between lines of text and even the letters themselves can be adjusted.

Graphic Design was once the exclusive province of trained professionals. Today, many programs contain templates including typestyle information and layouts for a variety of standard design functions, like newsletters or business cards. While not appropriate for the design professional, this is especially helpful to the many users of digital layout and design programs who do have not have extensive training in design, but who, with these new tools, are able to design serviceable documents on their own.

0 tracking

The principal element that distinguishes a digital layout and design program from a sophisticated word processing program is the way in which it handles type. Unlike a word processing program that processes type in rows of letters much like a typewriter would, digital layout and design programs see type as blocks of information that can be picked up and moved around much like designers a few decades ago picked up and moved around cut pieces of printed typography and pasted them to boards (hence the phrase "cut and paste"). Professional digital layout and design programs offer extensive capabilities for type treatment and layout variables. Text can be wrapped around a curved line or shape, distorted or skewed and the spaces between lines of text and even the letters themselves can be adjusted.

Graphic Design was once the exclusive province of trained professionals. Today, many programs contain templates including typestyle information and layouts for a variety of standard design functions, like newsletters or business cards. While not appropriate for the design professional, this is especially helpful to the many users of digital layout and design programs who do have not have extensive training in design, but who, with these new tools, are able to design serviceable documents on their own.

+20 tracking

Figure 6.32

Tracking changes the density of type on the page by expanding or contracting the spaces between letters and words. This dynamically effects type "color."

Leading 12 point type

Hundreds of years before we in the west were scraping hides to make parchment and painstakingly copying documents one at a time, the Chinese had discovered that a fibrous material like cotton could be mixed with water and heated until it became soft and pliable. Pouring it over fine bamboo screens allowed the water to escape, leaving the cotton fibers nesting together on the surface. This primitive paper was pliable and held ink well. Traditionally the invention of paper has been attributed to Cai Lun, who lived in the Eastern Han Dynasty, and presented the new writing surface to Emperor He Di in 105 AD. However, it is very likely that this primitive form of papermaking was in use several hundred years before that date.

auto leading

Hundreds of years before we in the west were scraping hides to make parchment and painstakingly copying documents one at a time, the Chinese had discovered that a fibrous material like cotton could be mixed with water and heated until it became soft and pliable. Pouring it over fine bamboo screens allowed the water to escape, leaving the cotton fibers nesting together on the surface. This primitive paper was pliable and held ink well. Traditionally the invention of paper has been attributed to Cai Lun, who lived in the Eastern Han Dynasty, and presented the new writing surface to Emperor He Di in 105 AD. However, it is very likely that this primitive form of papermaking was in use several hundred years before that date.

18 pt leading

Hundreds of years before we in the west were scraping hides to make parchment and painstakingly copying documents one at a time, the Chinese had discovered that a fibrous material like cotton could be mixed with water and heated until it became soft and pliable. Pouring it over fine bamboo screens allowed the water to escape, leaving the cotton fibers nesting together on the surface. This primitive paper was pliable and held ink well. Traditionally the invention of paper has been attributed to Cai Lun, who lived in the Eastern Han Dynasty, and presented the new writing surface to Emperor He Di in 105 AD. However, it is very likely that this primitive form of papermaking was in use several hundred years before that date.

10 pt leading

■ **Figure 6.33**

Leading allows you to change the space between lines of type.

in minute amounts so that type will fit into the space you want. *Baseline shifting*, however, allows you to select and then move individual characters above or below their *baselines*, the imaginary line upon which all letters would normally sit, by minute amounts. This is accomplished without affecting the leading of the overall sentence or paragraph. As with kerning, positive values shift characters up and negative values shift characters down.

The spacing of text and its density (how close together it is) will create different tonal values or what is known as *type color*. In discussing type color, it is not the color of the ink under discussion but the overall tone of the text on the page. The size and style of the typeface, the amount of space around the characters, and the space between the lines all affect typographic color.

However, typographic color is not the only way in which character spacing plays an important role. In addition to the flow of the text, *copyfitting* (the adjustment of type to fit into a given space or number of pages) can be adjusted to accommodate *widows and orphans*. Widows and orphans are words or short lines of text that become separated from other lines in a paragraph. Widows occur at the bottom of a paragraph and orphans occur at the top of a page. Using the many type adjustment tools in a desktop publishing program can eliminate problems like these.

Master Pages or Style Sheets

Although digital layout and design programs contain a default document master as a starting template, you can create your own templates for publications. Master pages are templates created for documents in which you can set a series of preferences that dictate any design element you want to appear on every page, from the number of columns to the way in which the pages will be numbered. Almost everything we have discussed so far can be adjusted and set in a master page template. You have the option of creating master pages from scratch or you can use an existing document that you have modified in order to create a master.

If creating a two-page master spread, you can also specify the *gutter* (the space between columns of type) in the spread, as well as set different attributes for the left and right pages. By creating master pages, especially for long documents, not only will you save time, but the finished product will be more consistent in terms of layout and design. If you have a publication already designed but wish to change the document to reflect the new master pages you have laid out, the new master pages can be applied to all or part of an existing document. This flexibility allows for a variety of design solutions to be created and compared.

Images on Your Desktop

One of the most important elements of digital layout and design programs is the ability to add photographs or other graphic elements to your page layout. The file format most often used for scanned photographs that are to be imported or placed in the document is the TIFF file. Once placed, text can be made to flow around the image in a variety of ways or even over an image. Using text standoff guides, text can even be made to flow around irregular shapes. Once a photograph or other graphic is placed in the document, it can be resized (proportionally or not), rotated, cropped, and otherwise modified. However, as mentioned earlier, the ability of a desktop publishing program to modify an image is limited compared to that of an image-editing program.

Image Limitations

The primary limitation of images incorporated into digital-layout-and-design programs is their lack of transparency. In an image-editing program, the use of layers allows an image to have all or part of it transparent. However, when images containing transparent areas are brought into a desktop publishing document, they lose their transparency and become opaque images once again.

In order for an image to appear in a digital layout and design program as an irregular shape instead of a rectangular one, a *clipping path* to isolate the image is necessary (see Figure 6.34). Paths, created with a special pen tool, are primarily used to make precise selections in image-editing and illustration programs. Where other image-editing tools create bitmaps, paths are vector objects that contain no pixels. A clipping path defines the area of an image that will be visible when placed in a digital-layout-and-design program.

image without clipping path

image with clipping path

■ **Figure 6.34**
An image imported to a digital-layout-and-design program without and with a clipping path.

When saved as an EPS file, or a tiff with clipping path, the image can be brought into a digital-layout-and-design program with the surrounding areas "clipped out." Some programs, like PhotoShop, will take an object on a transparent background and export the image as an EPS file with an eight-bit preview. This automatically creates a clipping path to define the transparent areas. While the eight-bit preview image will appear somewhat coarse in the digital-layout-and-design program, it will print acceptably to a PostScript printer.

Despite the ability of a clipping path to create a hard-edged vector outline that is filled with a bitmap image, the result is far from the more sophisticated capabilities available in most image-editing programs. Until a more sophisticated program evolves, irregular-shaped bitmaps in a desktop publishing program will continue to require some form of clipping path.

Color and Desktop Publishing

The production of a final printed piece progresses from an RGB (red, green, blue) system (the computer screen) to a CMYK (cyan, yellow, magenta, and black) ink system on a printing press (see Figure 6.35). One difference in the way these two color systems work is that colors appear brighter on screen than when printed. The *color gamut,* or range of

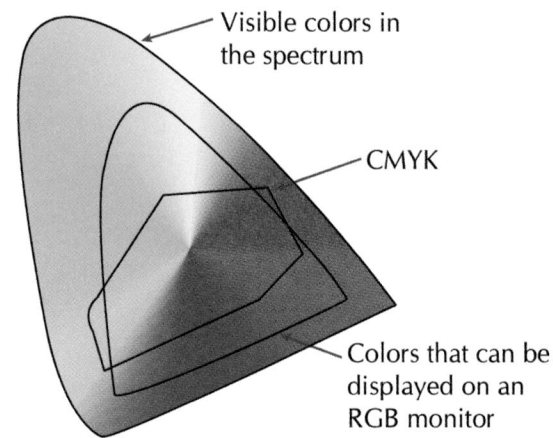

Visible colors in the spectrum

CMYK

Colors that can be displayed on an RGB monitor

■ **Figure 6.35**
RGB versus CMYK color gamut.

colors that can be displayed or printed, is less in CMYK than in RGB. Another way of thinking about this is that a computer monitor can display more than 16 million colors while a printed piece might only reproduce the equivalent of tens of thousands.

The difference in color from what you see on a computer monitor to what can be printed has sparked the pursuit of new systems of color reproduction that might better match the images on your computer screen (see Box 6.3).

In order to print a full-color (more accurately known as "four-color") image on an offset lithography press, individual pieces of film need to be exposed through special filters in order to separate the full range of colors into individual components created specifically for each of the ink colors to be used—cyan, yellow, magenta, black, and additional separation films for any spot colors (see Figure 6.36). Printing plates are then made from these separation negatives, which are created as halftones containing a screen pattern for offset printing. When the halftone separations are printed, even though the image is limited to a combination of dots of the four main *process colors*, your eyes mix the colors together to create the full range of hues one would expect to see in nature—the overlapping dots of color combine to create the illusion of a full color image. ■

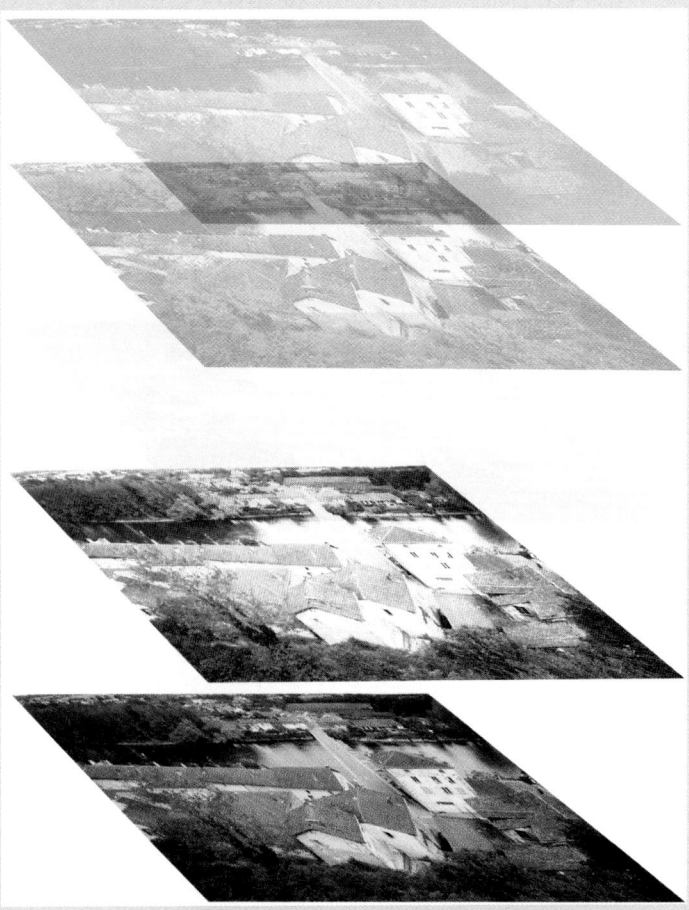

■ **Figure 6.36**

Sample of CMYK color separations.

Spot Color

Individual colors can be selected and printed in addition to the process colors (CMYK) noted on the previous page. *Spot colors* are special premixed solid colors used in addition to the process colors or independently to emphasize or create a point of interest on the page. This adds to the expense of a printing project because each spot color requires its own printing plate when the publication is printed on press. The clearest way to communicate the exact color you want is to select a color from a *Pantone* sample book that contains actual color chips. Each Pantone color has a specific CMYK mixture equivalent. The Pantone color system is only one of many similar systems for choosing spot colors. It can typically be found in the color library section of your digital-layout-and-design program.

Hi-fi color

Hi-fi color uses additional colors to supplement the process colors. One example of a hi-fi printing system is Pantone's *Hexachrome* inks. The Hexachrome process uses six printing inks instead of the traditional four. By adding a special orange and green to the standard CMYK color set, the color *gamut,* or range of colors the printing press is able to reproduce, is increased dramatically. The result is more lifelike and natural color.

Commercial Printing and PostScript

When you move from printing work on your own desktop to working with a professional printer, the level of complexity increases dramatically. Not only must your work translate to the professional printer's system, it must then be translated once again into *color separations,* where the colors you see on your screen are separated into separate components: cyan, magenta, yellow, black, and/or spot colors (see Box 6.3). While it is possible to do this within a digital-layout-and-design program, it is often easier and more accurate to produce a PostScript file containing all the information in your document and let a service bureau specializing in this area make the conversions. In fact, many printers and service providers prefer to create their own PostScript files in order to minimize problems with printed output. Among other things, failure to include the proper PostScript font information will result in your entire document printing with the wrong typeface. Failure to compensate for *dot gain* (the tendency of ink dots to spread as they strike and are absorbed by the paper) in an image-editing program can result in photographs that appear too dark.

To compensate for potential misregistration of solid side-by-side objects and colors, most desktop publishing programs include *trapping controls.* Trapping safeguards against the common small degree of misregistration in the printing process by slightly overlapping adjacent colors. An error in using these controls can result in colors that do not line up properly, leaving gaps (see Figure 6.37).

■ **Figure 6.37**

Example of trapping misregistration.

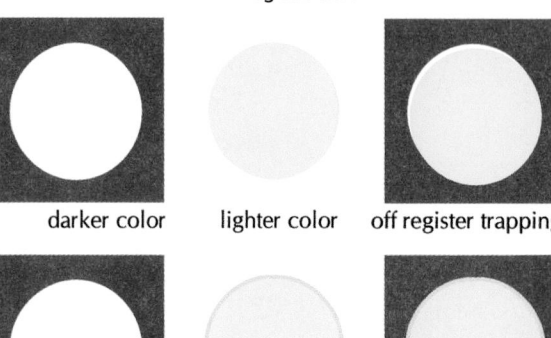

darker color　　　lighter color　　　off register trapping

darker color | additional dimension added to lighter color | overlapping color creates in register trapping

PostScript Basics

The language of the computer and the language of printed output are quite different. PostScript, a page description language introduced by Adobe in 1985, is a method of communication that links the two together. With this standard format, what you save through the PostScript driver on your computer is what will be decoded and finally printed. It is not even necessary to own a PostScript printer; you must, however, install a PostScript printer driver in your computer. Fortunately, most digital layout and design programs will do this for you automatically as you install the software.

The nature of PostScript, and a key to its success, is that it is device independent. It doesn't matter what sort of computer was used to save the document or what PostScript printer driver was used to create it. Once saved, the file can be printed on any PostScript printer, from desktop laser to professional imagesetter. Because it can encode everything from vector graphics to photographs to text, PostScript has become the standard in the professional printing world.

When you print to a file using a PostScript driver, a PostScript description of the page you have designed is created as a file. That file contains all color, font description, image, and layout information needed to print an accurate representation of your document. It is essentially a description of the page in the language of a printer (see Box 6.4).

BOX 6.4

PostScript fonts versus TrueType

Type 1 PostScript fonts are actually composed of a set of font elements. This set includes a bitmapped font used only to display the font on the computer screen, and a vector-based printer font composed of mathematically configured smooth curves and sharp lines for printing. The bitmapped screen font is made smoother and clearer on the screen by Adobe Type Manager software. This software will only work for Type 1 PostScript fonts. If the printer cannot access the printer/PostScript part of the font, it will substitute a bitmap version of the font instead. This bitmapped substitute is far below the crisp vector quality of a printer/PostScript font and will appear jagged when printed.

TrueType fonts have both the screen and printer information built into a single font. However, when a document is printed, even though the PostScript information built into the font goes to the printer, the printer must still be able to access the font with which the document was created. If it cannot, other fonts will be substituted that will reformat the document. In addition, less expensive versions of some TrueType fonts often do not provide the more sophisticated *hinting* (rules that tell the computer what to do with portions of the typeface to optimize their appearance on the printed page) that Type 1 PostScript and more expensive TrueType fonts have.

It is generally not a good idea to combine PostScript fonts and TrueType fonts in a single document. While this is technically possible, and is often done at home, it can confuse some printers and imagesetters when more complex documents are being processed. ∎

It is important to keep in mind that once the PostScript file is created, no further changes or corrections are possible. Unless you have a printer capable of printing PostScript, *proofing* your file—reviewing a document or design for errors before it is actually printed—is also very difficult. For this reason, unless you are skilled in prepress production (creating color separations, trapping colors, and so on) these areas are best left for a professional.

EPS

EPS files are actually small self-contained programs that contain a sequence of PostScript language commands. These commands mathematically interpret or describe all the individual elements that make up the content of the image within the file and include a preview of what the EPS graphic looks like. When an EPS graphic file is printed, its program is launched and the graphic is accurately recreated. This PostScript format is called *encapsulated* because it describes only a single page or image. When used in a digital layout and design program, it can be resized and placed anywhere within the design. It then becomes part of the PostScript description of the entire document. Strong, hard-edged graphics are especially well suited to this format, although bitmaps can also be included. EPS is the best choice for printing to a PostScript printer.

Despite the strength of the EPS format, there are certain problems that must be addressed. EPS files often appear on screen as blank, gray boxes with an X through them to signify their placement. While they will still print wonderfully to a PostScript printer, it can make proofing a difficult task. Even if an eight-bit (256 color) bitmap file is created as a preview image, it cannot reproduce the full quality of the image. Only the final print from a PostScript printer can accomplish that feat.

Printing PostScript and especially EPS files to a non-PostScript printer can also create unpredictable results. Colors may print inaccurately or fonts may not print as expected. Lines or boxes may reproduce with the wrong thickness or a host of other problems may occur. Fortunately, another PostScript format is growing in its ability to address these problems.

PDF Portable Document Format

The Adobe (portable document format) PDF is one way artists and designers are dealing with the complexities of PostScript production. When you save a file as a PDF, your entire design, including typography, fonts, layout information, graphics, and photographs is created as a single file that can be viewed and proofed on a computer screen using Adobe's free Acrobat Reader program. By using PDF files with Acrobat software, the person viewing the file does not need to own or know how to operate the software the original file was completed with or have the actual fonts that were used installed on his or her computer. For example, a file created in Quark or InDesign can be viewed by virtually anyone with Adobe Acrobat Reader installed on his or her computer, and the complete layout will be intact exactly as the designer intended it. Fonts will not be substituted and the layout will not be altered if the size or resolution of the monitor it is being viewed on changes. In addition, PDF documents will always appear exactly the same, whether viewed on a Macintosh, PC, or Unix operating system.

The ability of a PDF file to be hardware independent, operating-system independent, and even application-software independent makes it an excellent choice for publishing on the Internet, publishing digitally, or even for use in multimedia CDs. Estimates place users able to read PDF files at well over 200 million worldwide.

In the publishing industry, the qualities outlined above have made it easier for documents to be prepared for printing, even to non-PostScript printers. Because a PDF file is essentially a description of a page and maintains the integrity of that page's layout, typography, and vector and raster information, it can provide many of the positive elements of PostScript printing to non-PostScript printers and is fast becoming the de facto standard.

CONCLUSION

In digital layout and design, the once clear line between the production artist and the graphic designer has continued to blur. Due to the capabilities of digital layout-and-design-programs, what used to be the exclusive province of the graphic artist or production staff has become at least the partial responsibility of the designer. It is important to keep in mind that what may be an easy trial and error process for printing at home becomes a costly transaction once it moves outside of your control to other working professionals. For this reason, further study should include not only mastery of the specific program you have chosen to work with but also more detailed information concerning pre-press preparation and printing technologies.

Producing work for publication is an art in itself, and one that requires an awareness of what happens when the piece you produce on your desktop goes into production. Consideration of everything from image resolution to color trapping to dot gain to paper and type of press must be taken into account and resolved. It is the understanding and ability to deal with the complexity of these issues and many others that separates the professional designer from the desktop enthusiast.

Projects: Digital Layout and Design

1 Postage Stamp

Design a mock-up for a new postage stamp, celebrating a native animal from a particular nation, to be submitted to their postal service. Scan an image, then size and crop it to fill a 2″ × 3″ rectangle. Label the image in italics, add the country's name in normal style, and write the value of the stamp in bold style.

2 CORPORATE IDENTITY

Using type and objects, design a two-color logo for a digital design firm that is at least 4" in one dimension. Then, resize and utilize the logo in a 3 1/2" × 2" business card, 8 1/2" × 11" letterhead, and a business-size (4 1/8" × 9 1/2") envelope, with typical text information.

3 DIGITAL DOLLAR: NEW CURRENCY DESIGN

In a 6" × 3" format with a 1/4" border around the edge, design a new world currency for the United Nations. Both front and reverse should include images that symbolize international unity and progress. Invent a new monetary denomination and be sure to make it easy for users to see the amount quickly.

4 GALLERY ANNOUNCEMENT

Create an announcement for an exhibition of a past artist. Your approach to design and typography should try to evoke the era of the artist, whether he or she is from the Renaissance or the 1960s. Create a two-page spread, totaling 14" × 7" overall, with 1/2" borders all around and a 1" gutter. Divide one of the pages into two columns.

5 TRAVEL POSTER

Choose a famous city or exotic locale and create a poster of 11" × 17" that encourages tourists to fly to that location. Combine several images of various sizes and shapes with typography that not only grabs the attention of readers but evokes the tourist site. Use colors and tints that harmonize with the images. Wrap text around the images and include a box with reverse lettering.

Image Editing

Introduction

The words *image editing* seem rather mundane compared to the wide range of exciting techniques and approaches that fall under this heading. While the term might mean simply correcting the tonal value of an image, removing dust spots and cropping the composition, or correcting the color of an image prior to printing, it includes all of this and much more. Various filters can be used to enhance the image or even radically change its appearance. For many digital artists it means *image compositing*, where several images are combined to create a greater imaginative whole. This chapter will examine the various ways in which an image can be corrected, adjusted, and manipulated to enhance its ability to communicate the artist's vision.

The traditional techniques of photography are reflected in all image-editing programs. Most programs have a range of tools that mimic those used in a conventional darkroom. For example, if an area of an image is too light, it can be selectively darkened. If one were working in a traditional darkroom, one might *burn in,* or add more light to, that portion of the image. If an area needs to be lightened, one might *dodge out* that part of the image, blocking the light from hitting the area that was too dark for a certain amount of the overall exposure time. Digitally, this can be done with "burning" and "dodging" tools, which can be used like a brush to darken and lighten an area of the image. As in the darkroom, the effect is cumulative. Since it is easy to overburn or overdodge if one isn't careful, setting the opacity of the tool low and working gradually is the safest way to work.

We often use the term *dpi* to refer to the overall quality of a digitized image. However, this is not the only way to define image resolution as it relates to the process of image editing. When we scan an image, we are sampling a number of points using an x-y series of coordinates. The more samples per inch (spi), the higher the resolution will be. By sampling more points we obtain more information to use in representing the image. The image resolution, coupled with the image's physical size, determines the file size, which is usually measured in megabytes. Screen resolution is measured in pixels per inch (ppi) and print resolution is measured in dpi. Image resolution must contain sufficient information to allow the printer to fully utilize its ability to deposit ink or toner to the areas described in the print. If an image's resolution is too low, softness and a lack of sharp detail will result. ■

■ **Figure 7.1a**
RGB additive color model.

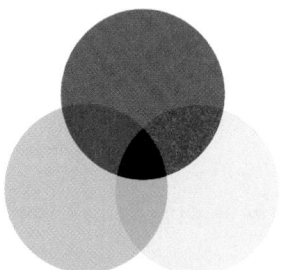

■ **Figure 7.1b**
CMYK subtractive color model.

Color Models

Most image-editing programs allow you to choose the color mode you wish to work in. Digital artists generally work in RGB mode—the default in most image-editing programs. As noted in Chapter 3, scanners sample images using red, green, and blue filters to create an RGB image, and computer monitors create color by emitting light through a screen containing red, green, and blue phosphors. In RGB mode, the visual spectrum is created by projected light, mixing the three visual primary colors. When all three colors of equal value and intensity overlap, white is the result. This is called an *additive color model* (see Figure 7.1a).

The CMYK color model is rooted in the way in which images are printed on a press. When printing, cyan, magenta, yellow, and black inks are printed one after the other to create full-color images. Unlike RGB, CMYK utilizes a *subtractive model* based on the reflected light of inks rather than projected light. As light strikes the ink, a portion of that light is absorbed. The light that isn't absorbed is reflected back to the eye. CMYK model image files are about one-third larger than RGB files due to the extra color (black) channel. Most artists edit their images in RGB mode and, if planning to print, convert to the CMYK model after all image editing is finished (see Figure 7.1b).

While RGB and CMYK are the most common models used, image-editing programs usually provide artists with other options. Artists often define a color by *hue, value,* and *intensity,* with hue being the color itself, value representing the lightness or darkness of a color, and intensity identifying the chromatic purity of the color. In image-editing programs, this is called the *HSB* (hue, saturation, brightness) model of color.

$L^*A^*B^*$ color is a result of a 1931 attempt to create an international standard for color measurement. The Commission Internationale d'Eclairage's (CIE) original standard was later revised and, in 1976, was renamed *CIE $L^*A^*B^*$*. The $L^*A^*B^*$ color model attempts to resolve the problem of varying color appearance on different monitors, printers, computers, and so on used to output an image. Designed to be device independent, $L^*A^*B^*$ color has a lightness component (L), and two chromatic components, A and B channels. The A channel controls the color from green to red and the B channel controls the color from blue to yellow. Most importantly, however, is that the $L^*A^*B^*$ color model is often the internal color model used to convert images from one color model to another.

In addition to the color models previously described, most imaging programs also have a *grayscale* mode that uses 256 shades of gray to represent the image. Pixels in a grayscale image have a value ranging from black (0) to white (255). *Indexed color* limits the use of a maximum of 256 colors to represent a full-color image (see Figure 7.2). Options within an indexed color format include the selection of a variety of color palettes to maximize the image for a Windows or Mac system, Web use, and other selections based on how the image is to be used (see Box 7.2).

a   b   c

■ **Figure 7.2**
Comparison of indexed color options.

BOX 7.2

Gamut

Gamut describes the range of colors available in a certain color space that can be displayed on a monitor or printed. The RGB gamut contains the colors that can be accurately viewed on a color monitor. The CMYK model has the smallest gamut, and represents colors that can be printed with cyan, magenta, yellow, and black process inks. By far, the $L^*A^*B^*$ color model has the largest gamut of all the color models. It contains all the colors in both the RBG and CMYK color models.

Out-of-gamut colors are colors that can be approximated on a computer screen but not printed accurately using the CMYK color ink set. Part of preparing an image for print is the process of "correcting" out-of-gamut colors, usually by reducing their intensity or contrast (see Figure 7.3). ■

■ **Figure 7.3**
RGB CMYK color gamut.

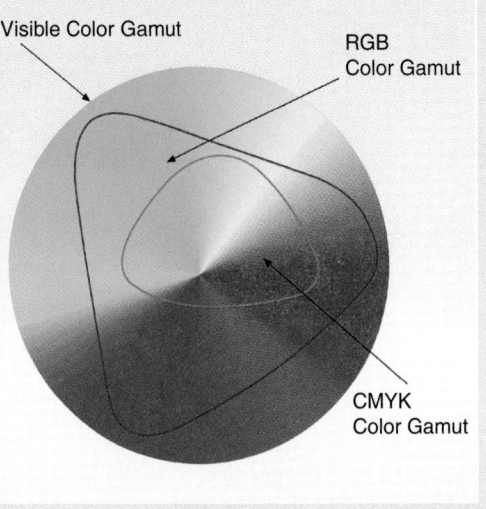

Visible Color Gamut

RGB Color Gamut

CMYK Color Gamut

Image Editing   147

Vector and Raster Images

Vector images are created from mathematically defined lines and are resolution independent. As a result, vector-based drawings can be drawn, rotated, and resized without diminishing their quality, and retain their smoothness and crispness even when greatly enlarged. Vector images work best for graphics that don't require subtle tonal gradations. While they may appear on the computer screen as pixels, the mathematically determined shape will print clear and sharp. (See Chapter 8 on painting and illustration for a more complete explanation.)

Unlike vector images, raster images are composed of a grid of small squares or pixels (picture elements). If a raster image is resized, the pixels are moved further apart or closer together in order to accommodate the resizing. The further apart the pixels get, the more jagged and less detailed the image becomes. On the positive side, raster-based images allow for a more natural, smooth gradation of tonalities within an image compared to vector graphics. Understandably, the more pixels present in an inch, the smaller the image elements are and the smoother color or tone gradations become (see Figure 7.4).

For example, a 1″ × 1″ image at 72 ppi will contain 5,184 pixels. If that same 1″ image contained 300 ppi, it would contain a total of 90,000 pixels, which would allow more detail as well as more subtle gradations of color. It would also result in a significantly larger file size.

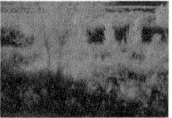

■ **Figure 7.4**

Pixel counts in an image affect the overall quality of both screen and print resolution.

Digitizing an Image for Editing

Digitizing your own images usually means using a scanner to convert an analog image into a digital one (see Chapter 3 for more information on scanners). There are three things that can help determine a successful scan: available optical resolution, bit depth, and dynamic range. A scanner's maximum optical scanning rate will determine the number of samples per inch (spi) it is capable of making without *interpolation*. The scanner's bit depth will determine its ability to define differences in value and color. Dynamic range refers to the scanner's ability to detect a greater range of tonalities.

Sample Rate

Initially, the most important consideration when scanning is to determine the sample rate (spi, but often called dpi) at which you should scan an image. This will be decided by your intended use of the scan. If you are preparing images for the Web (see Chapter 13), then your scan doesn't need to be 300 spi, as a small file size is important. If you know your inkjet printer works well with an image at 150 dpi, then anything more or less will create a file that either lacks information or one that has more information than you need. Generally, a 200 spi scan can capture all the detail contained by a traditional, machine-made color photograph. Scanning at a higher resolution might allow you to resize the image so a larger print can be made, but it won't provide additional detail. Scanning at 300 spi is certainly a good safety margin for most purposes. If you are starting with a small image that you know will be enlarged, then scanning at a higher sample rate is absolutely necessary—up to the scanner's maximum optical resolution.

Bit Depth

Another important element that affects the appearance of a digital image is bit depth, which determines how much color information can be used to define the pixel itself and is a measurement of the number of bits of information stored in each pixel. The greater the bit depth, the more subtle and accurate the color can become. A pixel with a bit depth of one is either black or white. If the bit depth increases to eight, then 256 values are possible. When the bit depth increases to twenty-four bits per pixel (eight bits each for R, G, and B), then over 16 million possible colors become available. This is referred to as *true* color. Many scanners today have the capability of scanning at thirty, thirty-six, and even forty-two bit depths. This allows them to separate more subtle tonal values into billions of colors. Several small variations of a color that a twenty-four-bit scan might read as the same color will be seen as slightly different shades at a higher bit depth. This represents more detail, especially in the shadow areas.

However, very few programs are capable of working at a bit depth greater than twenty-four, so when an image is brought into an image-editing program, extraneous information is deleted from the image. Still, images scanned at these higher bit depths often prove superior to those scanned at lesser bit depths. In addition, higher bit depths increase the potential to represent greater dynamic range.

Dynamic Range

Often rated as the scanner's *D-MAX*, dynamic range indicates the scanner's ability to correctly interpret the full tonal scale of a particular film or artwork. In conventional photography, this measurement is accomplished by using a densitometer to measure the lightest area of the film and then the darkest area. By subtracting the density of the lightest area from the darkest area, we get the range of values in the film itself. In a similar way, the scanner's *D-MIN* (lightest values the scanner can represent) are subtracted from the scanner's D-MAX (darkest values the scanner can represent) to arrive at the scanner's dynamic range. Having a scanner that is capable of capturing the true range of tones of the material being scanned is very important. While a photographic print might only have a density range of about 2.0D, a negative might have a range of 3.0D, and slide film might have a density range approaching 4.0D. The higher the dynamic range of the scanner, the better its ability to distinguish subtle tonal and color variations as well as its ability to separate values in difficult-to-read shadow areas.

Making Images Larger and Smaller

Image-editing programs give you the opportunity to make images larger or smaller after scanning. This is sometimes confusing due to the options provided. Making an image larger or smaller while maintaining its file size is known as *resizing*. This usually does not affect image quality but does change the ppi of the image. Changing the size of an image by eliminating or adding pixels is known as *resampling*, and allows the computer to interpolate new data. Resampling occurs when you make an image larger or smaller by adding or deleting pixels, which accordingly changes the file size. Generally, it is wise to avoid this sort of interpolation, which can degrade image quality.

Resizing

The physical dimensions of an image are determined differently for the monitor screen than they are for the printer. Once the number of pixels in an image are fixed (after scanning, for example) we can only increase the printed size of an image by spreading out or bringing closer together the number of ppi. Let's use the example of a 6″ × 6″ image which has been scanned at 300 spi. If we resize that image to 12″ × 12″ inches, we will find that the pixels have spread further apart in order to do so. The number of pixels per inch will drop from 300 to 150 ppi although the file size will remain the same. Making the 6″ × 6″ image (300 ppi) a 3″ × 3″ image by resizing will move the pixels closer together and make it a 600 ppi image. Again, the file size remains the same although the print size changes.

Resampling

Attempting to increase or decrease the number of pixels in an image while maintaining the physical size of the image requires *resampling*. When a program resamples an image up, in order to increase the print size without changing the ppi, additional pixels must be created. This is not the same as simply resizing an image. Creating new pixels by comparing existing pixels really means that the computer is making up new information. This results in diminishing the sharpness and overall quality of the image. This comparison and creation approach is known as *interpolation* and can be done in a number of ways. The most common choice is *bicubic,* a relatively sophisticated method that samples all existing pixels in the area in which new information must be created. New pixels are then added based on an averaging together of that information. *Bilinear* interpolation averages the pixels to either side of the area in which new information must be created. The least accurate but fastest method is called *nearest neighbor,* in which a single pixel is sampled and then duplicated.

Interpolation is not only used when resampling images in order to make them larger. When we make an image smaller or *downsample,* we delete information from the image. It is important to note that this information cannot be recovered if we change our mind later and decide to make the image larger. In addition, every time we resample an image larger or smaller, rotate an image, resize a layer, or use any special effects that change the size or dimension of an image, new color values are created for added pixels. This continued process of interpolation takes its toll on the quality of an image.

Strategy

It is probably wiser to work on a copy of your scanned image rather than the original scan itself. That way, if something goes wrong, you can go back to the archived scan to start again. Once an image is resampled and saved, the changes cannot be undone.

Global Changes

Value and Contrast

One of the most powerful features of image-editing programs lies in their ability to make changes that affect an entire image. Global adjustments for tone and color include brightness/contrast controls; a levels control to adjust an image's *histogram* (a visual representation of the tonal and color range of an image); curves, which can be used to adjust both tone and color balance; and actual color balance tools. In addition, many programs contain a variety of specialized filters that can mimic other media to create painterly effects, blur, sharpen or distort, add textures, and far more in order to change the appearance and quality of an image.

Many of the global tools designed to affect an image's tonal values do similar things with varying degrees of sophistication. Brightness/contrast controls, levels, and curves all have the capability to *remap* or shift values within an image to correct for poor contrast, or an image that is too light or dark. As digital artists become familiar with image-editing programs, they soon see there are many different but related ways to accomplish the same objective. In addition, some tools have the ability to accomplish more than one task.

Brightness and Contrast

In a traditional darkroom, a photographer can change from one contrast of photographic paper to another to correct an image that is too "flat" (lacking in

■ Figure 7.5

Linear nature of brightness/contrast controls shown in curves dialog box.

contrast) or too "harsh" (having too much contrast). The digital artist, when faced with an image lacking in contrast, or an image that is too dark or light, can correct the image by using a program's brightness and contrast controls. The brightness control lightens or darkens an image and the contrast control increases or decreases the number of tonal values in an image. While this is the simplest way to adjust an image's brightness and contrast, it adjusts highlights, midtones, and shadows all at the same time. It does not allow the artist to select specific areas in which to change tonal values, and it doesn't allow for adjustment to individual value ranges. Because this command is *linear* (see Figure 7.5), these controls have the potential to remove information in shadows or highlights that cannot be recovered.

Levels

As a better alternative to brightness/contrast controls, most programs have the ability to shift tonal values by adjusting an image's histogram. The levels command is an easy and powerful tool to use for this purpose. The levels dialog box (see Figure 7.6) builds on the visual nature of the histogram

■ Figure 7.6

Histogram control (levels) with parts labeled.

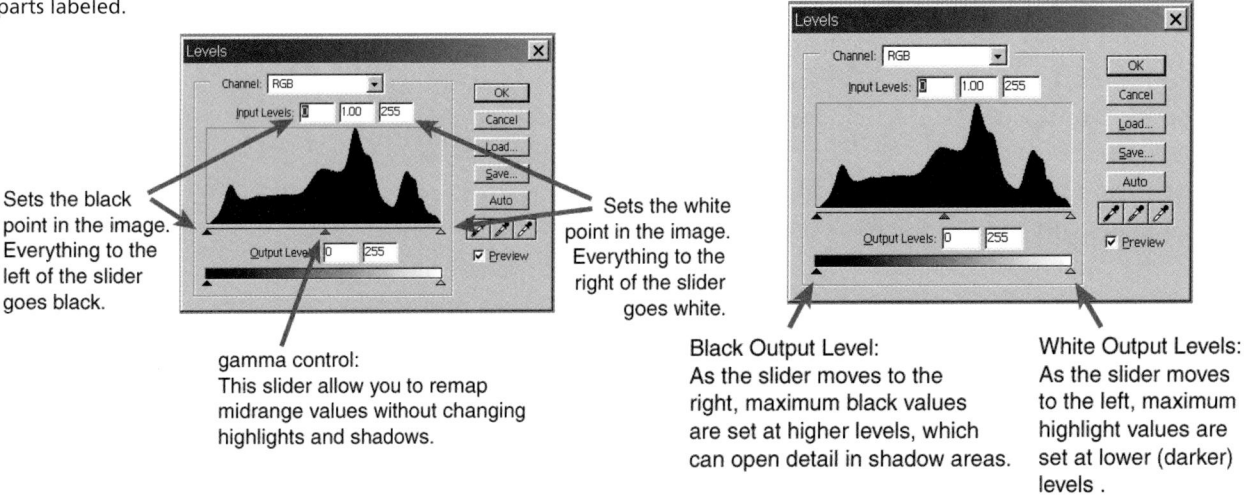

Sets the black point in the image. Everything to the left of the slider goes black.

Sets the white point in the image. Everything to the right of the slider goes white.

gamma control: This slider allow you to remap midrange values without changing highlights and shadows.

Black Output Level: As the slider moves to the right, maximum black values are set at higher levels, which can open detail in shadow areas.

White Output Levels: As the slider moves to the left, maximum highlight values are set at lower (darker) levels .

As the black and white sliders move towards each other, contrast increases, tonal range decreases.

Moving the black and white output levels towards each other results in a lowering of apparent contrast.

and provides a series of movable controls, which allows one to redistribute an image's tonal values. Histogram controls allow the user to change highlight, midtone, and shadow values separately in order to remap tonal areas.

A good-quality image generally has a histogram that is fairly evenly spread out from one end of the scale to another (see Figure 7.7). An image with blank space to either side of the histogram (see Figure 7.8) indicates an image lacking in contrast. This can be corrected by moving the sliders at the bottom of the histogram. The slider on the left controls the dark values while the slider on the right controls the light values. The slider in the middle controls the midrange or *gamma* of the image.

By moving the sliders on the left and right to the beginnings of the histogram (see Figure 7.9), one can shift the range of tonal values in the image and correct for an initial lack of contrast—or even for too much contrast. The center slider or gamma control allows one to shift the midrange of an image to make it darker or lighter. An important advantage of this approach versus the contrast-control tool is that you are merely shifting tonal relationships—reassigning values, not eliminating them.

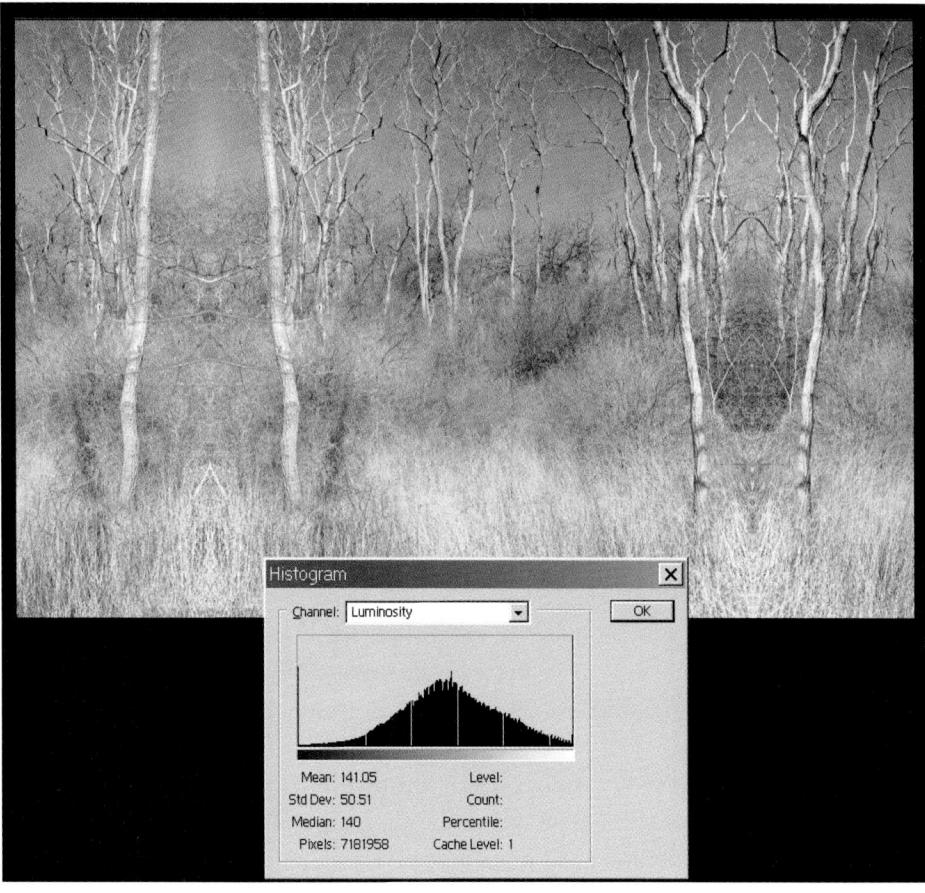

■ **Figure 7.7**
An image with its Histogram.

Figure 7.8

Low-contrast image with histogram.

Curves

The *curves* dialog box in most image-editing programs allows you to selectively raise or lower values in specific areas of an image. In the initial dialog box one will see a straight line running on a diagonal which represents the current value "ramp" of the image. The curves adjustment allows for far more precise control of values than does the levels tool. Along the curves' initial straight line are specific areas that relate to highlight values, quarter-tone values, midtone (fifty percent) values, three-quarter-tone values, and shadow values (see Figure 7.10). You can even use the eyedropper to click on the area of an image you wish to adjust and see its corresponding point on the curves line. That point can then be adjusted by dragging it up or down to raise or lower the value (see Figure 7.11). Sophisticated users of the curves tool actually read the numerical values of the areas they wish to adjust and shift their numbers to represent their target reproduction values.

Nevertheless, even simply clicking on the midrange area and dragging it upward or downward will show you the curves tool's ability to shift tonal values dramatically. Shifting just one point is very similar to using the levels tool. However, the curves tool's ability to target a specific range of tones in a print while others are left unchanged demonstrates its flexibility.

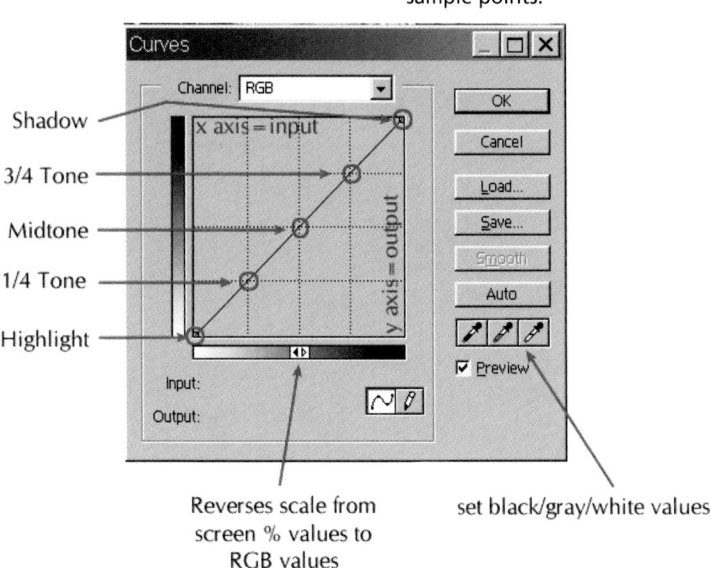

Color Balance

An RGB image has three eight-bit *channels* (separate eight-bit images) that
the computer mixes together to create a full color, twenty-four-bit image
(see Figure 7.12). Each of these independent eight-bit images (representing

the tonal values for red, green, and blue)
is available for editing as a separate
channel. Color correction in CMYK, or
any of the other color modes already discussed, is also possible.

■ **Figure 7.10**

Curves dialog box with labeled
sample points.

One thing remains constant, however. As with traditional color darkroom
filters, each color channel you adjust
makes a change not only to that color
but to its complement as well. The red
channel controls red and cyan, the green
channel controls green and magenta,
and the blue channel controls blue and
yellow. Each color model will work
in a similar fashion and you will find
that the complements remain essentially

■ **Figure 7.11**

Curves dialog box—targeted
point being adjusted along with
resulting image change.

unchanged. For the CMYK model, for example, you will find the color balance controls will still modify cyan and red, magenta and green, and yellow and blue.

Like most of the other options in image-editing programs, there are many ways to balance color. Very often, it will take several options together to arrive at the final color balance you wish to see. There is no one best option. Different people will find their own way of working or becoming comfortable with their favorite tools. Levels, curves, color balance, and hue/saturation controls are the most common interfaces for color modification. No matter which tool you choose, it will do essentially the same thing through a different interface with varying degrees of sophistication. Each allows individual color channels to be selected and adjusted to change color relationships.

Working with Color Balance Controls

As a general guide, when editing an image in RGB color mode, you can decrease a color by adding its complement or by increasing the two colors that mix together to make the color's complement (which is the same as decreasing the two colors that make the color you wish to reduce). For example, to remove red from an image, you can either increase the amount of cyan, which decreases the amount of red, or increase the amount of green and blue (which make cyan). This is the same as decreasing the amount of yellow and magenta (which make up red). All of these adjustments result in an image that will contain less red (see Figure 7.13).

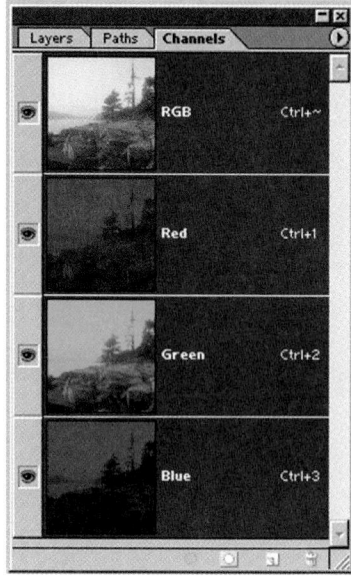

■ **Figure 7.12**
Channels dialog box.

Color Balance Using Levels

The *levels* control also allows you to select each color channel independently so that adjustments can be made to each color's highlight, midtone, and shadow areas. As a starting point, adjustments can be made to bring the sliders for each channel to the beginning and end of the visible histogram. Once this has been done, fine-tuning can be finished using further modification in levels or in any of the other controls previously listed (see Figure 7.14).

Hue/Saturation Controls

The *hue/saturation* control brings up a dialog box in which the *saturation* or intensity of an image's color can either be increased or decreased. Often color that appears to require major correction can be fixed by simply reducing the saturation. The hue or color control allows the shift of the entire spectrum of color in an image and provides the option of selecting a particular part of the color spectrum to move. This is usually accomplished with the use of sliders that make it possible to shift the original color to another part of the color wheel. All similar colors in an image will then change to the new selection (see Figures 7.15 and 7.16).

Some programs—most often scanning or simple image-editing programs—provide a color ball representing the full spectrum of available hues. By identifying the color cast you want to remove and then moving a dot from the center of the ball in the opposite direction, the color can be modified and "corrected." The further from the center of the ball, the stronger the color change effect will be. Whichever tool you use, recognizing the color you are attempting to shift and knowing its complement will help you accurately modify the image (see Figure 7.17).

Figure 7.13

Color balance controls allow you to adjust color balance for highlight, mid-tone, and shadow areas.

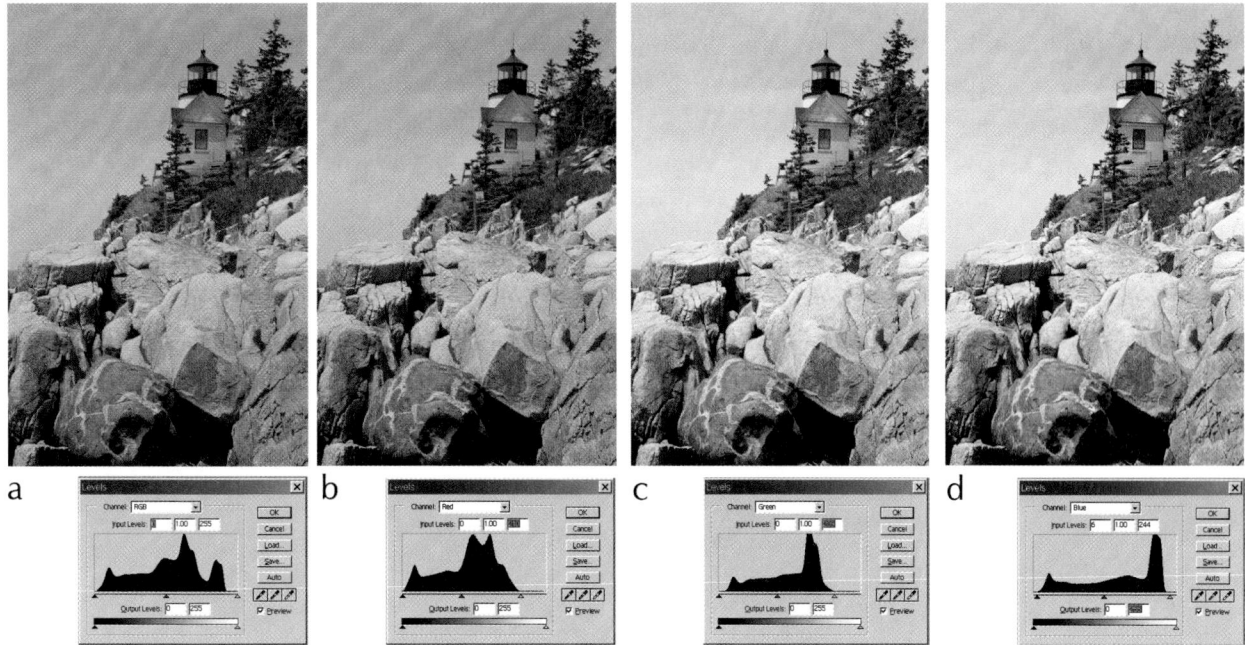

Figure 7.14

Simple color correction can be accomplished by bringing the highlight and shadow sliders to the edge of the histogram in each channel.

Figure 7.15

Often, simply decreasing saturation can bring colors into a more acceptable relationship.

Figure 7.16

Using hue/saturation can allow you to target a specific color to adjust. In this case, the greens have been adjusted in the top image and the reds in the bottom image.

Figure 7.17

Some scanning and image editing programs provide a color ball for color adjustment. By identifying the color we wish to change and then moving the center marker in the opposite direction, we can change and correct color dramatically.

Using Filters

All image-editing programs have sets of filters which will allow you to apply different effects to your image. You can change an image into one that looks like a pen-and-ink drawing or a watercolor, or create a multitude of other effects. Beyond what is included in the software, there are companies that specialize in creating special filters for image-editing programs.

Filters are relatively simple to experiment with and use. The challenge for many students is to use filters both creatively and wisely. It is far too common to allow filters to create interesting effects unrelated to the content of the image or the context in which an image is to be reproduced. Filters might seem new and interesting to the novice but the effects will appear quite obvious and cliched to the more sophisticated viewer. The selective application of filters to portions of an image is generally a more effective use.

Filter sets are usually classified by the function they perform. One group of filters mimic other art media. These include filters to create watercolor and other painting effects, pen-and-ink drawing effects, charcoal-and-pastel drawing effects, and many more. These filters usually provide dialog boxes that allow the user to control the impact of a filter by adjusting its strength, brush size, or opacity (see Figure 7.18).

Other filters blur an image, or parts of an image, in a variety of ways. These filters often include a simple-blur filter (to soften an image), a motion-blur filter (to recreate the streaky quality of an image photographed by a camera with a slow shutter speed), and a radial-blur tool (to mimic the effect of a camera zooming in on a subject or creating a radiating effect circling the subject).

■ **Figure 7.18**

Many image-editing programs provide special filters to mimic other media or otherwise modify an image. In this case a watercolor filter has been applied to the image of the castle.

Figure 7.19

The two figures in this image have shadows applied using two different methods. The figure on the left uses an image-editing program's built in shadow effect, which can change the size, distance, and opacity of the shadow. The figure on the right has a manual shadow created by duplicating the figure, filling it with black, reducing its opacity, and then distorting it with a layer transform command. Sometimes this can appear more realistic.

The one especially useful filter in the blur set is the Gaussian blur tool. It can soften parts of an image to create the illusion of a shallow area of focus or *depth of field*. By using the Gaussian blur tool to blur part of an image, the viewer's attention is focused directly on the main subject of the photograph. In addition, among its many uses, this filter can be used in the creation of *drop shadows*, and in correcting *moiré* patterns in images scanned from magazines that carry with them the dot patterns created by the printing process (see Figure 7.19).

The noise filters allow you to create an overall grain-like pattern throughout an image. This is useful when attempting to match film grain or textured areas after other image-modifying techniques have been applied. Usually available in this filter subset are the *despeckle* and *dust and scratches* filters. Both are useful in removing image flaws such as dust (see Box 7.3). However, it is important to note that these

BOX 7.3

Dust and scratches

The dust-and-scratches filter helps to disguise flaws in an image that appear as anomalies in particular tonal areas. It extends the pixels immediately surrounding the anomalous pixels in order to disguise them. An image with a large amount of dust or scratches in a particular area can be "repaired" by selecting the area with the dust specks, and then feathering the boundaries to soften the edges. After selecting the dust-and-scratches filter, review the dialog box. You will find two primary controls for this filter—radius and threshold. The radius controls how far from the edge of the defect the filter will go to find differences in pixels. The higher the value, the more the image will "blur." The threshold, with settings from 0 to 255, determines how different the defect has to be from the surrounding pixels before it is affected. The higher the setting, the more threshold sharpens the image. The goal is to find a balance between these two settings that disguises the dust while still leaving the image relatively sharp (see Figure 7.20). ■

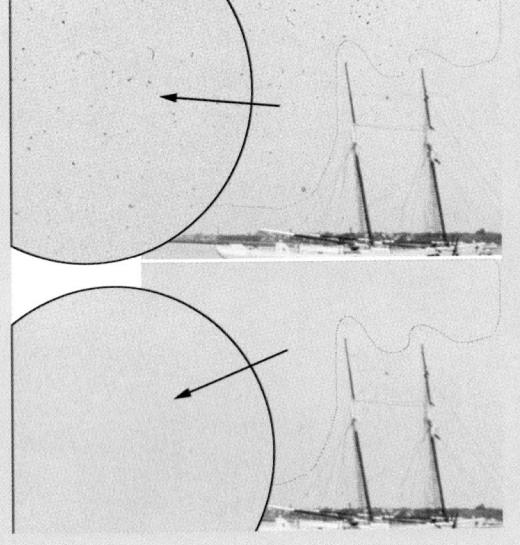

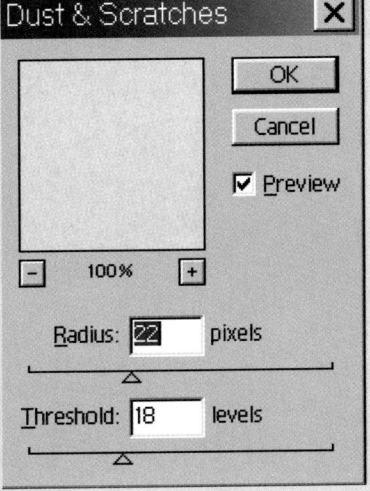

Figure 7.20

The dust-and-scratches filter can make dust disappear as it blurs and then creates "noise" in the areas selected for application.

filters add derivative information made up by the computer and actually disguise flaws more than remove them.

Sharpen filters provide a counterpoint to the blur filters. The *sharpen* and *sharpen more* filters intensify the differences in value between adjoining pixels. *sharpen edges* and *unsharp mask* filters increase the contrast along the edges of differently valued pixels. Pixels that are similar in value or show only gradual changes are left alone and not sharpened. The unsharp mask filter (see Box 7.4) is the most useful because it allows you to precisely determine the amount of sharpening to take place and the areas to protect from sharpening.

Some programs also provide filters that produce a large range of special effects. These filters can create ripples, the effect of looking through frosted glass, or twirl-and-twist images. Some special transformation filters can pinch and expand an image as if viewed in a fun house mirror. Filters can emboss an image, extrude it into blocks, create mosaics, and almost anything else you can imagine. Used in combination, the results can be quite expressive and creative, with results that can make the original image unrecognizable.

BOX 7.4

The unsharp mask

Most images require some form of sharpening after scanning or at the completion of various forms of manipulation. Every time your program resamples, rotates, or completes an operation affecting the file size of an image, there is some form of interpolation that can degrade its sharpness. Additionally, scanners, regardless of their resolution, tend to soften the contents of an image.

The unsharp mask filter takes its name from a traditional technique used in making color separations for printing. A piece of frosted mylar (coated plastic) was used as a photographic mask through which separation negatives were exposed. This process created an increase in contrast that appeared as an increase in sharpness. We use this term in digital imaging to describe this filter's ability to increase contrast between light and dark pixels and, thereby, create the illusion of greater sharpness.

When using this filter, there are three areas that can be set to control the amount of sharpening to take place. The amount, which ranges from 1 to 500 percent, controls the strength of the sharpening effect—between 100 and 200 percent works well for most images. The radius command controls the number of adjacent pixels that will be sharpened. This can range from .1 to 99.99 pixels, although a setting of 1 to 2 pixels creates appropriate contrast for most images. The higher the value selected, the more pixels will be affected by the sharpening. If too high a value is set, oversharpening might occur and the resulting image will appear granulated.

The threshold command, with a range of 0 to 255, is essentially a mask that protects certain portions of the image from being sharpened. It determines how different pixels must be before they are selected as edge pixels and sharpened by the filter. The larger the number entered here, the more pixels in an image are protected from being sharpened. An amount of zero sharpens the entire image. The higher the threshold is set, the more accepting of value differences the filter is. Threshold settings

(Continued on next page)

BOX 7.4

The unsharp
mask

continued

are highly variable and dependent upon the nature of the image being sharpened. If one wishes to maintain subtle differences and variations, a low setting is best; to emphasize only the edges of objects in an image (larger variations in pixel value) and increase edge contrast, then a higher threshold setting may be needed. Generally, the larger the image, the more sharpening it can use. A smaller image with a lesser dpi would require less sharpening (see Figure 7.21). ■

■ Figure 7.21
Before and after with unsharp mask filter.

Image-Editing Tools

The variety of tools provided to edit an image can range from the simple to complex but, in almost every case, have counterparts in the nondigital world. All of the effects already described, the global changes and filters that can be applied to an entire image, can also be applied to sections of an image. In order to accomplish this, parts of an image must be selected, or *masked,* which then allows the artist to make changes to only selected areas while leaving the remainder of the image intact.

Selection/Masking Tools

It is very important to master the basic selection tools and their modifying palettes. Whether selecting part of an image to lighten or darken, or selecting part of an image to copy in order to move it into another image, the quality of the selection process is critical to the final result.

Conventional selection tools usually include a *lasso* tool for freehand selections, a *rubber-band* tool which allows selections to be made in a series of straight lines much like snapping a band from point to point, *rectangle* and *oval* selection tools, and a *magic wand* tool which selects pixels of similar values and colors depending on the sensitivity you set in that tool's dialog box.

Some programs also have *magnetic free-form* tools that follow along pixels of dissimilar values to make a selection easier. These are used in a similar fashion to the *lasso* tool but cling to the edges of pixels that are different from one another, usually at the edges of objects in a picture.

The only controls available for most selection tools are *feathering* and *anti-aliasing*. Feathering allows the selection of a certain number of pixels with which to soften the edge of the selection or mask. This is helpful when selected areas need to be blended in with their surroundings at some point in the editing process. Anti-aliasing will smooth the edge of a selection but will not soften it as extensively as feathering has the capability of doing. Curved selections will benefit the most from anti-aliasing.

For conventional geometric shapes, the rectangle and oval (ellipse) selection tools are the easiest to use. After clicking in a corner of the area to be selected, the rectangle or oval tool is simply dragged to make it larger or smaller until the desired area is enclosed. While keyboard commands will constrain the selection to a square or circle, or start the selection from the center instead of the edges, the dialog boxes for these tools provide even greater flexibility. After an initial selection is complete, it can be modified by keyboard commands that allow you to add to or subtract from the selection. This is true for all selections.

The *lasso* tool is used to select areas that are irregular in shape. There are many variations of this free-form section tool. While holding down a mouse button, the tool is dragged around areas to be selected.

The *polygon lasso* or *rubber-band* selection tool creates a series of straight line segments. When you click the mouse, move to a new location, and click again, a selection is stretched between the two points. This can be useful for selections that are more geometric in nature, although curves can be selected with a series of short lines that follow an arc.

By clicking on an area with the *magic wand* selection tool, pixels of similar value will be selected. The magic wand selection tool has greater flexibility and additional control settings than the other selection tools. In addition to the choice of anti-aliasing, the magic wand also allows the choice of tolerance, which allows you to select the number of pixels that will be affected (from 0 to 255). The lower the number, the fewer the pixels that will be affected by the selection. There is also an option, depending on your program, of making the selection *contiguous*. A contiguous setting only allows similar pixels that are touching one another and within tolerance to be selected. If this box is unchecked, then all similar pixels within tolerance in an image will be selected when you use the magic wand.

Newer image-editing software includes *magnetic selection tools* that follow the edges created by tonal or color differences. By clicking the tool at the beginning of your selection and then floating the tool along the area to be selected without holding the mouse button down, the tool will follow along the edge while laying down points to fasten it to the selected area. The dialog box for this tool will display some form of options for the *lasso width*, which will determine the width of the area in which the tool will look for edge information. The smaller the width, the greater the eye-hand coordination required. In addition, frequency and edge-contrast settings are available. Frequency determines how often a fastening point is established as the selection is made and edge contrast determines the amount of contrast the tool looks for in establishing an edge. The more complex the selection to be made, the greater the frequency should be. For images with a lot of contrast between the object being

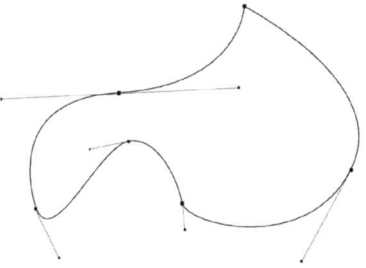

■ Figure 7.22

Creating paths is perhaps the most initially difficult but, ultimately, the most precise method of selecting portions of an image. Paths can be saved and then converted to selections at any time and can also be made into clipping paths for importing images into digital-layout-and-design programs.

selected and its surroundings, a high edge-contrast setting can be selected. Images with little contrast require a lower setting.

The *pen* tool utilizes a vector approach to provide a more exact way of selecting portions of an image for masking or later manipulation. Clicking with the mouse sets anchor points which are connected by a visible line or path. The shape of the path is adjusted by dragging handles on the anchor points to control the direction of the curve. This creates a series of path segments (see Figure 7.22). Additional pen tools allow you to modify path directions, add or remove points from a segment, or change from curved segments to straight line segments or vice versa. Paths have many advantages, including the fact that they can be stored in their own native vector format, which requires very little memory. They can be converted to selections at any time or activated as paths and edited at will.

Conventional selections or masks can also be converted to paths. However, when a selection is converted to a path, any feathering in the original selection process is lost. Saving a selection as a path requires you to set a tolerance value for the path. The higher the value, the fewer the number of anchor points and the smoother the path will be, although edge details may be lost. Once a conventional selection is saved as a path, it can be activated and edited as any path would (see Chapter 8 for more information on vectors and paths).

Whichever selection tools you elect to use, there will almost always be some cleanup after the initial selection is made. Once your initial selection is complete, parts of the selection can be added or deleted easily by a combination of keyboard commands and mouse movements. Selection modification tools will allow you to expand or shrink the selection, feather the edges, and much more, depending on the program you are using. Selections can also be *inverted* or switched so that the selected area becomes unselected and the unselected area becomes selected. This is helpful when the area you want to select is on a plain background. The background can then be selected (magic wand) and then inverted to switch the selection to the object you wanted to select in the first place.

Selection as Masking

When using a selection tool to capture part of an image, the result is a mask that blocks out part of the image. If a selection is saved, the effect of this mask can be seen in the channels dialog box. The channels dialog box shows the individual channels for each of the colors in the color model being used. A stored selection will show up as an *alpha* channel. This will not affect the color of an image. The alpha channel mask can be re-loaded at any time to bring the selection back into the image for further editing (see Figure 7.23).

Some programs also provide special selection-editing modes. For example, in PhotoShop, a feature called *QuickMask* creates a red mask around the areas selected. This can be changed to any color and level of transparency you wish for ease of viewing. You can then add to the selection by painting areas using any of the paint tools and the color black in the foreground or remove parts of the selection by painting with any of the brush tools and the color white in the foreground. Once you have cleaned up your image with the painting tools, you can click on the "selection" icon and your mask will convert back to a selection, complete with the proverbial "marching ants." Many people find it easier to use the brush tools to make selections on the alpha channel or in QuickMask mode due to their larger size and perceived ease of handling (see Figure 7.24).

If you are interested only in correcting an image's tonal or color flaws, selecting parts of an image for localized modification can be very important. If

■ **Figure 7.23**

Alpha channel and corresponding selection mask.

■ **Figure 7.24**

QuickMask tools allow you to make a selection by painting around an object instead of using a more traditional selection tool.

you are interested in image compositing or combining several images together to create a new reality, the selection tools will become a key component of the creative process.

Paint Tools

The *paint* tools in an image-editing program are relatively basic. Almost all include a brush tool, pencil tool, and some form of airbrush tool. Often a palette will allow you to choose the size of the brush and whether it has a sharp or soft edge. In addition, the rate at which the brush repeats can also be changed so that the space between individual brushstrokes can be made larger or smaller. This results in everything from a smooth flowing brushstroke to a staccato-like repetition of the brush character (see Figure 7.25).

The *basic brush* tool is circular but in many cases can be changed to an oval or even a flat brush and then rotated in any direction. The color and opacity of the brush can also be changed. Most programs offer several different ways of selecting the color of a brush. A box representing the color model you have selected can be used to make any color needed by moving sliders back and forth under each of the hues represented. The color the brush will apply will show up on the toolbar as the foreground color.

An *eyedropper* tool can also be used to select a color already in an image. The color clicked on with the eyedropper tool will then show up as the foreground color. A box containing predetermined color swatches can also be used for color selection. Finally, clicking on the foreground color in the toolbar will often bring up a more sophisticated color selection utility, allowing the choice of hue, value, and intensity (see Figure 7.26).

Choosing the *opacity* of the brush will allow control of the relative opacity and transparency of a color. With the conventional brush tool, once the set opacity is reached, further build-up of the color stops unless you stop and start again. The *airbrush* tool, however, can be set to a lower *pressure*, but will build color opacity or density as long as the mouse button is held down. Other than that, the airbrush tool is very similar to a regular brush tool.

■ **Figure 7.25**

Brush shapes can be modified in a variety of ways, including opacity, size, hardness, and direction in the case of oblong brush shapes.

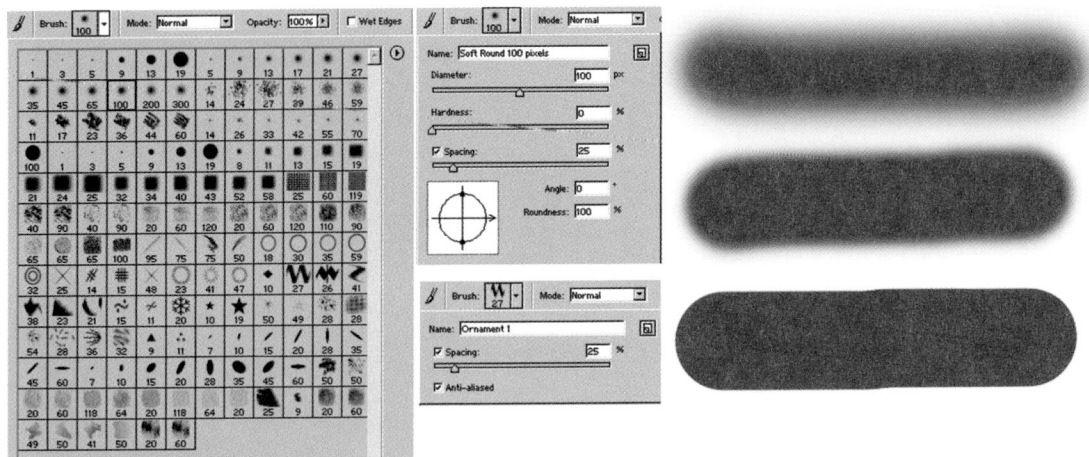

The pencil tool is also similar to the regular brush tool except that it always has a crisp, hard edge through the full range of sizes. The orientation of the brush can be changed from round to chisel point, but it is always hard edged.

Gradient tools are very useful for filling sections of an image with a range of color that changes smoothly from one hue to another. While most programs have at least one straight gradient option allowing for the selection of colors to run in a linear fashion, many programs also provide a selection of different types of gradients (for example, a radial gradient) along with numerous preset gradient colors. Most useful are the tools that allow you to edit gradients and select the points at which gradients blend colors. Many programs even allow you to create your own gradients.

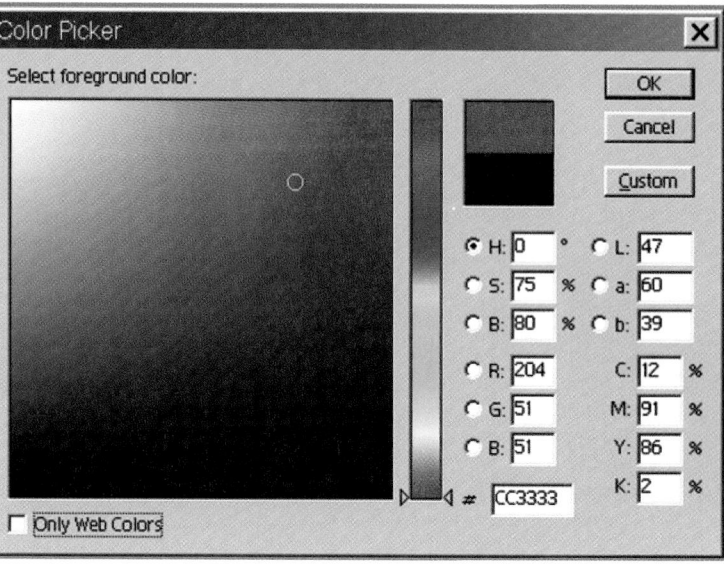

Figure 7.26
Color selection utility showing color modes.

Local Controls

Local controls allow for small changes to portions of an image without the need for masking or selecting areas first. These controls include tools that allow the user to blur, sharpen, or even smear portions of an image with a brush. In addition, similar local controls can be used to *saturate*, *desaturate*, and *burn and dodge* areas of an image.

Like the brush tools previously noted, the blur tool can be chosen directly from the program's toolbar. In most cases, similar tools are *nested* together in a roll-down or flip-out bar which is activated by holding the mouse down over a specific tool. Both the blur and sharpen tools can be made larger or smaller by choosing a different brush size. Varying pressures can also be set in their respective dialog boxes, which will determine the amount of change that will take place when the tool is activated. The *smudge* or *fingerpainting* tool works in a similar fashion but will smear the image as though you have moved your finger through wet paint. This can be an effective creative tool when used judiciously or just great fun for rearranging and exaggerating features.

Earlier in this chapter we discussed the burn and dodge tools, but it should be noted that the dialog box for these tools allows users to set the area that will be most affected by the tool—highlight, midtone, or shadow. In addition, the percentage of exposure determines the power of the tool to affect those areas. Like the other localized tools already mentioned, selecting different brush sizes from the brush menu changes the size of the affected area.

The saturate and desaturate tools will selectively intensify or subdue the intensity of a colored area. Setting the pressure in the dialog box for

Figure 7.27

The clone or rubber-stamp tool allows you to copy pixels from one part of an image to another. This can be used to fix damaged portions of an image or to copy parts of one image to another with ease. The second "Nike" image was cloned in a more transparent mode.

this tool will allow you to control the degree of change that takes place. However, like the airbrush, the effect of this tool is cumulative so it will continue to build saturation or eliminate it as long as you hold down the mouse button.

The Rubber-Stamp/Clone Tool

The *rubber-stamp* or *clone* tool is in a category all its own. This tool is designed for duplicating portions of an image from one location to another. One starts by setting the beginning of the clone point (the sample point) and then moving to another portion of an image and clicking a destination point. Information from the sample point is copied to the destination point and, thus, "cloned." The size of the clone tool is determined by selecting a brush size from the brush palette. Options include setting the opacity of the newly cloned or rubber-stamped area, and determining whether or not the area is *aligned*. If you do not select aligned, then each time you reclick the mouse, a new clone image will begin.

This tool is especially useful for correcting dust and other imperfections in an image. By starting the clone point near the image defect, those pixels can be copied over the defective ones and, thereby, eliminate them. By constantly resetting your beginning clone point, new "good" information is copied over bad (see Figure 7.27).

Basic Image Manipulation

Layers

The advent of *layers* in image-editing programs was a major advance. Layers are like sheets of clear plastic upon which new information is added. Any image scanned into or opened in an image-editing program is automatically opened as the first or background layer. In addition, new layers can be added as often as necessary to support new image elements and will be created automatically whenever you paste an image or part of an image into a document.

Figure 7.28

Perhaps the most powerful feature of most image editing programs is the incorporation of layers, where each portion of an image can be placed on an individual layer for editing.

Each layer is independent of other layers and can be set to varying opacities so that an image on one layer may show through another. In addition, the order of the layers in the layer palette can be changed so that the corresponding layer in your image can be placed over or under whatever layer you choose—much like shuffling images on pieces of acetate (see Figure 7.28).

Layers can also be duplicated, deleted, merged together in groups, or merged as an entire image. This is important since the more layers an image has, the larger the file size will become. In order to save an image with layers, and to keep those layers intact for additional editing sessions, the image must be saved in the program's native format, although recent developments in programs like PhotoShop allow tif files to also save layers. Saving an image in a file format other than the program's native format will flatten the layers into a single background layer. This should only be done when you are sure no further editing or compositing must be done.

The independence of layers is one of the greatest assets in image editing. In order to work on a layer, the layer must be active. Once the layer is active, anything you do to the image will take place only on that layer and will not affect any of the other layers in the image. Any of the image modification tools we have discussed in this chapter can be applied to the document and they too will only affect the active layer.

Rotate and Transform

If an image is to be turned or *rotated*, then a program's general rotate command will bring up a dialog box which will typically allow choices of 180 degrees, 90 degrees CW (clockwise), 90 degrees CCW (counterclockwise), arbitrary, flip horizontal, and flip vertical. These commands will affect the entire image, not a single layer. In order to make the same changes to a single layer, the edit/transform or layers/transform dialog box must be accessed. Information on layers can also be scaled to be made larger or smaller, rotated in a freehand method that will allow you to spin them incrementally, distorted into strange polygonal shapes (great for shadows), or even skewed and shifted in a "natural" perspective. This is very useful for those artists combining several images into composites, emphasizing creative exploration. These transformation commands can be applied directly to selections as well as layers.

The Layer Mask

One of the most powerful features of layers is the *layer mask*. The layer mask tool allows you to literally mask portions of a layer to reveal the layer underneath (see Figure 7.29). This works in a similar fashion to the

■ **Figure 7.29**

Photoshop provides a layer mask feature which allows you to paint directly on the mask (in black) to reveal whatever image is underneath. Painting with white reverses the effect.

QuickMask tool but it is an invisible addition to a layer. When activated, you can paint on it using the brush, pencil, airbrush, and just about anything else from the toolbar. Choosing black to paint with will cover up or erase the image, revealing what is underneath. Choosing white to paint with will restore the image, bringing back what is underneath. You may even want to choose the gradient tool (black to transparent with black as the foreground color) to allow the image to slowly fade out. While you can get a similar effect by simply using the eraser tool on an image—erasing it to reveal the image below—it does modify the actual image and is difficult, if not impossible, to undo once you move past that point. A layer mask is much more flexible; one can make modifications without affecting the original image.

The Undo

Most image-editing programs allow the artist to undo the last action undertaken in the editing process. If a mistake is made and discovered later, several options are available. If a snapshot, checkpoint, or other command is used frequently which allows an image to be temporarily saved at that stage of the editing process, it is a simple matter to go back to the last point at which that was done. If an error is made that does not allow the temporary save to resolve the problem, then it is possible to *revert* to the last fully saved version. Some programs also provide the option of multiple undo. That is, information about each action you take is stored in a chart. You can then click backwards on each step to undo as many things as are necessary. The number of undo steps stored as you work on an image can be set in an options box for this feature.

CONCLUSION

Image-editing programs today can overwhelm a user with the rich variety of their features, some immediately apparent and some that you might not discover for some time. Many digital artists work almost entirely in image editing and find it completely sufficient, even intoxicating. Still, it is important to remember that image editing is only one segment of the digital-media world.

As image-editing programs become more and more sophisticated, they begin to integrate components usually associated with other types of programs. Sometimes the division between a raster-based image-editing program and vector-based illustration program become blurred as an image-editing program's text handling becomes more advanced, or its vector-based pen tool evolves into a more sophisticated tool. Nevertheless, at the heart of image editing is the ability to work seamlessly with images—especially photographs—of all kinds. Digitizing, correcting, balancing, integrating, and creating new realities that stretch the imagination are part and parcel of these exciting programs.

Projects: Image Editing

1 THE NINE-SEGMENT PROJECT: INTRODUCTION TO LAYERS AND FILTERS

Select a single image. Using guidelines, break the image into nine relatively equal parts. Select one of the nine segments and cut or copy it to a new document. You may want to use the rectangle selection tool for this. Do this for each of the nine segments. Once you have each of the nine segments saved as an individual document, create a new, separate document the same size and resolution as your original image. Reposition the layers so that they recreate the original image. You will have to activate the layer before you can move it by clicking on it in the layers palette. Apply a different filter or effect to each one of the nine individual layers that now comprise your image. Experiment. If you don't like what has happened to an individual section, discard it and replace it with the original saved section so you can start again.

2 IMAGE CONVERSION: COLORIZE A BLACK-AND-WHITE IMAGE

Starting with a grayscale image, convert it to RGB. Select parts of your image, feather them to soften the edges (experiment with the amount), and then use any of the tools that can change color to "colorize" that portion of the image. Try color balance, hue/saturation, or curves. Avoid using the paintbrush tool.

3 IMAGE COMPOSITE: OLD MASTER PAINTING

Start with a scan of an old master painting. Add elements to redefine it and change the context of the image. Would Whistler's Mother really be watching TV? Copying and pasting new elements from one image into a painting background offers you an opportunity to try matching color values and even adding shadows to complete the illusion.

4 PLAYING CARD: EXPLORING SYMMETRY AND TEXT

Scan an image you feel might make a good jack, queen, or king play-ing card. Take a look at a conventional playing card to identify the major characteristics playing cards should have. Are they symmetri-cal? Symmetrical and flipped over? How can you "blend" the two images together using the layer mask tool? Add text elements to iden-tify the playing card. The final image should be 4" × 6" at 300 dpi.

5 SCANNER AS CAMERA

The scanner is a great camera. See what happens when you scan natu-ral objects like crumpled paper, feathers, and bubble wrap. What hap-pens when something moves while being scanned? Can you create a still life in the scanner or afterwards in an image-editing program?

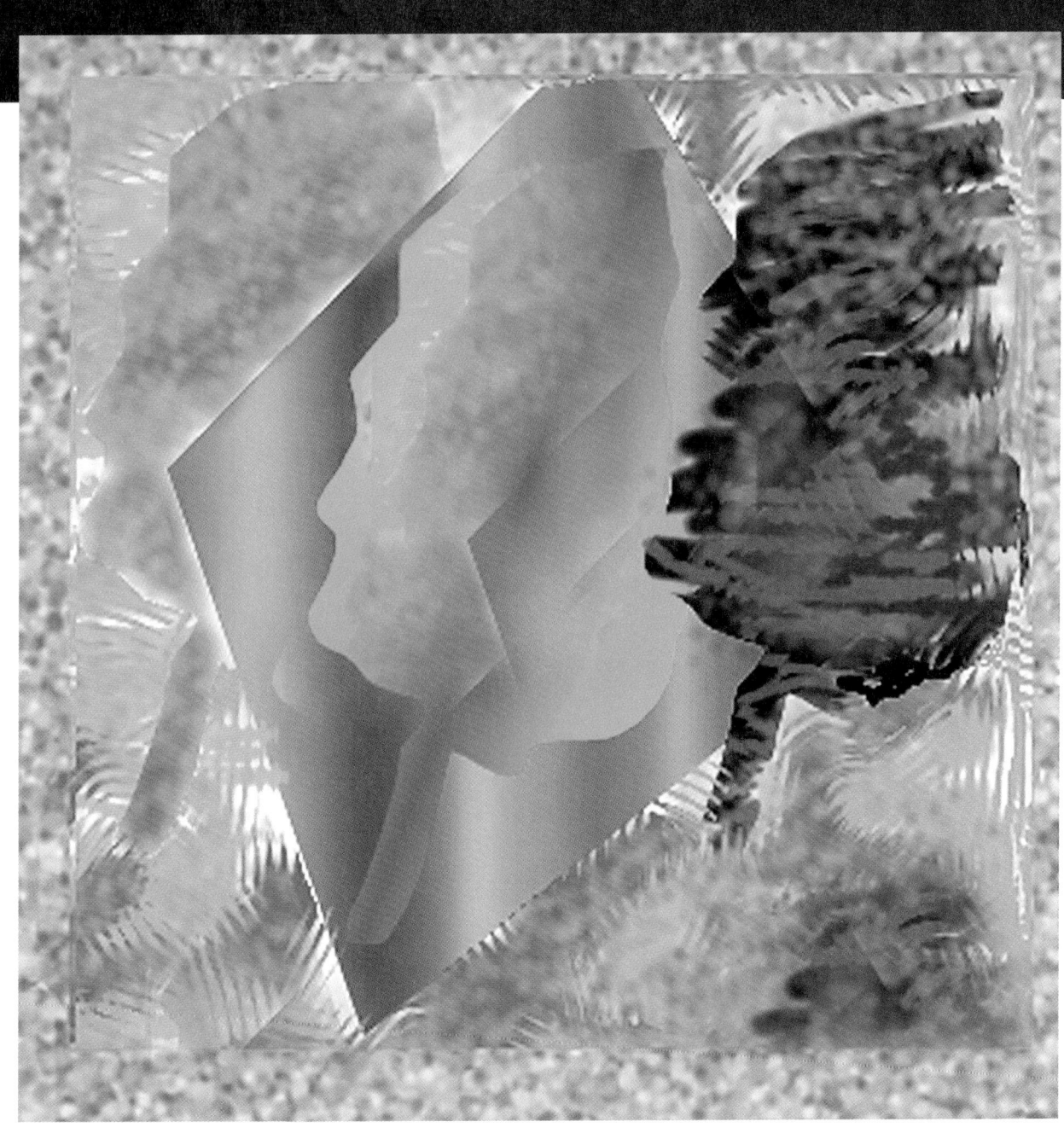

Digital Painting

Introduction

ike most software, digital media programs continue to increase in power and range. Some have become quite complex, even muscle-bound, by adding features of very different kinds of art programs with the goal of becoming a comprehensive "solution." Despite the impressive depth of today's digital media software, most digital artists and designers continue to use more than one program to create their works. The particular software an artist or designer chooses to use at any moment depends on the effect he or she is looking for. Experienced artists and designers know that each type of software has its own unique strengths and capabilities and when to use them.

This chapter focuses on one of the very important and distinct approaches to the creation of 2-D images: bitmap painting software. Along with the subject of the previous chapter (image editing) and the next (vector illustration), it forms one side of the triumvirate of 2-D digital imaging.

Bitmap painting software is the ideal choice for the many artists whose goal is to create digital pictures that have the look and range of traditional painting, as well as other artist materials. Like bitmapped images discussed in the last chapter, evocative, soft forms, and naturalism are its strengths (see Figure 8.1). But painting software can also be used to create rich, dramatic abstractions.

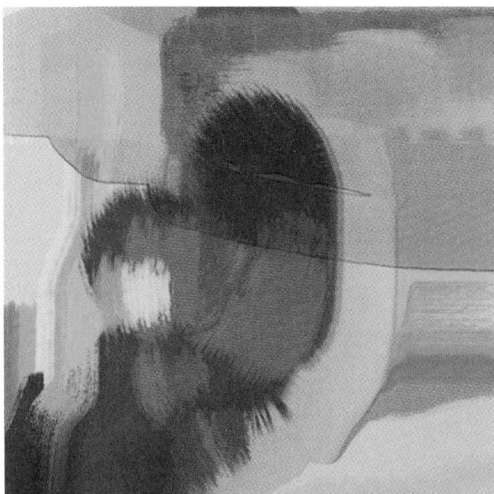

■ **Figure 8.1**
Close-up of a richly colored
digital painting.

Traditional and Digital Tools

All of today's bitmap painting programs are direct descendents of the first, Richard Shoup and Alvy Ray Smith's SuperPaint, created at Xerox PARC in the 1970s (see Chapter 5). While Shoup and Smith were true pioneers who saw the exciting potential of art software, their inspiration came from looking to the past. According to Smith, their goal was the "digital simulation of classic painting with a brush on a canvas." While bitmap painting software has certainly developed in depth and complexity in the last thirty years, it has retained Shoup and Smith's philosophy and remains the most closely connected of the digital media to the tools of the traditional artist.

Bitmap Painting

Basic Concepts and Tools

As in image editing, when working with bitmap painting software, you are redrawing each pixel on the screen. However, the focus of the tools is quite different. Their primary goal is to recreate traditional drawing and painting tools, like pencils, chalk, crayons, watercolors, and oil paints. That is why bitmap painting programs are also called *natural media* software.

What many artists find particularly exciting is that they can create art that does not look like it was made with a computer. Since every pixel on the screen is described in terms of color, value, and transparency, natural media brushes can paint the very subtle shades and complex color transitions of both convincing landscapes and vividly expressionistic abstract digital paintings. In addition, digital painting allows one to combine media that cannot be used together in the real world (for example, a picture with watercolor on top of oil paint).

For artists who have only previously worked in traditional media, bitmap painting smoothes the transition to the digital world. Combined with a digitizing tablet and a stylus, bitmap painting software feels more natural and direct than any of the other digital media (see Box 8.1).

The Workplace

When first opening a bitmap painting program, you will see much in common with other digital media software. The screen's work area includes menus at the top, a toolbar with the typical buttons found in art programs (like zoom and the paint bucket), and a large window where the new image will be created, called the *canvas*.

The strength of digital-painting programs can be found in their unique palettes. One houses an extensive collection of natural media brushes. There is also a separate control palette for modifying each brush's attributes. Other palettes are for selecting colors, gradients, and patterns. Like other art programs, the palettes can be hidden so you can see your work without distractions (see Figure 8.3).

BOX 8.1

The digitizing tablet

More than any of the other digital media programs, bitmap painting software is designed to take advantage of the features of graphics or digitizing tablets (see Figure 8.2)—though most other software can also take advantage of them. Digitizing tablets are pressure-sensitive input devices for artists. Rather than moving a mouse, the artist holds a pen-shaped stylus and draws directly on a tablet. A wire grid inside the tablet reads the position of a small transmitter built into the stylus. This information is sent to the computer as x and y coordinates of a location on the screen. Unlike a mouse's approach to location, these are absolute coordinates—each spot on the tablet corresponds to a specific place on the screen. Therefore, you do not have to roll over to a spot as you do with a mouse. You can just pick up the stylus and start making a mark in another location.

For a hand-drawn look, a tablet is essential. It works almost as easily as a pen and paper. The effects you are able to create can range from exuberant to subtle. The tablet is very sensitive to both the pressure of the stroke being made and its angle (this is done by modifying the strength of a stylus's signal.) As one increases the pressure of the stylus against the tablet, a line on the screen thickens and gets darker. Working with a tablet and the calligraphy pen tool from your painting software, you can smoothly change the angles of your hand-drawn script from wide to narrow and then back again. Without a tablet, effects like this are nearly impossible.

Tablets include software to personalize them to the user's preferences. You can adjust the feel of the pen and its response to pressure. Buttons along the top of the tablet are designed to trigger frequently used commands like copy and paste—and the indispensable undo. Some tablets also come with a firm plastic sheet that lays over the drawing area, where you can place pictures underneath for tracing.

Today, most painting software is designed around the use of a stylus and tablet. In fact, without a tablet, the programs lose some of their built-in functionality. With one, brushes, charcoal, pastels, and pencils of all sizes and shapes respond naturally to your hand's movements. ■

■ **Figure 8.2**

Digitizing tablets: standard and with imbedded monitor for painting.

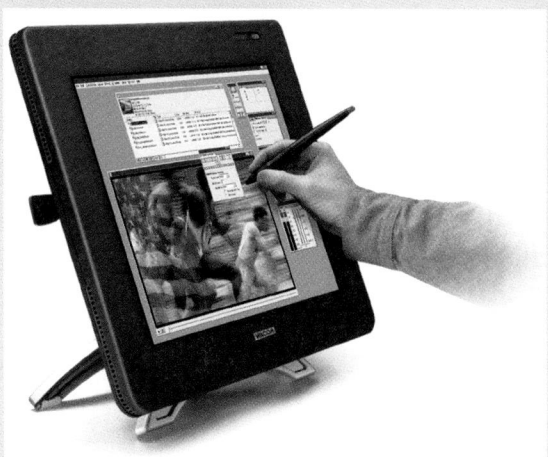

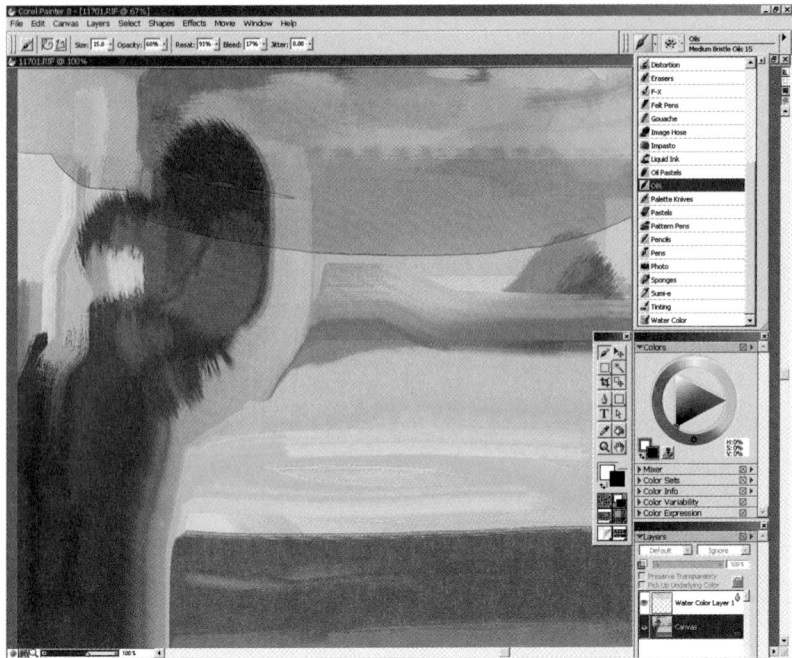

Figure 8.3
Painter's workplace.

The Brushes

The heart of any natural-media software is in its imaginative collection of brushes. The brushes are organized into categories based on traditional media, but within each one you can explore a wide assortment of variations. Think of each media button as a box for tools of that kind. For example, the pen tool includes pens of all sorts, from calligraphy to a leaky one. The chalk box contains soft and sharp chalks, dry pastels, and oil pastels.

Since the brushes are meant to respond like their traditional models, each has its own unique characteristics (see Figure 8.4). Some of the brushes work cumulatively, allowing you to build up areas with successive strokes. Others make transparent washes that appear to soak into the canvas. One brush may lay its paint independently of what is already there, while another will pick up nearby paint and smear it into the new stroke.

When using a stylus and digitizing tablet, you can make strokes that fade in and out as you vary the pressure of your marks. For example, if you are going to draw a shaded object, you might first trace its form lightly with a hard pencil, then begin shading with a sharp chalk held at a slant. To finish, you could aggressively deepen the shadows with thick, soft charcoal. The materials respond to the surface of your drawing as they do in real life. For example, when using chalks or charcoal with textured papers, the grain of the paper can be seen (see "Paper Textures" on page 183).

While the number of brushes at first seem to provide an overwhelming number of choices, eventually most artists find they want to adjust them to their own preferences. A separate control panel allows you to change the size of the marks made, their opacity, and the amount of grain from the paper that is revealed. Even more subtle variants can be created, from the shape of the brush, its angle, the ways color bleeds from it, and even the number of bristles. Advanced digital-painting software allows you to create your own variations and save them as new or *custom* brushes.

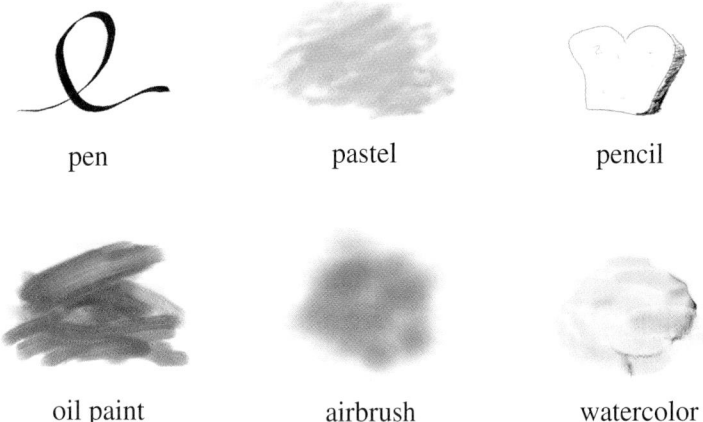

| pen | pastel | pencil |
| oil paint | airbrush | watercolor |

Figure 8.4
Marks from different brushes.

Color

The combination of color and brushes has excited artists for centuries and made painting one of the most popular of all the arts. In digital painting, while you can certainly create an impressive, finished drawing in black and white, adding color can make an image blossom (see Box 8.2).

BOX 8.2

Chet Phillips is a Dallas, Texas-based artist and illustrator who works predominantly in natural-media software. Before his discovery of digital media in 1992, he used the traditional tools of an illustrator: colored pencils, scratch-board, and airbrush. Today, his work utilizes the digital versions of those media and combines them in new ways. His clients include newspapers, magazines, airlines, department stores, and movie production companies (his art was featured recently in a line of *Harry Potter* merchandise like mugs and coloring books.)

Frankenscan (see Figure 8.5) was created for a service bureau that specializes in scans. Animals are characters in much of Phillips' work, in this case a mad cat scientist. Like many digital artists, he begins his work just like traditional artists—by making a pencil sketch. After the sketch is approved by his client, the drawing is scanned into his computer and opened in his natural-media software.

By placing a black layer above a white one, Phillips is able to recreate the process of scratchboarding (similar to carving a woodcut panel) by erasing the black areas until all the details emerge. The tracing-paper function of his software allows him to use the original sketch as a reference while he scrapes away the black areas.

Once the scratchboard image is finished, a new layer is added below it so he can add colors, but not cover up his drawing. His use of color adds richness and depth to the picture. In *Frankenscan,* Phillips used the pastel tool, rubbing in soft colors that heighten the drama of the dark night and the flashes of lightning. The final act was the placement of his client's logo on top in a new layer.

In addition to his work for clients, Phillips regularly exhibits his own personal work in galleries and on the Web. An example of it, from the series *The Life of An Imaginary Friend,* can be seen in Chapter 1. ∎

■ **Figure 8.5**
Chet Phillips, Frankenscan.

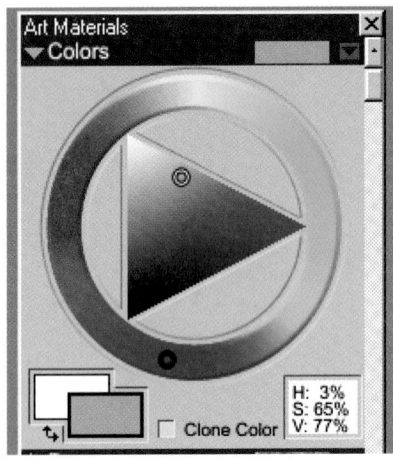

Figure 8.6

Color palette.

Three variables shape color in bitmap painting: hue, value, and saturation. The hue is the name of the basic color, as in "red" or "purple." Once the hue is selected, you can choose from the range of values, how dark or light the color should be (also known as *shades* or *tints,* respectively). You may also choose how saturated or intense it is.

Colors are placed on your brush in a two-step process. There are two large colored shapes in the color palette (see Figure 8.6). One has the color spectrum, where you select the hue. The color you've chosen will then appear in the other shape as a range of intensities and values. There you can choose how saturated the color will be and how light or dark it will appear.

Most painting software has alternative ways to select colors. You can choose to work in an optional RGB palette with variable sliders for the red, green, and blue components of projected color. Like most digital media programs, you can select a color already in your image by clicking on or *sampling* it with the eyedropper tool. This is particularly useful in digital painting, where it is often difficult, after much smearing and layering, to recreate how an existing color was made. In addition, there are sets of pre-selected colors in libraries, like Pantone color sets. You can also create your own sets.

More Than One Color and Gradients

With natural media software, you can paint with two or more colors at once. Unlike most other art programs, the two small rectangles at the bottom of the color palette are not foreground and background colors, but the primary and secondary ones (see Figure 8.7). Some painting brushes are designed to use both at the same time. For example, the oil brushes combine the two to create a more convincing recreation of painting in oils. There may also be specialized oil brushes with multiple colors that recreate the brushstrokes of famous artists like van Gogh. You can make your own multiple color brushes by adjusting the amount of color variability in a custom brush, adding a range of values, intensities, or colors for each stroke.

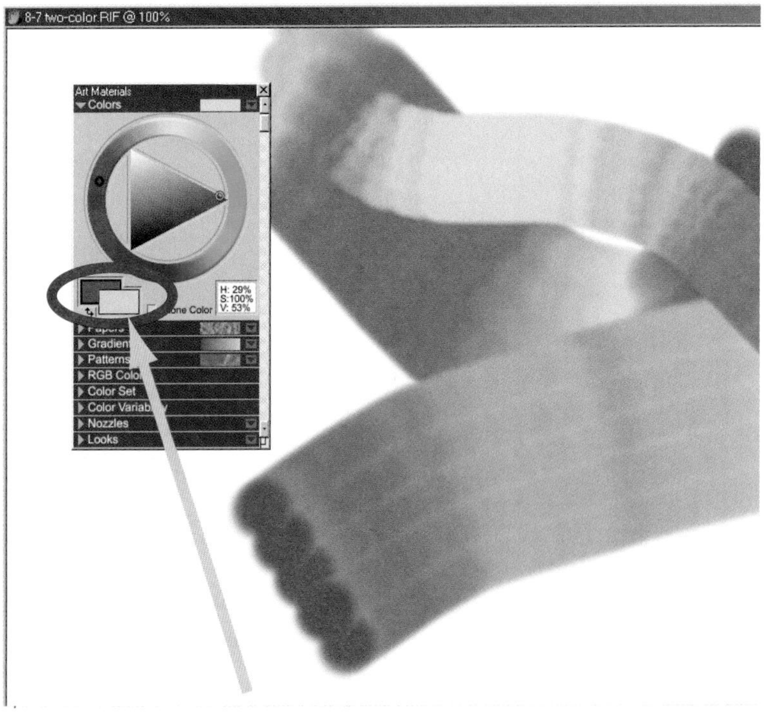

The use of *gradients,* a gradual blend of a range of colors, is a more common way to apply multiple colors in digital media software. Depending on your choices, these smooth blends can give a clean and professional, or atmospheric and natural, look to your images. Most bitmap painting programs have a large collection of gradients in a special palette, with even more in separate libraries. Custom gradients can be created by editing a preset gradient (for example, by adjusting its angle or by adding more colors to it). You can also start new ones from scratch and save them.

Figure 8.7

The color palette's small foreground and background rectangles.

Gradients can be linear or radial, and in some programs, spiral or circular (see Figure 8.8). They can be left to right or right to left, doubled or mirrored, or a combination of these. With so many fascinating choices and possibilities, the danger is you'll forget to work on your painting. Gradients are usually applied to shapes or selections with the paint bucket tool, but some digital-painting programs let you create interesting effects by using the brushes to paint directly with gradients.

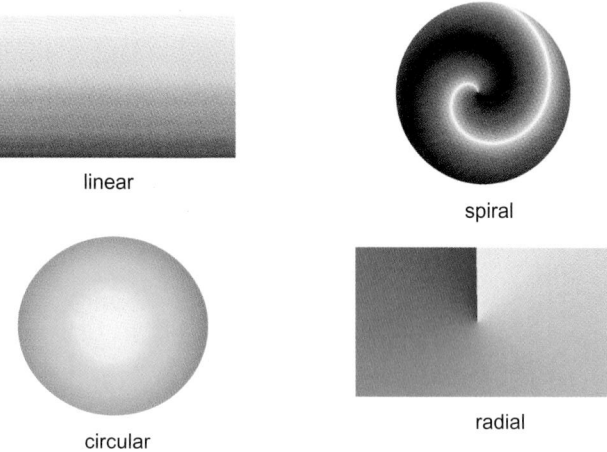

linear

circular

spiral

radial

■ **Figure 8.8**
Examples of linear, radial, spiral, and circular gradients.

Paper Textures

The simulation of paper textures is one of the most impressive ways digital painting software recreates traditional media. In most digital media programs, a new file is simply an empty white field. At most you can change the background color. In bitmap painting, while a new file may look empty and white when you begin, it has texture, like a fresh sheet of artist's paper or a stretched canvas. You can see this, for example, as soon as you use any of the tools that normally show the grain of a paper, like charcoal.

There are many textures available that simulate a variety of art materials, like newsprint and watercolor papers. In additional libraries, you may also find strange, unique ones, with names like "plastic pebbles" and "spider on caffeine." The size of the grain of each texture is adjustable. You can also modify most brushes to increase the visible effect of a paper's texture (see Figure 8.9).

■ **Figure 8.9**
Close-up showing grain.

Cloning and Tracing

Cloning, as in image-editing software, allows you to paint with a part of another picture or another part of the one you are working on. It is an excellent way to combine images with more control and subtlety than simply cutting and pasting. In digital painting, your clones can easily take on a painterly look even if your source is a photograph. Special cloning brushes transform your selection as you brush with them. For example, if your source is a color photograph of a tree and you draw in a new file with the chalk clone tool, the tree will appear in your new picture as if it was originally in pastels (see Figure 8.10).

Tracing is another way of retaining a natural look for your art while working from photographs as a source. Some digital-painting programs will place a pale clone of an entire image on a separate bottom layer, making it appear as if it is below a sheet of tracing paper. You can then trace over it with natural media tools. Just by clicking a button, you can turn the pale image on and off to check your progress. The pale tracing paper image is only a source; it will not be part of the final image or print.

original

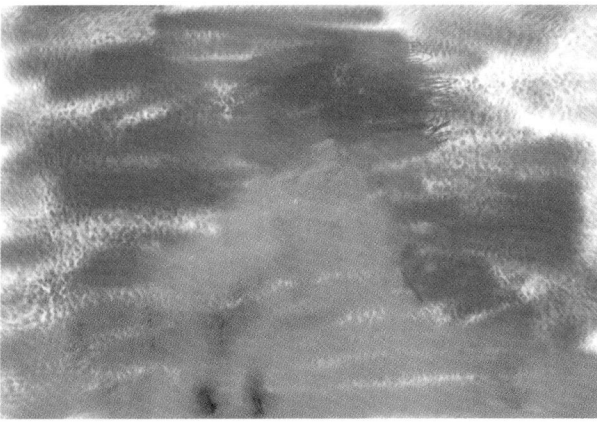

chalk clone

■ **Figure 8.10**

Photo and chalk cloning effect.

Layers

Layers allow you to keep elements of your picture in separate levels, so you can work on them independently. Each digital-painting program varies in how it utilizes layers. In the most limited software, there are only three layers: the canvas itself (where most drawing and painting takes place), a place for a selection or type to "float," and a wet layer above the canvas for the wet media (like watercolor painting). Once a selection is deselected, it drops back into the canvas. When the "dry" command is applied to a wet layer, it also becomes unified with the canvas.

More powerful painting programs utilize layers much like image-editing software (see Chapter 7 for a detailed explanation of how to use layers) with some special features. For example, one program has a reference layer with low-resolution versions of a layer's contents, to make rotating and resizing quicker. A complex painting program may even have special layers to separate vector from bitmap elements.

Selecting and Masking

The goal of making a selection is to isolate one part of your image from the rest of the picture. However, that simple act is a gateway to a whole range of operations that give you increased control over specific parts of your picture. An artist's skill in creating selections can have a big impact on whether a final work looks crude and clumsy or seamless and polished.

The basic selection tools in bitmap painting programs (arrow, lasso, marquee, and magic wand) are usually identical to those in image editing. Selections are used in three basic ways: to limit the area you can work on, to protect that area (or mask it), or to choose it for cutting, copying, or moving. While selected, the area will "float" above the canvas in an overlay, separated from the rest of the picture. You can paint wildly across it, rotate or resize it, change its opacity, apply a special effect like embossing, or all of the above, and not affect any other part of your image. Some programs allow you to save a selection for later use.

As in image editing, masks protect an area and prevent you from accidentally changing it. Masks are made in two basic ways. One is making a selection and transforming it into a mask. Another is to paint a new mask using brushes. This painterly approach is often more in keeping with the style of a digital painting. As in image-editing software, by painting your mask with a semi-transparent color, rather than an opaque one, you can allow changes but limit their impact.

Corel's *Painter* includes quick-masking buttons (see Figure 8.11), which allow you to choose to draw only outside or only inside a selection (known as *stenciling*). By clicking the "draw anywhere" button, the selection is released and you are free to work all over the canvas.

Special Effects

Like image-editing software, digital-painting programs include filters and plug-ins that create special effects. A wide range of exciting changes can be made quickly, such as transforming the whole image into a mosaic. The glass distortion filter will make your picture look like it is being seen through the glass of a shower stall. These changes can be applied to an entire picture or limited to a selection, masked area, or layer. Some painting plug-ins are designed to make special effect brushes; for example, giving you the ability to paint in liquid metal (see Figure 8.12).

Filters can also add texture to a whole image by selecting from different paper types and using the "apply surface texture" command. Your picture can appear more 3-D by applying filters that can either add a subtle sense of depth to your brushstrokes or make your whole image appear as if it was embossed in plastic.

Special lighting effects are another way to make your picture seem more 3-D. They can also be used to unify a picture with a simple wash of light across the surface, or create a sense of drama, with a focused spotlight in a field of darkness. There are many preset lighting effects to choose from, as well as custom settings that affect where a light is aimed, its color, brightness, angle, and "distance" from your image. You can have one light source or several.

As in all digital media, experimenting with filters presents the danger of losing track of what your aesthetic goals were. They may give your picture an artificial or computer-made look. To make sure you and not the software is in control, it is often better to rework your picture with brushstrokes after you finish applying filters.

The fade filter, however, is an excellent way to maintain control of your image. If your last brushstroke's effect was stronger than you had expected, you can reduce its strength. While looking at a preview window, you can use sliders to adjust the effect of your brushstroke and make sure it fits well with the rest of the picture. Fading adds transparency to the stroke and is, in essence, an "undo" of variable strength (see Figure 8.13).

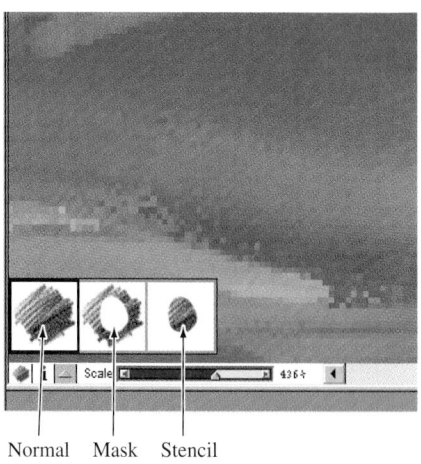

Normal   Mask   Stencil

■ **Figure 8.11**
Quick-masking buttons.

 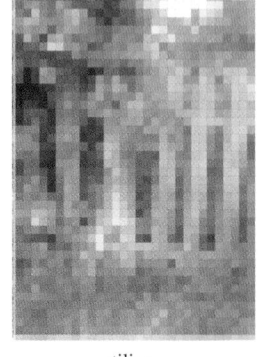

original   tiling

surface   lighting

■ **Figure 8.12**
Special effects.

Digital Media

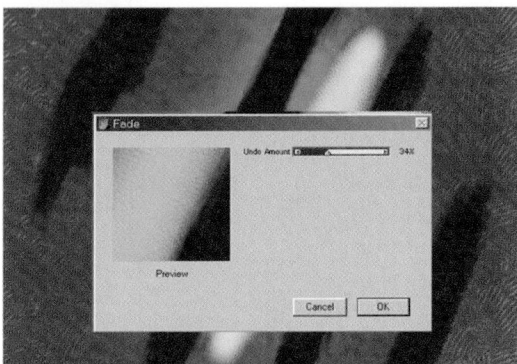

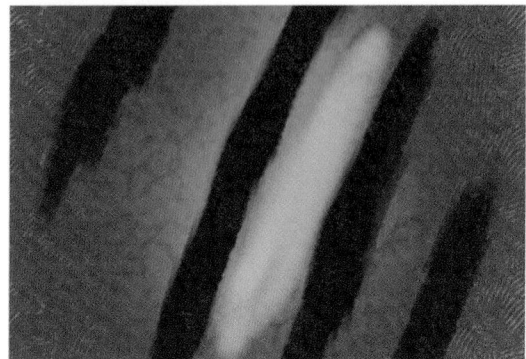

■ **Figure 8.14**
Type special effects.

■ **Figure 8.13**
Example of fading effect.

Working with Type

Because digital painting, like all bitmap software, breaks up shapes into fine dots, it is not a good choice when laying out large amounts of small text that needs to be crisp and legible. That's the strength of digital-layout-and-design software (see Chapter 6) or vector illustration (see Chapter 9). However, if you are designing large display text, digital-painting software has superb tools for creating imaginative and dynamic type for logos, signs, headings for a Web page, or film titles.

All painting programs include the basic tools of type manipulation. After the text is typed in, it floats above the canvas. Text can then be rotated, scaled, and repositioned. Spaces between the letters can be adjusted throughout the entire phrase (tracking) or between individual letters (kerning). Type can also be made transparent. Drop shadows can be added as a special effect.

More advanced software with multiple layers allows you to apply a wider range of special effects. Text can be filled with gradients and patterns. The letters can be blurred or given textured edges. By applying lighting effects, letters can glow like neon or appear embossed in the paper. Working carefully with selections and masks, you can zoom in and airbrush directly onto your letterforms to shape and bevel them (see Figure 8.14).

Of course, you can create letters without using the text tool at all. With the control you have with a stylus, along with the many kinds of pens, brushes, and lighting and texture effects, you can hand-letter your own exciting text. Rather than typing, why not use the creative freedom of painting software to create liquid metal chrome nameplates or furry spotted signatures?

Printing and Exporting

Printing is the moment of truth for many digital painters. The fidelity and quality of color printers, even those for home use, have improved to astonishing capabilities compared to the early years of the first color thermal inkjet printers (see Chapter 4). Nevertheless, all artists should prepare to be disappointed or, at best, surprised when seeing the first trial print of a newly finished image.

What is seen on the screen is rarely what appears printed on paper because they are very different ways of displaying images. The colors from the projected light seen on a monitor are often more luminous and saturated compared to those that appear on a printed page. Color management software (see Chapter 6) will calibrate the colors between your monitor and printer to minimize these differences, but you should still expect to spend some time adjusting an image so it prints to your satisfaction. Because these adjustments are often quite subtle, many artists prefer to export their paintings into an image-editing program to have more control over how an image is going to print.

Nonetheless, in the last few years, personal printers have become much more suitable for fine-art printing. One of the most important advantages of printing an image yourself (besides cost savings) is that it remains under your control and the studio computer can be calibrated directly to your printer. Another advantage of personal printing is the ability to see results immediately and to make necessary adjustments. Previously, only professional printers could produce archival prints. Today, archival inks and papers are now available for personal printers that have a life span far beyond typical color prints.

In the hands of many artists, personal printers have also become a medium for creating experimental prints. Some like to combine media, printing a digital image on fine papers and then reworking it with traditional media like watercolors or pastels. Others collage small digital prints into larger works. Unusual papers fed into the printer by hand can create imaginative variations of screen images.

Even with the expanded capabilities of personal printers, many artists still prefer to use a service bureau or professional printer to create a unique copy or edition of their digital paintings. The advantage of this approach is access to the finest quality printing equipment like IRIS printers (see Chapter 4), which are far beyond the financial capacity of most artists. You can also have your image printed directly to a slide or large-format transparency. Service bureaus can print much larger sizes than the largest personal printers and on a greater variety of materials (for example, canvas). Some service bureaus even have the equipment to print high-resolution images on vinyl large enough to cover a bus.

Painting for the Web

While digital painting is an artform in itself, no successful art program today can ignore the impact of the World Wide Web. Besides saving files in a bitmap-painting software's own native format, you can easily save them in the compression formats most commonly found on the Web: GIF and JPEG (see Chapter 13). Some of the more advanced painting programs now include built-in functions that make Web image and page construction more simple. For example, they allow you to limit colors to a Web-safe palette or define images as image maps. While these tools are very helpful, many artists continue to save their paintings as uncompressed TIFFs and then export them to a dedicated Web image-processing program for more sophisticated fine-tuning.

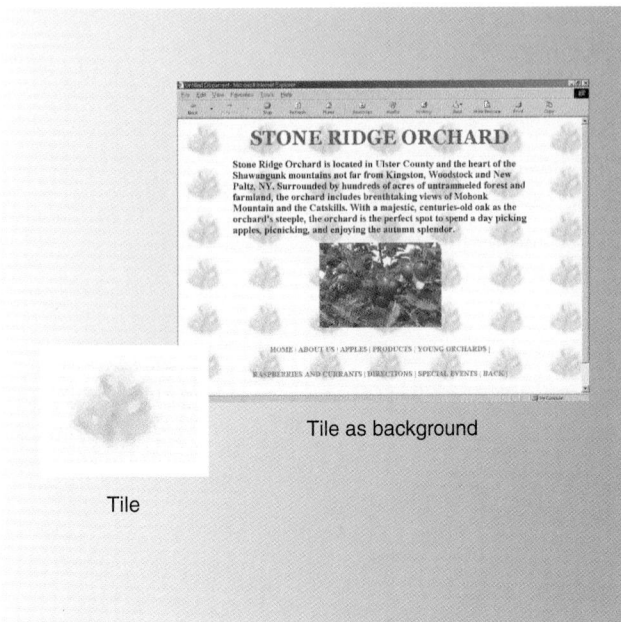

Figure 8.15

Painted tile and Web background.

Painting programs are excellent choices to enliven the standard elements of websites. Lively logos can be made using digital painting's type tools or by using hand-drawn letterforms. The organic, naturalistic shapes that are easily made with digital-painting software can be used as graphics for buttons that will stand out from the typical geometrical ones found on most websites.

For a Web page's background, many designers use painting software to make small *tiles* that Web browsers automatically repeat to form a seamless background behind the whole page (see Chapter 13). The advantage of these tiles is they download much more quickly than a large background image. The painterly brushes, textures, and lighting effects found in painting programs are great ways to create interesting and unusual background patterns (see Figure 8.15).

CONCLUSION

In the 1970s, Richard Shoup and Alvy Ray Smith's SuperPaint first took computer graphics beyond a fascination with geometry and recreated "classic painting" techniques. Their vision and dedication made it possible for today's digital studio to be a place where the techniques of the old masters can be combined with ones from a new age.

Natural-media software's hand-drawn look and its ability to simulate traditional painting techniques have drawn many artists and designers to this new medium. If you already love the way colors can smear together in unexpected ways in an oil painting or how an evocatively drawn line can bend, disappear, and re-emerge, then you will find bitmap-painting programs to be a satisfying and exciting method of creating digital works. Whether you are preparing an archival print to be displayed in a New York City gallery or images for an online one, digital-painting software provides the tools for a wide variety of painterly approaches to image-making.

Projects: Digital Painting

1 *Working in a nonrepresentational manner, paint a 5" × 7" image on the theme of "storm." Experiment with a variety of brushes to capture the feeling of being in the midst of a violent storm.*

2 *Paint a pair of 5" × 5" abstract images on the themes of "calm" and "anxiety." Use a different color scheme and brushes to increase the contrast between your two paintings. Experiment with contrasting paper textures as well.*

3 *Using the tracing feature of digital-painting software, begin a picture with a tracing of a landscape photograph that you have scanned. The goal is not to create a photo-realistic painting, but to use the photograph as a source of inspiration only. By the time you are finished, no trace of the original image should be apparent. Experiment with lighting to increase the mood of the scene.*

4 *Create an 8" × 10" illustration based on a favorite line of poetry or song lyric. Utilize the type tools in the painting software to integrate the words into your picture in a way that makes visual sense.*

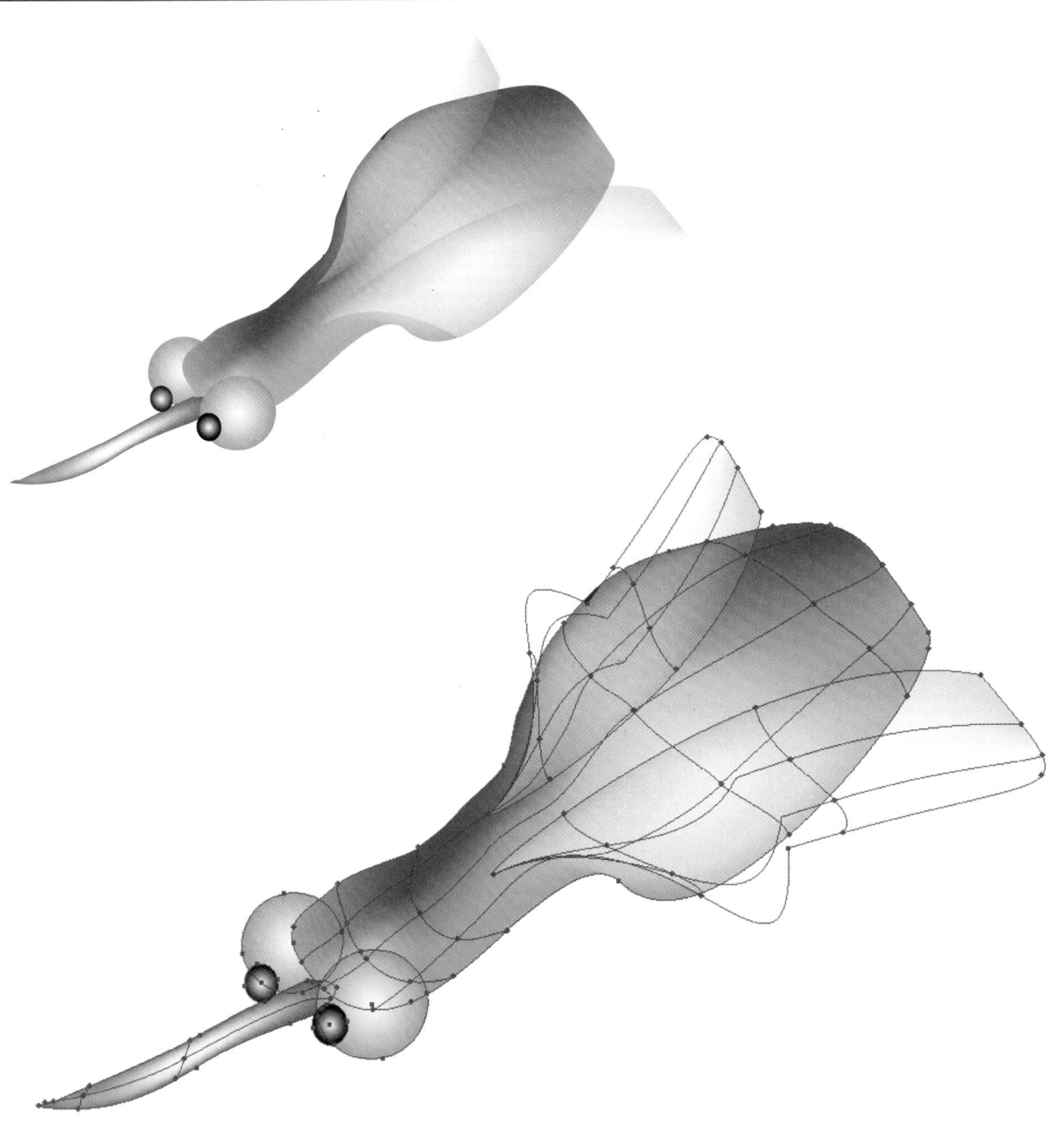

Vector Drawing and Illustration

Introduction

From the beginning, painting software was consciously designed to mimic a traditional painter's tools and palette. Image-editing programs included digital equivalents of many darkroom techniques, such as dodging and burning. Vector drawing, however, had no equivalent because it simply did not exist until the era of computers. As discussed in Chapter 5, Ivan Sutherland's Sketchpad, the first interactive art software, invented this new mathematical approach to line and shape creation (see Box 9.1).

Vector illustration is, in other words, the firstborn of the digital media. Today's software has an impressive collection of tools designed to create clearly defined forms, utilize patterns, manipulate typography, and much more. It is the first choice for artists and designers whose work requires elaborate geometrical shapes, precise control, bright colors, smooth gradients, and the imaginative arrangement of type.

BOX 9.1

Father Ivan

■ **Figure 9.1**
Ivan Sutherland.

If vector drawing is the firstborn of the digital media, it's no wonder that many people call Ivan Sutherland the father of computer graphics (see Figure 9.1). So much of what would come to define the field can be traced to his innovations, starting with Sketchpad.

Born in Hastings, Nebraska, in 1938, Sutherland was probably the only high school student in the 1950s who had a computer to play with. The SIMON, a relay-based mechanical computer, was lent to his father, an engineer. SIMON was so powerful that it was capable of adding all the way up to fifteen. It could be programmed—by punching

(Continued on next page)

BOX 9.1

Father Ivan

continued

holes into paper tape fed into a tape reader. Young Ivan's first program "taught" SIMON to divide and required an eight-foot-long roll of tape.

As a graduate student in engineering at MIT, Sutherland was once again one of the few young people in the nation to have a computer available for his research. And this one was much more powerful than SIMON. MIT's TX-2 was built for the Air Force to demonstrate that transistors could be the basis of a computer. One of the fastest machines of its day (320K of memory!), it had Xerox's first computer printer, one of the first display screens (nine inches in width), and a lightpen.

It was at MIT that he wrote Sketchpad, a graphics program, as his doctoral thesis. Sutherland utilized vectors based on geometry to create forms that could be rescaled and zoomed in on. His graphics were the first capable of being stored in computer memory and the first that could be changed by redrawing on the screen.

Interestingly, Sutherland created the first interactive drawing software not for art's sake, but with the goal of simplifying the exchange of information between people and machines. This goal, and the design of his program, are why many also consider him the grandfather of the Graphic User Interface or GUI (the father being Alan Kay, one of Sutherland's students). The width of the TX-2's small screen was treated by his program as a "window," so when one zoomed in on a form, its outer parts would go beyond the edges of the screen. His program even allowed him to copy parts of his objects, move them, and delete them.

While Sketchpad was a 2-D program, later versions utilized 3-D wireframes, the forerunner of modern CAD systems. Sketchpad 3 even included the now-customary division of the screen by all 3-D software into four views (above, side, front, and in perspective). Sutherland utilized this kind of software in another innovation. As a professor at Harvard, he developed a head-mounted display inside a helmet to project an immersive 3-D graphics environment. The movements of the wearer's eyes or bodies were tracked and the perspective of the image would make corresponding changes—in short, it was the first virtual reality display (see Figure 5.16).

At the University of Utah and at a company he co-founded with Dave Evans, Sutherland continued his research in computer graphics. This research helped lay the foundation for the simulators used to train pilots, as well as 3-D computer modeling. Their company's hardware and software systems were among the first graphics systems made available to the public. Both men extended their influence even further as teachers. As discussed in Chapter 5, their students at the University of Utah would make many of the most important contributions to 3-D modeling and animation.

In the 1970s, he joined the faculty at the California Institute of Technology and shifted his research and teaching away from graphics to integrated circuit design—helping to create the foundation for the modern computer chip industry and Silicon Valley. In the 1980s, he formed a new company which was later merged with Sun Microsystems. Today, he is exploring new technologies as a Sun Fellow, vice-president, and as a self-described "engineer, entrepreneur, capitalist, professor." ■

Basic Concepts and Tools

Vector illustration or *object-oriented* software utilizes a very different approach to image-making compared to bitmap software like digital painting or image editing. A simple explanation of the difference is that vector drawing is geometry based, while the other two are pixel based. Images are made up of geometric descriptions of points, lines, and shapes and their relative positions, rather than a large collection of pixels.

Every line and shape is created by placing endpoints. The software then calculates the *path* or connection between the points, creating forms that are always sharp and clear. They will be mathematically perfect, because their nature is geometric. That's why type in vector programs is always crisper and cleaner than in bitmap ones (see Figure 9.2). This makes illustration programs excellent choices for logos and other creative typography, as well as line art.

All forms are built with paths composed of anchor points and the lines between them (see Figure 9.3). Since outlines of shapes are created by points and the lines between them, rather than many pixels, the results are typically smooth and geometrical.

While this mathematical approach can put off many artists, it also means you can have a remarkable amount of control over an image. Placement is precise and editing is specific.

Another benefit of this form of imaging is that when images are resized, there is no change in the clarity of the forms. No matter how much vector images are enlarged, their edges will remain smooth and distinct, because the change is made mathematically. This is why they are also known as *resolution-independent graphics*. You can even re-scale an image many times, either larger or smaller (and back again), and it will not suffer from the blurring or "the jaggies" common to overenlarged bitmapped images.

Resolution independence also means that whether a vector object is seen on a high-end 21″ monitor or a Palm Pilot's 5″ one, it remains smooth and clear. Another benefit of the mathematical approach to image-making is that elements can also be rotated, distorted, and recolored quickly.

Perhaps the most exciting difference for those who normally work in imaging or painting software is the difference in file sizes. Unlike a bitmapped image, a vector file does not need to include information on every pixel on the screen. A vector file is composed of equations storing data on placement, size, color, and width; therefore, much less information is stored. File sizes in vector art, therefore, are considerably smaller than bitmapped images, sometimes astonishingly so. It is not unusual for a vector drawing to be one-tenth the size of a comparable image created with pixels.

The Workplace

On first look, the workplace of vector drawing and illustration programs resembles those in other digital media software. The basic commands are retained, as well as the motif of menus, toolboxes, palettes, and windows. As

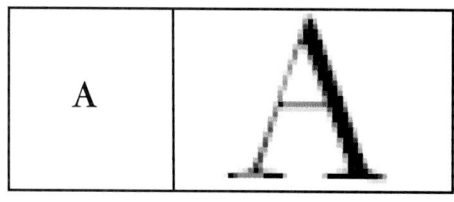

Bitmap type enlarged

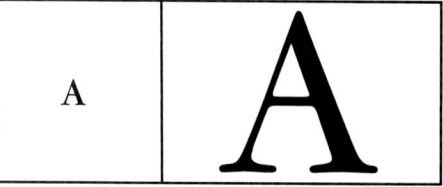

Vector type enlarged

■ **Figure 9.2**

Type created in vector programs retains its sharpness and clarity, even when enlarged significantly.

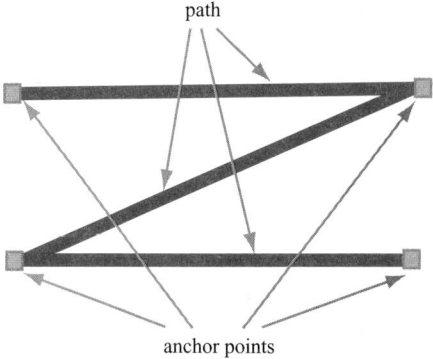

■ **Figure 9.3**

Vector drawings are made of anchor points and the paths between them.

in bitmap painting, the canvas or drawing area is generally kept at the center, with the toolboxes and palettes in the working space surrounding it (see Figure 9.4). Usually, the canvas will have blue, nonprinting guides near the edges that show what part of the page is in the printable area.

A closer look at the toolbox will reveal the more unique aspects of vector drawing and illustration. Some drawing tools will be unfamiliar; there are more shape tools than in bitmap software, and often two selection arrows. Beyond the toolbox, there is a window with precise x-, y-, and z-axis locations and a menu called "Object."

Path, Stroke, and Fill

The vocabulary of vector graphics contains terms that are distinctly different from those that describe bitmapped images. As previously mentioned, all vector forms are made up of paths, the connection between two points. There are two kinds of paths: *open* and *closed*. Open paths have endpoints that are not connected. A line, whether it is curved or straight, is an example of an open path. Closed paths begin and end at the same point and describe a shape. A rectangle or circle are examples of closed paths (see Figure 9.5). More complex forms can be made from connecting a collection of paths.

In vector drawing, shapes are made of *strokes* and *fills*. The stroke is the linear portion of the path and its characteristics. In an open path, it is the line itself. In a closed path, it is the outline around a shape. A line or outline's width, color, and style are all part of its stroke. For example, a stroke might be a violet dotted line, four points wide. Most illustration programs include a variety of stroke styles, from a simple line to snowflakes. A collection of arrowheads and tails can be applied to a stroke as well.

The fill is applied to the open area inside a closed path. A fill might be a color, gradient, or pattern. While an outline is necessary for any closed shape, a fill can appear to stand alone without an apparent outline. By setting the color of its stroke to "none," the outline, although still there, will become invisible. A sphere composed of only a smooth radial gradient could be created this way. Most illustration programs also include a variety of custom patterns to use as fills, from checkerboard patterns to blades of grass.

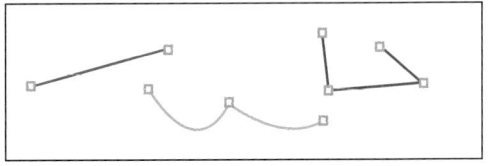

Open paths

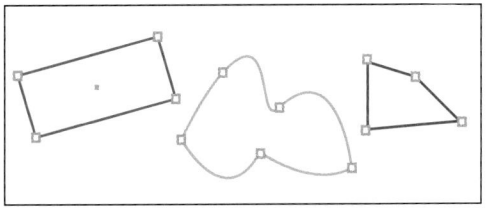

Closed paths

■ **Figure 9.5**
Open and closed paths.

Creating Simple Shapes

While any shape can be drawn by placing points (see "Drawing with the Pen Tool" later in this chapter), vector illustration software includes tools for basic, common forms to simplify the process. These are a good place to start when first exploring an illustration program. On the toolbar, you will find rectangle, ellipse, polygon, spiral, and star tools. These shapes are made by clicking on the drawing area and dragging until they reach the desired size. Combined with a keystroke, you can *constrain* (force) a rectangle to be a square or an ellipse to be a circle. By opening a special window, you can modify more complex shapes like polygons, spirals, and stars. For example, you can select the number of sides to a polygon or the number of points on a star (see Figure 9.6).

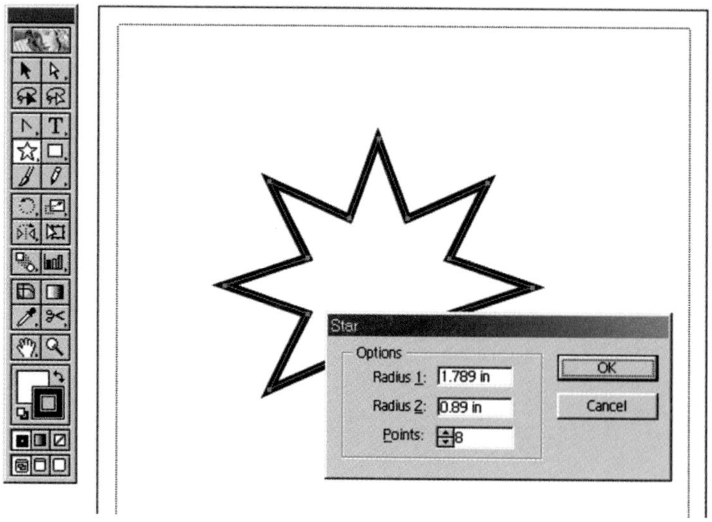

Selecting and Transforming Shapes

Of all the digital media, vector illustration is perhaps the most dependent on the process of selection and modification. Because of this, vector programs contain both standard and special selection tools. The basic selection arrow operates very much as it does in most digital media software. After selecting an object, you can move or manipulate it in many ways, either through commands in the menu or with special transformation tools in the toolbar. Among the many transformations possible are resizing or scaling, rotating, stretching, and skewing.

As in most digital media programs, multiple objects can be selected by holding down the shift key while clicking on them. Another common approach is to use the arrow to draw a marquee box over two or more objects. Once several objects are selected, they can be moved as a temporary group. To make a group permanent, choose the group command from the appropriate menu.

Objects can also be selected in a freehand way by the lasso tool. In some programs, simply by drawing a selection over part of one or more paths, each entire path is selected. In others, the lasso tool can simply select parts of an object or path.

The *direct selection* tool (usually displayed as a white arrow) is designed specifically for selecting parts of a path and individual anchor points. One of the most important editing tools in illustration software, it is used for making precise modifications to open and closed paths. With it, you can reshape any form by selecting its individual parts (see Figure 9.7).

After clicking on a straight line or edge, its anchor points and segment will be selected, visible, and ready for modification. By selecting just one of a straight line's anchor points, you can reposition the point and reshape the form (for example, skewing one side of a rectangle). Any path can be split with the scissor or knife tool by clicking in its middle. The knife tool can also be used to cut curves through closed paths, making two new closed paths. By pulling on one of the parts with the direct selection tool, you can separate the two paths.

Editing Curves

It is after clicking on a curve with the direct selection tool that vector graphics's most unique (and often frustrating for new users) aspects are revealed. Along with a curve's anchor points, its *direction lines* are made

Figure 9.6
Star modification window.

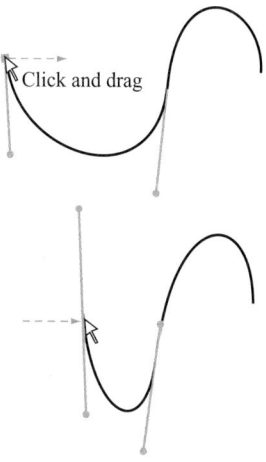

Click and drag

Figure 9.7
Direct selection in action.

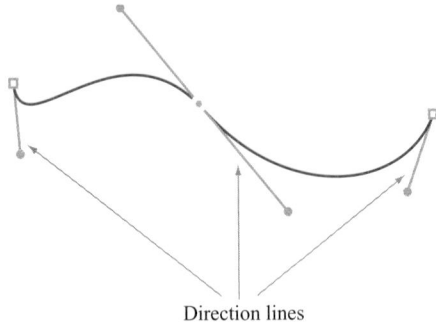

■ Figure 9.8

Direction lines of a curve.

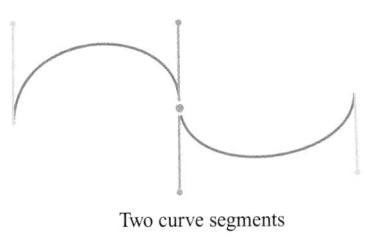

Two curve segments

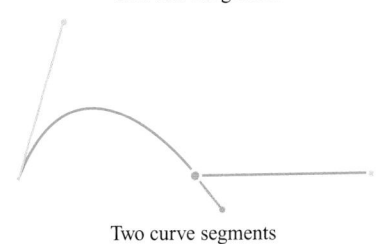

Two curve segments

■ Figure 9.9

Direction lines for curved and
straight segments.

visible (see Figure 9.8). As with a straight line, the direct selection tool can simply reshape a form by moving individual anchor points. However, much more comprehensive and complex changes to curves are possible when you modify the direction lines.

Direction lines are connected to each of a curve's two anchor points. These lines control a curve's height and slope. An anchor point between two curved segments will have two going off in two directions. Anchor points located where a curve and a straight segment meet have only one direction line. At the end of each direction line is a small control point, which can be clicked on and dragged to edit a curve (see Figure 9.9).

As you click and drag on a control point, the curve will quickly reshape, so it is best to move slowly. If you drag the control point further away from the anchor point, the direction line will get longer and the curve will bulge more and more. If the direction line connected to the anchor point at the other end of the curve is shorter than the one you just edited, the curve will lean toward the higher direction line (see Figure 9.10). If both direction lines are equal in height and placed symmetrically, the curve will be uniform and balanced. By dragging a direction line away from the curve at an angle, you can increase the lean of a curve in one direction.

Even with illustrations, it is not easy to describe how dragging a direction line's control point redraws a curve. It is best to experiment in order to become familiar with how to edit vector curves.

Working with Type

Illustration software is ideal for handling type. Unlike bitmapped type forms, type created with vectors will remain crisp and sharp even after being rescaled and manipulated many times. In addition, the type tools in vector illustration programs are the most sophisticated of all the digital media. In fact, for short documents, like an ad or brochure, many designers prefer them to layout and design software. (A longer document, like a book, does require a layout program's specialized page handling tools.)

Because you are working in a vector program, type can, of course, be rescaled, skewed, and rotated easily. But the strength of illustration software in handling type goes far beyond this. In other programs, to go beyond simple horizontal text boxes and layout type in an imaginative way, you have to

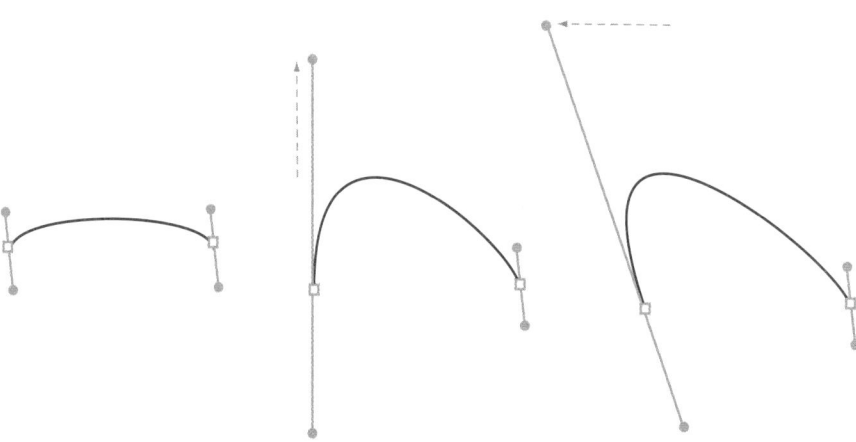

■ Figure 9.10

Effects on curves when direction
lines are modified.

cut and paste letters and experiment with spacing keys. In vector software, type can be placed vertically, along curving paths, and inside any shape by simply clicking on a special tool in the toolbar. These paths and shapes are editable with the direct selection tool. You can even slide type along a path to reposition it.

Along with these specialized tools are the standard page layout ones: kerning (the spacing between two letters), leading (the spacing between lines of text), and tracking (the spacing between groups of letters). Text can be wrapped around graphics or scaled as a group. These are the tools that allow many designers to forgo the use of desktop publishing software on many projects.

By converting type to outlines, the forms of individual letters can be modified. As in other programs, this converts the type to shapes, which means one loses the ability to edit them as type. However, because they remain vector forms, the vector program's sophisticated and precise editing tools can be used to manipulate their curves and outlines. When complete, the transformations will retain a clarity and geometrical nature that is superior to those in bitmapped ones. This is why designers prefer illustration software for creating logos (see Figure 9.11).

Today, some of the more powerful image-editing and painting programs include vector typography tools. Still, the dedicated vector illustration

■ **Figure 9.11**

Imaginative logos created by Leslie Cabarga with illustration software.

software packages remain the designer's choice for the ultimate clarity of type, along with the speed and full range of capabilities in manipulating typography.

Painting and Color

Color can be applied to a vector object's stroke and fill after the object is selected. In most illustration programs, there are a variety of ways to choose colors similar to those in bitmap programs. There are panels where you can mix colors. The eyedropper tool can select a color instantly from any place already in your picture (and sometimes, if a window from another program can be seen, even from pictures in other programs). There is also a panel with a collection of color swatches. This assortment of standard colors can be supplemented with selections from color libraries, like Pantone, or with new ones that you create. As in layout and design software, tints of any color can be made by adjusting the percentage of a color.

New colors can be mixed by any of the standard digital media approaches: CMYK, RGB, or HLS (see Chapter 7 for an explanation of these color models). Whatever color model you choose, you can either adjust a color's components with sliders (for example, ones for red, green, and blue) or by simply picking a color by clicking in a circle or rectangle filled with the wide spectrum of colors and values. After a new color is created, it can be added to the swatches panel and even given a unique name (like "nacho yellow").

Drawing with the Pen Tool

As powerful as the many tools included in a vector illustration program may be, the heart of the program will always be the pen tool (sometimes called the Bézier tool). Drawing with the pen is the essence of vector graphics, but also its most challenging skill to master. The precise control you have when creating paths and editing them are beyond any of the alternative line and shape creation tools found in other software. This may be why more and more other kinds of digital media programs are now including the pen tool. Still, because of the way lines are generated and then edited, it takes most artists and designers some practice to become comfortable with using it.

Clicking down and placing one endpoint, moving the mouse, and then clicking down again will create a simple straight line. The path must then be ended or the pen tool will automatically connect a new line to the old one when you begin using it again. Many beginners find this difficult to remember and end up with unexpected results (often resembling a tangle of hairs). One way to end a path is to connect it up to its beginning—making a closed path. Open paths are ended by either clicking on the pen tool's button in the toolbar or by deselecting the path. You can always continue an open path later by clicking on an endpoint with the pen tool and drawing.

Vector curves are also called Bézier curves. To create them, click down with the pen tool to place a starting point and drag to make it the first curve

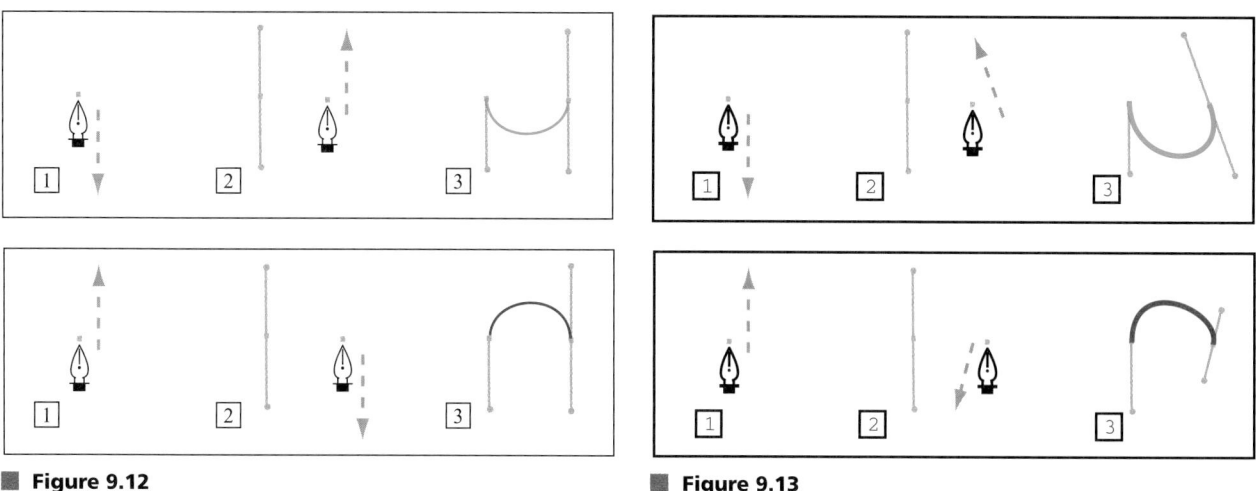

Figure 9.12
Drawing a simple curve with the pen tool.

Figure 9.13
The effect of different dragging movements with the pen tool on curves.

anchor point. The first click places the point, while the drag draws its attached direction line or handle. The curve will not become visible until you place the second curve anchor point (again by clicking and dragging). The direction in which you drag will determine two things—if the curve will be upward or downward and the angle of its slope (see Figures 9.12 and 9.13). How far you drag before releasing the mouse button will determine the height of the curve. As with all lines made with the pen tool, the path will continue to be added to until you decide to end it.

As discussed earlier, once you've created curves, you can reshape them with the direct selection arrow. You can drag anchor points or the handles at the end of direction lines. For example, by changing the angle of a direction line, you can increase its inward curve. When a curve becomes too complex, it can be simplified by deleting some of its points. Special pen tools are used to delete or add points in most software.

As you draw a line, the pen tool creates two kinds of anchor points. *Smooth points* are for drawing continuous curves, as in rolling hills. *Corner points* are where the direction of a curve changes, as in a collection of waves (see Figure 9.14). You can also convert smooth points (points within continuous curves) to corner points with a special tool or the pen tool and a keystroke. This will change the direction of the next curve to make it the opposite of the earlier one (for example, upward to downward).

smooth points

corner points

Figure 9.14
Curves with smooth and corner points.

It will take a while to feel comfortable using the pen tool. Dragging and clicking to make curving paths is not like drawing with a pencil. If you are using a mouse, rather than a digitizing tablet, it's easy to make a less-than-smooth movement and create a new point accidentally. But the hours of practice will be time well spent. There is no better tool to create smooth, curving forms. And once you've mastered the pen tool in a vector illustration program, you will be able to use it in any software package that includes it, even bitmap ones.

Brushes

The more powerful illustration programs have evolved over the years to include more tools that imitate natural media. A variety of brushes from the painterly to the calligraphic can create more "artistic" effects but retain the benefits of the vector format. Because of the underlying geometry, even with brushes that splatter, results tend to be less rough edged and smoother—helping to create a more polished look. And of course, file sizes remain small.

Patterns and Gradients

In addition to colors, vector objects, including type, can be filled with patterns and gradients. A selection of standard patterns can be found in the swatch palette. New ones can also be created, which can later be saved to and named in the swatch palette.

Any of the standard patterns can be modified and then applied as a new fill. In the fill panel, you can scale the size of the pattern, change its colors, vary the angle, or set it to tile. Some illustration programs allow you to create a pattern from scratch. You simply draw the shapes you would like to use as a pattern, fit a rectangle around them, and either save it as a pattern in the appropriate menu or just drag it into the swatches palette.

In the gradient panel, you can either redesign preset gradients to transform them or make entirely new ones. Basic variations include choosing between the two categories of gradients (linear and radial) and adjusting the angle of any gradient. Simple gradients are created by selecting two colors for either end of a linear gradient or for the center and circular edge of a radial one. The program immediately calculates the smooth color transition between the two colors. By adding more colors and adjusting their relative positions, more complex multicolor gradients can be created.

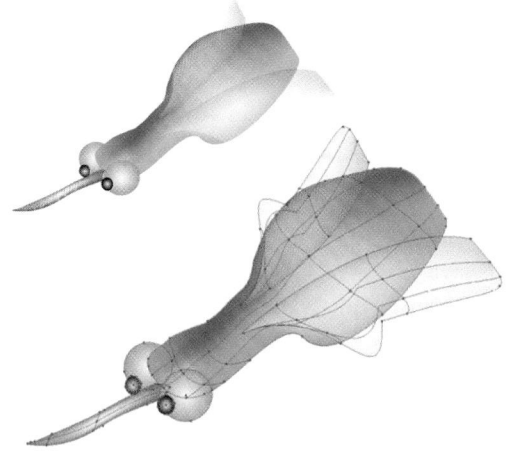

■ **Figure 9.15**
The gradient mesh: hidden wireframe and wireframe views.

Gradient Meshes

Gradient meshes are a unique feature of Adobe Illustrator, which, by smoothly combining multicolored gradients, allow you to create a 3-D look for your forms. A mesh looks like a net applied over your object (see Figure 9.15). Any object can be converted to a mesh one through the object menu or by selecting the gradient mesh tool from the toolbar and clicking on the form. Whatever color is current is then combined with the object's original color to form a gradient across it. To add an additional color to the gradient mesh, simply choose one and click on another spot in the object. Simultaneously with adding the color, new mesh lines appear. The more colors you add, the more mesh lines that will crisscross the form.

With the direct selection tool, you can grab mesh points at the intersection of each mesh line and drag them to reshape the mesh and its gradients. Mesh points, like anchor points, have direction lines that can also be used to reshape the curves of the mesh. By using lighter and darker colors carefully and manipulating the lines of a mesh, you can use gradient meshes almost like a sculptor. For example, an apple can be modeled into a pepper by adding colors and reshaping the curving mesh lines.

Layers and Stacking

Like many other digital media programs, most vector illustration software allows you to divide an image into layers, a collection of transparent and independent overlays. Layers can be hidden or locked, added, deleted, and merged. The locking function is particularly useful when working with the pen tool. Because of its propensity for adding unwanted points or segments, it is wise to lock all but the layer you are working on.

You can rearrange the position of the layer itself just by clicking and dragging it to a new position in the layer menu. In addition, individual objects on a layer are stacked as they are created. They can be rearranged with commands like "bring forward" or "send to back."

The most valuable attribute of layers is their independence. As in bitmap programs, special effects and other transformations can be applied to the forms on just one layer without affecting objects on any other one.

Combining Forms to Make Complex Shapes

One of the special features in vector illustration programs is their ability to make a *compound path;* a new, more complex shape made from two or more overlapping shapes. A whole new object can be made from a group of closed paths in a variety of ways (see Box 9.2). They can be combined or *united* and become one form sharing the same overall outline. On the other hand, the new form could be made where the forms *intersect* only, eliminating all other parts. *Exclude* does just the opposite, eliminating only the areas where the shapes overlap (see Figure 9.16).

Other possible transformations of a group of shapes vary depending on the particular program. *Merge* will combine only the overlapping shapes that share the same fill color. *Crop* removes any parts below the top shape. *Punch* or *minus front* cuts away the topmost shape from the group. The command *divide* increases the number of sections by splitting the shapes into smaller ones wherever they overlap.

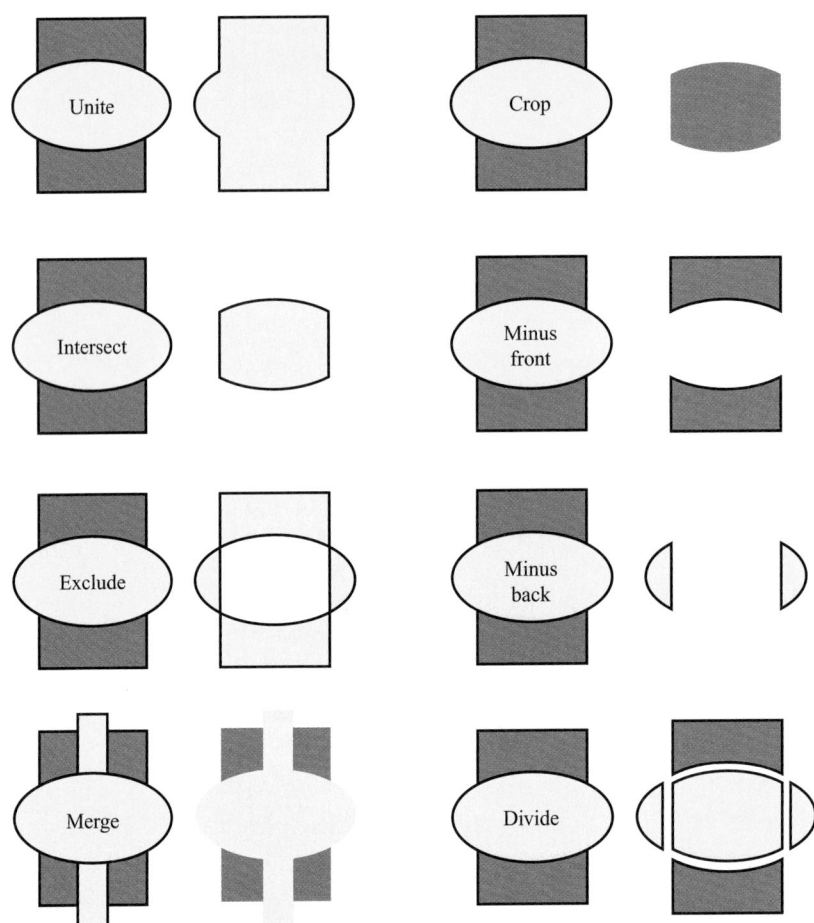

■ Figure 9.16
Compound path effects.

BOX 9.2

Making a gear with compound paths

While the effect of compound path commands may be difficult to visualize for the beginner, they are well worth exploring. Applied with creativity, they can save you a great deal of time in drawing complex forms. For example, to create a simple gear with the pen tool could mean hours spent trying to get the teeth along its rim even. However, if you plan with the punch or minus front command in mind, the process is much simpler. First, make a filled circle, and then place a smaller circle in the center. Next, create an even arrangement of small ellipses passing over the circle's outer edge. Finally, give the transformation command, and all that was in front of the circle will vanish as it removes the parts of the original circle it overlapped like a cookie cutter (see Figure 9.17). ■

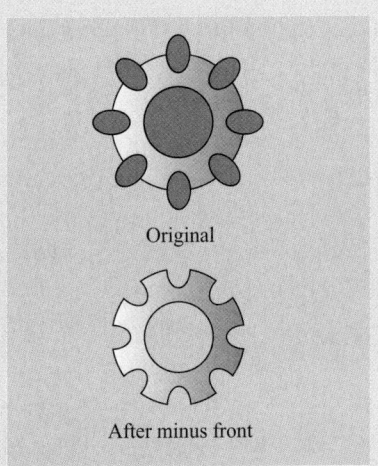

Original

After minus front

■ Figure 9.17
Making a gear using *minus front*.

Printing

When you are ready to print your image, you'll generally be pleased to see how quickly a file in vector format prints. However, there are some illustration techniques that can slow down the process. Among them are using excessive patterns, gradients, complex paths, or special effects. Gradient meshes and other gradient blends are known culprits for increasing file size and slowing the printing process. Before you print an image, it makes sense to look closely at it and make sure which of these elements are truly necessary and whether some simplification will improve the image.

Because printers print in dots, all vector images have to be translated in the process of printing. As might be expected, the higher the resolution of the printer, the smoother the ultimate appearance of the vector graphics. High-resolution PostScript printers are generally the best choice for printing vector images. It is a page description language that is especially designed for the graphics professional and includes support for many of the special effects used by digital illustrators.

If your final image is to be printed by a service bureau or professional printer, as with layout-and-design programs, you can also produce color separations (a separate page for each color plate) or have your image print in specific lines per inch settings. You should rely on a printing professional to tell you what settings should be used.

Vector Illustration and the Web

Because vector images are resolution independent and are usually much smaller than their bitmapped counterparts, they should be ideal choices for images on web pages. Unfortunately, the native formats of vector programs are not the standard ones universally understood by Web browsers. Therefore, it is necessary to export the vector images into other formats.

Luckily, most vector software makes it easy to export images in formats that work well on Web pages and keep file sizes small. In fact, some have a special "Save for Web" choice under the file menu. Exporting in the GIF format will make the most sense if your image has many flat colored areas and sharp edges (as many vector images do) or type. If you have used many gradients and blends in your image, saving it as JPEG will produce more faithful results. While the flat colored areas and edges may blur a bit, JPEG is a format designed to display the continuous tones of gradients and photographic images. Whether you choose GIF or JPEG, most software today includes tools to optimize an image file; in other words, reduce its size for faster downloading. Chapter 13 discusses how to optimize your images for the Web.

If, instead of one image, you want viewers to see one or more pages that you have designed in your illustration program, you can export the pages as a PDF file. This will retain your layout just as you originally designed it. However, your audience will need to use the Acrobat Reader, which is free and easily downloaded, to see these files. Most current browsers will support the Reader inside the browser itself.

Another way vector illustration is used on the Web is for making elements for vector animation programs like Macromedia's Flash (see Chapter 10). This approach makes sense particularly when you want to create complex backgrounds or forms that are more easily created with the sophisticated drawing tools of an illustration program. To make the process even easier, most illustration programs now include a module to export images in vector animation software's native format.

CONCLUSION

Artists and designers utilize vector illustration in many ways. Illustrations can be a fine art image, a page design for an ad, a whole brochure, or just one piece of a bigger project, such as elements for a layout, animation, or Web page. While some of the tools are not very intuitive and can be frustrating to learn, when your conception requires creating strong, colorful, and graphic imagery with precise control or complex geometric forms, digital illustration has few competitors. Combine that with its flexibility in handling typography and it is easy to see why some artists and designers use this kind of software exclusively.

Bitmap painting, however, puts tools in your hand that will feel natural and enable you to create images that have the texture and complexity of traditional paintings. Combined with a digitizing tablet, it will respond to subtle nuances of pressure and angle. For creating images with a hand-drawn look, painting software has few competitors.

Nevertheless, there are many artists who have built very successful careers by using only image-editing software. The strengths of image-editing include a whole range of ways to adjust color, value, and opacity, utilize filters, and, of course, edit and combine photographic images imaginatively. It has been for many years the most popular of all the digital media.

You may wonder which kind of program to choose for 2-D imagery. In some ways, this is the wrong question to ask. For most artists the real issue is to understand the nature of the project they are working on and the strengths and weaknesses of each kind of software. Digital artists who work in only one program tend to find themselves spending a lot of time trying to find a way to make the program do what it wasn't designed to do. While the most powerful programs now include tools from other types of programs, these added tools are limited versions of more sophisticated ones. When you know the real strengths of each kind of digital media program and use them intelligently, you will spend less time trying to work around a problem and more time simply solving it. Just like building a house, nothing can replace having the best tools at hand.

Projects: Vector Drawing and Illustration

1 *Design a logo for a chain of stationery stores that are located in malls. You may use black and white and one other color. The logo should include a strong graphic symbol and dramatic typography to make sure the store is easily identifiable at a distance and can attract customers in the visual competition for attention inside a crowded mall. Scale the symbol and typography in various sizes for the various purposes of a logo (e.g., signage, letterhead, clothing, and so on) and label them.*

2 *Design a 14" × 7" menu cover for an imaginary restaurant that serves your favorite food. Choose a name for the restaurant and create a sense of its ambiance by your style of drawing and choice of type. Include patterns in your design.*

3 *Create a full color, full page (8" × 10") illustration for a magazine article called "Helping Grandma and Grandpa Use Their First Computer." Your illustration should express the confusion that some senior citizens feel when first confronted with computing.*

2-D Animation: Up and Running

Introduction

Animation is a magical process that has enchanted generations of audiences around the world. Few are immune to the fascination of seeing drawings come alive and move. The illusion of animation depends on a visual phenomenon called *the persistence of vision*. Because we see images for a split-second longer than they are actually in front of us, a series of pictures drawn in sequence appear to be one continuous picture in motion. The illusion is powerful. Even the knowledge that we are seeing only a collection of quickly changing drawings cannot prevent us from feeling that what we are seeing is real.

Today, we are in the midst of an animation renaissance, with digital techniques leading the way. Commercials, cartoons, videos, full-length films, multimedia CDs and DVDs, websites, and video games all make extensive use of digital animation. Beyond the entertainment industry, animations are being used to enhance corporate presentations, as evidence in court (for example, recreations of car accidents), and for scientific visualizations.

In this chapter, we will enter the exciting world of animation. "World" is not an overstatement because once you've added the element of time to 2-D art, there is a whole new vocabulary to learn and a different way of seeing. For many experienced 2-D artists and designers, shifting to this new world is quite a challenge. Unlike other 2-D art forms, it doesn't make much sense to carefully build a single image for days or months since images will fly by at ten a second or faster. Animation requires a different approach and philosophy. It even has its own laws of physics. As disconcerting as these differences may be at first, animation's unique methods and principles are well worth studying, since your art truly comes to life when you make pictures that move.

Figure 10.1

Scenes from one of Thomas Edison's first movies, *The Enchanted Drawing*, 1900.

In the Beginning

Our fascination with animation has a long history. It was not long after Thomas Edison's invention of motion pictures that animation made its debut (see Figure 10.1). His *The Enchanted Drawing* from 1900 combines both live action and animation. In it, a gentleman makes a drawing of a man's head on an easel, which appears to come alive. When the artist pulls the man's hat out of the drawing and puts it on himself, the drawing starts to frown. When he returns the hat, the face smiles again. Being given a cigar increases the drawing's pleasure; he appears to puff contentedly.

Even before the first films, however, the magic of animated pictures had already fascinated both young and old. In the nineteenth century, toys that created animated effects were popular. The *thaumatrope* is the earliest known toy that played with persistence of vision. It was a round disk with different pictures on each side. A child would hold both ends of a string threaded through it with both hands and spin the disk as fast as he or she could. The thaumatrope's most famous subject was a bird on one side and a cage on the other. When twirled quickly, the pictures would blend visually and the bird would magically appear to be in the cage.

The *zoetrope* (see Figure 10.2) created a more truly animated effect. The toy was an open metal cylinder with evenly spaced slits, which rested on a pedestal. To make it work, a strip of paper with drawings was placed inside and the cylinder was rapidly spun. By looking through the slits as they sped around, a child could see the drawings come to life by moving in sequence. Children could buy drawing strips to put in their zoetropes with many different subjects, from elephants to Indians, at toy shops all over Europe.

Figure 10.2

Zoetrope.

As quaint as the thaumatrope and zoetrope seem today, one antique animated toy continues to enchant—the hand-drawn flipbook. With one drawing quickly superimposed on the next, it is a simple and low-cost method to animate that even a child can create. Yet it remains an excellent introduction to the basic principles of creating animation.

Pioneers of Traditional Animation

Winsor McKay

Seeing one of his son's flipbooks inspired Winsor McKay to make what he called "modern cartoon movies." In the early 1900s, McKay was already one of America's favorite cartoonists. His most famous comic strip, "Little Nemo in Slumberland," depicted the fantastic dreams of a little boy. Based on his son, the scenes were beautifully drawn hallucinations, like Nemo sliding down a never-ending bannister in a mansion that ultimately flings him off into outer space, or Nemo finding himself in a world where everyone is made of glass. In the last panel, the little boy always woke up.

McKay's *Gertie the Dinosaur* (see Figure 10.3) was one of the most influential films in the history of animation. In the film, a combination of live action and animation, McKay is with a group of friends at a natural history museum and bets that he can make a dinosaur come alive. Six months later, they reconvene at a gentleman's dinner and McKay begins sketching on a pad on the wall. Gertie sticks her head out of a cave and then emerges as a huge brontosaurus. More a gigantic dog than fearsome creature, she responds to McKay's commands (but is not always well behaved).

First completed in 1914 after two years of work, McKay created sixteen drawings for every second of animation, matching the film speed of the era. In 1916, he later added the live-action segments mentioned above plus one showing the animation process. In a slapstick moment, an assistant falls down the stairs as a huge stack of drawings goes flying in all directions.

McKay took the first version, which only included the animated sequence with Gertie, on a vaudeville tour around the country. Standing on the stage next to the screen with a whip, like a lion tamer in a suit, he'd "attempt" to control the dinosaur's actions. The crowning moment of his act was when Gertie would stick her head down and McKay appeared to get on it and was carried into the film.

It was the sight of Gertie in vaudeville shows that inspired many of the pioneers of animation. Among those whose lives were changed by seeing a dinosaur come to life were Otto Messmer and Pat Sullivan, the creators of Felix the Cat; Max and Dave Fleischer, the creators of Betty Boop and Popeye; and Walter Lantz, the creator of Woody Woodpecker.

Otto Messmer

By the 1920s, cartoons had already become a regular part of an afternoon spent at the motion pictures. The king of cartoons was Felix the Cat (see Figure 10.4), a mischievous creature whose fantastic silent film adventures were more like Little Nemo than his later, tamer incarnation on television. For example, in one cartoon Felix travels to Mars by shooting an arrow that is attached to his waist with a rope and then wins the presidency by convincing all cats to join him there for a better life. A product of Otto Messmer's fertile visual imagination, Felix might be grabbed by a robot, squished into a nail, and hammered into the ground one moment, and then take off his tail and use it as a cane in another. Produced at the Pat Sullivan Studios, he was the first animated character to have marketed merchandise. There were Felix toys,

handkerchiefs, and china. Felix even had popular songs and classical music written about him.

Many of the basic techniques of early animation can be seen in the first Felix silents. Messmer designed Felix to have a clear, strong silhouette, which made his actions easily understood. Felix's arms and legs were completely flexible—like rubber hoses. In fact, his whole universe sometimes seemed as if it was made of rubber; most objects stretched as they move and squashed when they banged into something else. Messmer also made constant use of repeated actions or *cycles*, which saved him time when animating. One character bicycling would usually be joined by hundreds of identical bicyclists; a jumping and cheering cat would be repeated to form a crowd.

The Fleischer Brothers

As with Messmer, the animated films of Max and Dave Fleischer emphasized visual imagination more than the story (see Figure 10.5). To this day, very few animators have ever exploited the imaginative possibilities of the medium more fully. Their first successes utilized an original Fleischer invention, the *rotoscope* (see page 249). Dave was photographed moving while in a black clown suit against a white sheet. After tracing the frames onto paper, his drawn silhouette was transformed into the cartoon character Koko the Clown. Koko starred in a series of shorts called *Out of the Inkwell* beginning in 1919. Each short began as a live action film, with Max working at his drawing table. Koko would climb out of the inkwell and find ways to torture Max.

Another innovation of the Fleischers was the *Car-tunes* series, which put the words of popular music on the screen and encouraged the audience to sing along by following the bouncing ball. However, it was the entrance of a floppy-eared female dog with a suggestive dance style into a cartoon with Koko and a male dog named Bimbo that led to the greatest Fleischer success.

■ **Figure 10.5**

Max and Dave Fleischer's Koko the Clown.

With the sweet voice of Mae Questel, a singer and comedienne, she captured the audience's imagination. The Fleischers transformed the floppy-eared dog into Betty Boop, a 1920s flapper in a revealing dress and visible garter. Her adventures rarely made sense, but were opportunities for the Fleischers to demonstrate their extraordinarily creative approach to animation. Logic was not important and anything could happen. One moment in their version of *Snow White*, a masterpiece of visual imagination, exemplifies the richness of their work. After the jealous stepmother yells, "Off with her head," she points at Snow White (played by Betty Boop), and to make the point, one of her fingers curls around, becomes saw-edged, and cuts off her own thumb.

Among the many animators influenced by the Fleischers' approach is John Kricfalusi, the creator of *Ren and Stimpy*, who said their films "best illustrate the purest essence of what cartoons are about."

Walt Disney

Kricfalusi also sees the emergence of Walt Disney as the beginning of a sad decline of animation from its early wildly imaginative years. Nonetheless, there are millions who would disagree. Disney's name has become synonymous with cartoon animation, and his company's methods defined the standard process for animation production (see Figure 10.6).

Walt Disney created his first animation company, Laugh-O-Gram Films, in Kansas City during the early 1920s. He was always very conscious of the business aspect of cartoons, and early on planned his productions carefully so that the lowest possible number of drawings was required. In 1923, close to bankruptcy, he left for Hollywood with a one-way ticket and $50. There, Disney made a series of increasingly popular cartoons about a rabbit named Oswald. But in 1928, just as he was enjoying his first successes, Universal Pictures (the distributor of his films) took control of the rights to Oswald and hired away most of Disney's animators.

■ **Figure 10.6**
Walt Disney in 1930.

To recover from this disaster, Disney decided to create another character, which he copyrighted. It was a mouse, originally called "Mortimer." His wife didn't like the name and suggested the now world-famous name "Mickey." Designed by Ub Iwerks, one of the few animators who had stuck with Disney after the Universal fiasco, Mickey was a pleasant collection of simple circular shapes traced from quarters and half-dollars. For long shots, the animators used nickels and dimes.

Like Felix, Mickey was black and white with a strong silhouette. But Disney's overall approach to cartoons was fundamentally different. Even in his earliest films, Disney insisted that his staff tell a story. Unlike Messmer's and the Fleischers' cartoons, his characters inhabited a pleasant country environment. While Mickey could be mischievous, it was always just gentle fun.

The first two cartoons featuring Mickey Mouse didn't attract any distributors. The third, *Steamboat Willie*, like the others was initially released as a silent cartoon and was equally unsuccessful. But in 1928, with the arrival of sound in motion pictures, Disney decided to redo his previously silent film with sound, using a washboard, slide whistle, harmonica, and banged-on cans to test their idea. It cost $15,000 to add a soundtrack with professional musicians and his brother, Roy, the business manager, protested. Disney wrote to him and said, "I think this is Old Man opportunity rapping at our door. Let's not let the jingle of a few pennies drown out his knock."

The rerelease of *Steamboat Willie* was a landmark in cartoon history (see Figure 10.7). Adding synchronized sound to cartoons became the standard and was even called "Mickey Mousing." Reportedly, Max Fleischer and Pat Sullivan were unimpressed by Disney's new work, although they would soon be struggling to compete with him.

As the Disney Studios grew over the next decades, their understanding of animation principles evolved. The careful planning procedures that are the standard process today, with detailed storyboards, model sheets, and pencil tests, were Disney innovations (see Box 10.1). Different teams were responsible for different characters. He

■ **Figure 10.7**
Sketch from the storyboard for *Steamboat Willie*.

BOX 10.1

How traditional animation was made at the big studios

As anyone who has watched the credits after a full-length animated film knows, the production process in a professional studio is a huge enterprise. In filmed animation, twenty-four frames are used for every second of action. Tens of thousands of drawings are needed just for a typical seven-minute cartoon. Teamwork and coordination among many different staff members is essential for success. Since the 1920s, a basic structure for organizing work has evolved in the large studios, outlines which are still followed whether working digitally or not. An understanding of these approaches is also important because much of the vocabulary used by digital software refers to the older techniques.

After the concept, script, and storyboards (see pages 220–222) are approved, it is actually the soundtrack that comes next. Prepared from the script, the sounds and actions heard will be important inspirations to the animators designated to work on individual sequences.

Once the soundtrack is completed, a very detailed work schedule, sometimes called the *exposure sheet,* is made (see Figure 10.8). In this chart, every frame of the film and every piece of art is described in terms of the general action (such as "man walking in field"), detail of action ("five-frame cycle of walking"), if there are any special effects, and sound ("crunching with sound of airplane in distance"). *Tweeners* (also known as In betweeners) working from this schedule, the storyboard, model sheets (see page 222), and key poses created by the lead animator or director begin making pencil sketches to fill in the action on *onion skin* (semi-transparent) pages, which allows one to see earlier drawings placed over a light board. These are then given to the clean-up artists who correct lines and make sure the work of various animators conform to the director's model sheets. After the pencil sketches are cleaned up, they are photographed and made into a film called the *pencil test.*

Meanwhile, the backgrounds are created and will later be compared to the action (see Figure 10.9). Once the pencil tests are accepted, they are scanned and printed or photocopied to cels. In many studios, even today, painters then paint colors and shadows on the back of each cel. These painted cels are placed on top of the backgrounds and photographed, frame by frame.

The film is then carefully synchronized with the soundtrack. The director and film editor preview the film and make the final editing decisions. Copies of the film are made for distribution. After that, it is up to the publicity and marketing departments to bring the film to the public. ■

■ **Figure 10.8**

Exposure Sheet from Don Bluth's studio, the creator of *An American Tail* and other animated feature films.

■ **Figure 10.9**

Elaborate background scene from Disney's *Pinocchio*.

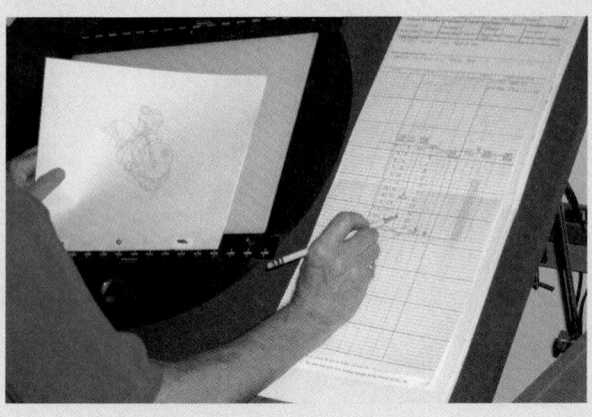

also made sure his company led in technology; for example, being the first to use a multiplane camera, which could vary the focus on different layers of a scene as it zoomed in. A tough taskmaster, Disney constantly pushed his animators to greater challenges. In order to ensure quality, he hired drawing instructors who worked with his staff at regular model sessions.

Disney's first full-length animated film, *Snow White and the Seven Dwarfs,* released in 1937 took nearly three years to complete. Known during those years as "Disney's Folly," it cost $1.5 million, an unheard of amount for a cartoon in the 1930s. What he aimed for was nothing less than art. In Technicolor with a fully orchestrated soundtrack, each scene was more complex and beautiful than any that had ever been seen on the screen. In the years since its release, it has earned more than $1 billion and will undoubtedly continue to earn profits for years to come.

Chuck Jones

Chuck Jones is the leading figure of the second generation of pioneer animators (see Figure 10.10). Jones grew up around Hollywood and, as a child, regularly peeked over a fence to see Charlie Chaplin making his movies. He worked for Ub Iwerks and Walter Lantz, and even had a short stint at Disney Studios. In the depths of the Great Depression, he was hired at Warner Brothers Studios to wash animation cels. He moved up to being a *tweener,* and then became a lead animator in 1938. Along with his older colleagues Tex Avery and Friz Freleng, Jones was the guiding spirit of the animation division of Warner Brothers known as "Termite Terrace," the home of Bugs Bunny, Daffy Duck, Elmer Fudd, and Porky Pig.

■ **Figure 10.10**
Chuck Jones.

In a long career at Warner Brothers, MGM, and as an independent director, Jones worked on over three hundred cartoons. He believed in the fundamental importance of each and every frame being carefully drawn and designed. The backgrounds of his cartoons were just as carefully planned as Disney's but far more modern and geometric, his characters more ridiculous and wittier. His original creations include Pepe LePew, Marvin the Martian, Wile E. Coyote, and Roadrunner. The winner of many Academy Awards, his most acclaimed cartoons include *What's Opera, Doc?* and *Duck Dodgers in the 24 1/2 Century.* His longer films from the late 1960s include *How the Grinch Stole Christmas* and *The Phantom Tollbooth.*

Tezuka and Anime

Anime (pronounced "annie-may") is the Japanese style of animation. Compared to cartoons in the United States, anime has much greater variety in subject matter. In fact, anime is enjoyed by all age groups in Japan, from children to adults.

The sources of anime go back to the nineteenth century artist Hokusai and what he called *manga.* Hokusai is best known for his woodcut prints, like "The Great Wave," which inspired the French Impressionists. His manga (meaning "easy, silly pictures") were sketchbooks (see Figure 10.11) that caricatured all sorts of activities in Japan, some real, some pure fantasy. For example, one page showed overweight men taking baths. Another imagined games

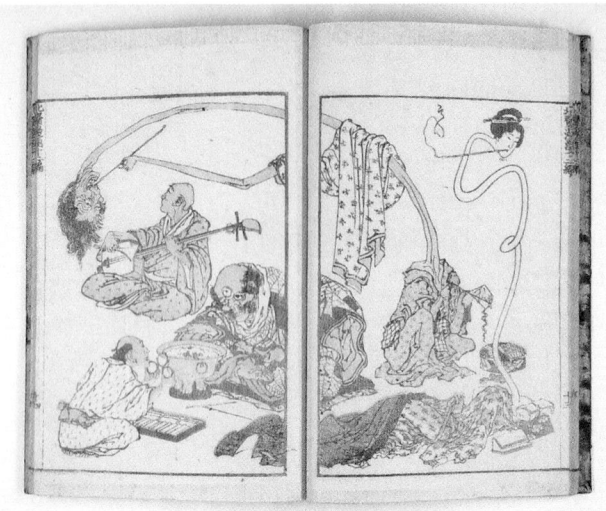

■ Figure 10.11

Two-page spread from Hokusai's manga.

■ Figure 10.12

Astroboy.

people with very long noses might play, like tossing rings from nose to nose.

In the twentieth century, manga came to mean comic books. Japanese comics were strongly influenced by those from the United States, particularly Walt Disney's. During World War II, manga were suppressed by the dictatorial regime, but in the war's aftermath they flourished as one of the few low-cost entertainments available in poverty-stricken Japan.

Anime's founding father was a former medical student, Tezuka Osamu, known in Japan as "the god of manga." He brought a more sophisticated, cinematic style to the manga, using close-ups and "camera" angles. He also expanded the subject matter. "The potential of manga was more than humor," Tezuka said. "Using the themes of tears, sorrow, anger, and hatred, I made stories that do not always have happy endings."

Ironically, he is most famous for his manga created for children, particularly *Tetsuwan Atomu* (Mighty Atom), a robot boy who fought crime (see Figure 10.12). In 1958, Tezuka founded his own animation company and turned Mighty Atom into an animated cartoon for television. In the 1960s, the robot boy came to the United States with another name—Astro Boy (the original name might have reminded Americans of Hiroshima). The anime industry had begun.

Tezuka's influence on anime is far reaching. In his cartoons all humans and animals have big, expressive eyes and simple, rounded features. One can see Tezuka's style in the faces of today's Sailor Moon and *Pokemon's* Ash Ketchum. The action in most anime reflects his method of using rapidly changing close-up stills rather than smooth animation to show a character's reaction. The success of his Astro Boy created an international interest in Japanese anime. In the 1960s, new programs came to the United States such as *Mach GoGoGo*, or *Speed Racer*. Another show, *Gigantor*, created the genre of giant robots controlled by humans, like the very popular *Gundam*.

Katsuhiro Otamo's 1988 landmark *Akira* brought anime in the style of the adult manga to an international audience. These animated stories had more complex emotions and a more sophisticated design. In them, convincing and fluid movement was less important than dramatic effects, details, and stylized forms. In the last decade, this approach has begun to influence many animators outside of Japan (for example, Peter Chung, the creator of the MTV series *Aeon Flux*).

Animation Goes Digital: John Lasseter and Pixar

New technologies have affected the shape of animation since its beginning. The arrival of sound added a new arena for the animator's imagination. The multiplane cameras in the 1930s led to new ways to create a sense of depth. In the 1960s, copier techniques, which used Xerox cameras to create cels, sped up the animation process and allowed a more hand-drawn look throughout.

Like many young people interested in animation in the early 1980s, John Lasseter began experimenting with computer animation, although his career already had an auspicious beginning. After an internship at Disney Studios, Lasseter was hired straight out of college in 1979, where he worked on *The Fox and the Hound,* among other films. Enthusiastic about the possibility of creating animation on a computer, but finding little enthusiasm at Disney, he left what many would have called a dream job in 1984.

■ **Figure 10.13**
Still from Pixar's *Luxo Jr.*

Lasseter joined the new computer graphics division of Lucasfilm, which focused on special effects for motion pictures like *Return of the Jedi.* The division was soon sold to Steve Jobs, one of the founders of Apple (see Chapter 5), and renamed Pixar. Jobs poured millions into his new company, allowing it to develop the latest technologies, among them *RenderMan,* still regarded as one of the finest photorealistic rendering software systems. In this fresh environment, and with the assistance of some of the best available digital tools, Lasseter created his own totally computer-animated short film.

Luxo Jr. (1986) (see Figure 10.13) was the story of a parent desk lamp, a child lamp, and an ill-fated bouncing ball. It became the first 3-D computer-animated film to be nominated for an Academy Award. Two years later, Lasseter's *Tin Toy,* the story of a metal drummer chased by a baby, brought home his first Oscar.

These successes led to the ironic situation of the once-disinterested Disney Studios hiring Pixar to develop their first full-length computer-animated film. Taking four years to complete, *Toy Story* became the highest-grossing film in 1995. A completely digital production, each character's design was the result of some of the most extraordinarily complex 3-D models ever created. For example, Woody, the toy cowboy, had more than a thousand control points. A room full of workstations, stacked like pizza boxes, handled the chore of rendering the complicated models, scenes, and action. *Toy Story* won a Special Achievement Academy Award in 1996.

While the technical achievement of Lasseter's films *is* impressive (Chapter 11 discusses the complex and specialized techniques of 3-D modeling and animation), underlying his great success is a mastery of traditional animation techniques. This is what gives them life. Lasseter's approach is the product of what is now a century long development in the art of animated films. All animators, whether traditional or digital, need to understand the basic principles and techniques of animation to be effective, in order to have success creating, as Thomas Edison did in 1900, enchanted drawings.

Traditional Animation Techniques and Production

Working in Time

One of the challenges visual artists face when planning animation is moving from carefully developing a single image to working on a series of images which may not be seen for more than a tenth of a second. Working in the fourth dimension, time, requires a very different approach. Over the decades, since the first hand-drawn film animations were created, a unique visual language has evolved with its own rules of design.

Animation's language and laws are known intuitively to anyone who has spent hours watching cartoons on television. Compare in one's mind a punch to the face in an action movie to one in an animated film. In one, a head jerks back sharply, sweat flying. In the other, the head flies back several feet, the neck stretches like a rubber-band, and the shape of the fist becomes imprinted on the victim's face. The normal rules of physics do not apply in an animation and, in fact, appear abnormal.

The "Natural" World of Animation

The first rule of animation is that it is an artificial world. The more naturalistic the forms, the more unnatural they will appear. This is why *exaggeration appears normal* in an animation. In the language of animation, action is communicated by overstatement. Winds are rarely gentle zephyrs; they bend trees. Animators use the technique of *squashing* to represent the power of an impact and also give a sense of an object's material. Therefore, when a rubber ball hits a wall, it squashes and expands as it hits a barrier (see Figure 10.14). A ping-pong ball wouldn't squash as much and would spring up quicker.

Sympathetic movement or *stretching* is utilized to better convey action, too. For instance, a fast-moving object will change its form to accentuate its path. A superhero will stretch out as she sweeps across the sky.

It is important to understand when one plans an animation that *reality is much too slow to remain interesting.* This is something all filmmakers know. While the pop artist, Andy Warhol, thought it would be an interesting statement to film twenty-four hours at the Empire State Building uncut and with one camera angle, a successful animator will only include the essential moments necessary to tell a story. Filmmakers know a character that is waiting a long time for a companion can convey that by checking his watch two or three times. The viewer does not have to wait twenty minutes. Successful animators utilize other conventions of film such as fade-outs, close-ups, and changing angles to hold the interest of the viewer.

Finally, remember that *animation is fundamentally a visual medium.* Whatever your story, it should be understandable simply from the images you create. While sound can make important contributions to your film (see Box 10.2 on page 223), it should never be the main focus. It should enrich the images. If you find yourself creating a great deal of dialog to explain your story, then animation might be the wrong medium for your project. Your animation should be a work of visual imagination.

■ **Figure 10.14**
Bouncing ball sequence.

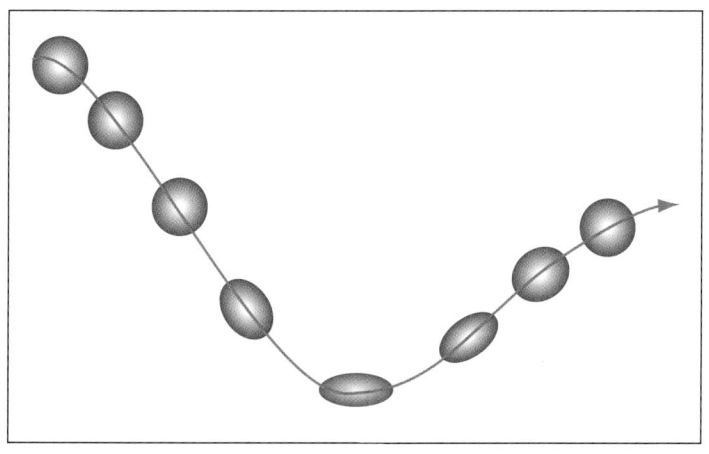

Cinematic Techniques

Understanding basic film techniques can enhance even the simplest animation. Over the past century, directors have developed a language for cinema that viewers have come to understand intuitively. Animators use these concepts, too. Effective use of these techniques provides variety for viewers and retains their interest.

Close-ups are among the most effective film techniques. A close-up not only adds variety, it also forces the audience to pay attention to what the director wants viewers to look at.

The earliest films followed the conventions of plays and did not use close-ups. Viewers watched the entire scene as if they were watching live theater. When the director focused on one character, that character was shown from head to toe. One of the first directors to use close-ups was D.W. Griffith, and they are reputed to have been terribly startling. Audiences screamed as if a character had just been decapitated. Charlie Chaplin was another early director who used close-ups. By focusing on his tramp's face, viewers were drawn into sympathy with his character and felt they understood what he was feeling.

Generally, new subjects are not first seen in close-up but whole, in what is called an *establishing shot*. The camera then *zooms in* or moves in closer. Zooming in intensifies the action or emotion of a scene while *zooming out* tends to have a calming effect. *Panning* is another form of camera movement, usually used at a distance from the main subjects (see Figure 10.15). It is a slow movement across a wide scene, which feels as if the viewer's head is turning with the camera.

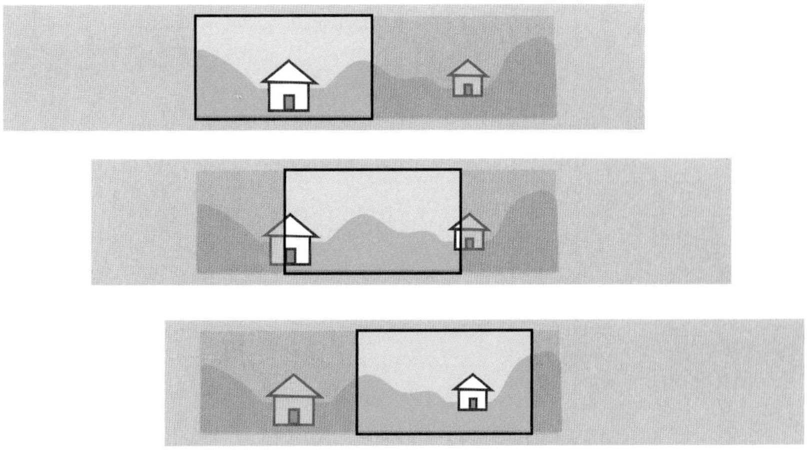

Every animator should consider carefully the *point-of-view* of each scene. Viewers' feelings are strongly affected by whether a camera is tilted or straight on or how far from a subject someone is seen. For example, a character seen with a camera placed low to the ground will seem huge and menacing. If that same character is shot from high above, looking down into a pit, our impression of his situation would be quite different.

Figure 10.15
Panning sequence.

Transitions

Transitions between scenes play a crucial role in helping retain the interest of the audience. Each kind of transition not only moves the action along, but means something different to viewers. *Cuts,* or quick shifts of view, are the most common transitions. They allow the filmmaker to radically compress time, so the events of an hour can be shown in a few minutes. They may also be edits of previously animated material that only slowed down the action. Rapid cuts create a feeling of intense energy.

Figure 10.16
Dissolve sequence.

Another common transition is a *fade*. Fading in or out indicates to viewers that there has been a complete change in time between the two scenes. A *dissolve* is when one scene fades-in as the other fades-out. This implies a logical connection between the two scenes. A dissolve might be used when the first scene shows the main character as a baby and the second as a young girl (see Figure 10.16).

One of the earliest transitions used in films was the *wipe*, where one scene is cleared off the screen at an angle by the next scene. Wipes are rarely used in live-action movies today unless the director wants to give the film an old-fashioned look. However, animations still use wipes to tell the viewer that a change in location is happening.

The Importance of Planning

Even with the assistance of computers, animation is an extremely time-consuming, labor-intensive medium. All professional animators know the importance of careful and thorough planning. Every artist and company has their own approach but all generally follow a standard series of steps in developing a final animation.

Concept

Animations begin with the *concept,* the idea behind the film. It should be able to be expressed in no more than a sentence or two. Examples of a concept are "young mermaid falls in love with a human prince" or "a strange substance turns four young turtles into teenage ninjas." A good concept suggests something interesting and full of possibilities. In the professional world, it is called the *high concept;* this is what's presented or *pitched* to possible financial backers.

Script

Once a good concept is settled on, it is then developed into a script or *treatment*. Like the concept, this is written rather than drawn. The story is outlined from beginning to end and each of the characters is described. A good script will be one that boils the story down to its essentials and manages to keep the interest of the audience every step of the way. It will limit the number of scenes and make sure everything shown has meaning and importance. Ham Luske, who worked for many years at Disney Studios, wrote a very clear explanation of the challenge facing scriptwriters:

> Our first job is to tell a story that isn't known to the audience. Then we have to tell a story that may cover several days or several years. . . so we have to tell things faster than they happen in real life. Also we want to make things more interesting than ordinary life. Our actors must be more interesting and more unusual than you or I. Their thought process must be quicker than ours, their uninteresting progressions from one situation to another must be skipped. . . . Is that not what drama is anyway, life with the dull parts cut out?

While it is written, the treatment forms the foundation for the next step—the artist's *visualization* of the film. After reading the script, artists begin making the first sketches of scenes and characters.

Storyboard

The storyboard (see Figure 10.17) shows the key moments of an animation in a series of small boxes with written notes below. Each major change of action should be illustrated. The notes below the pictures should include any sounds or dialogue. The storyboard is used to plan changes in camera angles and transitions between scenes. At a major film company, this can mean a detailed storyboard of more than ten thousand frames. A smaller company might make storyboards with quick black-and-white sketches.

Storyboarding is a creative process during which new ideas will be generated. This is when the flow of the story is determined and fundamental editing decisions are made. When preparing a storyboard, one should think like a director. The sequence of "shots" needs to be decided upon. Is there enough variety in the camera angles? Will the viewer be confused? Is there too little or too much information? Is the pace right? The shifts of scene should appear natural but, ultimately, you are responsible for what viewers see and what they don't. Viewers should feel that what they are seeing is what they would want to see—unaware that the director is actually in control.

While new animators might be inclined to plunge into animating once the script is decided on, experienced ones agree that the storyboarding is the most crucial part of the planning process. It is while the storyboard is being made that the animator truly visualizes the look of the film. Sketches are made over and over again so that each frame of a storyboard has a strong composition. Most importantly, an animator wants to limit the number of scenes that are animated and have to be cut later. Both the emotional and financial cost of cutting a scene is much less during storyboarding than after weeks of work on an ultimately nonessential sequence.

■ **Figure 10.17**

Just a fraction of the extensive storyboards for Shrek.

Model Sheets and Character Design

After a good story, the success of an animated film probably depends most on strong character design. In professional animation companies, the lead animator creates *model sheets* (see Figure 10.18) as a guide for the other animators. Each character is drawn at various angles, colors and costumes are carefully detailed, and any notes the animator thinks would be helpful to colleagues are added.

Because each image of animation flies by faster than anyone can see it, it is best to use easily drawn, simple shapes with clear structures. The silhouette of each character should be easily recognizable. Characters with clear outlines communicate best with viewers. This is a good thing for the artist, because these kinds of shapes are also the easiest to recreate over and over again during the length of a film. This is not a small consideration, since even a short cartoon for the Web will require a minimum of 240 separate images for a length of just two minutes. One designed for film would need almost 6,000. It is important to make sure they are easily drawn from every angle.

The most famous and successful character in animation history, Mickey Mouse, illustrates this principle. As mentioned earlier, he was first drawn as a series of circles by tracing quarters and half-dollars. Open, round shapes like his strike viewers as likable and appealing. Long shapes with sharp angles usually signal an evil and dangerous character.

■ **Figure 10.18**
Model sheet for Mickey Mouse.

Backgrounds

In the larger studios, while the main actions are being animated, other artists are at work creating backgrounds for the film (see Figure 10.9). They provide a stage for the characters and help set the mood of each scene. Because they are seen by viewers for longer periods of time than any one image of a character, they are generally more complex and developed than the character drawings.

However, it is important that a background not be a finished composition in itself. It should always seem a bit empty, as if it is missing something. Then, when a background is shown without any characters, viewers will have a sense of anticipation that some action is about to begin. The arrival of your actors will seem natural as they complete your composition.

Soundtrack

The soundtrack plays an important supporting role in an animated film. Used imaginatively, it helps amplify the action. The sound of the sea will give depth and weight to the simplest pictures of waves. Sounds can also be important time-savers for animators because they help "draw" scenes that are never actually seen. If we hear a car crash after a car has driven across the screen, our imagination completes the picture.

A soundtrack should be chosen carefully with your themes in mind. Viewers will make associations between the images they see and the sounds they hear. Sounds can set the mood of a scene, such as a moonlit night with a wolf howling. Sounds can also create a sense of anticipation because viewers listen for clues to the action ahead. A young woman swimming is a pleasant image until ominous music begins to play. Add a quick image of a shark's fin and a beach party has been transformed into a horror film.

Most animation programs include simple tools for synching the images with the soundtrack. Modest editing of sounds is sometimes possible. However, before sounds are added to an animation, it is best to edit them first with dedicated sound software (see Box 10.2). Sound-editing programs have sophisticated editing tools and filters, which can produce a variety of sound effects.

From the silliest sound effects to lush orchestrations, sound and animation have gone together for more than seventy-five years. Even in the era of "silent pictures," cartoons were usually shown in theaters accompanied by a piano with a prepared score. That's because every image, from the slap of a face to the start of a car, is made more vivid by the addition of sound. As the masters of radio drama knew, sound can create a world in the listener's imagination, even when that world is never seen.

■ **Figure 10.19**
Sound wavegraph.

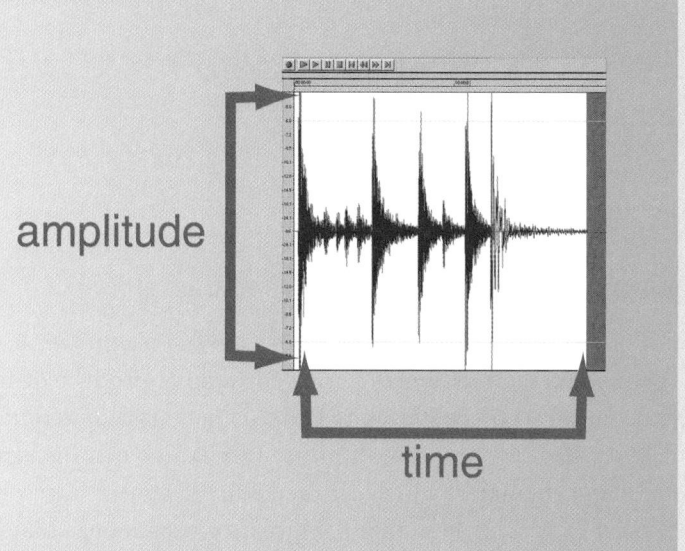

On the other hand, a poor soundtrack can make even the most professional animation appear amateurish. Care and effort need to be taken when adding sounds. Luckily, there are many sound-editing programs available to manipulate and transform sounds in the digital environment.

Sounds are composed of waves. In sound-editing software, each recorded sound is pictured as a *sound wavegraph* (see Figure 10.19). The graph shows the wave itself, the length of the sound over time, and the wave's *amplitude*. Amplitude is technically how much change in pressure a sound creates. While we don't usually think of sound as pressure, you may have experienced it at a loud concert. You can feel the huge sounds against your body; the pressure even hurts your ears. The taller a wavegraph's amplitude, the louder the sound.

Digitized sound comes in two formats: *synthesized* and *sampled*. Synthesized sound is computer generated from formulas. Its most common format is MIDI. Like another mathematical format, vector graphics, synthesized music even with an orchestra full of

(Continued on next page)

BOX 10.2

Orchestrating
sounds
continued

instruments can often come from files of surprisingly small sizes.

Sampled sound is made with digital recording equipment (for example, speaking into a microphone connected to your sound card). Among the standard sampling file formats are WAV (for PCs), AIF (Macintosh), AU (Sun), and MP3. Like a scanned bitmap image, a sampled sound can result in a very large file size depending on the quality of the recording. In fact, if you zoom into a sampled sound closely, you will see the same "jaggies" as you would in a bitmapped image. That's because digitized recording is made in steps that are known as "sound samples." The number of samples per second is called the *playback rate*. The higher the number of samples, the truer the sound (just as an image with higher dpi will appear more realistic). Average sampling rates for digitized recordings are 8,000 to 44,100 per second.

CD-quality sound is not necessary for many digital productions. In fact, in order to limit your overall file size it's wise to keep sound files as small as possible. One common method to eliminate the need for a lengthy sound file for background music is to use a *loop*, a short sequence of music that can be repeated over and over again.

Most sound software allows you to add several audio streams or *tracks,* like layers in graphics programs. These can be *mixed* (layered on top of one another). Sounds can also be cut and pasted. You can use cutting to clean up a sound file, such as the sound of the narrator's breath before speaking into a microphone. Once it has been located on the wavegraph, it can be quickly edited out. Sounds can then be altered or *processed* with filters (for example, adding echoes or changing the pitch).

Simple sounds can have big effects, like the "whoop" of a slide whistle as a character slips and falls. That's why sound effects have always been popular with animators. More complex ones can add to the excitement of a scene, like footsteps coming closer and closer as sinister music gets louder and louder. Any animator will tell you that the time and effort spent in developing a soundtrack is well worth it. You'll know it the first time you put a sound in one of your animations. ■

2-D Animation

Cel or Keyframe Animation: Traditional and Digital

What most of us think of as animation is *cel* or *keyframe animation*. In the traditional process, cel animation is a time-consuming product of filming drawings made on sheets of clear acetate or *cels*. One frame of action might be several cels stacked on top of one another (for example, a background, middle-ground, and character) which are then photographed. Careful registration is ensured by placing cels on a fixed platform with pegs that match punched holes in the cels. The most common peg and camera system during the Golden Age of animation was the *Acme*, a name immortalized in cartoons as the manufacturer of all incredible and improbable machines (see Figure 10.20).

In cel animation, whether you are working traditionally or digitally, a series of drawings is made that show a subject's small and regular changes of position. For example, in a traditional animation, a boat moving across the screen from left to right might require ten drawings, with the boat's position changing an inch to the right in each one. In digital animation, the process is a bit simpler. Ten blank frames are created. The boat is drawn, copied, and then pasted to a new position in each frame. Most digital software provides an *onion skin* function that allows the animator to see pale versions of previous drawings as if they were on semitransparent pages.

Traditional animators draw on clear cels and then lay them over any elements that do not change (like a background). These can be seen below the cels and used for several frames. In the moving boat example, one drawing of a lake and shoreline can be used in all ten frames. If animating a talking head, a drawing of a character's head without a mouth could also be used for several frames while only the mouth is animated on another layer of cels.

In digital animation, the equivalent of the stacking of pages of clear cels is the use of layers. In each layer, any part of the frame that is not drawn on remains transparent. So, a background with no animation simply is drawn once on a layer and left on screen for the necessary number of frames. It will be seen behind the other layers that contain characters and other elements.

The Timeline

The timeline is the backbone of all animation software (see Figure 10.21). This is where one works with the frames and layers that make up an animation. Individual frames or entire segments can be shifted in time by cutting and pasting. Layers can be repositioned so that, for example, a fish passes behind a rock, not in front of it. The stacking of multiple layers, therefore, is an important aid in creating a sense of depth. The timeline is also where soundtracks are synchronized with images; each track of sound will appear as a separate layer.

■ **Figure 10.21**
Timeline and layers.

Tweening

Most traditional animation studios have a division of labor where lead animators create *keyframes,* or moments of important changes in action. *Tweeners* then have the more tedious responsibility of drawing the in-between frames. Digital animation software automates this time-consuming process. After one has drawn

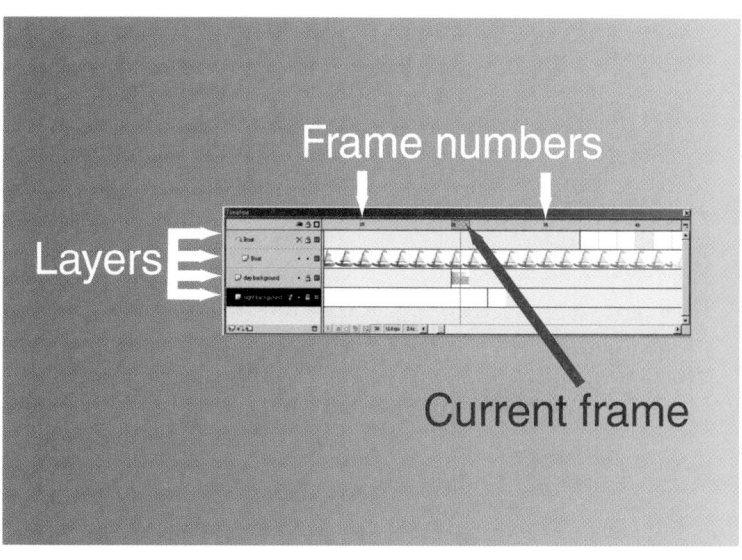

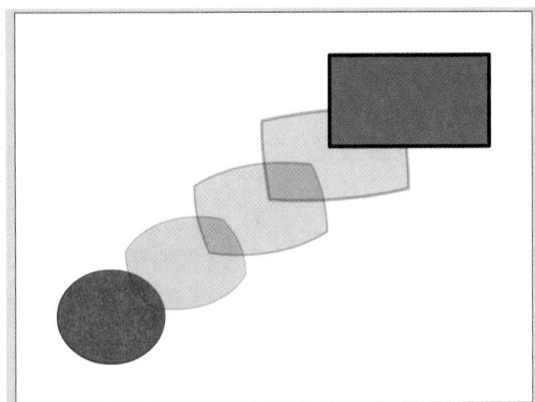

Figure 10.22
Tweening of two shapes.

Figure 10.23
Simple cycle of a flying bird.

an element on the first keyframe, a specific number of frames are created for the tweening sequence. Changes are then made to that element in the last frame. The program will calculate the differences between the first and last frame and *tween* them; in other words, create the in-between frames, making a smooth transition over time (see Figure 10.22). Tweens can be used for changes in shape and size (usually called *morphs*), position, rotation, color, and transparency. Since the tween will be absolutely smooth and mathematical, most animators edit tweened sequences to make them appear more natural.

Cycles and Sprites

Because of the tedious nature of creating animated action, all animators have looked for shortcuts to simplify the process. One of the most time-honored is the *cycle*, where a short sequence is repeated several times to form a longer action. For example, only three changes are necessary to make a bird flap its wings. The wings should be drawn in the up, horizontal, and down positions. This sequence of three drawings can then be traced over and over again and simply moved to different positions across the screen to create the illusion of a bird flying around. The key to success in a cycle is to create an end frame that leads naturally to the first.

In digital animation, these repeating cycles are known either as *sprites* or *animated symbols* (see Figure 10.23). They are saved with a project's file and can be reused over and over again in different places. A shuffling walk, clocks with moving hands, fishes with swishing tails, and spinning car wheels are all examples of animated sprites.

Creating and Importing Elements

Most animation software contains basic painting, text, and selection tools that are familiar to anyone who has worked with image-editing, drawing, and painting programs. Elements can be created that can be resized, rotated, or grouped. However, the main purpose of animation software is the complex task of creating movement and combining the various parts in a timeline. As with all digital projects, it is best to make use of a variety of programs, utilizing each software package's unique strengths. Complex and detailed shapes are often best created in programs dedicated to that purpose and then imported into animation software.

Many digital animators actually begin by drawing their elements by hand with traditional tools like pen and ink, which they then scan. Most animation software has a function that will import these drawings and allow them to be used directly as animatable forms or permit the animator to convert them into animatable forms by tracing.

Masking Techniques

Masks in animation software can be used to create a wide variety of special effects. As in other programs, masks are placed on separate layers and can conceal or reveal what is below them on other layers. In some programs, by changing a mask's alpha (opaqueness) settings over time by tweening, other elements below the mask can appear to fade in or out.

Masks can be animated as well, revealing different portions of frames at different times. Multiple animated masks can be used to create professional looking credits, where titles and names are slowly revealed and then disappear (see Figure 10.24).

GIF Animations

In the last few years, animation has made an increasingly significant impact on the Web. However, because of the large size of bitmapped images and the limited bandwidth of many web users, special software has had to be developed to keep the file sizes of animations with multiple images relatively small. One of the first answers to small web-sized animations was *GIF animation,* also known as the *GIF 89A* format.

■ Figure 10.24

Masking to create animated credits. Left: the mask revealed; right: the mask hidden.

In GIF animation, several bitmapped pictures are linked together and appear animated as they play sequentially. Normally, they are no more than fifteen separate pictures. The software allows the animator to specify the pace of the animation.

The critical issue in GIF animation is achieving a significant impact while keeping the overall file size small. No matter how interesting your sequence is, web users will not wait patiently while an animation takes minutes to download.

One way an overall file size is reduced is by keeping the frame size small by cropping right up to the size of the largest element. Another is to keep the number of colors used to a minimum (for example, by having all frames share a few colors rather than using the GIF format's maximum of 256 colors in each frame). Clever use of traditional cartoon techniques, like streaking lines or spinning a simple form that gets larger, can create the illusion of 3-D animation and maximize a small GIF animation's effect. In addition, several web design and image-editing programs have optimization features designed to minimize the overall file size.

Vector Animation

A newer method of creating animations for the Web, which utilizes vector forms rather than bitmapped ones, has begun to surpass the use of GIF animations. Two of the most popular vector animation programs are Macromedia's Flash and Adobe's LiveMotion. As discussed in Chapter 9, because vector graphics define forms by mathematical equations, they result in much smaller file sizes than bitmapped images. One way vector animation software keeps file size low is by reusing single versions of an object in a library rather than saving multiple copies of it. When an object appears again, only the later reference, not the object itself, is added to the file. Because of the much smaller file sizes, more complex and longer animations can be created that download quickly (see Figure 10.25).

Recent releases of vector animation software have expanded beyond animation to providing more interactive multimedia experiences on the Web. Clickable buttons can be added that supply information, jump the user to other points, and activate sounds. By *streaming* the files (see Chapter 13), users receive the multimedia experience progressively, thereby allowing them to start seeing effects immediately while the rest of the file downloads in the background.

Vector animation is not only for the Web. It can be used to create traditional length cartoons with surprisingly small file sizes or entire multimedia productions to be distributed on floppy disks or CD-ROMs.

■ **Figure 10.25**

Scenes from *Banzai!* a flash cartoon for the Web by Joe Cartoon.

CONCLUSION

Animation is in the midst of a renaissance. The impact of animation can be seen in commercials, hugely successful feature films, and entire television networks devoted to showing cartoons. Animation has also found a new worldwide theater with the ability to distribute work via the Web. Sadly, ubiquitous banner ads and pop-up windows have recently come to epitomize animation on the Web. In the hands of skilled artists and designers, however, Web animation can be a stimulating and gratifying experience or an integral and useful part of a website's design.

The trivialization of animation on the Web by some may simply be an unfortunate by-product of what is perhaps the most exciting recent development in the history of animation. Animation is no longer the exclusive domain of specially trained professionals with high-priced machinery. Animation can now be a mode of expression for any digital artist who has access to relatively inexpensive hardware and software.

Nevertheless, as seen in this chapter, even with the aid of digital techniques, animation remains a time-consuming process. Effective animation requires the study of time-honored animation principles and procedures. It has its own visual vocabulary and physical principles. For success, nothing can replace diligent study and practice. With them, you can move beyond concepts, techniques, tips, and tricks into fluency in the language and citizenship in the world of animation.

Projects: 2-D Animation

1 *Make a flipbook animation using twenty-five 3" × 5" index cards. Drawing in pencil on the cards, show a simple boat moving from right to left, hitting an iceberg, and sinking.*

2 *Create your own version of a short digital animation of a bouncing ball (see Figure 10.14). In fifteen frames, have a ball enter from the left, hit bottom, and spring up and out of the frame at the right. To make your animation more convincing, draw the ball when it hits bottom as a flattened ellipse. To show the effect of gravity, increase the distance the ball travels in each frame as it moves downward. After it springs upward, slowly shorten the distance between frames. By the fifteenth frame, the ball should be beyond the edge of the frame. Set your animation software to play your film as a loop and the ball should smoothly repeat its bounce over and over again.*

3 *Using layers, create an animation of an aquarium. Show a variety of fish moving in different directions. Make a background with typical home aquarium items. Put plants in different layers, so the fish can pass in front of some and behind others. If your software has this capability, a semi-transparent blue gradient can be located in the front layer to increase the sense of looking through water to see your characters moving.*

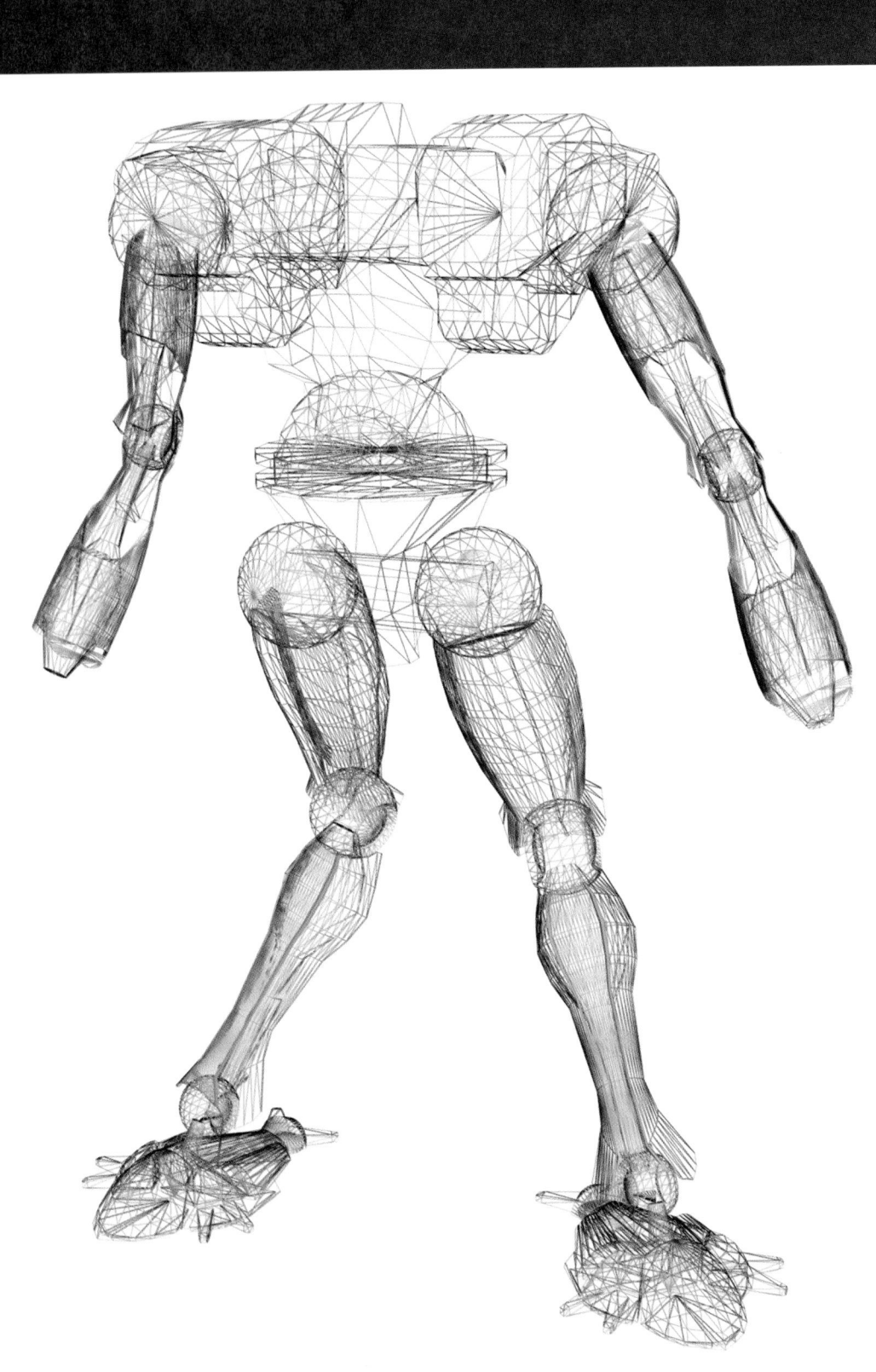

3-D Modeling and Animation

Introduction

Because of the popularity of computer games and motion pictures like *Jurassic Park* and *Toy Story*, *3-D modeling* (the construction of digital objects that can be viewed at any angle) and *3-D animation* (the movement of such objects in virtual space) have become the best known of the digital media. Their basic procedures have been demonstrated in numerous "The Making of . . . " videos. Digital artists are usually portrayed in these promotional films as people creating convincing representations of incredible creatures with the ease of a magician. By adding color, texture, and lighting to wireframed forms, they conjure up a fully rounded image of their imagination with a few clicks of the mouse.

Of course, in reality the process is quite complex and demanding, as demonstrated by the lengthy credits following any film featuring 3-D animation. The many professionals who create these marvels spend years learning their skills. Manuals for the most powerful software run into volumes.

Professionals know that success in this exciting field depends on artists continually learning and improving their skills. The power and capability of software is constantly increasing. This chapter is designed only as an introduction to this new arena for the imagination. The range of techniques and approaches is probably more than any one person can learn in a lifetime.

For beginning digital animators, simply visualizing a group of objects in three dimensions and simultaneously moving them over a period of time is in itself quite a challenge. For those with experience in 2-D software, a few of the tools in 3-D programs will be familiar. Typically, there are pencil and pen tools, selection tools like a lasso, and simple geometric shape tools like a circle and rectangle. As in 2-D programs, objects may be grouped so they move together or combined to create more complex shapes. However, there are many other tools and techniques that are unique to 3-D modeling and animation.

The basic steps of modeling and animating in three dimensions can be seen as the digital version of traditional clay, or stop-action, animation. First, as in the older form, the objects are constructed, in this case from virtual wire that is wrapped in color and textures. Then, lights are positioned.

Cameras are placed that will "film" the scene. Finally, the animators control the action as the entire scene is recorded or, in 3-D animation terms, *rendered*. The process is time-consuming; however, because it is done entirely on computers, with time and effort you can create nearly anything you can imagine.

Before anyone begins learning the specialized techniques of 3-D modeling and animation, he or she must first understand the unique qualities of the stage where the creations will perform. Compared to the world of 2-D art, it is a very different kind of space.

The View in Three Dimensions: the z-axis

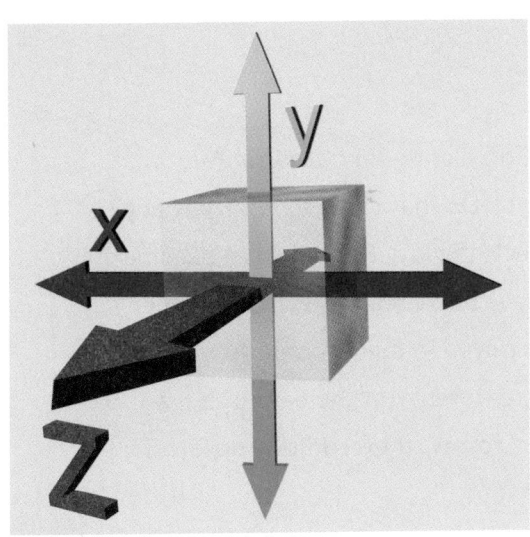

■ Figure 11.1

Imaginary box of space with x, y, and z-axes.

Since our lives are lived in a 3-D world where there is constant movement, why should creating and animating in that kind of world be so difficult? First, we are not required to create very much of what we experience in our world. The sun, the sky, and the mountains are already there. Most of us have not built our houses or our cars. We buy dishes and televisions. In 3-D modeling and animation, however, everything that is seen has to be created from scratch.

Secondly, we will be working in a virtual world. Even though both 3-D and 2-D space on a computer are an illusion, there is a profound difference between them. Mathematically, this is explained by saying that the width and height of the x- and y-axes are joined by the z-axis, or depth. Artistically, this means that those experienced in 2-D techniques like imaging or illustration are forced to make a significant shift in what has to be considered. Instead of working on a flat surface, the computer modeler works in an imaginary box of space (see Figure 11.1).

To do this effectively, the modeler has to see an object from more than one angle. Most 3-D programs provide *viewports* (see Figure 11.2), different views of the object for creating and editing forms. The viewport is usually a 3-D grid with a wireframe version of the object or objects. There are usually four, with views from the front, top, bottom, and either left or right side. As you work, you can zoom in and out in each of the viewports, moving quickly from being close to the object to being almost infinitely distant from it.

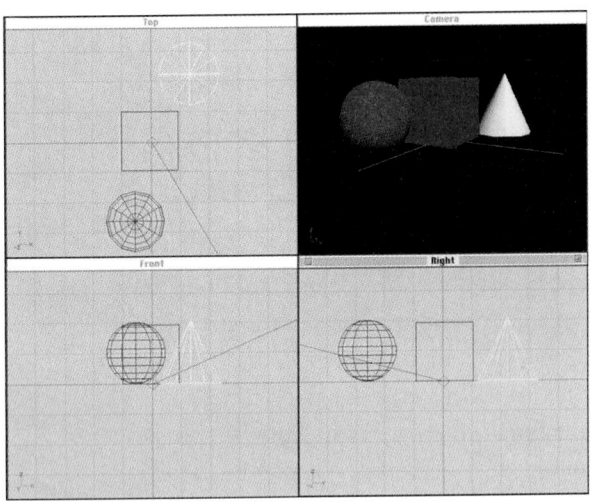

■ Figure 11.2

Multiple views of the same objects in 3-D software.

However, the almost god-like view of the modeler is not the same as the audience who watches the finished animation. Generally, only one angle will be seen at one time and much will be cut-off at the edges of the screen. Hence, it is important as you work to keep in mind what will ultimately be in the *viewing plane*—what the audience will see in the monitor.

Viewing Modes

In addition to the viewports, modelers need to choose the kind of *viewing mode* they will work in. *Smooth textured* mode shows each sculptural form in color as well as how it is lit; in terms of details, it is very close to how it will be ultimately seen by viewers. While it might be the most helpful for the modeler, this mode is very demanding on the computer. Even with the great increase in computing power of today's processors, each change to a scene will be rendered or redrawn slowly. Waiting for the screen to redraw while manipulating a form can become very frustrating.

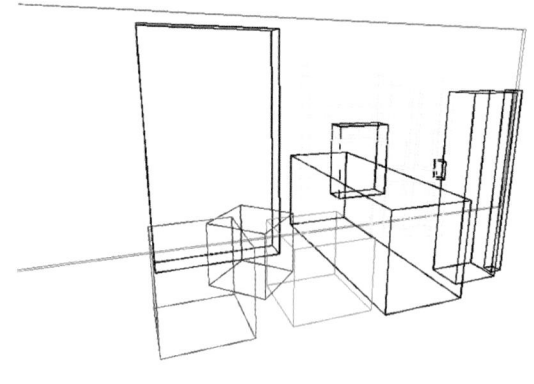

This is why most modelers choose to work in *wireframe mode* rather than smooth textured mode. In wireframe mode, objects are displayed like a mesh sculpture wrapped in netting. Each line and vertice is represented and the overall form can be seen. Unfortunately, as the wireframe forms increase in number and complexity the scene before the modeler can become fairly confusing. By going to *hidden line* mode, only the outer edges of each wireframe are seen. Any facets that would normally be blocked from view if the object was shaded are hidden.

Bounding box is an even less demanding display mode used to animate but not model. Only a simple box, large enough to contain the object, is seen. Processing power is conserved by simply moving the box's position.

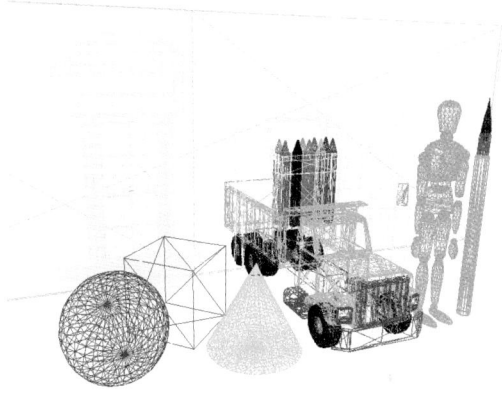

From time to time, most modelers will choose to check their progress by closing their multiple viewports and looking instead at the camera's view of the scene. At the same time, they'll switch the program to either *simple shaded* or *smooth shaded* modes, creating fuller renderings of the scene in order to better gauge its effect on the audience (see Figure 11.3).

Modeling: Digital Sculpting

Every element in 3-D animations has to be built or modeled. The construction of convincing 3-D forms in virtual space is an art in itself. While most beginners assume that animation is the most time-consuming part of the process, experienced 3-D animators know about two-thirds of their time on any project is spent creating the models. Some professionals make this their specialty, leaving animating to others.

■ **Figure 11.3**
Three viewing modes: bounding box, wireframe, and simple shaded.

Each 3-D shape must be planned carefully. The first step is to analyze the shape you ultimately desire and break it down into its simpler components. Generally, each part is created separately and then assembled later. The collection of parts for a complex 3-D object (like a jet fighter before it is assembled) is not unlike what you might see when you first open a modeling kit sold in a hobby store.

In 3-D modeling, objects are constructed out of a series of connected polygons, called a *polygon mesh*. Even a form as simple as a cube has six interconnected squares or *faces*. More complex objects will be made from thousands of

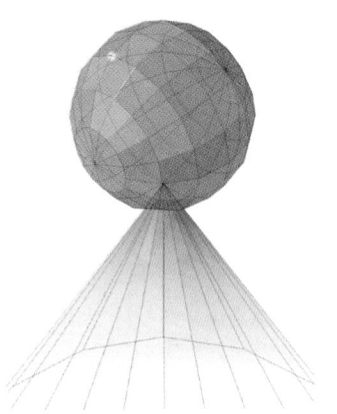

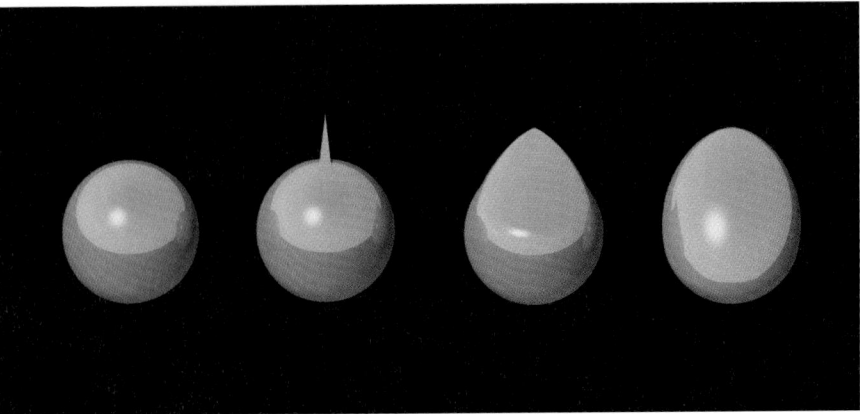

■ **Figure 11.5**

Dragging a sphere's polygons will create new forms.

small polygons. A closer look at the smooth surface of a sphere, for example, will reveal something more like a disco ball covered with many facets (see Figure 11.4). The modeler digitally sculpts by adding and subtracting from objects. Like an artist working with clay, the modeler stretches and pushes the forms by dragging the polygons to new locations (see Figure 11.5).

Working with Primitives

Most 3-D modeling begins with *primitives*, basic geometrical shapes supplied by the animation program. Typically, these shapes include cubes, spheres, cylinders, and cones. Primitives can be repositioned, resized, and rotated in all three dimensions. Altering or combining these simple shapes can create a surprisingly wide array of forms (see Figure 11.6).

For example, by stretching a cube along the x-axis, it can be transformed into a shoebox. By compressing or *squashing* the height of a cylinder, it will take on the shape of a can of tuna. These kinds of changes are called *deformations*. Other kinds of deformations include bending, twisting, or skewing in one direction (see Figure 11.7).

■ **Figure 11.6**

Primitive shapes (cube, box, sphere, cylinder, and cone) and simple deformations of them.

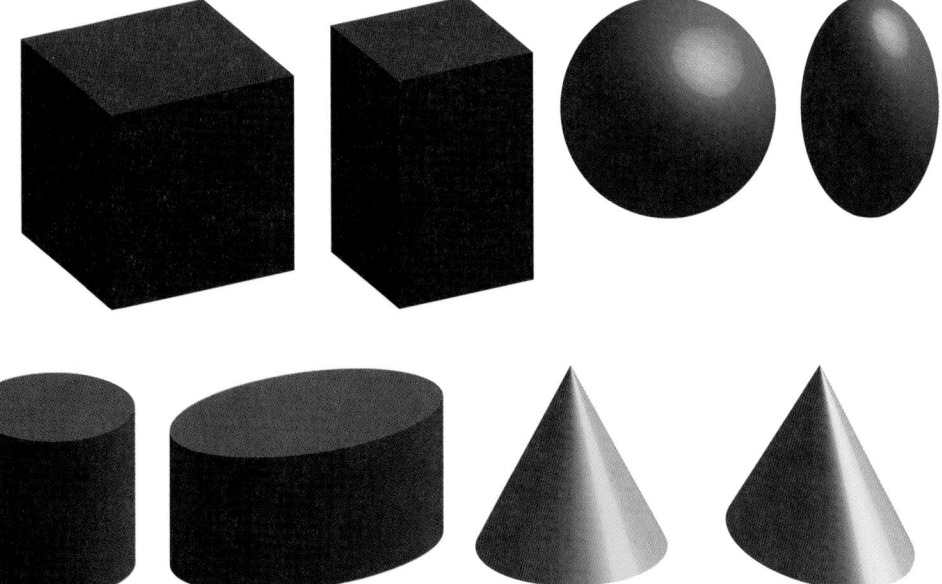

■ **Figure 11.7**
More complex deformations of a cube: stretch, bend, and twist.

Techniques for Modifying 2-D Forms

Another way to model in three dimensions is to start with a 2-D form. Many modelers begin by drawing with the pen tool and creating a simple shape made up of Bézier curves. As in vector drawing, points can be added and subtracted until the shape is satisfactory. Some programs even allow you to draw free-hand with the pencil and then convert the form to a Bézier-curved one.

Once a flat shape is created, the modeler can use a variety of techniques to transform it into a 3-D shape. The most commonly used method is *extruding*, sometimes called *lofting*, which gives the shape depth by pulling it out into 3-D space. Extruding gives a flat shape volume by adding a z-axis to the flat shape and extending the shape along it. For example, by extruding a circle vertically upward, you can make a column. The process is much like the children's toy that forces clay through a cutout shape to make long snake-like forms. The outer edge of the extruded form is determined by the outline of the cutout shape. Like those toys, extrusion is generally used for fairly simple solid forms that will later be edited. In essence, it is a technique to use 2-D shapes to create your own 3-D primitives (see Figure 11.8).

Beveling is a simple and very common variation of extrusion. Even many 2-D programs include a beveling function to give text a 3-D look (see Figure 11.9). Sometimes called *face extrusion*, the process pushes a flat shape forward and adds angled edges along its sides, so the original shape becomes the front face of the new 3-D object. This technique first caught the public's eye when "flying logos" began to appear at the beginning of sports telecasts in the late 1980s.

In *sweeping*, sometimes called *lathing*, a simple shape is spun around its center to create a new object with volume. The classic example is the sweeping of a wineglass (see Figure 11.10). The profile of the glass is drawn as a thin, flat shape. It is then spun along its center by the program to make a 3-D glass with its open-cupped top, thin stem, and rounded base. This process can be used to create simple shapes (for example, a swept right triangle would create a cone) or many complex 3-D forms, like elaborate chair legs, with relative ease.

■ **Figure 11.8**
Simple extrusion of a letter.

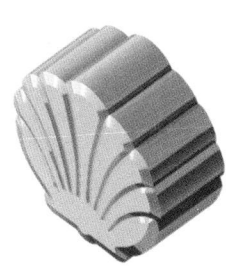

■ **Figure 11.9**
Extrusion of a shape with and without bevel.

Boolean Operations

To create more complex solid forms, modelers overlap solid shapes and combine them in a variety of ways. These methods are called *Boolean operations* and the various techniques used are similar to the ways compound forms are created in vector illustration (see Chapter 9).

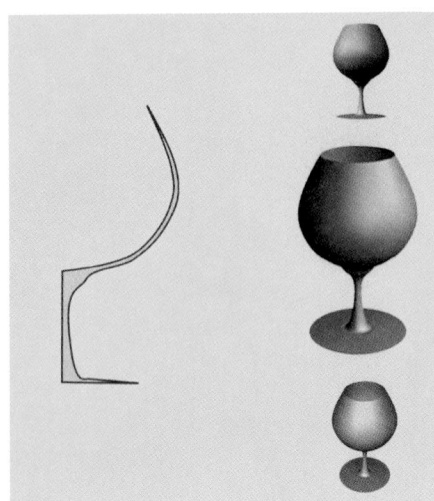

Figure 11.10

Sweeping a wineglass.

In a Boolean *union*, the outer forms of two volumes are added together and whatever intersects internally is eliminated. For example, the rough form of a derby hat could be made from a half-sphere unified with a dish-shaped disc. One of the most useful Boolean operations is *subtraction*, where one form is cut away from the other. If the above example was done as a subtraction rather than an addition, the dish-shaped disc would end up with a circular opening. Another kind of Boolean operation is the *intersection*, where only the overlapping parts of the two shapes are preserved and every other part is eliminated. In this case the combination of the half-sphere and the dish would result in a smaller dish (see Figure 11.11).

Digital Sculpting

All of the previous techniques are designed to create fundamentally geometric forms that are quite far from the more free-form shapes that amaze viewers of films like *Monsters, Inc.* Unless you are creating an architectural scene or machinery, these basic volumes are usually just a starting point. Like a traditional sculptor's block of wood or lump of clay, their geometry will then be digitally sculpted by hand to realize more remarkable visions. This is called *free-form modeling*.

Most modeling software allows you to shift and pull the polygons that make up the wireframe mesh that covers all 3-D objects. This can be a very effective technique to create modeled forms. However, advanced modeling software is required to sculpt 3-D objects in finer detail.

Spline-based modeling applies more subtle changes to solids. Rather than moving and pushing whole polygons in a wireframe, the curved *splines* that make them up are individually edited. Splines are similar to the Bézier curves found in vector illustration programs (see Chapter 9). Each curve has control points that can be pulled and dragged to reshape curves.

In *direct-point* or *surface modeling*, individual vertices in the wireframe mesh can be dragged and stretched to reshape the surface of a form. By clicking and pulling many points, a sphere can become a head, or a cone can take on the appearance of a mountain (see Figure 11.12).

Figure 11.11

Boolean operations: subtraction, intersection, and union.

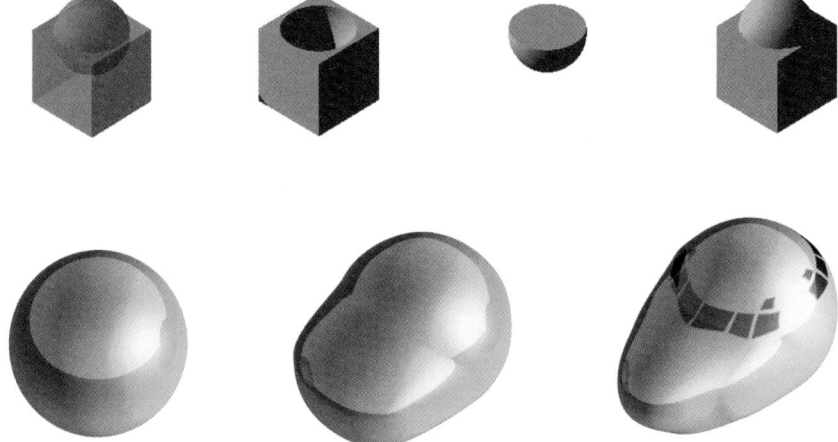

Figure 11.12

Simple form created by direct-point modeling of a sphere.

NURBS (non-uniform rational b-splines) are a special kind of spline
designed for modeling organic forms. In most splines, each control point has
an equal impact on a curve. But a NURBS spline has adjustable weights
attached to each control point so you can increase or reduce the impact of any
change by individual control points. Weighting control points permits the finer
modifications to a spline curve necessary to make the more subtle, complex
curves found in natural forms.

Procedural Processes

For recreating the almost infinite complexity of nature, many modelers
depend on special techniques, called *procedural modeling,* available in
high-end software or as plug-ins. The software relies upon elaborate
formulas that take into account the randomness of natural phenomena.
Organic forms like mountainsides or trees can be created with *fractal
geometry* (see Figure 11.13), a mathematical process developed by
Benoit Mandelbrot (see Chapter 5). Another kind of procedural modeling is used in *particle systems,* which can recreate smoke, explosions, and tor-
nadoes, and thereby eliminate the need to describe and control thousands of
elements at once (see Figure 11.14).

■ **Figure 11.14**
Particle systems are used to
create complex effects like smoke
and dust.

BOX 11.1

CAD and
digital
architecture

Computer-aided design or CAD is a special kind of 3-D modeling used by industrial and fashion designers, engineers,
and architects to create models for manufacturing and architecture. Sometimes
called a *drafting* program, CAD uses a
vector-based approach, combining elements of digital illustration and 3-D
modeling programs to make wireframe
drawings of 3-D forms. In higher level

versions of these programs, the wireframe drawings can then be rendered as
bitmapped images using such photorealistic techniques as ray tracing (see
page 244). Material libraries and a
library of objects, such as those for land-
scaping, may also be included.

With a CAD program, you can
design machinery based on engineering

(Continued on next page)

BOX 11.1

data or draft detailed models of a building based on floor plans (see Figure 11.15). Because CAD technical drawings are used for industrial production, they have a level of precision far beyond 3-D modeling programs. In fact, those who import CAD drawings for use in modeling and animation usually have to simplify them before they can be used.

High-end CAD software also includes project management software that links electronically to the Internet. With digital technologies, the whole process from design to completion moves faster. Project proposals have become more dramatic, with animations that swoop over proposed buildings. Clients can see photographic renders of designs, make comments, and see changes made in days rather than weeks.

One of the biggest impacts of CAD software has been on architectural design itself. Architects today are able to go far beyond the boxes and cylinders of the past. Right angles are giving way to once unimaginable curving forms. The complex infrastructure necessary for buildings like Frank Gehry's Guggenheim museum in Bilbao, Spain (see Figure 11.16) would have been impossible to build only a decade ago. Fabrication of its parts was done by contractors around the world, working from CAD-generated information. Step by step, builders assemble these complex structures working with CAD databases, containing information on each part's angle and position.

Liberated from old constraints, architectural design is becoming a more sculptural medium. Architects can imaginatively model unusual geometric forms and see how they interact. With clicks of the mouse, a model can be refined and polished. Some visionary cyber-architects are now designing architecture that only exists in a virtual environment, unfettered by logical constraints or gravity. These buildings can morph into new forms as a visitor enters, changing depending on one's movements and actions. Even with buildings designed for the real world, the new freedom in design is allowing architects to explore what was once impossible, leading to a new era in architecture. ■

■ **Figure 11.15**
Three views of machinery in AutoCAD, one of the most popular CAD software packages.

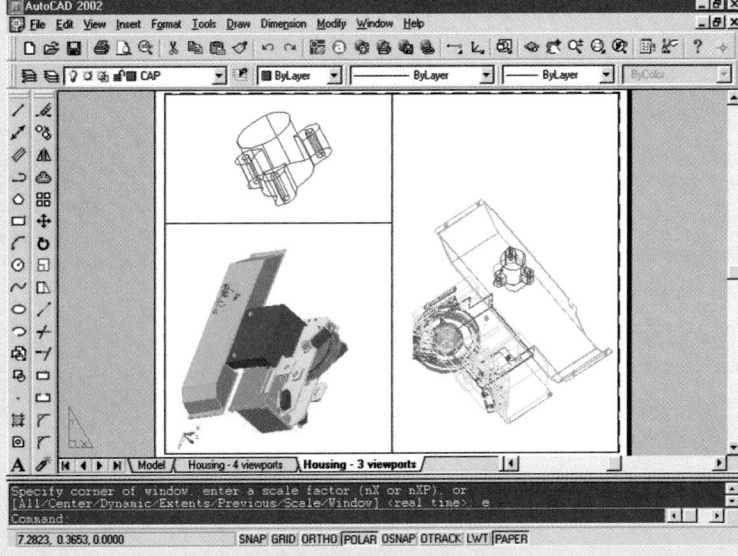

■ **Figure 11.16**
The Guggenheim museum in Bilbao, Spain, designed by Frank Gehry.

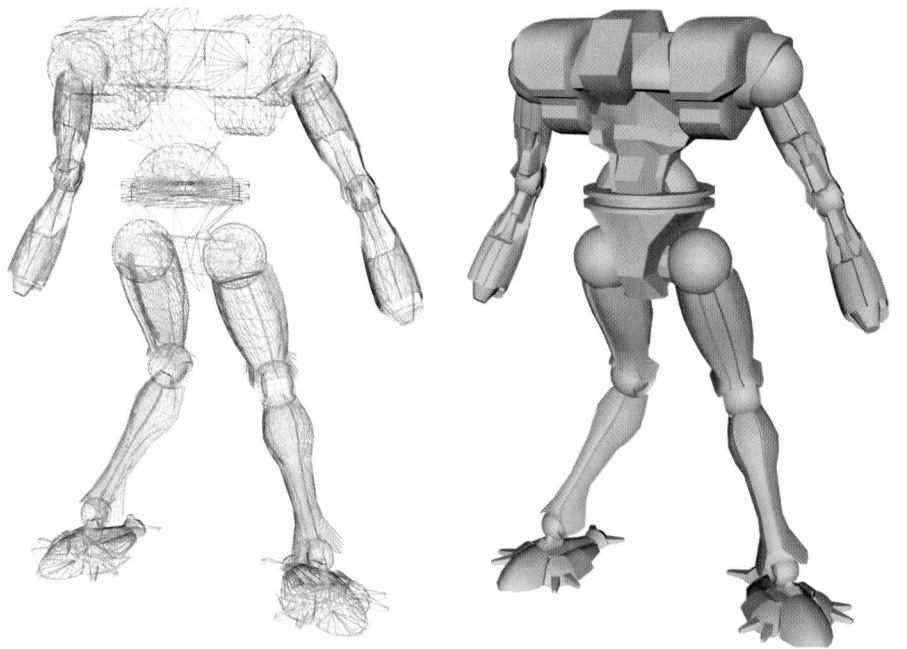

Figure 11.17

Complex wireframe for a Battlemech available commercially
left: wireframe;
right: rendered.

If the many modeling processes previously outlined seem far too complex at first, it may be reassuring to know that you can purchase mesh models from many companies who sell libraries of all kinds of forms to animators. Some of these are made by using expensive 3-D scanners that are far beyond the finances of most artists. Free mesh objects are also available on the Internet. Some specialized programs like CAD (see Box 11.1) come with libraries of useful elements like trees and ponds for a modeler's use. Rather than spending hours to painstakingly recreate a jet fighter with its many elaborate shapes, you can order a wireframe model of an F-14 and spend your time in the next import steps: coloring and adding textures (see Figure 11.17).

Mapping

Once a wireframe model is finished, the next step is to add a surface or skin to it. This is called *mapping,* and includes the addition of colors, patterns, materials, and textures, as well as properties like shininess and transparency. Mapping is an almost magical process; one wireframe shape can take on many skins and become the parent of many different and equally convincing objects. A wireframe of a simple sphere, for example, can become a rubber ball, a marble, or a ball bearing depending on how it is mapped (see Figure 11.18).

Figure 11.18

Spheres mapped with four different textures.

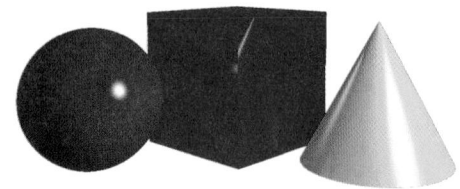

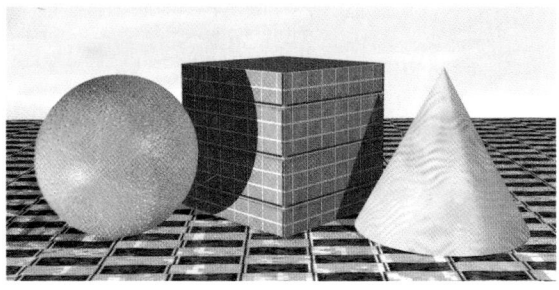

■ Figure 11.19

Changing skins with surface mapping: three simple solids with glossy surfaces, bump maps, and texture maps.

Many modeling programs include a large collection of preset textures to make this process easier. Among the categories you can choose from are plastics, woods, metals, and glass. Applying the preset texture automatically adds the special qualities of that material, such as its colors, whether it is transparent, or how it reflects light.

Texture mapping is one of a modeler's most important time-saving tools. In this process, a bitmap image is wrapped around a wireframe form. By choosing a picture of a texture, a primitive shape can appear to have a very complex, modeled surface without a modeler having to go through detailed point-to-point editing of the wireframe mesh. It also eliminates the long processing time necessary to render such complicated forms. For example, instead of the time-consuming effort to reproduce the rough texture of a brick in a wireframe model, a convincing brick can be made by simply wrapping a picture of a brick's texture around a basic rectangular box shape. A column can become a complexly textured tree trunk with just an image of tree bark (see Fig. 11.19). Textures for mapping can be created from scratch using paint or image-editing programs. Some modelers will simply grab their digital camera and take a photograph of a surface, like the bark of a tree in their backyard. In addition, thousands of texture images are commercially available in stock libraries on CD-ROMs.

Texture mapping is often utilized in video games to ensure that scenes are rapidly rendered. If a vehicle is going to speed by a brick wall, it doesn't make sense to do more than create a flat wall shape with a bitmapped picture of brick on it. Experienced modelers know that in many parts of any scene, it is only necessary to create an impression, not a literal representation. Complex models are reserved for important objects that audiences will study extensively and appreciate, like the racecar the gamer is driving.

What many call texture mapping is not limited to creating the illusion of texture. In a raceway scene, the modelers will wrap images or *decals* of numbers and company logos across cars and use bitmaps of a small collection of faces, for example, to create crowd scenes from simple wireframe forms.

Bump maps are a step beyond texture mapping in realism. This technique alters the way light reflects off a surface, simulating the way an actual textured surface would reflect the light without actually changing the geometry of the outside of the model. The illusion of the texture's depth is based on the contrast between the bright and dark parts of the image. For example, the dark areas of a wood grain bitmap would appear indented while the light ones would be raised. By embossing a bitmap of an orange's dimples to a sphere as a bump map, you can create the illusion of an orange's texture without tedious modeling.

With modeling and texture techniques, you can create objects with complex and remarkable surfaces. However, for a 3-D scene to be truly effective, it has to be more than a collection of objects, as marvelously realistic as they may be. To bring an entire scene together and unify it, artists use the power of light.

Lighting

Lighting a 3-D scene is an art in itself, often meaning the difference between ordinary and dramatic expression. A single candle, a fireplace, or a child's innocent face transformed into something quite different by applying a flashlight just below the chin are all examples of the impact of lighting. Just like on a stage, the 3-D modeler will place lights to establish the appropriate mood and focus the audience's attention. Well-placed lighting will enhance the objects in an image and the theme of the picture.

There are three basic kinds of lights: *ambient, fill,* and *spot. Ambient lighting* is not focused, spreading light across an entire scene. The objects in a scene lit by ambient lighting alone are easily seen but tend to appear flat and dull. *Fill lighting* (sometimes called *omnidirectional*) is somewhat more focused, spreading light from one general direction, but does not cast strong shadows or make highlights. *Spot lighting* (sometimes called *key lighting*) is the most focused. It is emitted from one point and directed at another, usually as a cone of light. Spotlights create strong shadows and concentratedly lit areas. Changing their angles can dramatically change the effect of a scene. The most effective lighting combines at least two of these types (see Figure 11.20).

For example, the harshness of a spotlight can be moderated by adding a global light, which will add light to the shadows so the contrast between light and dark is not as harsh and appears more realistic. A flatly lit scene with ambient lighting can be given more drama by lowering the ambient light and adding a spotlight on the main subject in the scene to emphasize its importance.

Most 3-D modeling programs provide many more options beyond choosing between the three types of lights and adjusting their angles. The brightness and distance from the scene or target can also be adjusted. This allows the modeler to distinguish between the light cast by a lamp on a desk and the broad power of the sun on a summer's day.

Pure white light is rare in the natural world; most lighting has a *cast* to it or a tendency toward one color. One of the most important choices a modeler makes when lighting is adjusting the colors of the lights. The color of interior lighting will have a significant impact on a scene. It can determine whether a room appears cool and forbidding or warm and inviting. For example, the blue cast of fluorescent lighting will seem more appropriate in a large department store than in the warm study of a home. Colored lights are also an excellent way to depict the time of day in exterior scenes. Morning light has a red cast, while the light at noon tends to be more yellow.

■ **Figure 11.20**

A scene lit by three lighting types: ambient, spot, and fill.

As important as lighting is, it should be used carefully and not excessively. A scene with many lights and shadows will not only appear unnatural but also will greatly increase the scene's complexity and considerably increase its rendering time.

The Camera and the Audience

As discussed at the beginning of this chapter, most 3-D programs provide four viewports, different views of the object for creating and editing forms. The viewport is usually a 3-D grid with a wireframe version of the object or objects seen from the top, bottom, and sides.

However, this is not the point of view of the audience. The viewer can only see what is in the frame of the finished image. To be successful, the 3-D modeler should never lose sight of this. As in photography or any of the other fine arts, choosing what will be in a frame, how a scene will be cropped and presented, is decisive. A table setting of beautiful objects, lit dramatically, can lose all its impact if seen from too great a distance. A happy couple dancing in a garden turns nightmarish if all we see is a close-up of their teeth. The placement of the viewing plane can determine not only what the audience sees in a scene but how they understand it.

In order to set the edges of the frame, the modeler first places the camera *target*—a marker that shows where the camera is focused—on the wireframe drawing. Surrounding that marker is the *viewing plane,* the rectangular field that contains the only section that the viewer sees in the frame. This widens or shrinks depending on how distant the camera is located from the scene. It is important to take the time to set the camera and the ultimate viewing plane carefully. Rotate and adjust them until the scene is framed in a strong, meaningful composition.

Focus

■ **Figure 11.21**

Using different camera lenses for different effects: normal, wide angle, and telephoto.

Another way to influence what the viewer is focusing on is by adjusting the camera's *focal length*. This is a term borrowed from conventional cameras, where the changing of lenses on cameras achieves different effects by altering what is in focus. The focal length controls both the *depth of field* and *field of view*. Depth of field is how far back things can be seen in focus. Field of view is how wide or narrow is the area seen in focus. The shorter the focal length, the wider the view. Among the choices that 3-D software recreates are wide angle (for distant scenes), macro (for extreme close-ups), and telephoto or zoom lenses (see Figure 11.21). Creative use of focus is another important technique 3-D artists use to direct the view of the audience and affect how they perceive a scene's meaning. For example, in a churchyard, depending on your use of the depth and field of view, your audience will see either a sharply focused hand reaching for another, with vague stonework in the background, or a shadowy couple at the entrance of an old medieval church covered with beautifully carved figures.

Rendering and Shading

After the models have been created, the lights set, and the camera positioned, the moment of truth for a 3-D image has arrived—rendering. Rendering is the computer generation of the finished scene from the viewer's point of view. A bitmapped image is created from the polygons of the wire meshes, the mapped colors, and the textures, along with the lights, shadows, and reflections. If special effects, like smoke and fire, have been added, their impact not only on the atmosphere but on every surface needs to be calculated by the computer, too.

Even in an age of ever faster and more powerful computers, this is usually a lengthy process that requires the patience of the modeler. As with much of the digital media, just as the hardware has increased in capacity, so has the software increased in complexity. Modeling procedures, which recently were only possible on mainframes, are now commonly available on a digital artist's desktop. Rendering intricate models with many textures and effects remains a demanding, highly intensive processing operation. For many scenes, the old 3-D artist's joke remains true—after you enter the command for rendering, it's time to go make dinner. In some cases, it's also time to eat dinner and go to bed.

Before rendering begins, there remain some important choices for the modeler that will affect the quality of the final image. What resolution should it be? What should be its color depth or number of colors? Your decisions should be based on your ultimate goal. What kind of output is planned? Is the image going to be a high-resolution print or a 35mm slide? Is it going to be featured on a website? (Chapter 7 provides a discussion of resolution, color depth, and output.) Another decisive factor in the ultimate quality of the image is what method of *shading* will be used to render the 3-D image.

Shading Options

Shading transforms the geometrical net of polygons in a wireframe model into an object whose surfaces have color and tone. With more complex *shaders*, objects can become shiny and have highlights and reflections.

There are several standard ways to shade surfaces. *Flat shading* (sometimes called *facet surface shading*) is a simple approach that applies one tone and color to each facet or polygon on the surface of the model. Because of its simplicity, it renders faster than other methods but results in very geometric, almost cubist, looking 3-D forms. Surfaces tend to be flat and dull, and edges often have the "jaggies." The first 3-D video games were dominated by this method. Today, few final images are made with this method, but most modelers will make "quick renders" with it during the modeling process to check on their progress.

Gouraud shading (or smooth shading) was developed by Henri Gouraud, a graduate student at the University of Utah in 1971 (see Chapter 5). This rendering mode results in much smoother tonal blends by mathematically interpolating and, hence, smoothing the edges of the polygons. It approaches shading as a series of colored lines. A model rendered with the Gouraud shader will have a surface that appears to be shaded with gradients.

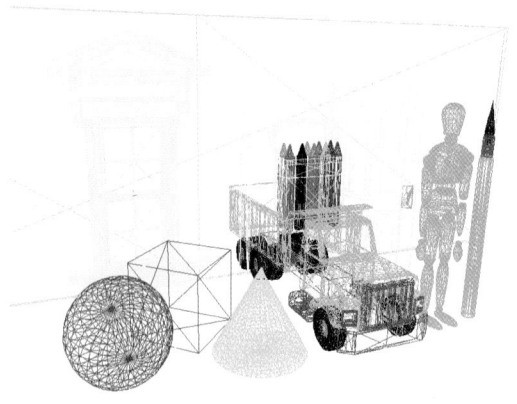

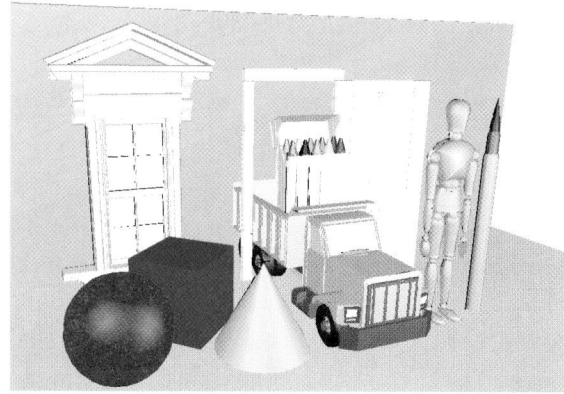

■ Figure 11.22

Rendering a wireframe model with different shading options: Flat shading, Gouraud shading, Phong shading, and Ray tracing.

Another graduate student at the University of Utah, Bui Tuong Phong, developed an even more complex form of shading, known as *Phong shading* (or *specular shading*) in 1975 (see Chapter 5). His approach smoothes the polygons of a wireframe pixel by pixel, rather than line by line. This makes it possible to add shiny highlights and reflections to 3-D models but also results in much more time-consuming renders.

Ray Tracing

Ray tracing is one of the most realistic rendering approaches. It recreates the reflections of light and color that we use to see objects in the real world. A line of light is traced from the light source to every pixel of an object and then bounced to the camera as a light ray. Depending on the nature of the model's surface, the light will bounce in different ways. For example, a brick and a metal pipe reflect light differently, while transparent glass filled with colored water will bend the light rays. Ray tracing calculates these differences as it renders the scene. This mode of rendering is used for many of the special effects we are familiar with in movies, like fog and smoke.

As might be expected, the more complex the reflections or the bends of light, the more computer intensive the renders become. Still, the convincing photorealism of ray-traced images is well worth the extra time (see Figure 11.22).

The Final Render

To save processing power and time the final rendering of an image will not include all sides of your models, only those visible in the viewing plane. This is called *backface elimination*. Each polygon in a wire-mesh is tested to see if it ultimately will be visible to the viewer. Any polygons outside the viewing plane will be ignored. Once that is done, the rendering of each object in the scene begins. Colors and shading are applied, materials and bitmapped textures are wrapped around surfaces, the amount of light on any surface and how it bounces is determined, and highlights, shadows, and reflections appear. When these calculations are finished, special effects like motion blur or fog are applied and much of the earlier work is recalculated and reapplied. Then, the long hours of work and waiting are over and a finished image is created (see Figure 11.23).

■ **Figure 11.23**
Complex rendered image.

For some artists, a fully rendered 3-D model, like a mountain landscape in the Alps or the interior of the living quarters on a distant planet, is the finished work. However, for many others, modeling forms, placing the lights and the camera are only preliminary steps in a longer process—in essence, they just set the stage for *action*.

3-D Animation

Movement in 3-D Space: the z-axis

While most of the basic techniques and concepts used in 2-D animation apply to all animation, the world 3-D animation moves in is quite different. Because 2-D animation is based only on the x- and y-axes, each element is fundamentally flat. One has to create the illusion of changes in depth. The addition of the z-axis in 3-D animation not only provides a much more convincing sense of depth and solidity but a whole other dimension for movement. The camera can soar over and under objects. When a boat roars past, we can see its bow; when a dragster's front end rears up, we zoom in on its undercarriage to see the dripping fuel. Because of sophisticated 3-D modeling software, these movements can be combined with photorealistic objects and create remarkably convincing effects (see Figure 11.24).

■ **Figure 11.24**
"Rock 'n Roll", a Shell Oil commercial by R/GA in 1994, brought fuel pumps to life.

Keyframes and Motion Paths in Three Dimensions

As in 2-D software, 3-D animators create movement by positioning objects in keyframes and utilizing timelines to keep track of the animation. Markers indicate the keyframe on the timeline. The software *tweens* the frames in-between keyframes. The main difference between 2-D and 3-D animation in this regard is that the position of objects can vary on three axes, rather than two, so an object can move across the screen, as well as under and away from the viewer. More powerful software and hardware are needed to calculate these kinds of changes. Once the animator has taken the time to draw an object in three dimensions, the software will take care of redrawing the object as it changes its position.

Motion paths can be drawn to guide an object's movement. These, too, are seen along three different axes. In 3-D wireframe mode, one can see the relation of an object to its surroundings over time by studying its path.

Having objects follow paths make more fluid movements possible. The paths can be drawn with either free-form or geometric tools. Editing the path is done by *curve editing*, clicking and moving points on the curves or splines (see page 236). New spline points can also be added to create more complicated movement.

Motion paths can be used to control more than objects. Just about anything can be moved with motion paths, including lighting and the camera. In a very active sequence, an animator will even use a motion path to create a sense of the observer moving, along with the action in the scene.

Point of View and Camera Movement

As mentioned earlier in the chapter, the camera is the eye of the viewer taking in the scene. Intelligent use of point of view is important in any animation. However, it is even more of a challenge in a 3-D animated environment because of the variety of possibilities. Like a play's director controlling which actors are on stage or off stage, the animator chooses what is in the viewing plane at any moment in time.

The movement of the camera can be an extremely dramatic element in an animation. 3-D software recreates and utilizes the vocabulary of traditional film camera movement to create imaginative effects. For example, when a *dolly,* or moving platform, is attached to a track in a film studio, the camera can follow the subjects as they walk down a hallway. In 3-D programs, *tracking* will keep the camera dolly at a set distance from an object as it moves along a scene. *Dollying* moves the camera toward or away from objects to zoom in or out on subjects.

Unlike 2-D animation, *panning* in 3-D animation follows a curved motion, similar to a head turning to take in different parts of a scene. Cameras can also be *rolled* and *banked* to create effects like riding on roller coasters or spinning in an airplane. Today, 3-D animation software provides the animator with an almost unlimited range of interesting, wild, and even strange uses for positioning and moving the camera. As exciting as they may be, animators should first think about the purpose of the animated sequence before positioning their cameras. Ultimately, camera angles should be chosen for their dramatic effect only if they support the story (see Figure 11.25).

■ **Figure 11.25**

The same scene from three different points of view.

Morphing

For many of us, one of the first computer animations that captured our imagination was a *morph* (see Figure 11.26). Derived from the word *metamorphosis,* morphing creates smooth transitions from one physical form to another. While simple geometric forms are relatively easily morphed in 3-D software, it is the transformation of photographic and video imagery that appears the most spectacular. These kinds of transformations have been used successfully in music videos, commercials, and films. One famous music video showed men and women of all races gracefully changing into one another, making a compelling statement of the unity of all human beings. Morphing can also make inanimate objects appear to come alive. Horror films often use this technique for chilling transformations; for example, a whole room can appear to breathe in and out.

Creating a morph is a very time-consuming procedure. Both objects have to be outlined in wireframes that recreate the basic geometry of the subject (see Figure 11.27). Each vertice, or *control point,* needs to be linked from the first object to a corresponding control point on the other and both wireframes need to have the same total number of vertices. The morphing program (usually part of a 3-D animation package) will calculate the difference between each pair of control points and between transitional frames over time. While the process is painstaking, the more control points used, the less crude and more convincing the morphed transformation.

In practice, rather than making two separate wireframe models, only one is usually made. A copy of the wireframe is then placed on top of the second image and adjusted to fit the contours of the second object. In this way, the vertices are already linked between the two wireframe forms. Next, the animator marks the start and end keyframes on the timeline for the morphing sequence. The software then calculates the in-between frames. When rendered, one form will appear to dissolve into another.

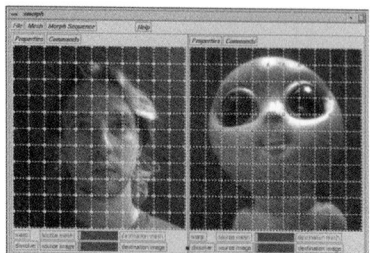

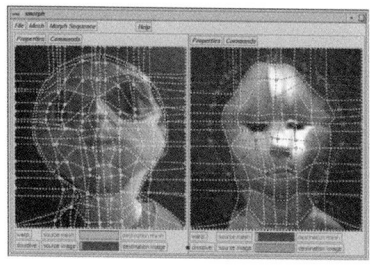

■ **Figure 11.27**
Wireframes of the morphing sequence shown in Figure 11.26.

■ **Figure 11.26**
Morphing sequence.

The Search for Realism

In stark contrast with 2-D animation, the history of 3-D modeling and animation software continues to be largely a search for more and more realistic effects (see Chapter 5). More convincing shading, lighting, and motion have been placed in the hands of artists because of innovations in software and more powerful processors and video cards. As these effects become ever more sophisticated, so do the challenges.

Physics and Gravity

Calculating the impact of the physical forces of the real world, like gravity and the wind, on 3-D models in motion is an extremely complex enterprise. Luckily, most 3-D animation software has built-in tools to simulate these effects for you. Once an object's characteristics or *attributes* are set, realistic animations can be created that take into account the rigidity of an object, its weight, and how friction and inertia might affect its movements. Without the addition of attributes, a character's feet might just pass through a floor as she walks.

Modules for Special Effects

Add-on packages, sometimes called *modules* or *third-party plug-ins,* can also be purchased to handle even more complex issues in physics. For example, how would soft objects like a flag react to a stiff wind? What would a car's headlights illuminate on a foggy road at night? In fact, animators gauge the strength and importance of 3-D animation software by comparing how wide a range of plug-ins is being developed by independent companies. As mentioned earlier in the chapter, many companies have created advanced particle systems, which generate realistic special effects like smoke, fire, fog, clouds, and explosions (see Figure 11.28). Other kinds of plug-ins create special lighting effects, like realistic neon lights, or provide special tools, like shaping tools that act like they are carving wood. Texture plug-ins might cover an object with fur or add a veneer of rust to metallic surfaces. Post-production plug-ins can change the whole look of a 3-D animation to the style of Japanese anime or look as if it is an old 1950s-style black-and-white television show.

■ Figure 11.28

Particle effects creating smoke, flames, and blown debris.

■ Figure 11.29

Linked motion of 3-D figures.

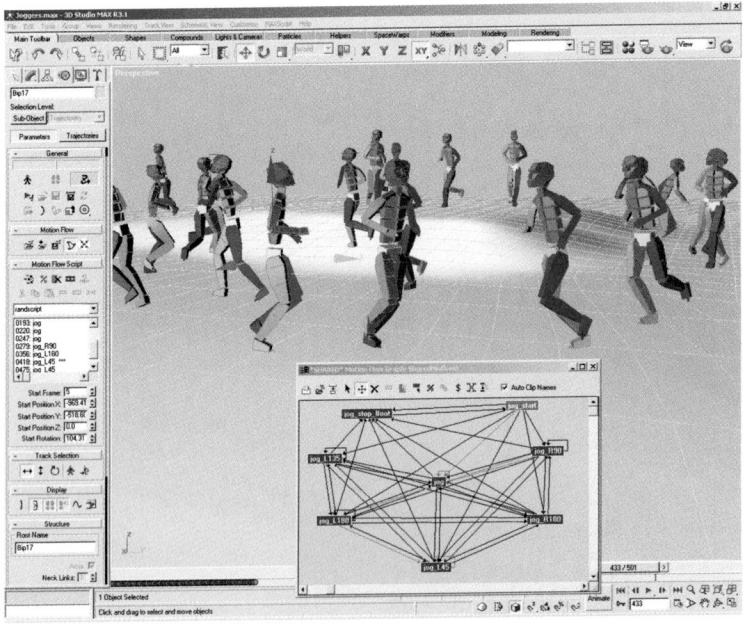

Linked Motion

While it is challenging to create convincing spatial forms, designing complex models with parts that move together is an art in itself. *Parent-child* relationships, where moving one part causes a second to move, are made by establishing *links* between the two parts. These links should be established in the model before animating. An example of a parent-child connection is a hinge, whether on a machine or a knee.

More complicated links are needed in objects like an arm, where a *chain* is established so that when an upper arm is moved, the elbow, forearm, wrist, and hand move with it. In this case, *constraints* are added to limit the range of motion to create more natural movement (see Figure 11.29).

Forward and Inverse Kinematics

A chain of parent-child links can be used for describing the movement of machinery. One mechanical part initiates the movement of other parts, a process called *forward kinematics*. The movement works only in one direction—for example, in the case of an arm, the upper arm must initiate the action. In order to move a finger, the animator must start first at the shoulder and move down through the chain of links.

Inverse kinematics, one of the most sophisticated animation tools, allows one to initiate actions at either end of the links. Once one has established the basic skeleton, one can move a finger and thereby create the normal chain of reactions in the hand, wrist, and forearm.

Motion-Capture and Roto-Scoping

The movements of human beings are extraordinarily complex and have frustrated animators since the beginning of animation. Kinematics creates very smooth movements, but much of the subtle nature of natural movement is lost. An important technique to create convincing natural body movement is *motion-capture*.

Early animators used a form called *roto-scoping*, where a live person was filmed while moving. The filmed frames were made into a series of large photographs which the animators used as references or even traced. The results can be spectacular; for example, the dance sequences of Walt Disney's *Snow White* were based on roto-scoping the dancer Marge Champion.

Today, movement can be recorded digitally and then interpreted with computer software. To do this, the subject wears a dark, skin-tight bodysuit. Little white spots or reflective balls are attached to the person at key juncture points and act as targets. When subjects move, an optical tracking system follows their movements. Strobe lights are flashed at over 200 times a second while cameras record their actions from several angles and feed the information into a computer (see Figure 11.30).

After the movement is captured, custom software translates the information into standard 3-D animation formats. Initially, what is seen on the screen is a cloud of white dots, like a swarm of bees. Animators translate these dots into fluid, natural movement. The higher the number of recorded points, the smoother and more convincing the final animation.

Not all motion-captures result in photorealistic action. In Riverbed Studio's *Ghostcatching*, an animation based on the movements of the dancer and choreographer Bill T. Jones, the forms are hand drawn and gestural (see Figure 11.31). The

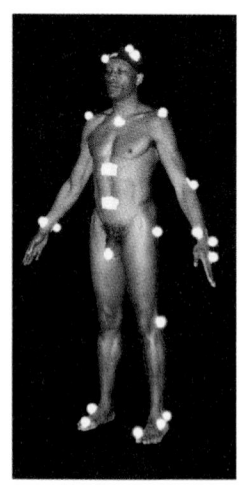

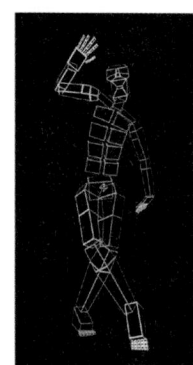

■ **Figure 11.30**

Four steps in the process of motion-capturing the dancer Bill T. Jones.

■ **Figure 11.31**

Two frames from the finished film, *Ghostcatching*.

stylized, luminescent lines move across the dark screen gracefully, like a 3-D dance of pastel figure drawings.

Motion-capture can also be used for other purposes. By placing dots along the critical muscles of a face, a person can be the model for very convincing facial animations. When combined with motion-capture for body movement, virtual actors can be created. The first applications for these virtual actors were for animal characters and aliens, but more recently virtual human actors created on high-end workstations have begun appearing in feature length films. While still beyond the capabilities of personal computers, as with most technologies, it is only a matter of time before these tools are placed in the hands of most digital artists.

Previewing and Rendering

Just like modelers, while animators spend most of their long hours of work in a wireframe environment with grids and multiple perspectives, they have to remain aware that, when rendered, the wireframes and grids will disappear. Their creation will become a smooth, lit world of movement and color with only one angle seen at any one time.

While making editing quick and efficient, working in a world of wireframes has its limitations. From time to time, to truly understand what effects are being created, it is important to preview the animation. Most software has one or two *preview modes* to allow the animator to see at least a simplified version of the animation with the colors applied. A higher level preview will show more detail using flat or Gouraud shading (see page 243). Unfortunately, anything more complex or detailed still takes a long time to be created on personal computers and is therefore unsuitable as a preview in the midst of animating.

Once the 3-D animation is complete, it is time to *render* it. Rendering an animation goes beyond the complicated application of all colors, textures, lighting, and reflections to wireframe models to computing their movements (and the camera's) in time. This is why rendering a 3-D animation is an even more time-consuming process, usually taking many hours.

Preparing for final rendering of an animation is the time for final choices. What will be the quality of the render? How detailed will the images be? As discussed earlier in the chapter, there are many ways to render a 3-D model, like ray tracing and Phong shading. With animation, there are new questions, like how many frames per second will the animation be? What special effects are truly necessary?

Knowing where the animation will be used affects many of these choices. Is the animation going to be used on video, a CD-ROM, or the Web? For example, output to videotape requires that frames be displayed at a rate of one-sixtieth of a second versus the typical one-thirtieth or less. In addition, special digital video equipment is needed to transfer digital animation files to videotape.

If the animation is headed for the Web or a CD-ROM, there are a variety of formats to choose from; for example, MP3, Microsoft's AVI (which has a variety of CODECs, or compression approaches), or Apple's QuickTime. Each format has its own specific requirements for how the file will be rendered.

3-D Animation and the Internet

Like all areas of digital media, animation has felt the influence of the Internet. The Internet has changed the working arrangements of animation studios.

Today, 3-D modelers and animators can be in different cities, even different countries, working on the same projects. More changes are ahead. As more powerful broadband connections become common, same time collaborations on animation files will soon be possible.

Surprisingly, for the general public, most 3-D modeling and animation on the World Wide Web is designed to be viewed passively, not unlike sitting in front of a television or in a movie theater. While many artists, designers, and computer scientists have made valiant efforts to bring the interactive 3-D experience common in video games to the Web, progress has been frustratingly slow. Virtual Reality Modeling Language, or *VRML*, has long been expected to be the method to fulfill this goal. Its promise, when finally realized (see Box 11.2), will provide online 3-D experiences for not just game players, but shoppers and virtual tourists. It may eventually even become the standard way of experiencing the Web.

BOX 11.2

3-D for the Web: where is VRML?

The VRML was designed in the mid-1990s to give programmers and artists tools to create a 3-D virtual environment on the World Wide Web. Since then, simulations of buildings and cities, 3-D games, and interactive visualizations of scientific data are among the many VRML experiences that can be found on the Web (see Figure 11.32). With the recent addition of Java support in VRML 2.0, users can interact more fully in these 3-D worlds and direct their own movement. In addition, they can trigger animations and sounds as they travel.

While there are many exciting VRML experiences on the Web today, it has not yet fulfilled the expectations of many of its advocates. It was once thought that VRML would be a common, if not the most common, way to experience the Web. But several things have held back VRML's universal acceptance. First, special software needs to be downloaded to view VRML environments, and most Web users do not take the time to do this. In addition, complex scenes take a long time to download. For most Web users, who have experienced the dynamic and rich world of video games, VRML is disappointing. Complex scenes change at speeds reminiscent of old silent movies and simple ones look rudimentary and clumsy. A long-time handicap for those interested in designing VRML worlds was that, originally, only programmers could create them. However, more user-friendly software packages are beginning to be available.

As bandwidth increases and more plug-ins come preloaded with browsers, we can expect more VRML worlds to be developed and appreciated. There is now discussion of Web-casting sports events in VRML. The ability to shop in a 3-D environment, join an interactive 3-D game, or visit a long-lost ancient site with ease should ultimately fulfill the great expectations of the pioneers of VRML. ∎

■ **Figure 11.32**
Walking through a VRML environment.

CONCLUSION

In less than twenty years, 3-D animation went from slow-moving boxy shapes "dancing" to disco music to lunging velociraptors convincingly attacking live-action actors. With the rapidly increasing capabilities and power of both hardware and software, even more complex and photorealistic 3-D animations are on the horizon. We are already seeing long-format 3-D animations created entirely digitally on television and film. The first virtual human actors have begun appearing in movies, with the real actors relegated to the roles of motion-capture subjects and lip-synching. News programs are already being located in lively virtual environments. What will be next? Virtual newscasters? Stories on wildlife with virtual elephants roaming the set?

3-D animators have been waiting for years for real-time finished rendering. Editing animations and seeing them fully rendered immediately will be a tremendous advance from today's limitation of seeing only crude previews while working.

One can be confident that today's rendering tools and other processes will soon seem antiquated. There are startling new software capabilities ahead, increases in data storage, more powerful video cards, and the arrival of broadband networks with the ability to quickly deliver 3-D animated films. To be successful, professional animators must be committed to constantly learning new techniques and updating their knowledge of new software and hardware.

Is it possible for the tools of animators to become too powerful and complex? Even with the incredible capabilities of the technology to come, the challenges of interesting storylines and drama will remain just as they have for more than a century. In fact, the greatest challenge for animators may not be how to learn to use the latest version of a complex piece of software. Rather, it will probably be to have the discipline to avoid the temptation to spend hours exploring new, complicated tools and, instead, keep one's focus on the creative issues that have always been central to successful animation.

Projects: 3-D Modeling and Animation

1 *Using a predefined solid primitive like the box, complete six variations using texture, mapping, and lighting to create six objects that appear very different.*

2 *By overlapping three different solid primitives, create three very different forms using the Boolean operations of union, subtraction, and intersection.*

3 *Using primitives, simple colors, and by applying plastic surface materials, model a child's toy boat. With camera movement alone, create a twenty-five-frame fly-over of the toy.*

4 *Animate a thirty-frame bouncing ball sequence with three different 3-D balls. By changing their appearance and how they bounce, make them appear as if they are made of three different materials with different attributes: a rubber ball, a ping-pong ball, and a bowling ball.*

5 *Create a short, fifty-frame animation of a dancing cylinder. Bend, squash, and twist the cylinder. Vary the camera position and viewing plane to add to the energy of the dancing. Move the lighting to create a dance club atmosphere. Add appropriate music.*

The Internet and the World Wide Web

Introduction

There have been only a few times in history when an innovation has revolutionized a culture and redefined the way in which average people interface with the world. Beginning in the nineteenth century, the arrival of new communication systems, each having a part in making the world a smaller and more accessible place by offering an unprecedented immediacy to mass communication, signaled such revolutions. First, the telegraph made almost instantaneous communication possible over wires strung across the continent. However, the telegraph, for all its speed, was essentially communication from one user to another, interpreted and delivered by a third party. Interpersonal communication took a major leap forward through telephones, as written communication was augmented by a more human and direct contact. The radio moved mass communication beyond the physical wires necessary for telegraph and telephone communication and touched the lives of many listeners simultaneously.

Each of these technologies was a revolution in its own right, but none of them compares to the Internet, a worldwide medium that has the ability to broadcast information and allow for immediate interaction between individuals separated by vast spaces. The implications of this new technology are still developing. In this chapter, we will discuss the many aspects of this revolution and the unusual way it came to be.

How Did the Internet Happen?

The Origins of the Internet

Sometimes it seems as though the Internet and what we now know as the World Wide Web came into existence almost overnight. Most users of the Web have only been able to access its features since 1994 when the introduction of graphical Web browsers made it more accessible. As with most inventions, what may appear to be an overnight success actually took a long time to develop.

As a direct response to the Soviet Union's launching of *Sputnik* (the first artificial satellite to orbit the earth) in 1957, and the fears it caused (potential military applications), the U.S. Department of Defense formed the *Advanced Research Projects Agency* (ARPA). Its goal was to re-establish America's lead in the development of science and technology applicable to the military.

In 1962, the Air Force commissioned the RAND Corporation (a major cold war think tank) to do a study to determine how the Air Force could maintain its command and control over its nuclear missiles and strategic bombers after a nuclear attack. The story commonly told indicates that the government wanted a decentralized military communication and research network that could survive a nuclear strike. If a particular city was destroyed, they wanted to be sure the network could survive. This would guarantee the United States' ability to launch a counterattack. This is a wonderful story, but nonetheless untrue. In fact, the federal government simply wanted to find a way to allow their many incompatible computers, in locations around the country, to communicate with one another. They wanted a nationwide network that would be capable of connecting every type of computer with every other type of computer. The final report from the RAND Corporation recommended the development of a packet-switched network dealing primarily with voice communication.

The Basic Technology

ARPANET (Advanced Research Projects Agency—NET), created by the Department of Defense in 1969, was originally intended to investigate various ways in which computers could be networked together. This first network was rather primitive and functioned more like a vast bulletin board than the Internet we know today. In addition, it was limited to military use only.

The technology behind this early experimentation centered on the concept of *packet switching*, a unique method of sending messages. In packet switching, *protocols* (standardized formats) divide data into *packets* or pieces (see Figure 12.1) before they are sent to another computer. Separate packets, each with part of a complete message, can be transmitted individually, even following different routes before arriving at their final destination. Each individual packet contains a header, much like a zip code for the postal service, which provides information about the source, destination, and how the packets are sequenced. Because they follow a particular protocol, they can be reassembled back into a complete message at their destination. Should a single packet get lost or damaged, that individual packet can be resent.

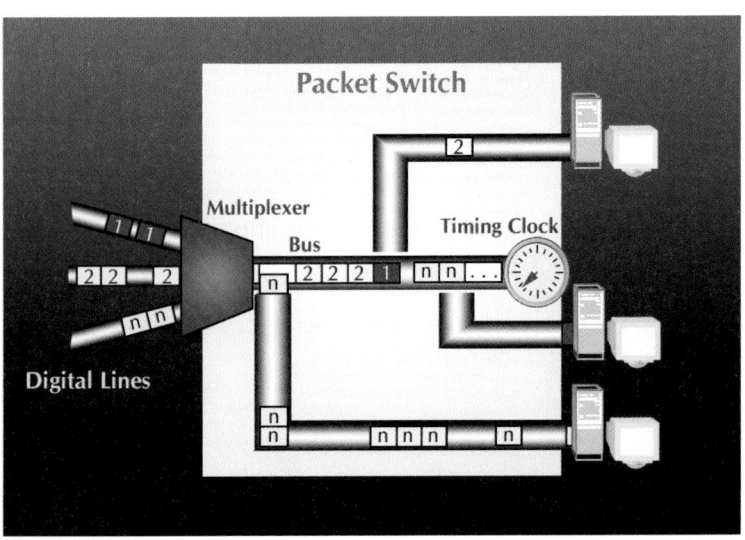

■ Figure 12.1

Packet switching, in which information is broken into small packets for transfer and then reassembled at their destination, made the Internet a reality.

Today, the most widely used protocol is Transmission Control Protocol/Internet Protocol or TCP/IP. Information that requires flexibility in speed of transmission or that often experiences delays (like real-time audio, video, e-mail, and so on) benefits from the technology of packet switching. The development

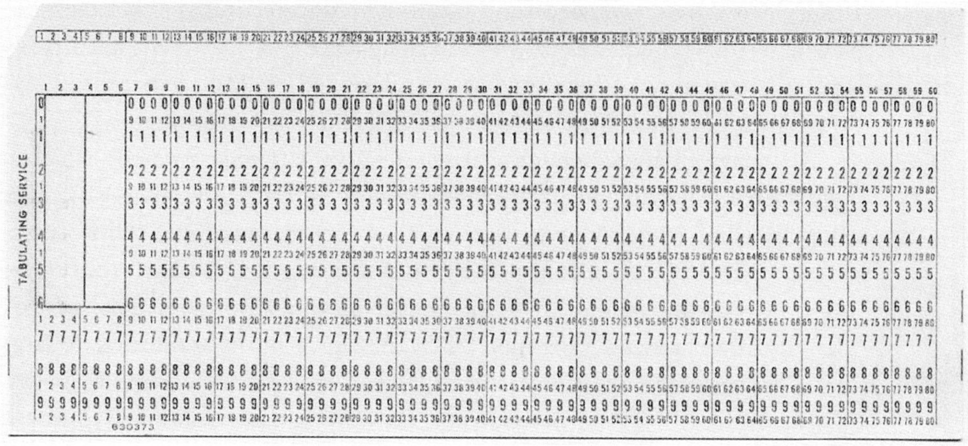

Figure 12.2

Punch cards like this one formed the basis for information coding and decoding for most of the early mainframe computers.

of networks using a packet-switched technology revolutionized the way in which computers shared information.

As a result of the RAND study, ARPA began to fund work to accomplish a packet-driven network and Dr. J. C. R. Licklider was selected to head the project. This resulted in a dramatic shift in funding from military to academic computing centers. Licklider felt that rather than simply finding ways to improve what was already being done, only new work on advancing the nature of computing was acceptable to the project. At the time, computers processed information via punch cards (see Figure 12.2), and the computer scientists working on this project felt that the computer industry still perceived the computer as an arithmetic engine (see Chapter 2). Licklider's vision of networking was almost prophetic. He envisioned a day when computers would be connected in a vast global network through which anyone could access data, share information, and use programs from any connected site. Due to the far-reaching nature of Licklider's investigations, his office was renamed the *Information Processing Techniques Office*, or IPTO. In keeping with his theories, he nicknamed his group of computer specialists the "Intergalactic Network." Licklider, however, would leave before his dreams came to fruition. In 1964, Ivan Sutherland (see Figure 12.3), one of the pioneers of digital media (see Chapter 5), was chosen to replace him. Sutherland was in turn replaced by Bob Taylor from NASA.

Figure 12.3

Dr. Ivan Sutherland developed Sketchpad (a pen drawing device) while at MIT and then lead the ARPANET project before going to Harvard, where he developed a head-mounted display—the first virtual reality simulation.

One day while sitting in his office, Taylor realized that he had three different terminals, each of which was connected to a different computer system by a telephone. He asked himself the question—why three? Why not one interconnected system? In one of the most successful meetings in history, Taylor met with the head of ARPA to outline the problem. Twenty minutes later, he was given a million dollars to explore networking solutions. He recruited graduate student Larry Roberts from MIT to direct the ARPA network project. Roberts assembled the ARPA researchers, many of them still graduate students, at a conference in Ann Arbor, Michigan, to discuss the issues facing them. At the end of the meeting, Wesley Clark suggested the use of interconnected *interface message processors*, *or IMPs*, (known today as routers) to manage the network.

As with many inventions whose time was near, several important groups were working on the same concept at the same time—each unaware of the other. In this case, work on secure packet-switching networks was proceeding at MIT, the RAND Corporation, and the National Physical Laboratory (NPL) in Great Britain. Most of the initial work on packet switching culminated in

1968 when ARPA awarded the ARPANET contract to Bolt, Beranek and Newman (BBN). BBN was to work on the packet switches, then called IMPs, while the structure of the network was designed by MIT researcher Larry Roberts with Howard Frank at the Network Analysis Corporation.

A Honeywell minicomputer was selected as the foundation upon which to build the IMP after an unusual demonstration of its durability. It was suspended from the ceiling while running, beaten with a sledgehammer, and still worked.

In 1969 the actual network was constructed. It linked four *nodes* or processing locations— the University of California at Los Angeles, Stanford Research Institute (SRI), the University of California at Santa Barbara, and the University of Utah. The network capability at that time was only 50 Kbps, very slow by today's standards, but the ARPANET had nonetheless become a reality. Each of the nodes had a unique address that would identify it to other computers.

Leonard Kleinrock's (see Figure 12.4) team at UCLA became the first functional node on the ARPANET. A month later, Engelbart's Stanford Research Center became the second node. With the addition of a second node, UCLA initiated the first host-to-host message ever sent on the Internet. Kleinrock and one of his programmers attempted to "logon" to the Stanford Host. Programmers at both ends wore telephone headsets so they could respond to the logon procedure by voice. Once the programmer typed in "log," the computer at Stanford would add the "in" to create the word command "login." Checking by voice as each letter was typed in, they got to the letter "g" and the system crashed. The second try was successful. The system worked (see Box 12.1).

■ **Figure 12.4**

Dr. Leonard Kleinrock, developer of packet switching and team leader at UCLA of the first functional node on the Internet.

Even though this first Internet was a simple text-only system, research into visual communication played a role from the early days of the ARPANET. The third and fourth sites were at research universities working on visualization application projects. The University of California at Santa Barbara set up a node to investigate methods for the display of mathematical functions, while the University of Utah set up a node to investigate 3-D representation. During the next several years the number of computers connected to the ARPANET increased. Beginning in 1970, new nodes were added to the ARPANET at a rate of one each month.

The first public demonstration of the ARPANET took place at the International Computer Communication Conference (ICCC) in 1972. However, the most significant event that year was the introduction of something most of us take for granted today—electronic mail. Written by Ray

BOX 12.1

The Request For Comments

In 1969 the Request for Comments (RFC) notes were established as a way for researchers to engage in the give and take of concept development. The memos, generated by network researchers, were intended to be informal reactions to the ideas of other researchers. Initially collected, printed, and distributed by regular mail, they were eventually accessed electronically. The RFCs often started a series of interrelated discussions. As the discussions began to gel around one particular idea, it would be investigated more thoroughly by a team of researchers. In time, the RFCs became the "documents of record" in the Internet community. ■

Tomlinson (see Figure 12.5) at BBN to allow ARPANET scientists to coordinate their efforts, electronic mail soon became the network's largest application.

Open-Architecture Networking

When Robert Kahn arrived at ARPA in 1972, the ARPANET was already a success. However, at that time the ARPANET was using an NCP protocol that allowed computers to communicate with one another, but not address networks or computers outside a destination on the ARPANET. Since the ARPANET was the only existing network, this was not a real problem. However, it limited the opportunity for future growth.

Kahn quickly introduced the concept of open-architecture networking, which he called *Internetting*. Under open-architecture networking, different networks could connect to the Internet without internal modifications to their hardware. It was this open-architecture concept that led to the development of a common protocol, which would become known as the *Transmission Control Protocol/Internet Protocol* or TCP/IP. The military adopted this protocol as a "defense standard" in 1980.

Several ground rules were established for the development of this new protocol. First, new networks could not be required to undergo internal changes in order to connect to the Internet. Second, transmission would be on a best-effort basis—if a packet did not arrive, it would automatically be retransmitted from the source. Three, the black boxes used to connect the networks (soon to develop into gateways and routers) would be kept simple and not retain any of the information that passed through them. Finally, operations would remain free of global control.

Vin Cerf, then at Stanford, was asked to join Kahn's development team in 1973 (see Figure 12.6). After nine months of intensive work the team published a paper that became a blueprint of the protocol Kahn had theorized. Cerf and his team of graduate students worked out the design details of the TCP protocol for several years. When it was finished, it was able to bring together computers made by Digital Equipment Corporation, IBM, Hewlett-Packard, and others, making it possible for them to communicate and transfer data to one another (see Figure 12.7).

Early in the testing process the discovery that some packet losses could not be corrected by TCP led to the reorganization of TCP into two separate protocols. One was termed IP (Internet Protocol), which controlled only the addressing and forwarding of the packets themselves, while a separate TCP managed flow control and recovery from lost packets.

It was the incorporation of Internet protocols like TCP/IP into a supported operating system throughout the research community that contributed to the widespread acceptance of the Internet. On January 1, 1983, all hosts connected to the ARPANET changed from the NCP to the TCP/IP protocol. It was also around this time that the ARPANET was divided into a MILNET for military use only, leaving the remaining ARPANET for research use.

■ Figure 12.5

Dr. Ray Tomlinson wrote the first electronic mail program in order to allow ARPANET scientists to coordinate with one another.

■ Figure 12.6

Dr. Vin Cerf is recognized (with Dr. Kahn) as co-developer of TCP/IP that allowed computers to talk to each other over the Internet.

As new networks came online throughout the world, the vast majority of them adopted the TCP/IP protocol. What had been the province of the military and selected scholars began to open to the rest of the world. In the mid-1980s, the British JANET (Joint Academic Network—1984) and the U.S. NSFNET (National Science Foundation Network—1985) made it their policy to serve the entire academic community and not just selected scholars. In fact, by 1985, in order to receive funding for an Internet connection, a university had to guarantee that the connection would be made available to all qualified users on campus.

The NSFNET program not only adopted TCP/IP but also formulated a number of other policy decisions that shaped the Internet, including policy decisions encouraging its regional academic networks to seek commercial nonacademic customers. These networks were also directed to expand their networking facilities to better serve customers. The resulting increase in users allowed the networks to lower subscription costs to everyone.

On the NSFNET itself, an *Acceptable Use Policy* (AUP) was implemented and enforced which prevented any use that was "not in support of research and education." By denying commercial traffic at the national level but supporting it at the local level, the growth of private, national, commercially oriented networks was encouraged. As a direct result, numerous private national networks were successfully established. This privatization of the Internet would accelerate during the next few years (see Box 12.2).

By 1995, with the defunding of the NSFNET backbone, the capital that would have been used to maintain it was redistributed to smaller regional networks to support their connection to privately owned, national Internet providers. In less than nine years, a transition from government-sponsored networks to privately owned and operated national networks was completed.

BOX 12.2

PSINet: beyond the educational community

In 1989 PSINet was the first company to organize specifically for the purpose of providing Internet access on a commercial basis. Initially working with a base of forty customers in its first year, PSINet was offering a nationwide leased-line service by 1990. As one of the first privately owned, commercially oriented companies with infrastructure designed specifically toward communication on the Internet, they hosted websites, offered design services, and worked to establish e-commerce.

PSINet Japan, Inc., was established in 1994, thus expanding its network and associated services overseas and becoming one of the first Internet service providers in Japan. They expanded to the United Kingdom in the following year and, in 1996, revealed their plans for PSINet Europe and their goal of building a European Internet backbone dedicated solely to the needs of corporate and institutional users. ■

The World Wide Web

As the Internet developed from its ARPANET roots to the decentralized series of interconnected networks we have today, one thing has remained constant—the expansion of access to an ever-broadening body of users. As cheaper, more powerful computers have become accessible to the public, use of the Internet has grown. This was, in large part, the direct result of a new kind of software designed to take advantage of the Internet's capacity to deliver images as well as text (and later, audio and video streams). What made this possible was the implementation of *hypertext markup language* (HTML) into point-and-click *browsers* that allowed the average user to navigate through a network in order to access information.

History of Hypertext

In an article published in the July 1945 issue of *The Atlantic Monthly,* Vannevar Bush (science advisor to President Franklin Delano Roosevelt) envisioned a device that could not only store information, but in which users would be able to link information in the form of text and images for future reference. Bush noted that finding information was often made more difficult by the various indexing systems currently in use, most of which worked either alphabetically or numerically. With the information located in only one place, it was very difficult to reference and connect data in other folders, much less at other locations.

In his article, "As We May Think," Bush made the observation that the human mind connects data by association, not alphanumeric ordering, and that as one focuses on a thought, a trail or web of associations is formed. Most importantly, however, those trails of associations can fade as they are left only in memory as a "mental picture." Using this template as a guide, Bush suggested that indexing by association should be used as a model rather than the forms previously used. While this would not reproduce the full range of the human mind's ability to connect information, it could create a private file and library that would be of greater use. He called his mechanical device *Memex,* and saw it as an intimate supplement to individual memory. The Memex machine was visualized as a kind of desk with translucent screens on which items could be projected and read or from which text (typed and in longhand) and images could be photographed onto special Memex film. All of this information could be coded within a document so that references could be called up easily and quickly (see Figure 12.7).

Despite the description of a machine with screens, a keyboard, and supplemental levers to move through data, Bush's description of Memex conceptualized the technology and approach to data integration far ahead of its time. It would be twenty years later before this concept was reintroduced in a practical form.

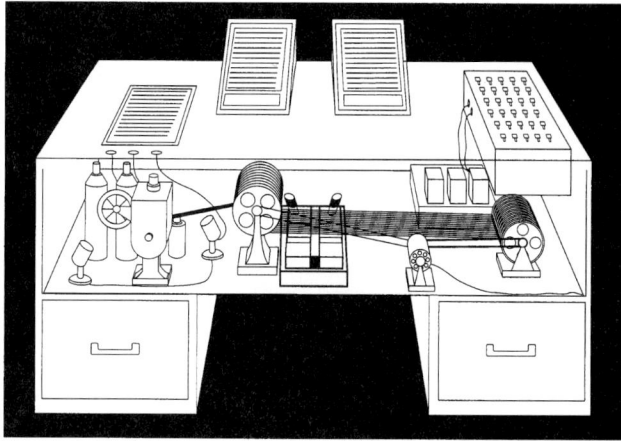

The Memex machine visualized by Vannevar Bush in an article for *The Atlantic Monthly* in 1945 as a kind of non-linear reference device.

In 1981, Nelson outlined his vision of the *Xanadu* project, which would create a global literary environment—a storehouse for everything ever written—available as a pay-per-document hypertext database. Containing basic hypertext features, Xanadu also contained a highly generalized link structure that would allow multiple links that could be followed in any direction. These links were also independent of editing changes because they would not be embedded in the data, but instead attached from a different part of the document. This allowed them to be addressed separately from the data. Documents would be composed of addresses and links pointing to unchanging base files. These virtual documents could be changed easily and offered great potential for collaborative referencing and editing.

A major part of Xanadu's design was called *transclusion*—a tracking of all connections or references to any data, while staying connected to their "virtual cosmic original" throughout Xanadu. This concept would allow users to follow ownership, track usage, and provide for micropayment depending on use or reference. To date, a workable version of Xanadu has yet to be perfected. However, in 1999 the Xanadu code became open source and available for continued development. ∎

Ted Nelson and Hypertext

The terms *hypertext* and *hypermedia* were first used by Ted Nelson in a paper to the ACM twentieth national conference in 1965. Hypertext describes a nonlinear approach to writing, allowing the reader to make choices about which threads of information are going to be followed. In order to accomplish this, hypertext language creates links in the text to other words, images, or documents that offer the reader a new, nonlinear way to seek information (see Box 12.3).

Englebart, van Dam, Nelson and the Hypertext Editing System

Andries van Dam created the first hypertext system in 1967 while at Brown University, and at the time gave full credit to the founders of the hypertext concept, Ted Nelson and Doug Englebart. Ted Nelson, a college friend of van Dam, had worked with him in developing the *Hypertext Editing System* (HES).

As mentioned earlier, Engelbart's laboratory at SRI was the second node hooked up to the ARPANet network (for more on Engelbart, see Chapter 5). It was his research group's responsibility to coordinate work over networks. As a result, they became the first Network Information Center to organize access to the network's resources. During the 1960s and 1970s, Englebart's lab initiated a large-scale hypermedia system (NLS for oNLine System). This led to the exploration of and, by the early 1970s, the deployment of hyperlinked data over the Internet—far before the evolution of the World Wide Web.

The Hypertext Editing System allowed for on-screen editing, links within documents that led to other parts of the same document, and even links that led to other documents. However, HES eventually left Nelson's hypertext ideas behind to concentrate on printout and formatting, eventually becoming one of the prototypes of today's word-processing systems. While Ted Nelson considered this a disastrous wrong turn, later versions of van Dam's hypertext system would allow for graphics to be linked to a document and laid the groundwork for the way in which graphical links on the World Wide Web work today. Still, many aspects of his system needed further development before hypertext systems would fulfill their promise (see Figure 12.8).

Inventing the Web

Tim Berners-Lee and CERN

Located in Geneva, Switzerland, CERN (European Laboratory for Particle Physics) is one of the world's oldest and largest scientific laboratories dedicated to research in the field of particle physics. Since no single European country can afford the extensive and costly facilities this type of research requires, CERN, along with several satellite sites, is a collaborative venture and a center for researchers from more than eighty countries. While much of the research takes place at one of the CERN sites, researchers also work at their own universities or government laboratories. They collaborate in research teams that may include hundreds of physicists, engineers, and other highly trained colleagues spread all over the world. In order for the experiments to proceed smoothly, constant contact must be maintained as data is shared.

In 1989, CERN connected their computers to the Internet so researchers throughout CERN could exchange information quickly over their network. In addition to e-mail, communicating over the Internet allowed scientists to analyze data in their own labs, and this in turn allowed them to continue teaching at their own universities. Throughout the 1980s, however, even as the Internet was evolving at dizzying speed, the system was becoming increasingly frustrating. The types of computers, operating and network systems being used throughout the academic community was widely varied. Common features were rare and users needed to be conversant with more than their own system in order to share information.

At that time, in order to share information and research data, researchers had to find the file they wanted by name from a list of files without any description on either a local or remote computer, connect to that computer using the current TCP/IP, and then download the file they wanted. If they were working on different types of computers, they would also have to translate the information in order for it to work on their native platform. It became clear that this unwieldy system needed to be replaced by a common user interface that could bring information across a network without the need to translate it before it could be read by differing operating systems.

Tim Berners-Lee (see Figure 12.9), a young programmer at CERN, wrote a program in 1980 called *Enquire* that organized information through open-ended relationships between documents by using links. In 1989 he proposed a hypertext system based on his earlier work with *Enquire*. Using prior experiences with developing multitasking operating systems and typesetting software, he wrote

Figure 12.8
Dr. Andries van Dam developed the first workable hypertext system while at Brown University.

Figure 12.9

Dr. Tim Berners-Lee introduced HTTP or hyper-text transfer protocol while a research scientist at CERN, opening the way for the World Wide Web.

the prototype software for a server and client for what later came to be known as the World Wide Web. His program could connect a collection of hyperlinked pages at different locations on the Internet by using a network protocol called hyper-text transfer protocol (HTTP).

Berners-Lee's system was refined from December of 1990 through 1993. In addition, in 1993 the International Standards Organization (ISO) established a standard for HTML which involved marking up text files with standard codes in order to format it. This was initially done with a basic text editor. In the early 1990s, researchers at CERN were using Berners-Lee's early Web browsers to access information on the Web and a variety of newsgroups in order to share information. Soon, these simple browsers spread to other research and scientific communities, and interfaces were added to provide additional access to other protocols like WAIS, Telnet, FTP, and Gopher (see Box 12.4).

BOX 12.4 PROTOCOLS FOR THE INTERNET: A BRIEF DESCRIPTION

♦ *WAIS (Wide Area Information System)* supported document retrieval from databases through a full-text search. WAIS also supported listings of directories of servers, which could then be searched for a particular source by name or topic.

♦ *Telnet* programs are similar to modem-based communications programs. They provide a type of terminal emulation program, but instead of needing to dial other computers directly, Telnet uses a "telnet protocol" to talk to other computers connected to the Internet. The protocol also allows for interactive text between computers in a manner similar to systems established for connection to bulletin board services (BBS). By using telnet, a user can access BBSs and similar systems that are connected through the Internet.

♦ *FTP (file transfer protocol)* software allows you to transfer files between your computer and a remote server. While files can be transferred as e-mail attachments or through HTTP, neither of these methods were designed for transferring large files. FTP not only allows you to transfer larger files but it can resume transfer, even if interrupted, from the point at which the interruption took place (see additional information about FTP in Chapter 13).

♦ *Gopher* is the earliest of the systems available for organizing and displaying files on the World Wide Web. Originally developed at the University of Minnesota, Gopher was named after the school's mascot. Gopher servers present information in a hierarchically structured list of files which can be searched by either Veronica or Jughead. Jughead is a simpler version of Veronica. Veronica uses a *spider* that crawls over the Web to automatically fetch Web pages to feed the search engine. Gopher has, for the most part, been replaced by more sophisticated systems.

In 1992, CERN published the source code for their Web servers and browsers and also began to promote the Web beyond the research and academic communities. It immediately became evident that the Web was providing a communication medium for users from all walks of life. Web pages began to appear everywhere—not just on academic topics, but on all sorts of subjects. Soon, software developers were creating second-generation Web browsers with more powerful tools and simpler interfaces for PC and Mac systems.

At this early stage in the development of the World Wide Web, there were only two kinds of browsers available. The first was Berners-Lee's original version, which was very sophisticated but only available for use on NeXT computers. The second browser was a *line-mode* browser (see Figure 12.10) which could run on any platform. This browser was not very powerful, was more difficult to use, and was limited to text only. It was at this point that Tim Berners-Lee placed a request over the Internet for other developers to participate in improving the software available for accessing what was becoming the World Wide Web.

As a result of Tim Berners-Lee's innovative work, by the end of 1994, the WWW had evolved to 10,000 servers and 10 million users. By 1997, the number of servers had exceeded 650,000 with approximately 1,000 new servers coming online every day. Today that number is escalating exponentially (see Box 12.5).

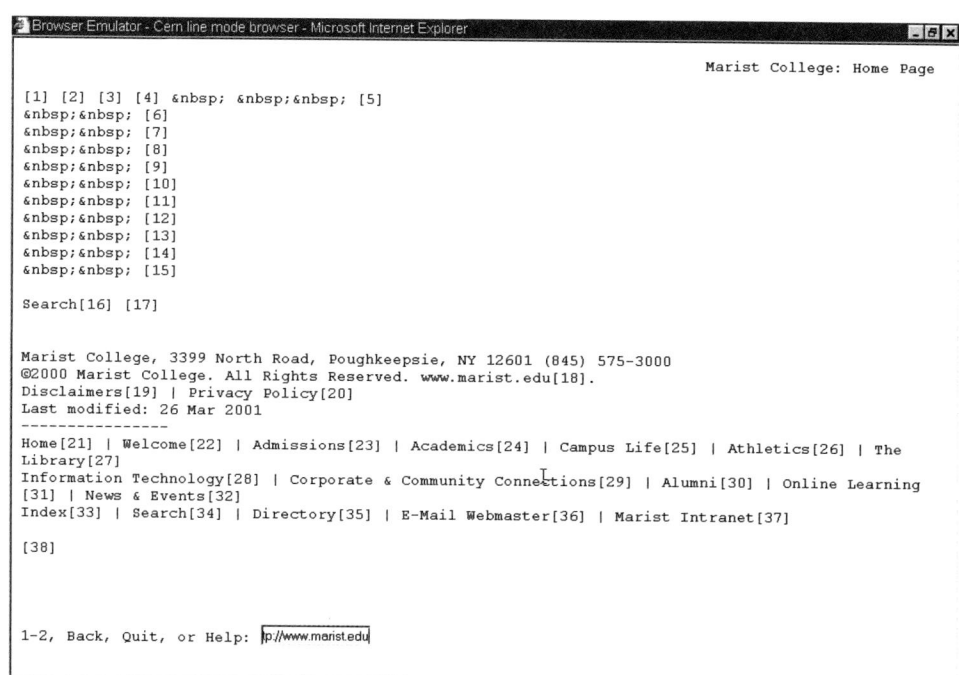

Figure 12.10

This is how the Marist College website would appear on a simple line browser similar to that developed by Tim Berners-Lee.

BOX 12.5

What is the World Wide Web?

The World Wide Web merges computer networks and hypertext into a whole greater than the parts—nothing less than a global information system accessed through a simple browser interface accessed through a keyboard and mouse. The use of hypertext to link information together—kind of a cross-referencing that can take you anywhere in that imaginary community we call the Web—allows data to be referenced to any existing document in the world (that is on the Web). By clicking from one link to the next, you can wander or browse from one page to another. ∎

Marc Andreesen and Mosaic

In 1992, Marc Andreesen was a student and part-time assistant at the National Center for Supercomputing Applications (NCSA) at the University of Illinois at Urbana-Champaign. The University of Illinois had been one of the first dozen nodes on the ARPANET and had been chosen to direct the NCSA. With researchers submitting work to the Cray supercomputers at NCSA around the clock over the NSFnet, which had replaced the ARPANET, an enormous number of students and staff were required to keep things running smoothly.

While working at NCSA, Marc Andreesen and a group of fellow students discovered the World Wide Web browser source code that CERN had just released that year. Andreesen was already familiar with the relatively difficult-to-use browsers connected to the Unix machines that researchers used, and wanted to work on something that would be simpler and easier to use. At this time, finding and downloading documents was a tedious and time-consuming process using complex Unix commands and protocols like FTP, Gopher, and Telnet. Enlisting the help of Eric Bina, also at NCSA, he began to work on a new browser that would integrate those separate functions within a single program, using graphics to make things easier. Initially designed to run in the X Window System environment in Unix, *Mosaic* offered a friendly window-based interface on a platform that many researchers shared. Suddenly, users could learn to navigate the Web in minutes instead of months (see Figure 12.11).

The new browser Andreesen created was far more graphically sophisticated than other browsers were at the time. It could not only display conventional HTML documents but also included a number of new formatting tags to organize text. Most importantly, however, was the addition of an *image tag*. Where earlier browsers could view images as separate files, Mosaic, for the first time, allowed images and text to appear on the same page. In addition, Andreesen's browser had a graphical interface with buttons that could be clicked with a mouse in order to move around more easily, as well as new controls that let users scroll through text.

■ **Figure 12.11**

Screen capture of the Marist College website on an early Mosaic interface.

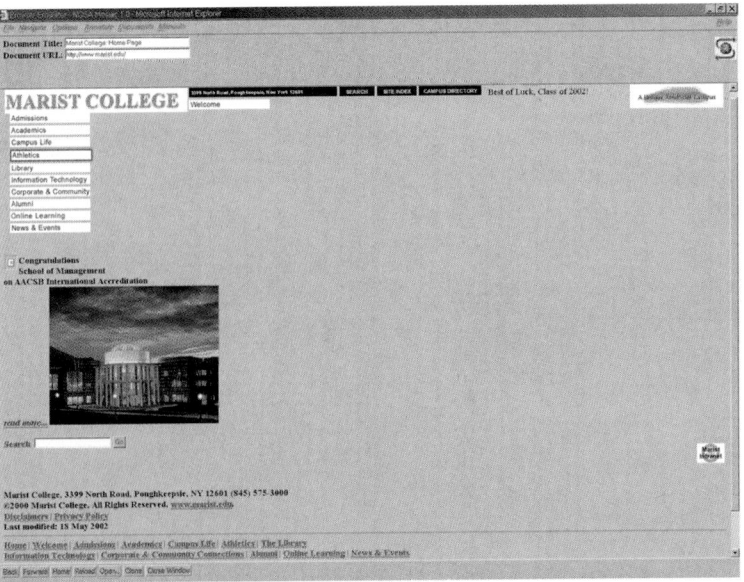

In addition to the user-friendly graphical interface, hyperlinks were handled differently. Hypertext links in earlier browsers were designated by reference numbers. To see the related information, users had to type the reference number into the browser to go to the linked document. In Mosaic, the user simply clicked on the hyperlink to move to the linked document.

In 1993, when the Unix version of Mosaic was made available for download on NCSA's servers, it was an overnight success. When the PC and Mac versions were released later that year, it was a sensation. It also started the paradigm we know today—the more users there are, the greater the creation of new and more varied Web content. The larger and more varied the Web content, the more the number of people using the Web increases.

Like many other industry innovators, Andreesen and Bina were never mentioned in news releases by the organization that controlled the innovation—in this case, NCSA. By the end of 1993 it became clear to Andreesen that NCSA, which was in reality a research environment and not a software company, was not going to be able to develop or maintain the software as part of their mission. It was at that point he decided to leave NCSA after graduation and move to Silicon Valley.

Coincidentally, Jim Clark, founder of SGI (Silicon Graphics, Inc), found that Andreesen was working nearby and decided to talk to him about his new Web browser. Clark, retiring from SGI, was interested in starting a technology company featuring interactive television, and he thought Andreesen's browser might be able to serve as an interface. However, Andreesen convinced Clark that the Internet represented a better market, and they decided to build on Andreesen's already successful Mosaic Web browser. Andreesen recruited six of the seven Illinois students originally involved in writing Mosaic and incorporated his new company. However, a surprise awaited: the University of Illinois claimed that Andreesen had stolen Mosaic from the university and demanded that he stop using the name Mosaic and also stop further distribution of the browser that he had developed. This was especially surprising to Jim Clark, who had started SGI after developing the technology that made the browser possible while working as an associate professor at Stanford. While Stanford accepted Clark's commercial implementation of technology developed at the university, the University of Illinois was not as generous. As a result, Andreesen changed the name Mosaic to Netscape, and at the end of 1994 agreed to a financial settlement of 3 million dollars with the University of Illinois to free Netscape from further claims.

Netscape

The fledgling Netscape Communication Corporation was founded in 1994 and immediately faced the problem of writing a new browser that would surpass the earlier Mosaic browser (now the sole property of the University of Illinois). With the Netscape team working around the clock, they soon came up with a superior browser that offered exciting new features. The question that remained, however, was how to profit from the new software. It was decided that market share was the key, and they decided to make Netscape a pervasive part of the Web.

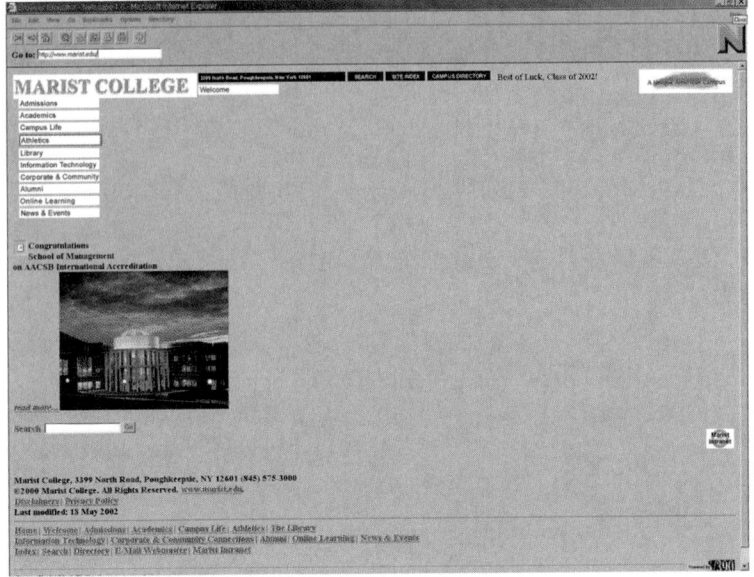

Netscape adopted a price structure for their browser that would charge for business use but allowed students and educators to download the software for free. Everyone else would pay $39 to download the software. While this was the plan, the reality was that almost everyone was able to download and use Netscape for free. Whether using a free beta version or new versions on a ninety-day unenforced trial period, Netscape was essentially free to the general public (see Figure 12.12).

Luckily, Andreesen and Clark were not as concerned about making money selling the browser as they were about selling advertising on their home page. The more people who downloaded the browser, the greater the advertising fees they could charge. In addition, they made more money with their basic server (the programs run on computers that served as network hubs for the Internet). Complete with Secure Socket Layer (SSL) technology for encrypting sensitive information like credit card numbers, it was priced from $1,500 to $5,000 for a commercial server.

The new Netscape browser included new HTML tags that made greater control of text and images possible. Designers immediately began to use the new tags to improve their pages. Of course, only the new Netscape browser could read the new tags, leading to notes on most Web pages indicating that the pages were best when viewed with Netscape. This often included a link to the Netscape home page where the browser could be downloaded. As a result, web pages became more interesting to view and easier to navigate and more people switched to the program that made that possible—Netscape.

Netscape released their second-generation browser, Netscape Navigator 2.0, in 1995. It included many new features that are common today, such as frames (which allowed the screen to be cut into separately controlled windows) and image maps (which allowed users to click on part of an image to move to another source). In addition, it featured Java support, LiveScript (Javascript), a plug-in application programming interface

(API), and SSL encryption technology to enable secure transactions. Netscape also included a Newsreader, a WYSIWYG HTML editor, and an e-mail program.

Browser Wars: The Sleeping Giant

Microsoft had already developed its own browser by 1995 and was including it as part of the operating systems they sold, but it lacked the sophisticated features Netscape was providing. However, when Netscape released their second-generation browser, Microsoft took notice and quickly introduced Internet Explorer 3.0, which offered many of the same features as the Netscape browser. They also gave Internet Explorer away for free, not only as part of their operating system but as a download from their website. The battle for market share was thereby joined (see Figure 12.13).

The jump from Microsoft's Internet Explorer 2.0 to Internet Explorer 3.0 was significant. Working in a fashion similar to their new operating system, the browser not only did most of the things Netscape could do, it also added support for *style sheets*. Style sheets define the elements of page layout and apply them to an entire series of pages in order to create a unified and consistent look to an entire website. This ability to definitively establish everything from font size to margin size to placement of images makes things easier for designers involved with overall site development. In addition to style sheets, where Netscape supported Java, Explorer upped the ante by adding ActiveX, which made it possible to place Windows applications directly on Web pages. Both Netscape and Microsoft were battling to establish de facto standards for the WWW before the World Wide Web Consortium could come up with official standards.

By the end of 1996, both Netscape Navigator and Microsoft's Internet Explorer had their fourth-generation browser in the late beta (testing) stage and ready for final distribution. From barely supporting frames and Java,

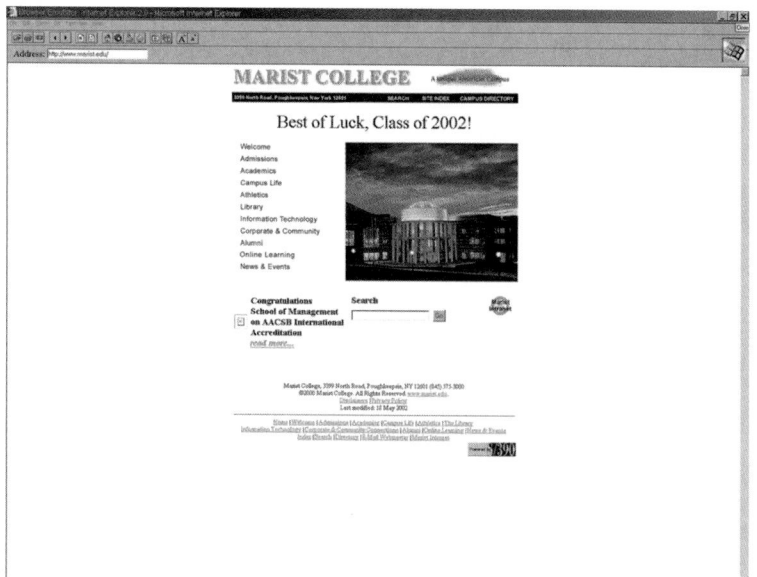

■ **Figure 12.13**

Screen capture Marist College website on emulation of Internet Explorer 2.

these new browsers now supported videoconferencing modules, streaming video technologies, and secure connection encryption.

Where Netscape's marketing strategy of giving away the software to the general public but selling server software to companies and service providers had been very successful in gaining them the lion's share of the browser market, Microsoft was able to upstage them by not only bundling a browser as part of their Windows operating system (already giving them a huge advantage in terms of availability and usability since every PC came with the software already installed), but also by giving away the server-side software that Netscape relied on for its profits. Commercial servers now had to make a very difficult choice—pay Netscape $5,000 for their server software or use the software Microsoft was providing free. Their choice changed the nature of browser use on the Web.

As a result of Microsoft's Web software distribution policy, Jim Clark, Netscape's CEO, accused Microsoft of "buying the market" and various other unethical business practices. This soon evolved into an antitrust battle charging that Microsoft was unfairly taking advantage of bundling its browser in the operating systems it was selling to approximately ninety percent of the market—that Microsoft was using its monopoly in one area to achieve a monopoly in another area. At this writing, this court case is still being resolved by the judicial system but the final decision may be moot. By 1999, Microsoft had already won a decisive victory on the WWW, as almost seventy-five percent of the market was using their browser.

By late 1998, as Netscape watched its share of the market dwindle, it was sold to America Online for $10 billion in stock options. Soon, many of the engineers that made Netscape into a powerhouse were leaving to find other jobs in the industry. However, AOL's takeover of Netscape (with 20 million registered users) meant its browser would live on as part of AOL's browser. AOL, which was often treated as a second-rate Internet service provider catering to the less-technologically sophisticated Web user, became an even more powerful force to be reckoned with.

What was the result of the battle between Netscape and Microsoft? A victory for Microsoft on the browser front but years of court battles, while Netscape was integrated into AOL's system. More important than these corporate issues, however, was the competition that spurred both Netscape and Microsoft to quicker, more imaginative innovations that helped make the Web what it is today.

Skirmishes Along the Web

In addition to the primary battle between Microsoft and Netscape for Web dominance, smaller battles were also being waged. VRML, ICQ, and PUSH, a few of the many new technologies that began to crop up throughout the Web, were all making their voices heard within the Web community. In each case, they would have an impact upon the evolution of the browser wars and even question whether browsers might be necessary after all. As the electronic industry geared up to respond to the new medium, Internet "appliances" were also hot topics of discussion and folded into the boiling pot of sometimes-conflicting technology.

VRML

In the 1990s many technology experts saw VRML as the next manifestation of the Web. VRML is not a true modeling language, nor is it really a virtual reality interface. VRML is a 3-D-file interchange format that defines things like light sources, different viewpoints, geometry, fog effects, basic animation, and textural properties, among other things. It is used primarily as an uncomplicated, multiplatform language for publishing 3-D Web pages. This is especially helpful for games, engineering projects, architecture, and so on. The true strength of VRML is in designing Web pages that engage the user in an interactive role beyond that which is capable through HTML. As VRML has grown, its specifications have become more sophisticated and its potential has been expanded; however, because of the need for plug-ins and its relatively slow speeds, it has not lived up to its promise.

PUSH

Where current Web browsers are user directed, allowing individuals to navigate by clicking on links to tunnel through to the information they want, PUSH technology broadcasts or pushes information to you. One of the first, mild examples of this was *Pointcast* (now part of Infogate), which used the Web to "push" information like news, sports, or ads across your computer screen while it is idle, much like a screen saver might. Nascent forms of PUSH technology can include things like stock market tickers that pop up to keep you abreast of current happenings, weather tickers, and similar informational windows.

PUSH technology has the capability of working without the user ever launching a browser, and it is not limited to the computer screen. Plans for PUSH include everything from use in wireless phones to whatever other devices might be connected in some way to the net. Beyond interactive media, PUSH as envisioned might not remain so simple. Many see it as broadcast, networked media that seeks you out, without invitation, as content is pushed at you like a telemarketer who never stops calling. People who don't like screen "pop-ups" will most likely find PUSH technology equally annoying. PUSH media is always on and is designed to seek you out twenty-four hours a day.

Microsoft Explorer and Netscape have already begun to include certain forms of this technology in their browsers. Microsoft's Active Desktop has introduced channels that frame ongoing streams of data rather than static single-frame windows. The content itself moves the information along without the user needing to do anything. Other technologies like Java, ActiveX, and WebObject are contributing to the evolution of this new technology, which is essentially directed by others rather than chosen by individual users. There are some prognosticators who believe that this technology has the capability of changing the way in which we access the net entirely—replacing conventional browsers with a constant stream of information flowing at you from every corner of your life.

Second Revolution of the Computer Age

AOL and Time Warner

Started as a bulletin board service (BBS) Quantum Computer Services introduced a GUI in 1985 and officially became America Online in 1989. As an Internet Service Provider, AOL had grown to 500,000 members by 1993. In addition to offering access to the Internet, AOL also provided unique services which took into consideration the interests and needs of their users. By 1997, as the World Wide Web became ever more popular, AOL had grown to 9 million members. After purchasing Netscape, its membership soared to over 20 million users in just a few years (see Figure 12.14).

CONCLUSION

The emergence of the Web as a dominating force in communication is best exemplified by AOL's purchase of Time Warner. In a labyrinthine melding of two media giants, one new, one old, an AOL/Time Warner merger was approved just before the start of the millenium—December 14, 2000. The largest merger in the history of the United States, Time Warner received $166 billion in stock from AOL in exchange for their communications empire. AOL now owned Time Warner's publishing business encompassing *Time*, *People,* and *Sports Illustrated* as well as Time Warner Trade Publishing; the Warner Music Group, including a range of recording artists; Warner's film and entertainment division, including Warner Brothers and New Line Cinema; their networks, including Turner Broadcasting, CNN, and Home Box Office; and Time Warner Cable. Time Warner's cable network provides Roadrunner—a popular broadband cable Internet provider. Add to this list CompuServe, Netscape, AOL Instant Messenger, AOL MovieFone, ICQ, TBS, TNT, the Cartoon Network, Digital City, Spinner, Winamp, Fortune, AOL.COM, *Entertainment Weekly,* and Looney Tunes— all owned by an Internet service provider little more than a decade old. It would appear that the Internet and its offspring, the World Wide Web, are in the process of changing the very structure of commerce in the world today.

Even as this merger was taking place, other entertainment giants were announcing plans to bring their product to the Web. Both Disney and Sony are looking for Web partners, as are Viacom, MGM, and others. We seem to be in a time of transition from traditional media, and their more conventional outlets, to entertainment content redefined by the Internet. Most importantly, the World Wide Web is only beginning to mature.

Projects: The Internet and the World Wide Web

1 *Create a visual timeline of Web browsers by finding images representing the milestones in Web browser history. These may be images of what a computer screen would have looked like when using a particular browser. See how far back you can go. Try to include the first nongraphical browsers.*

2 *Review the differences between Andreesen's original Mosaic (1993) and a recent version of Netscape or Internet Explorer. What can recent browsers do that Mosaic could not do?*

3 *Make a list of the characteristics that an ideal art department website should have. Compare the websites for the art departments of three different colleges or universities. Determine which is the most effective and make a list of the reasons why.*

4 *Create a list of elements you enjoy at the various websites you visit. Make a list of the elements you find most annoying or bothersome. Provide three examples of sites that represent each of these lists.*

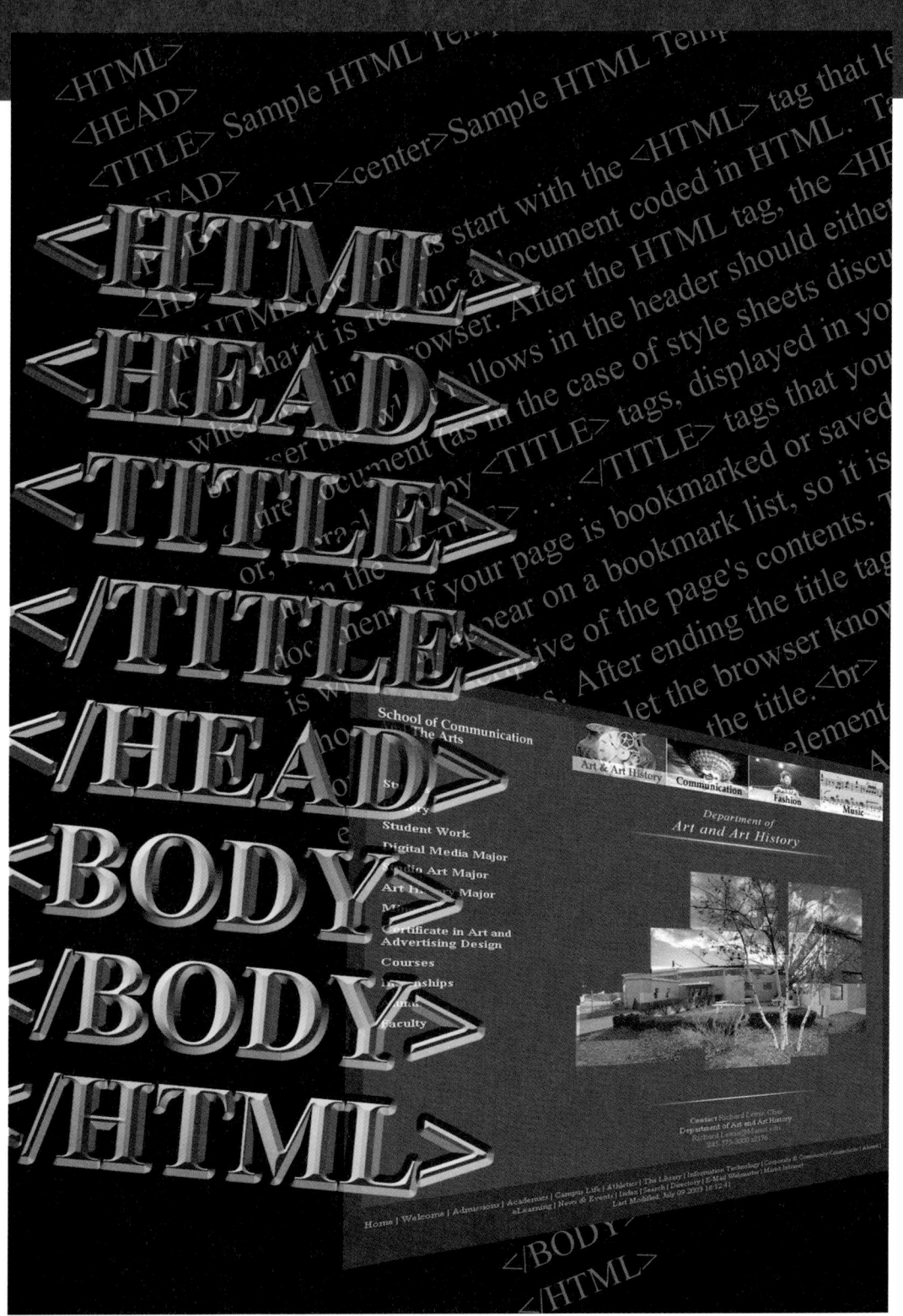

CHAPTER 13

Designing for the Web: Tools and Technologies

Introduction

The last chapter was a brief overview of the development of the Internet and, subsequently, the World Wide Web. As astonishing as it may seem, the World Wide Web has only been available to the general public since 1994. During that time, the ability of Web browsers to deliver complex information, including graphics, animations, and streaming video and audio, has grown dramatically. The growing use of broadband access to the Web, in the form of cable connections, DSL, and satellite access, has opened new horizons for Web content. This chapter is intended to give you an overview of how to create content for the Web and how to get that content online.

What Makes the Web Work?

What we refer to as the Internet is not a single network but rather a Web of individual networks tied together by modems connected through regular dial-up telephone lines, as well as a variety of higher-speed options, such as ISDN, DSL, cable, and other broadband connections (see Chapter 4 for more information). Early in the development of the Internet, an accurate picture of just how many networks were connected to the Internet was possible. Today, the number of interconnected networks throughout the world is so vast, and increasing so quickly, that it is impossible to keep track of them all.

Who's in Charge?

No one really controls the Internet. As strange as it may sound for something so expansive and powerful, the Internet is like a vast cooperative, with many different organizations and even countries supporting it with money, hardware, and technical expertise. Certainly there are "thicker" networks supporting the "thinner" ones. For example, the National Science Foundation (NSF) started the NSFNET, which is a nationwide network connecting universities, colleges, and other organizations. This can be likened to one of the information superhighways you may have heard about. These networks eventually connect smaller and smaller networks until one of them eventually connects to your house. However, the NSF does not directly oversee any of the smaller networks that it makes possible. Similar situations exist throughout the world. Internet technology has made the independence of individually connected networks guaranteed. However, while the technology has made it possible for individual networks to communicate seamlessly with one another, content and structure are another matter. There is no governing Internet agency. There is no set of absolute rules everyone must follow (outside of the communication protocols that allow the net to function). Organized chaos is the way many Internet experts describe the nature of the Web today.

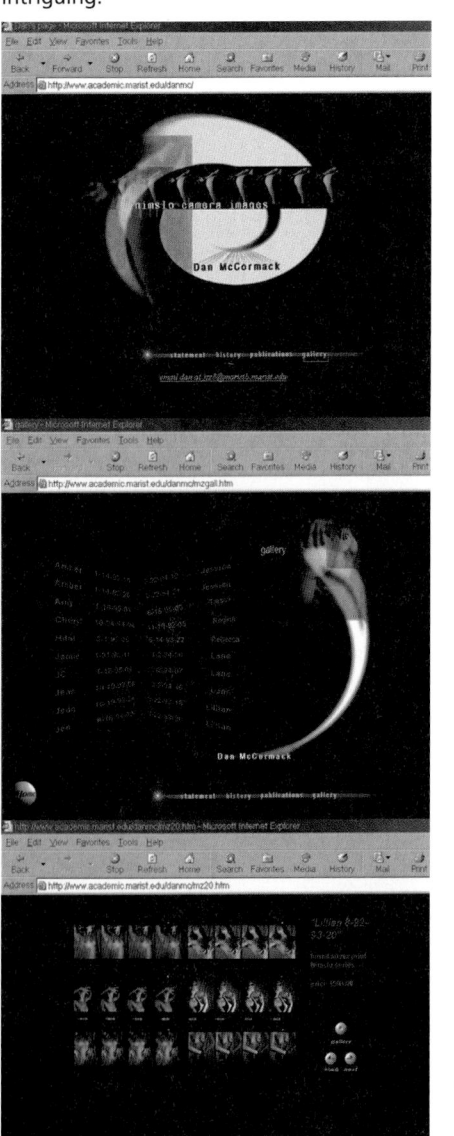

Planning a Website

Thinking It Over

There are many things that all come together on a website. However, even after you learn all the code, the different ways of preparing images, and perhaps even some JavaScript, the most important considerations come before you sit down at the computer. A website usually contains a series of inter-linked pages, each of which covers part of the particular content you wish to present. The first questions asked should not deal with HTML code, but with the nature of the site itself (see Figure 13.1).

As in any multimedia production (see Chapter 11), before you begin you should ask several important questions. Who is your audience? What do you wish to convey? What ideas do you have for the "look" of the page—the format of the basic design? While the Web does have its own special properties (many of which we will introduce during this chapter), you are still designing space that must not only make sense and be visually appealing, but must also convey the content (what the site is about) clearly and coherently with a minimum of distraction. A site for "John Smith: Party Clown" would not have the same look and feel as one for "John Smith: Corporate Law." All of the skills that a graphic designer brings to print publication—selection, size, and spacing of type; use of graphics and photographs; judicious use of color; and so on—apply to designing for the Web. Many students interested in Web design feel they should spend most of their time learning the latest in HTML code, JavaScript, and other Web languages. However, even the best HTML skills will be wasted if the underlying design is poor and navigational elements are difficult to use. Strong design skills still go a long way, and for art and design students, are absolutely the best preparation for Web design.

That said, consider the site's content. Who is actually going to write the information that will appear on the website? Clear, cogent writing that gets to the point quickly and without obvious errors in the use of language says something about the professionalism of the site you prepare. If you don't like to write, find someone who does. Many websites are the result of a collaboration between visual artists, writers, photographers, and technology experts.

The Website Interface

Once your content is clearly delineated, it makes sense to plan various ways in which that information can be presented within the website. As already mentioned, a website is usually composed of inter-linked pages, each of which conveys some portion of the information you wish to present. Based on the content of the page, how should the information be accessed? Usually there is a home or opening page, often referred to by professionals as the index page, which introduces the site and offers links to additional information/pages on the site. Because this is an HTML page, items will be linked to other information on later pages. However, once again there are questions to be addressed before jumping into the coding of the page.

Page Size

As noted in Chapters 3 and 4, different size monitors, while able to display various screen resolutions, have a default resolution for their relative size. A 14″ monitor's screen resolution is 640 × 480 pixels, while a 17″ monitor has a default screen resolution of 1,024 × 768 pixels. When designing a website, a decision has to be made to design for a particular screen size and its pixel dimensions. In the past, designers automatically designed for 14″ monitors because they were used by the majority of viewers. Evolving technology has changed that. Many people are now using a 15″, 17″, or larger monitor. Again, you must consider the purpose of your site when making the decision to design for a particular screen size. A site designed for the 800 × 600 pixel size of a 15″ monitor may look smaller on a 17″ monitor, but it will display just fine. A site designed for the 1,280 × 1,024 pixel size of a 19″ monitor will require someone with a smaller monitor to scroll from side to side to see the entire page, resulting in viewer frustration and perhaps loss of interest in your content.

Navigation

Once you have made a few of the decisions previously outlined, it often helps to draw out a schematic of the site you wish to create. This can be a simple series of boxes that indicates the "flow" of information on the website and how you intend to get from one place to another (see Figure 13.2). This *flowchart*, outlining how information is to be connected, can indicate when a website might be too "deep" (see Figure 13.3). In other words, users may have to click and click from one page to another to another and so on, making it difficult for someone to backtrack to an earlier page. However, a site that is too shallow (see Figure 13.4), with one page leading to a series of parallel pages, might not offer the depth of information necessary. Planning at this step is crucially important to creating a good site.

The schematic you prepare in planning your website will not only provide a clear sense of how information on one page will lead to another, but

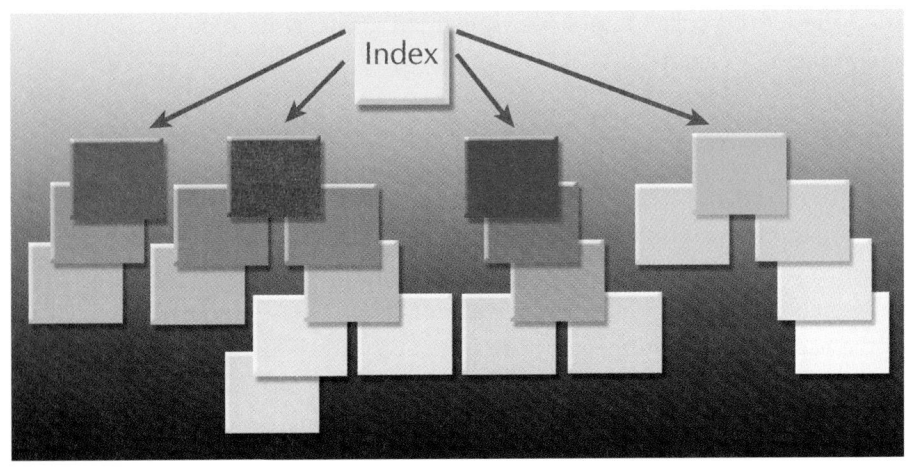

■ Figure 13.2

In planning a website it is helpful, even necessary, to have a Web outline/flow chart to help you organize information.

■ Figure 13.3

A website designed too deep will make it difficult for users to backtrack or know where they are.

■ Figure 13.4

A shallow website doesn't provide enough content development to keep users interested.

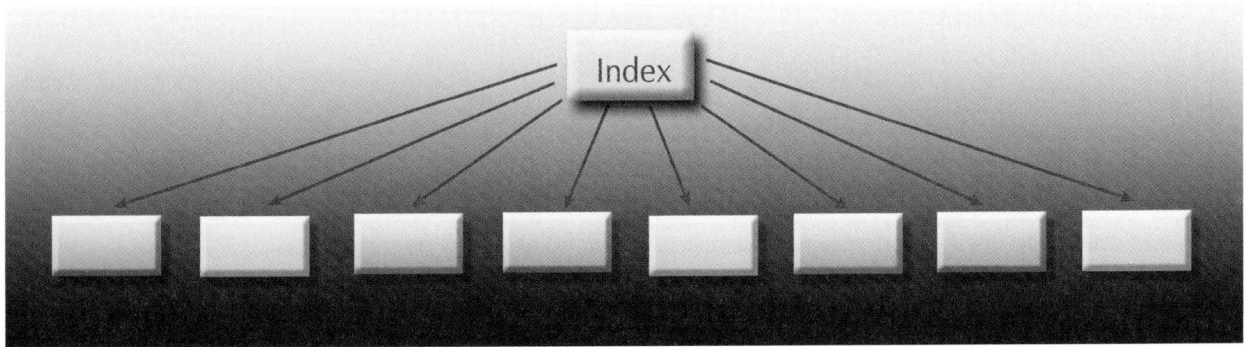

also a clear outline of the kinds of navigational elements that should be included on the page. Getting from one page to another and back again, without confusion, is an important element of Web design. If your pages are longer than a single screen, it makes sense to include navigational controls (see Figure 13.5) both at the top and bottom of the page. If your page is complex enough to require many pages of information, it is important to include navigational aids beyond the browser's back button. For example, in addition to clickable buttons that can move you forward and backward on the site, there should also be a button that will take you *home* to the main or index page of the site.

Bits and Pieces

As this chapter progresses, you will find many pieces of the puzzle for preparing a good Web page outlined and explained. The interrelationships between technical considerations and design considerations are inextricably wound together. For every design decision you make, a technical issue must be resolved; likewise, for every technical issue you raise, a corresponding aesthetic concern must be addressed.

Hypertext Markup Language (HTML): A Quick Look at the Basics

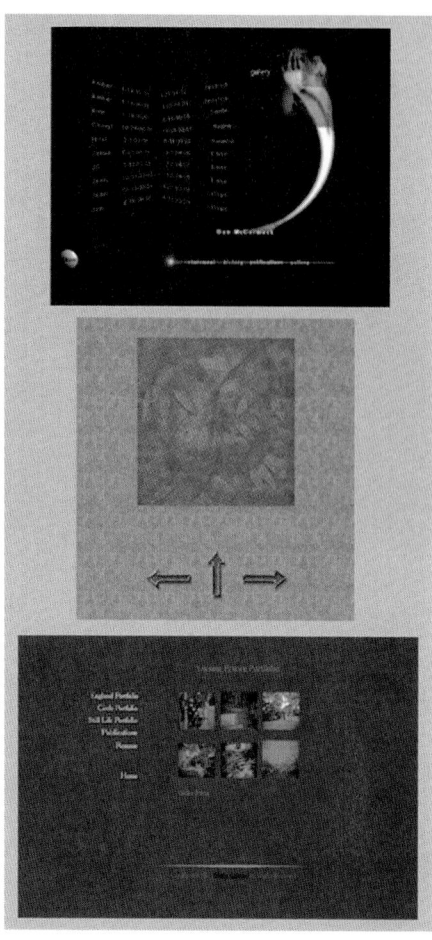

■ **Figure 13.5**

Navigational controls, whatever their form, should be consistent and easy to figure out.

HTML Web pages can become quite complex as items are added and "marked up" with various tags (codes) in order to change the nature of type, reference other pages or images, or organize information. A basic starting page, however, is quite simple. The sample template described below indicates all that is necessary for a simple, functional Web page.

Every HTML command, or tag, is placed in a set of bracket (< >) symbols. HTML tags can range from a single letter to several lines of detailed information. Each tag contains instructions that change the nature of an item on the page. Most tags work very much like switches, with one tag turning a setting on and another tag turning a setting off. The off commands are preceded by a slash. For example, **<TITLE>** indicates that what follows is the document's title and **</TITLE>** indicates the title is complete. **<B>** indicates that the type following this element is going to be bold and **</B>** indicates that the bolding of type should end here. Box 13.1 includes all the basic HTML tags you need to create a simple Web page.

It is worth noting that browsers don't notice spaces between the lines that you include when you type information during the coding of a page. When you space lines apart by hitting the enter key (so you can more easily keep track of code elements), those spaces disappear when the browser reads the document. Text will wrap continuously until you tell it not to. Any spaces you wish to have appear in the browser's version of your HTML document must be included in the code of the page. A <P> indicates a paragraph break with a

BOX 13.1 BASIC HTML DOCUMENT

`<HTML>`	Starts the HTML document.
`<HEAD>`	Starts the header element.
`<TITLE>title of page</TITLE>`	Names or "titles" your document. (Note the `</TITLE>` which says the title ends here.)
`</HEAD>`	Ends the header element. This lets the browser know that the information that follows belongs on the body of the page.
`<BODY>`	Starts the body element. Begin to enter the content of your Web page right after this tag.
`</BODY>`	After the page content is complete, ends the body element.
`</HTML>`	End the HTML document.

blank line of space after it, while a <BR> indicates a smaller line break, simply moving the text to the next line much like a carriage return (when you hit enter on the keyboard). If you need to add extra spaces between letters, words, or images, the "nonbreaking" character string ( ) can be used for each space you need.

Sample HTML Template

All HTML documents start with the <HTML> tag that lets an older browser know that it is reading a document coded in HTML. Tags are not displayed when seen in a browser. After the HTML tag, the <HEAD> tag tells the browser that what follows in the header should either be applied to the entire document (as in the case of style sheets, discussed later in this chapter) or, if bracketed by <TITLE> tags, displayed in your browser's title bar. It is within the <TITLE> . . . </TITLE> tags that you name or "title" your document. If your page is *bookmarked* or saved to be revisited, the title is what will appear on a bookmark list, so it is important to choose something short and descriptive of the page's content. Titles also identify your page for search engines. After ending the title tags, end the header element </HEAD> to let the browser know that the information that follows does not belong in the title.

After the header, start the body element. The content of your Web page comes right after this tag <BODY>. Add the content you wish to have appear on the Web page when someone views it. If this is your beginning or index page, then it will contain links to other parts of your site. After the body of your document is complete, end it with the </BODY> tag. Finish your document with the end HTML tag </HTML>.

All of the information previously described could be typed in a simple text editor and saved with an .htm or .html file name extension. If you apply all of the tags previously described, along with even minimal content, you will have a Web page that any browser can read. Of course, it doesn't contain hyper-

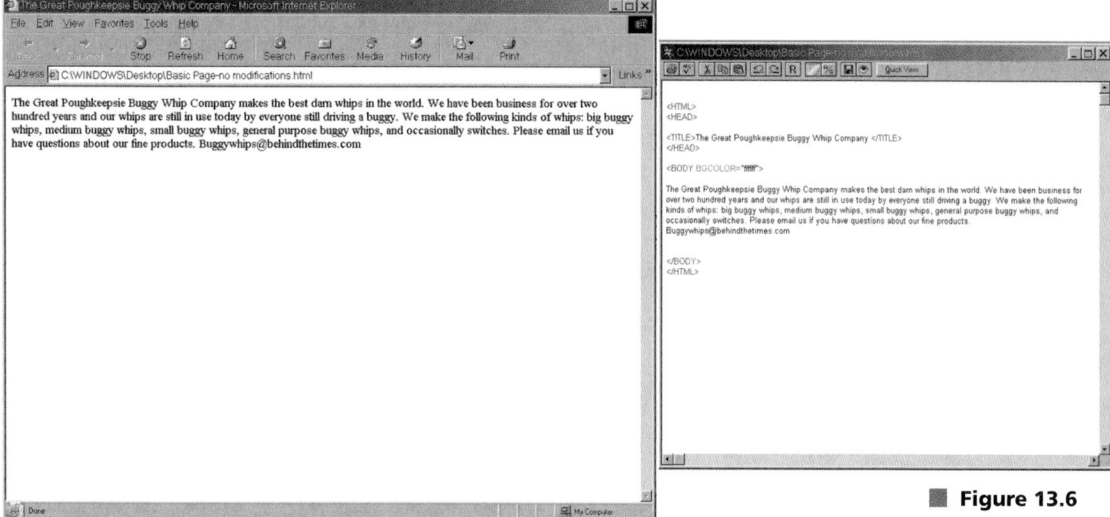

links, images, or any of the things which can make Web pages interesting, but it is a Web page nonetheless.

If we were to add the following sample text to the HTML template previously outlined, without further HTML coding, it would be rather hard to decipher and it would not be very visually appealing (see Figure 13.6).

> The Great Poughkeepsie Buggy Whip Company makes the best darn whips in the world. We have been in business for over two hundred years and our whips are still in use today by everyone still driving a buggy. We make the following kinds of whips: big buggy whips, medium buggy whips, small buggy whips, general purpose buggy whips, and occasionally switches. Please e-mail us if you have questions about our fine products: Buggywhips@behindthetimes.com.

The ways in which this text could be changed are many and varied and up to the designer of the page. One way to vary type sizes is through the use of simple codes called headings. Rather than specify a point size for type, a header simply indicates relative size. For example:

<H1>The Great Poughkeepsie Buggy Whip Company<H1>

<H2>The Great Poughkeepsie Buggy Whip Company<H2>

<H3>The Great Poughkeepsie Buggy Whip Company<H3>

<H4>The Great Poughkeepsie Buggy Whip Company<H4>

<H5>The Great Poughkeepsie Buggy Whip Company<H5>

<H6>The Great Poughkeepsie Buggy Whip Company<H6>

In addition to changing the size of the type, there are *physical styles* you can apply as well. In keeping with the types of commands we might find in conventional word processing software, we have:

Widget (no special tags applied)

Widget	**Boldface**
<i>*Widget*</i>	*Italics*
<u>Widget</u>	Underline
<tt>Widget</tt>	Typewriter font

In addition, there are other commands to help you place text. The simplest is the center command that centers text that falls within the **<center>. . . </center>** tags. There are also several easy ways to list items. You can present a bulleted or *unordered* list using the <ul> command.

<ul> Indicates an unordered list.
<li> First item in the list.
<li> Next item in the list.
</ul> End the unordered list.

Note that <li> does not have an ending bracket.
An unordered list might look something like this:

◆ big buggy whips
◆ medium buggy whips
◆ general purpose buggy whips
◆ switches

A numbered or *ordered* list is also possible using the <ol> command.

<ol> Indicates an ordered list.
<li> First item in the list.
<li> Next item in the list.
</ol> End the ordered list.

An ordered list might look something like this:

1. big buggy whips
2. medium buggy whips
3. general purpose buggy whips
4. switches

There are some other commands that do not require an ending bracket. These include:

 	The tag forces an immediate line break pushing text to the next line.
<hr>	The <hr> tag places a horizontal rule or separator bar between sections of text.
<p>	The <p> tag is a paragraph break, which again forces text to the next line and adds an additional line of blank space.

If we apply some of the previous coding to our buggy whip page, it might look something like this:

```
<HTML>
<HEAD>
<TITLE> The Great Pacific Buggy Whip Company</TITLE>
</HEAD>
<BODY>
<CENTER><H1>The Great Pacific Buggy Whip Company </H1></CENTER><p>
<B>The Great Pacific Buggy Whip Company</B> makes the best darn whips
in the world. We have been in business for over two hundred years and
our whips are still in use today by everyone still driving a buggy. We
make the following kinds of whips: <BR>
<UL>
<LI> big whips
<LI> medium whips
<LI> small whips
<LI> general purpose whips
<LI> switches
</UL>
<BR>
<BR>
<HR>
<H4>Please <A HREF="mailto:buggywhips@behindthetimes.com">e-mail</a> us
if you have questions about our fine products.</H4>
</BODY>
</HTML>
```

When you are finished encoding the document, it must be saved with the suffix .htm or .html (e.g., bugindex.htm) so it will be recognized as a document that a browser can read. It is also a good idea to use no more than eight letters in a file name. If longer file names are used, be sure to use an *underscore* (_) instead of blank spaces between words. If we save this as the main page of a website containing several referenced pages, we'll save it as the index page or index.htm. At this point the document should look something like this (see Figure 13.7):

Figure 13.7

Screen capture of page with basic coding to organize information.

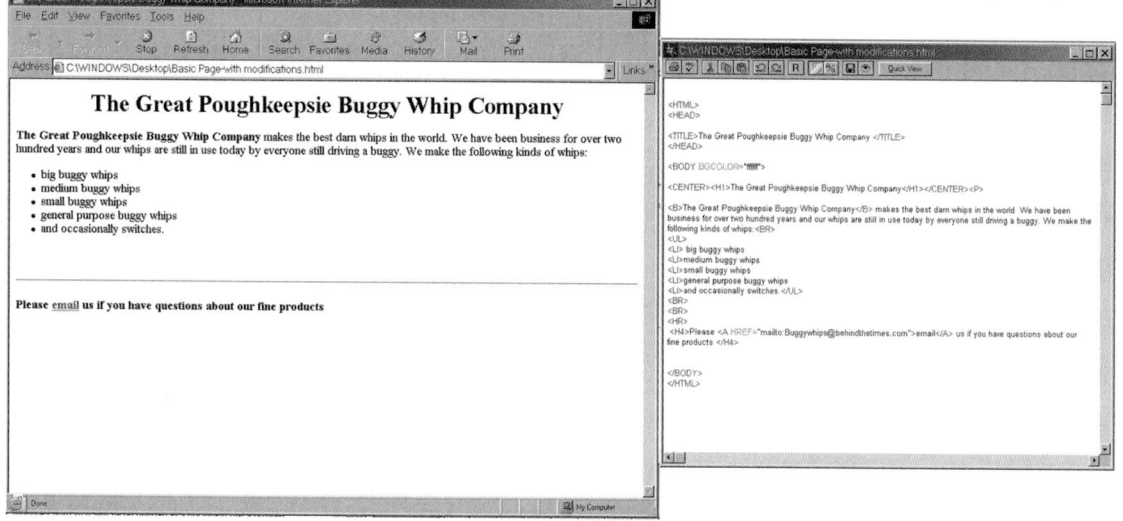

Adding Links

Hyperlinks (or hypertext) can be added to your Web page to allow the viewer to jump from information on one page to view new information on another page within your website, on another website entirely, or even to a new spot on the same Web page. Almost anything can serve as the source of the link, but usually it is a word or an image. For example, small thumbnail images can be clicked to open a larger version of the image or a new HTML page containing the image with information about it.

Linking to a Website or Web Page

The following code includes all the information you need to create links. In every case, the links start with an <A> *anchor* tag and end with </A> tag.

To link text to a website:

```
<A HREF="http://www.marist.edu">Marist
College</A>
```
Note: <A starts the anchor tag and HREF
 indicates the referenced
 site or file.

The url being referenced starts and ends with quotes. The words **Marist College** will show up as a blue, underlined link. When you click on it, your browser will take you to the Marist College website.

To link an icon to a website:

```
<A HREF="http://www.marist.edu"><IMG SRC=
"redfox.gif"> </A>
```

This will take you to the same site but you will be clicking on a red fox *icon* (small picture) to take you there.

To link an icon to a Web page:

```
<A HREF="english_castle.htm"><IMG
SRC="castle_icon.gif"> </A>
```

Note: When there is a space between words
(*english* and *castle*) use an underscore in place
of a blank space. This will make things go easier
when it is time to FTP your site to a server.

This is similar to the above, except that we are referencing (HREF) a particular HTML file "english_castle.htm" that contains further information about an English castle. We are going to click on an icon to launch us there.

Linking to Files in Other Directories

Unless you have a very complex site with many different kinds of files and images, HTML coding will be easier if all of your HTML files and Web images are kept in a single folder known as a *directory*. If your site is complex, and you have to keep files in separate directories, then a little more work is involved. The directory structure must be listed clearly for the link to be understood by the browser.

 If you have a single directory with subdirectories, then referencing a file in one of the lower directories is a matter of listing the entire directory structure when referencing your documents. For example, if you have a folder named "Castles," and nested within it a folder named "England," and within that a file called "Cornwall.htm," you would link to that file by listing the entire directory structure:

```
<A HREF="Castles/England/cornwall.htm">Cornwall</A>
```

Clicking on the word *Cornwall* would open the file "cornwall.htm." In order to move up a directory, use a dot dot slash (../) command to move to a higher level directory. To reference a page called salisbury.htm in the "England" directory from the "cornwall.htm" document, we would use:

```
<A HREF="../salisbury.htm">Home</A>
```

As you can see, things are much simpler if all files are kept in a single folder.

Adding Color

Web Color Palettes

One of the difficulties that often arises when selecting colors for Web pages is that different platforms (Mac and PC) have different color palettes. In addition to this, individual browsers often use their own Web palettes for displaying color. This means that when an image is displayed in one Web browser on a Mac it can look quite different than when displayed in the same Web browser on a PC. When you choose a specific color, the browser tries to use the closest color it can from the palette it is using. If it does not have the color you have chosen, it tries to reproduce it by *dithering* or mixing its own colors together to make it (see Figure 13.8).

Websafe Color: The Hexadecimal World

To address this difficulty, a group of *Websafe* colors has been agreed to that are similar on all browsers. They use a color model in which each of the three primary colors (RGB) is represented by its hexadecimal values of 00, 33, 66, 99, CC, and FF. The basic Web palette, which will work as a standard on all Web browsers and platforms, is composed of combinations of these hexadecimal values. This means we have the potential output of six shades of red, six shades of green, and six shades of blue. Multiplying $6 \times 6 \times 6$ gives us a total of 216 specific colors which can be used safely for all Web applications without fear of the colors changing from one application to another.

Unfortunately, converting from the decimal value of a particular color to its hexadecimal value is not that easy for us. While it is possible to learn the math of converting RGB color to hexadecimal, it is far easier to use the Web color

■ **Figure 13.8**

Sample of Web graphic with and without dithering.

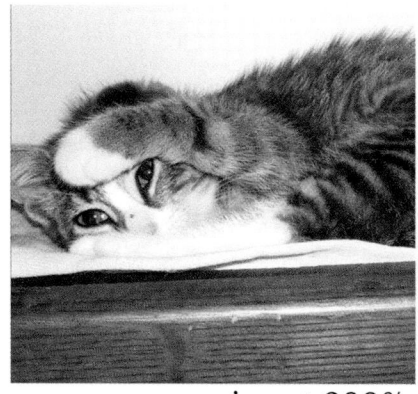  

jpg at 200%   dithered gif at 200%   undithered gif at 200%

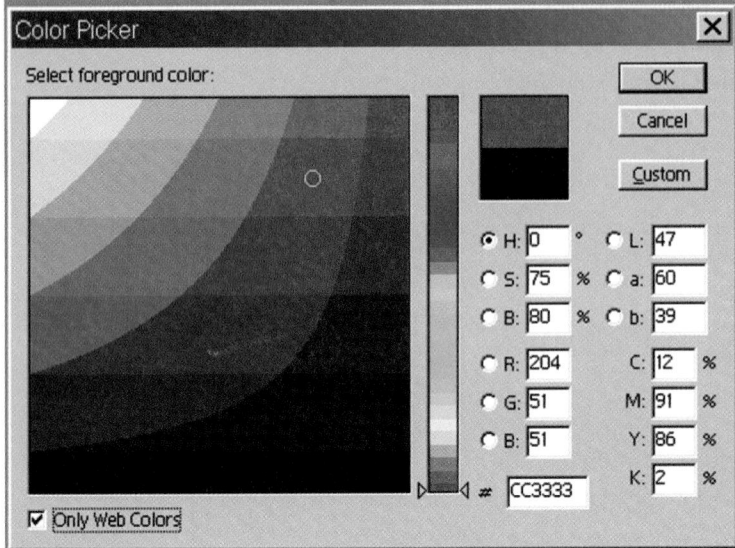

conversion tools available in most image-editing or paint programs. By using an eyedropper or similar tool, you can click on any color you wish, then go to the color picker to see the color represented numerically in RGB, HSB, CMYK, L*A*B*, and finally Hex. For example, in PhotoShop, if you click the "only Web colors" box, Websafe colors appear for you to choose (see Figure 13.9).

Figure 13.9

Web safe colors in PhotoShop's Color Picker.

Add Color to Almost Anything

As our earlier sample HTML document shows, the resulting page shows up with black text on a white or gray background, depending on the browser chosen. You can change the color of both the text and the background by coding in the color you wish to see it in. This is done by specifying the hexadecimal value of the color you wish to use. The code is quite simple—just add <BGCOLOR = "#CC3333"> (which is a dark red) right after the <BODY> tag in your HTML document. You can choose from any of the 216 Websafe colors. Most programs used for creating Web pages allow you to click on a color, automatically adding the hexadecimal information.

Besides the background, with <FONT> tags you can add color to specific text or set a text color for the entire document. You can also set the color of hypertext links, visited links and active links (see Box 13.2).

Using an Image as a Tiling Background

Small JPEG or GIF images can be tiled or repeated throughout the background of a Web page. However, be careful when choosing an image. If an image is too complex, text may be difficult to distinguish against the repeating pattern (see Box 13.2). In a similar fashion, be careful that text is legible against light or

BOX 13.2 SIMPLE COLOR TAGS	
<BODY BGCOLOR="hex number">	Specifies solid background color for page (default is white or #ffffff).
<BODY TEXT="hex number">	Specifies text color for page (default is black).
<BODY LINK="hex number">	Specifies link color for page (default is blue).
<BODY VLINK="hex number">	Specifies visited link color for page (default is purple).
<BODY ALINK="hex number">	Specifies active link for page (appears as link is clicked).

dark colored tiles. Not only must text be easy to read, but links must also show up clearly.

The code adding a tiling image is very straightforward. Instead of using a color background code like <BODY BGCOLOR="hex number">, substitute <BODY BACKGROUND="your tile image.jpg"> in its place. When you view your Web page, all text will appear over the tiling background image you have created (see Box 13.3).

BOX 13.3

Making a background image

You can create a background image from any texture or photo you wish to use. You can even use your scanner to scan bits and pieces of just about anything—coins, fabric, even insects. However, before you consider using messier objects, you may want to place them in a clear plastic bag to protect the scanner. Also, be careful about objects that could scratch the glass. Once you scratch the glass on your scanner, the scratch will show up in every scan you do from then on. Because this will be used as part of a Web page, and we want to have a relatively small pixel area for the tiled image, set your scanner for 100 spi to start.

Once your scan (from a photo or natural object) is complete, bring your scan into an image-editing program for further modification. Be sure your background image is fairly small—perhaps no larger than 150 pixels square. This is where you can lighten the image so that

it "ghosts" out behind your text, or darken it so you can use light colored text over the darkened image. You can even change its color, increase or decrease its color saturation, or apply any one of a number of special-effects filters to modify it further.

Most images used as a background will tile as a series of clearly defined rectangles. Most image-editing programs have a special filter to help fix this. PhotoShop, for example, has an offset filter (in the "other" category in the Filters menu) that will allow you to offset the image by a set number of pixels so that you can see where the clearly defined lines will take place. By using the rubber stamp or smudge tool you can minimize or eliminate the divisions in tone so that the image will tile more smoothly (see Figures 13.10 and 13.11). Be sure to save your small tile as a JPEG image at medium compression. ■

(Continued on next page)

■ **Figure 13.10**

It is necessary to prepare a small image for repetitive tiling.

Basic image capture

Offset Image

Offset image cloned

■ **Figure 13.11**

This comparison of tiled squares demonstrates the results of a properly prepared tile.

Adding Images to Web Pages

The addition of images to Web pages through the arrival of the Mosaic browser (see Chapter 12) led to the large increase of interest in the Web. Adding them to a website is quite simple.

Adding Images to Your Pages

Placing an inline image on your website is accomplished by adding the <IMG SRC="name_of_photo.jpg"> code in the body of your document. By adding this tag, whatever image you include after "<IMG SRC=" will be included on your page (e.g., <IMG SRC="name_of_photo.jpg">). If you want to have an icon or word linked to the image so that the image will appear when it is clicked, then you need to have the image in the folder containing your Web files (see section on linking files). If you want the image to appear on screen with a color background, then you need to prepare a separate HTML document to hold the image. That document can be very simple: just the basic HTML template with the <IMG SRC="name_of_photo.jpg"> included (see Figures 13.12 and 13.13).

Height and Width Tags

Placing height and width tags in your HTML document will tell the browser how large the image being downloaded should be displayed. It also allows the browser to begin downloading and displaying text while the image is downloading, which may keep the interest of less-patient Web users. Without the size specification, the browser has to complete the image download before it can display the text. This can be done by adding the HEIGHT= WIDTH= commands as part of the image tag e.g., <IMG

Figure 13.12

HTML code that references an image directly results in a page with an image in the upper left corner of a plain white background.

Figure 13.13

Preparing a separate page for an image provides more opportunity for design and formatting.

SRC="cats.jpg" HEIGHT="120" WIDTH="240">. The numbers refer to the size (in pixels) the images will fill, and their final size on the page will be dependent upon the size of the screen for which you are designing.

A related consideration to having things appear quickly on screen is whether or not to use *interlaced* GIFs or *progressive* JPEGs, especially when the image might be a bit large. An interlaced or progressive image appears in a series of images starting with a very low-resolution, blocky image that appears quickly, to successively more defined images, until the image appears in full resolution. Image-editing software has tools to choose these options.

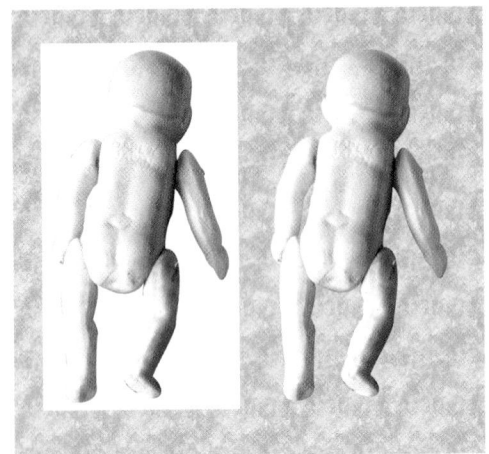

Figure 13.15

This series of screen captures shows JPEGS at different rates of compression. The image on the left has the least compression and the image on the right has the most.

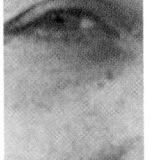 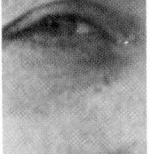 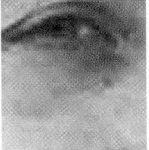

Figure 13.14

A basic GIF or JPEG image will display with a visible rectangular background. A transparent GIF image allows you to define a color or colors within an image to be masked out to reveal the background image or color of your Web page.

JPEG or GIF?

Each of the image file formats that can be displayed on the Web has its own strengths and weaknesses based on its particular file format and compression schemes. GIF files, for example, use a *lossless* compression scheme, which means that after the image is compressed and opened up, it will not lose any of the information it originally had. However, GIF files are limited to 256 colors (eight bit), which makes them unsuitable for color photographs, which look best in millions of colors. GIFs are best for solid color graphics with sharp-edged transitions between colors. Another strength of a GIF file is that you can define colors in the image that will appear transparent, allowing the background of the Web page the image is placed on to show through those areas (see Figure 13.14).

JPEG files use a *lossy* compression scheme that discards or loses information as the file is compressed. When the file is opened from its compressed state, that information cannot be regained. There is always a tradeoff between the amount of compression that takes place and the amount of information that is lost in the compression. However, JPEGs reproduce a photograph's subtle tonal gradation much better than GIFs and are generally much smaller in terms of file size (see Figure 13.15).

The newest file format that can be used on the Web is PNG (pronounced "ping"). It is similar to a GIF, using a lossless compression scheme and working best on graphics, line drawings, and text, but it uses a larger palette. However, it does so at the expense of file size. Like GIFs, certain colors may be defined that will appear transparent on your Web page. PNG also allows for differing degrees of transparency.

Pixel Size for Images

There is a common myth that all Web images should be 72 ppi. However, the size of an image in inches or dpi is unimportant (see Chapter 7 for more information). Converting an image to what has become a de facto standard of 72 ppi will not harm anything, but it misses the point. The only thing that counts in determining the size of an image for display on a computer monitor is pixel size. An image that is 500 × 500 pixels might be 1.667 × 1.667 inches at 300 dpi or 6.944 × 6.944 inches at 72 ppi. It makes no difference whatsoever to the file size, quality of the image, or how large it will appear on screen.

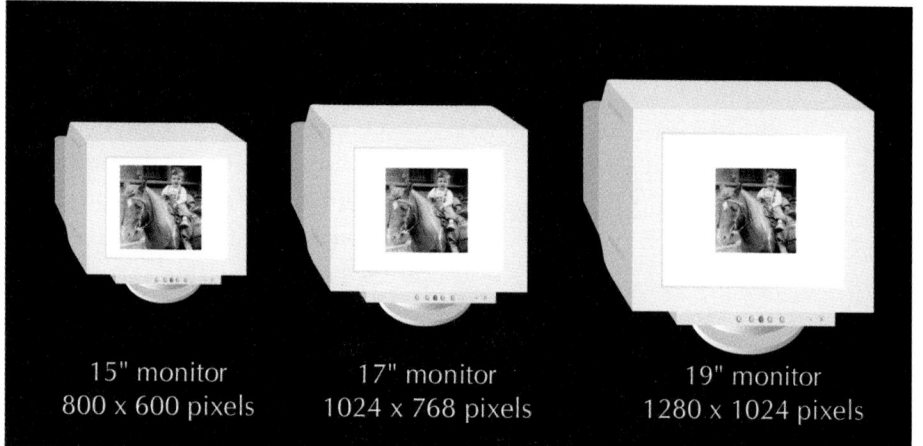

15" monitor
800 x 600 pixels

17" monitor
1024 x 768 pixels

19" monitor
1280 x 1024 pixels

A computer monitor can be set for any one of several pixel sizes, and we have already mentioned that different size monitors have traditional pixel sizes. A 500 pixel × 500 pixel image, displayed on a 17" monitor at 1,024 × 768 pixels, will appear to be much smaller than on a 14" monitor at 640 × 480 pixels. This is the sizing that really matters (see Figure 13.16).

When preparing your images in an image-editing program, be sure to set the pixel size rather than worry about the dpi of the image (see Box 13.4).

Using Tables

If your site contains data that needs to be in the form of charts, or information that needs to be aligned—perhaps a résumé, a budget report, or even a page of thumbnail images—then you might consider using *tables* to organize your Web page (see Figure 13.17). The tables used in an HTML document are very similar to tables found in word processing software. However, in an HTML document there is an even greater variety in the way in which tables can be formatted and used.

BOX 13.4

Design images for the Web at 72 ppi? Check your math.

The conventional wisdom that says all monitors have a screen resolution of 72 ppi (pixels per inch) is simply wrong. The number of pixels a screen actually accommodates is almost always higher. For example, a 17" monitor screen is usually 12.5" wide. If the screen resolution is set for the traditional 1,024 × 768 pixels, the actual screen resolution is 1,024 pixels divided by 12.5, or 82.24. So, the monitor is running at a screen resolution of 82 ppi. If the screen resolution is lowered to 800 × 600 ppi, when one divides 800 pixels (horizontal measurement) by 12.5", we discover that the screen resolution has dropped to 64 ppi. Things now appear coarser. As the pixels presented at any resolution are finite (a monitor set for 1,024 × 768 will have exactly 1,024 pixels horizontally) it is far more important to consider the size of an image in pixels rather than resolution in terms of dpi or ppi in order to control how large it will appear on screen. It really doesn't matter whether the image is 72 ppi or 300 ppi as long as the pixel dimensions are suitable for the screen size for which you are designing. ■

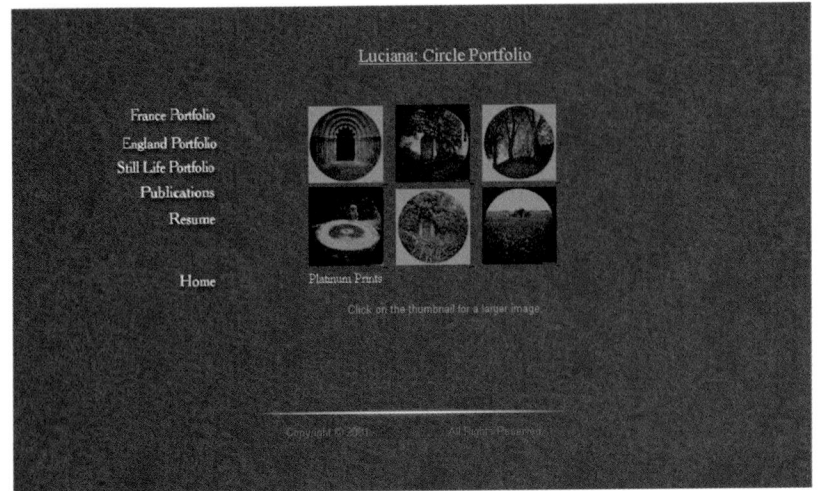

Figure 13.17

Tables offer the designer the opportunity to organize information in a more sophisticated and visually appealing manner.

The basic code for tables is not that difficult. While many use a WYSIWYG Web-building program to create tables, it is important to have a sense of how tables work so you can fix a Web page if it has problems. As with many of the other areas covered in this introductory chapter, this information will simply introduce the most common features and coding of tables, rather than attempt an exhaustive analysis of table construction.

Defining a Table

As in a word processing program, tables are composed of a group of vertical columns and horizontal rows. The boxes they form are called cells, each of which contains information. Tables have their own unique tags that define their structure. A table's opening and closing tags are placed within the body of a document as <TABLE>...</TABLE>. The underlying code for a simple table is straightforward.

Each of the table's horizontal rows is indicated by <TR>...</TR>. Each item of table data in a row is indicated <TD>...</TD> and forms a cell that actually holds the data.

There is no column tag. Columns are formed by the number of cells in each row, so that a row with three items would automatically have three columns. To establish a new row, add another <TR>...</TR> tag set. The code for a table with two rows and three columns would look like this:

```
<HTML>

<HEAD>                              Starts header.

<TITLE>A Simple Table </TITLE>      Title of page.

</HEAD>                             Ends header.

<TABLE>                             Indicates the beginning of a
                                    table.

<TR>                                This sets up a table that has two
   <TD>this is row 1 cell 1</TD>    rows and three columns.
   <TD>this is row 1 cell 2</TD>
   <TD>this is row 1 cell 3</TD>
</TR>
<TR>
   <TD>this is row 2 cell 1</TD>
   <TD>this is row 2 cell 2</TD>
   <TD>this is row 2 cell 3</TD>
</TR>

</TABLE>                            Ends the table.

</HTML>                             Ends HTML document.
```

Designing with Tables

There are very sophisticated ways in which the attributes of a table can be changed in order to design a Web page (see Figure 13.18). Many of these can mimic the ways in which a desktop publishing program organizes text and images. For example, once you understand the basic concept and coding behind tables, you can change the dimensions of the tables, their border sizes, and even their color. To widen the size of a table's border, use the <TABLE BORDER="8"> command instead of the simple <TABLE> opening. To hide the borders entirely, try <TABLE BORDER="0">.

The chart below lists a few of the commands that can be used to modify a table:

<TABLE BORDER="8">	Use whatever pixel amount you wish to change the size of a table's borders.
<TABLE WIDTH="300" HEIGHT="150">	Table specified in pixels. You can also use percentages.
<TABLE CELLSPACING="10">	Changes the two-pixel default space between cells.
<TABLE BGCOLOR="#CC9999">	You can change the color by using a Websafe hexadecimal color.

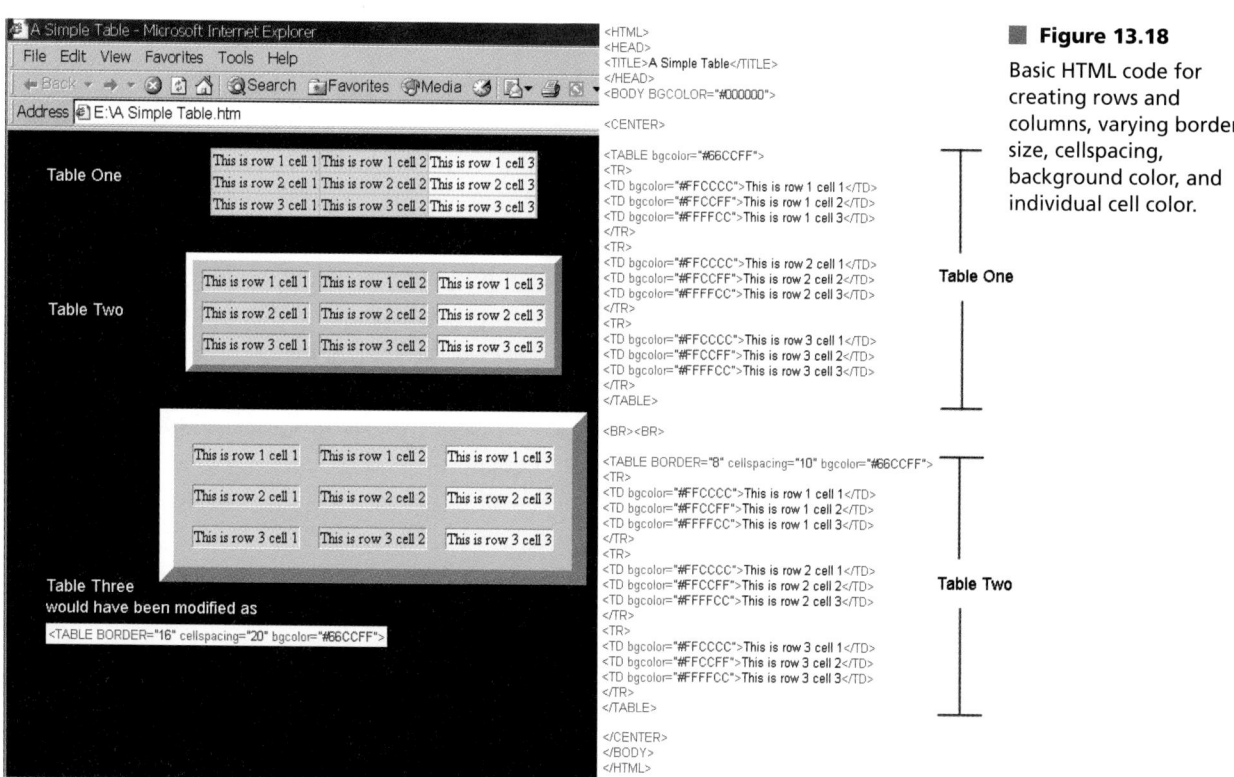

Figure 13.18

Basic HTML code for creating rows and columns, varying border size, cellspacing, background color, and individual cell color.

Figure 13.19

Basic code showing tables without and with the "rowspan" code included within a table cell.

Without Rowspan

```
<HTML>
<HEAD>
<TITLE>Rowspan</TITLE>
</HEAD>

<BODY BACKGROUND="bg3.jpg">
<CENTER>
<TABLE BORDER="8">
<TR>
<TD ><IMG SRC="rowspan2.jpg"></TD>
<TD><IMG SRC="fcross.jpg"></TD>
<TD><IMG SRC="fdianatree.jpg"></TD>
</TR>

<TR>
<TD><IMG SRC="frcross2.jpg"></TD>
<TD><IMG SRC="frchairs.jpg"></TD>
</TR>
</TABLE>
</CENTER>
</BODY>
</HTML>
```

With Rowspan

```
<HTML>
<HEAD>
<TITLE>Rowspan</TITLE>
</HEAD>

<BODY BACKGROUND="bg3.jpg">
<CENTER>
<TABLE BORDER="8">
<TR>
<TD ROWSPAN=2><IMG SRC="rowspan2.jpg"></TD>
<TD><IMG SRC="fcross.jpg"></TD>
<TD><IMG SRC="fdianatree.jpg"></TD>
</TR>

<TR>
<TD><IMG SRC="frcross2.jpg"></TD>
<TD><IMG SRC="frchairs.jpg"></TD>
</TR>
</TABLE>
</CENTER>
</BODY>
</HTML>
```

It is also possible to have individual cells expand to combine several smaller cells. Cells can expand to cover either rows or columns depending on your design needs. Row spanning extends a cell vertically to cover several rows (see Figure 13.19) while column spanning expands a cell horizontally to cover several columns. (see Figure 13.20) The command for both row and column spans take place within an individual cell. Rows are spanned with the code: <TD ROWSPAN=X></TD> with X being the number of rows to span. Columns are spanned with the code: <TD COLSPAN=X></TD> with X being the number of columns to span. These two can be combined in a single cell to create larger spaces for your design.

The chart below lists a few of the commands that can be used to modify an individual cell:

<TD ROWSPAN=X></TD> (X = the number of rows to span.	Allows you to combine several cells together to make a larger cell spanning a number of rows
<TD COLSPAN=X></TD (X = the number of columns to span.	Works similarly to Rowspan but spans columns instead of rows
<TD WIDTH=X></TD> (X= the number of pixels you want the cell (column) to be.	Can be used to fix the width of the columns no matter what size the browser window is.

```
This is frame one and will be used for
navigation by incorporating hypertext
links to frame 2<br><br>
```

`<A HREF="blue2.htm">Blue Frame 2"</A> `	Link to created HTML document.
`<A HREF="red2.htm">Red Frame 2</A> `	Link to created HTML document.
`<A HREF="green2.htm">Green Frame 2</A> `	Link to created HTML document.
`</BODY>`	
`</HTML>`	EndS HTML template.

This is the frame that will appear in the smaller navigational window on the left.

We have also created three other HTML documents, one with blue text (blue2.htm), one with red text (red2.htm), and one with green text (green2.htm). These are the documents that will be opened in the larger window on the right when the links are clicked in the Frame1.htm document.

It is important to understand that each frame in the browser window will act independently of the other. Unless you tell the smaller frame on the left that linked documents should open in the larger window on the right, they will open in the smaller window on the left that contains the links. The larger window on the right will remain empty. This is not very helpful if we want to use the narrower frame on the left as a navigation device. The solution is to edit the frames file so that each frame is clearly identified with a different name. We used "linkframe" and "mainframe" to designate the two separate windows.

`<HTML>`	
`<HEAD>`	Starts header.
`<TITLE>. . . </TITLE>`	Title of page.
`</HEAD>`	Ends header.
`<FRAMESET COLS="25%,75%">`	You can define the size of the frame by the percentage value or by the absolute pixel value.
`<FRAME SRC="FRAME1.htm"` `name="linkframe">`	We have changed the generic "filename1" to "FRAME1.htm" to help keep track of which frame goes where. Note the addition *name="linkframe">* to the FRAME SRC tag.
`<FRAME SRC="FRAME2.htm"` `name="mainframe">`	Again, the generic "filename1" from above has been changed to "FRAME2.htm" and *name= "mainframe">* has been added to the command line.
`</FRAMESET>`	Ends the frameset command.
`<NOFRAMES>`	Starts the tag set to identify this as a frames document for those whose browsers do not support it.

`If you do not have a frame-`
`enabled browser, you will not`
`be able to view this page.`	

`</NOFRAMES>`	Ends noframes tag set.
`</HTML>`	Ends HTML document.

```
<HTML>
<HEAD>
<TITLE>Basic Frameset Page</TITLE>
</HEAD>

<FRAMESET COLS="25%,75%">

<FRAME SRC="frame1.htm" name="linkframe">
<FRAME SRC="frame2.htm" name="mainframe">

</FRAMESET>

<NOFRAMES>
If you do not have a frames enabled browser, you will not be able to view this page.
</NOFRAMES>
</HTML>
```

Link Frame

```
<HTML>
<HEAD>
<TITLE>Demonstration Frames 1</TITLE>
<base target="mainframe">
</HEAD>

<BODY>
This is frame one and will be used for navigation by incorporating hypertext links to frame 2
<br>
<br>

<A HREF="blue2.htm">Blue Frame 2"</A><br>
<A HREF="red2.htm">Red Frame 2</A><br>
<A HREF="green2.htm">Green Frame 2</A><br>

</BODY>
</HTML>
```

Content

```
<HTML>
<HEAD>

<TITLE>Blue Image</TITLE>
</HEAD>
<BODY BGCOLOR="#59FFFF">
<BR>
<BR>

<CENTER><IMG SRC="harbor.jpg">

<H1><FONT COLOR="#0000ff">This is the "Mainframe" and will contain all content for
this frames document.</FONT></H1>
</CENTER>

</BODY>
</HTML>
```

■ **Figure 13.21**

HTML code for basic frames
navigation.

Now that the primary frames document is complete, and each frame is identified with a name, we must be sure that the linked documents will show up in the large "mainframe" window instead of the smaller "linkframe" window. We do this by adding <base target="mainframe"> to the header part of the document containing the links—in this case, "Frames1.htm". That document will now look like this:

```
<HTML>
<HEAD>
<TITLE>Demonstration Frames 1</TITLE>
<base target="mainframe">
</HEAD>
<BODY>
This is frame one and will be used for navigation by
incorporating hypertext links to frame 2<br><br>
<A HREF="blue2.htm">Blue Frame 2"</A><br>
<A HREF="red2.htm">Red Frame 2</A><br>
<A HREF="green2.htm">Green Frame 2</A><br>
</BODY>
</HTML>
```

Each of the linked documents in "Frames1.htm" (shown in the "linkframe" window) will now show up in the larger "mainframe" window (see Figures 13.21 and 13.22).

Frame Borders and Scrolling

As separate HTML pages, each frame will include both horizontal and vertical scroll bars if the information contained goes beyond the size of a viewer's screen. To remove the scroll bars

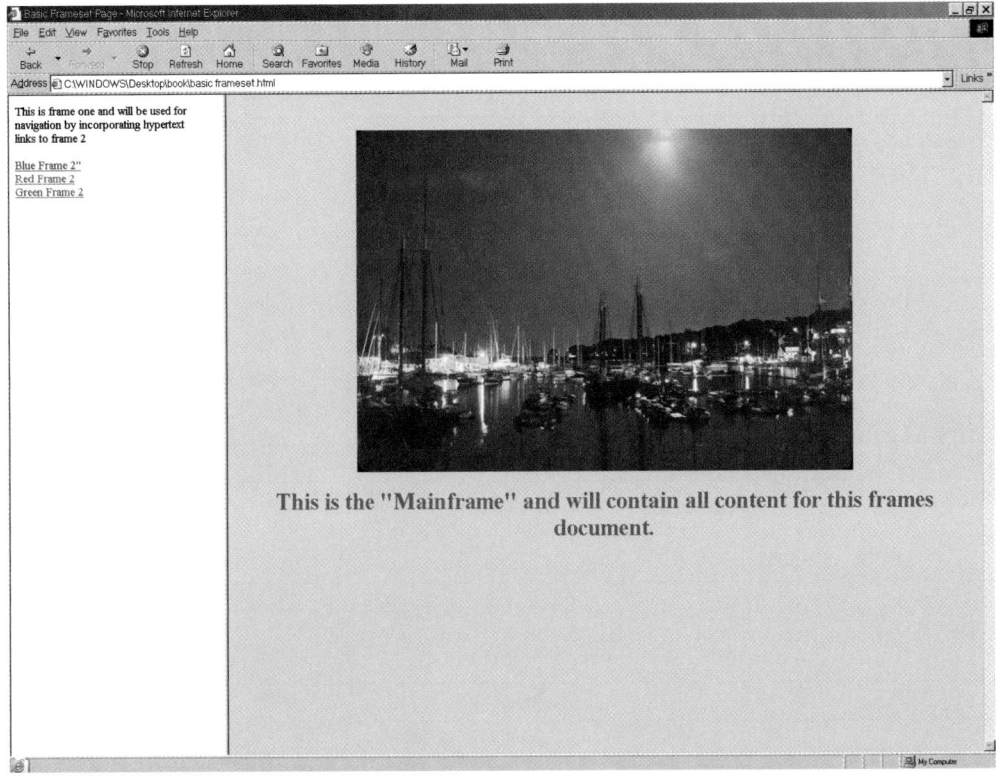

■ **Figure 13.22**

Results from frameset
page showing side-by-
side frames with
navigation frame on left.

from one or both of the frames, add the following attribute command to the <FRAME> tag.

```
<FRAME SRC="filename.htm" scrolling =no>
```

There is much more that can be done with frames, but navigation is certainly one of the easiest and most accepted forms of frame use.

Style Sheets

Internal Style Sheets

A more recent feature added to Web pages are style sheets. *Cascading Style Sheets (CSS)* allow you to assign properties to various elements of your Web page which then affect everything on the page. Style sheets can control everything from font size, face, color, physical style, weight, and line spacing (among many things) to the background color of the pages to which it is applied. This can help to provide a consistent look to a website's many interrelated pages.

The information that defines the way in which coded text in the body of the HTML document will appear is inserted in the <HEAD>. . . </HEAD> portion of your document. It starts with a <STYLE> tag and, after the styles are set, ends with a </STYLE> tag. At this point, you simply type the name of the tag you wish to define followed by a { symbol, your definition, and that tag's closing } symbol. The definitions can become very complex with text being defined by size, spacing, color, type of font, and so on. The simple HTML page below demonstrates one simple tag definition. Definitions are usually far more complex and complete than this example.

`<HTML>`	Conventional header code.
`<HEAD>`	
`<TITLE>CCS Demo</TITLE>`	
`<STYLE>`	Tells the browser that the following information defines parts of the document to follow.
`A:link {color:red}`	Defines a link as red.
	Note: When defining styles, a colon is used to separate definitions.
`A:visited {color:green}`	Defines a visited link as green.
`A:active {color:yellow}`	Defines an active link as yellow.
`</STYLE>`	Definition of styles ends.
`</HEAD>`	Conventional HTML document begins.
`<BODY>`	Anything that appears in styles will have the characteristics defined.
`Remainder of HTML document`	

External Style Sheets

External style sheets are almost exactly like internal style sheets except they are created as a separate text document. The codes are all the same, except that they do not contain any HTML code whatsoever. You do not start with an HTML document and you do not have to use the <STYLE> tag. You simply define the items on your page that you wish to make consistent throughout your website. When you are finished, save the file with a .css extension. At this point, in order to apply the page definitions to an HTML document, simply reference the .css document in the header portion of the code.

```
<HTML>                                        Conventional header code.
<HEAD>
<TITLE>CCS Demo<\TITLE>
<LINK REL=STYLESHEET TYPE="TEXT/CSS"          The link tag tells the HTML
HREF="docname.css">                           document to look for a style sheet.
                                              The HREF= command gives the browser
Note: This information takes place            the name of the style sheet
within the heading.                           to be used.

</HEAD>                                        Conventional HTML document begins.
<BODY>                                         Anything that appears in styles will
Remainder of HTML document                    have the characteristics defined.
```

Whatever Web page has this information present in its header will apply the styles defined in the plain text .css document. If you wish to change the look of the entire site, you simply need to change the information in the referenced style sheet.

Multimedia on the Web

The World Wide Web is fast becoming a portal to a world that includes more than the simple text and image combinations to which it started. It has become a synthesis of experiences as varied as seeing movie trailers advertising new film releases, listening to music from the latest CDs, viewing animations—even playing games with multiple opponents.

Audio on the Web

The quality of a sound file is based on the sample rate of sound waves and then how those sound waves are digitally recreated during playback. The higher the sample rate, the larger the file and the truer the sound. Typical sample rates are 11,000, 22,000, and 44,000 times per second. Typically, an 11,000 sample rate is often referred to as being similar to telephone sound, a 22,000 sample rate similar to radio, and the 44,000 sample rate closer to CD quality. Most dial-up Internet connections cannot convey sound at more than the lowest quality. Broadband connections can often provide rates at the radio or even CD level without much difficulty.

Musical instrument digital interface (MIDI) is a different type of sound file that uses prerecorded instrumental sounds that are resident in the memory of a computer's sound card. MIDI music relies on *wave table synthesis* to reproduce sound waves. MIDI sampling of the original music sends information to the sound card about the pitch, duration, instrument, and type of sound. The sound card reads this information and reproduces the sound from prerecorded instrumental sounds in its wave table. Because the sounds are already recorded in the wave table of the card, and the software only has to describe the sound, MIDI files are considerably smaller than those that attempt to reproduce the actual sampled sound waves of music (see Chapter 11 for more information).

Web browsers do not have built-in capability to play sounds or video. They rely on small programs called plug-ins that are added to the browser's own capabilities. If you try to play a sound or video for which no plug-in is present, the browser will either try to launch an external *helper* application or ask if you want to save the file to the hard drive in your computer. Many of the necessary plug-ins now come with newer browsers or can be easily downloaded.

Sound can be embedded in a Web page as a file that begins to play after being downloaded to the user's computer, or as a streaming file that begins to play as it continues to download. If the sound you want to play is a short, fairly small file, then it is far easier to use it as a nonstreaming file. You will recall from Chapter 11, however, that the higher the quality of the sound, the larger the file size will be. The larger the file size, the longer it will take the sound to download. While quality is always important, for short nonstreaming files, download time is also a key factor in their usefulness. When choosing a sound format for this type of file, .wav is probably the most useful as it can be read on both Macs and PCs without additional helper programs.

Sound Embedding

The easiest way to bring sound to your site is to place a link to the sound file. This will usually play the sound with an operating system's built-in sound software or the browser's plug-in player. A simple HTML reference code might be:

```
<A HREF="yoursonghere.mid"> Play Music </A>
```

Embedding a sound on a Web page is an even better alternative and is very similar to placing an image. Instead of <IMG SRC=, you can use the <EMBED SRC= command to place your sound. If you wanted to play the sound of a dog barking, and you had a sound file called dogbark.wav, the code would be <EMBED SRC="dogbark.wav">. The Controls command can install simple sound controls that allow you to turn the sound on and off. The options are smallconsole, console, playbutton, pausebutton, volumelever, and stopbutton. You can even set the size of the controls with width and height commands.

`<HTML>`	Basic HTML template.
`<HEAD>`	
`<TITLE>Demonstration Frames 1</TITLE>`	
`</HEAD>`	
`<BODY>`	
`Here are sounds my cats make when they` `are hungry. All different, all cute.`	
`<IMG SRC="pud.jpg"><EMBED SRC="pud.wav"` `CONTROLS="console"` `WIDTH= "60" HEIGHT="20" AUTOSTART=FALSE>` `</EMBED> `	Three separate, embedded sounds from Pud, Woody, and Stella, with consoles.
`<IMG SRC="woody.jpg"><<EMBED SRC="woody.wav"` `CONTROLS="console"` `WIDTH="60" HEIGHT="20" AUTOSTART=FALSE>` `</EMBED> `	*Note:* the AUTOSTART=FALSE prevents the sound from playing when the page opens.
`<IMG SRC="stella.jpg"><<EMBED SRC="stella.wav"` `CONTROLS="console"` `WIDTH="60" HEIGHT="20"` `AUTOSTART="FALSE"></EMBED> `	
`</BODY>`	Ends HTML template.
`</HTML>`	

At this point, the user can control the sound playback when and if he or she chooses to play it. Keep in mind that you must make the size (width and height) large enough to accommodate the sound utility you want to show up. If you choose console and have a very small button, then only the play part of the button will be available.

Streaming Audio and Video

If you intend to play extended sound—such as music or video—then streaming is the best approach. RealAudio, QuickTime, Shockwave, and Streamworks are some of the most common plug-in programs that make this possible. Streaming audio begins to play as soon as it reaches the listener's computer,

BOX 13.5

Copyright

There are an enormous number of misapprehensions concerning copyright infringements on the World Wide Web. It should be obvious that any copyrighted material that you wish to use on your site requires the permission of the copyright holder. However, it is sometimes difficult to determine just what is copyrighted material and what is not. Generally, if material is more than seventy-five years old, chances are good that it is no longer covered by copyright unless the owner of the material has specifically taken steps to extend the copyright. Material that is less than seventy-five years old, has not specifically been placed in the public domain, is protected by copyright. More specifically, work by a single author remains protected by copyright until seventy years after the author's (or artist's) death. If a work has more than one author, an anonymous author, or if the work is owned by an organization, it is protected for ninety-five years. Of course, there are always exceptions, but these guidelines should help in determining what you can and cannot use. Further, copyright exists from the moment a work is published. It does not have to be formally registered with the copyright office and it is not even important whether or not the copyright symbol appears on the work.

Finding something already on the Web does not mean that it is copyright free and can be copied for inclusion on your own site. This applies to text, images, music, multimedia, and anything else you can think of—unless the site specifically states that the material is copyright free. Even if you receive permission to use a work, there may still be problems. Often there are separate copyrights on items. If you receive permission to use a piece of music by the author, the performance you choose to use may still be copyrighted by the artist performing it. In fact, there may be many copyrights by various artists and recording companies on the same piece of music. Film or video is even more complex with copyrights extending throughout the world. Researching copyrights has become a growing business in the multimedia production profession.

Fair use, or limited use free of copyright restrictions, is often misunderstood. Outside of educational use, the only fair use applications that are relevant apply to small sections of an original work that is used for news reporting, criticism, and parody. Any uses outside of that may very well make you liable for copyright infringement. ∎

Multimedia, including the use of sound, animations, and even video, can enhance a site if used judiciously. Everything that can be an asset to a page also has the capability of being a detriment. Attention spans are short on the Web. Poorly prepared video can take a long time to download, and viewers may not want to wait. The same can be said for still images and animations. Each of these enhancements can be a wonderful improvement to a page but they must seem like a natural extension of the content if they are to work well.

If at all possible, you may want to avoid some of the things that do turn many viewers off. For a while, blinking text (available in conventional HTML code) was all the rage—but soon was just an annoying page element that could be stopped only by leaving the page entirely. The same can be said of poorly used multimedia elements. Scrolling text can be an interesting addition to a page or just an annoying banner that moves incessantly, telling us things we care little about, and taking our attention away from the contents of the page itself. Animations, while they can be interesting, often become an annoyance after the first few times they play. Audio that immediately starts playing when the web page loads can be an unwelcome, even startling, intrusion if it is not in some way part of what the site is about or is featuring. ■

and continues to download while the sound is being played. Unfortunately, to move beyond simple wav files to streaming audio is far more complex and beyond the capabilities of beginning Web designers.

Streaming audio or video requires an expensive separate server in addition to a regular Web server. The separate server will support dynamic bandwidth compensation that will allow the rate at which sound and video are streamed through a system (called bit rate) to change depending upon the speed of the modem being used by the listener.

The audio must also be encoded, which means purchasing an encoding program and knowing how to use it to get the best sound out of the files to be compressed. In addition, unless the listener has a broadband Internet connection, the quality of the sound will be quite low. Also, your audience must have Navigator 3.0 or later or Internet Explorer 4.0 or later. RealAudio, or a similar plug-in software program, must also be installed on their computer (see Box 13.6).

JavaScript

Many people confuse JavaScript with Java. Apart from the word "Java" they have nothing in common. *Java* is a powerful programming language with the ability to create actual applications or aplets for insertion into a Web page, as well as stand alone applications. It can also run the programs it creates on PC, Mac, and Unix computers. *JavaScript*, however, is a relatively easy programming language that can be embedded in an HTML document to open the range of possible interactive features. It allows you to embed special effects, open new

BOX 13.7   TRY A MOUSEOVER

In order to create a mouseover, two images of the same size are created. One of the images will be visible when the page initially loads. The second image—changed to whatever form the designer wishes— will become the rollover image that will result when the mouse action triggers it. Even though your browser will assume the script language you are using is JavaScript, many designers suggest adding a set of tags in the header of your document to define the script language in the event other scripting languages are introduced.

In the body of your HTML document, you can insert the JavaScript that will trigger the mouseover event:

`<A HREF="circle1.htm"`	References the HTML document that will be opened when the mouse click actually takes place on the mouseover.
`onMouseOver = "document.sample.src='itest.jpg';return false;"`	When the mouse moves over the icon, it changes to this.
`onMouseOut = "document.sample.src='itestb.jpg';return false;">`	When the mouse is not over the icon, it looks like this.
`<IMG SRC="itestb.jpg" name="sample" border=0>`	The image (icon) that first shows up when you see the page with the rollover.
`</A>`	Ends the anchor tag.

Note: For a series of mouseovers, the "sample label" must be unique. This is often accomplished by adding successive numbers for each of the mouseovers after the sample (e.g., document.sample2.src).

■ Figure 13.23
Icon changing with mouseover.

message windows, perform calculations, write interactive games, and more. The JavaScript we tend to see most often is used for cause and effect activities like mouseovers (also called rollovers) where, as the mouse rolls over an item, it changes (see Box 13.7 and Figure 13.23).

Oops! It Doesn't Work

During the process of creating Web pages with HTML, most designers expect some errors to creep in. HTML is very literal and expects perfection. Most pages with elements that don't work can be traced to a spelling error, a missing tag, or even a missing bracket from a tag. It takes a lot of time to work out a complete site without frustrating errors. Certainly, in the beginning, keep it simple. Tables, frames, and style sheets usually take a bit of time to get to know well. Even experienced Web designers encounter problems having to do with code that will work in one browser and not on another. The more complex your code, the greater the likelihood there is of this happening.

As mentioned earlier, to make things easier, keep all your files in one directory. It removes the possibility that you are not referencing the complete command line in directing the browser to your file. Still, your website will more than likely contain different HTML files, GIF files, and JPEGs. Are you spelling them correctly? Are you using .htm or .html to designate your HTML files? A link to "anyfile.html" that is saved as "anyfile.htm" will result in a broken link. Did you try to link to an "image.gif" when it should have been an "image.jpg? Did you use .jpg or .jpeg? Often, it is the smallest things that prevent a page from working correctly.

Test Your Site

The most important rule is to test your site and test it often. Test your site on Netscape as well as on Explorer. Click all the links and make sure the linked documents appear the way in which you want them. Check the photos on the page to be sure they are the ones you want to appear. Have you included information about who to contact about the site? You should. There are many users who will provide both good and bad feedback on a site—especially if something really annoys them, like that huge image you forgot to resample and compress.

Finding a Host

Once your page checks out thoroughly, determine where to place your site. There are many hosts that will carry your website free of charge. If you are a student, most colleges and universities provide space for student websites. Most Internet service providers, including local telephone and cable companies, will provide free space for subscribers' websites. If you are producing a commercial site, then there are thousands of companies that will host your site for a monthly fee.

The main point to consider in finding a host for your site is the amount of disk space available to use. Most websites are quite small and don't need much space unless you are storing video and sound files. You also want to find out how fast your host's connection to the Internet is. A slow server with few access connections will not serve your site well. Does the host support advanced features like streaming video and audio? If your site is built around streaming media' this is an important question and one that ties directly to the speed of the host's connection.

Domain Names

The *Domain Name System* (DNS) is how websites are commonly addressed. Domain names exist in a kind of categorical hierarchy which groups different types of sites together. There are commercial sites (.com), educational sites (.edu), government sites (.gov), military sites (.mil), organizations (.org), and more. Organizations register for domain names based on the type of site they will maintain. It has become fairly easy to purchase a *domain name*. Having your own domain name makes it easier for users to find and remember your site.

FTP: Uploading Your Site to a Server

There are many file transfer protocol (FTP) programs available both commercially and as freeware and shareware. The major differences between them are speed and ease of use. Whether using Fetch for the Macintosh or WS_FTP for Windows, the result will be the same—files uploaded from your computer to the Web host computer.

Figure 13.24

Basic FTP program.

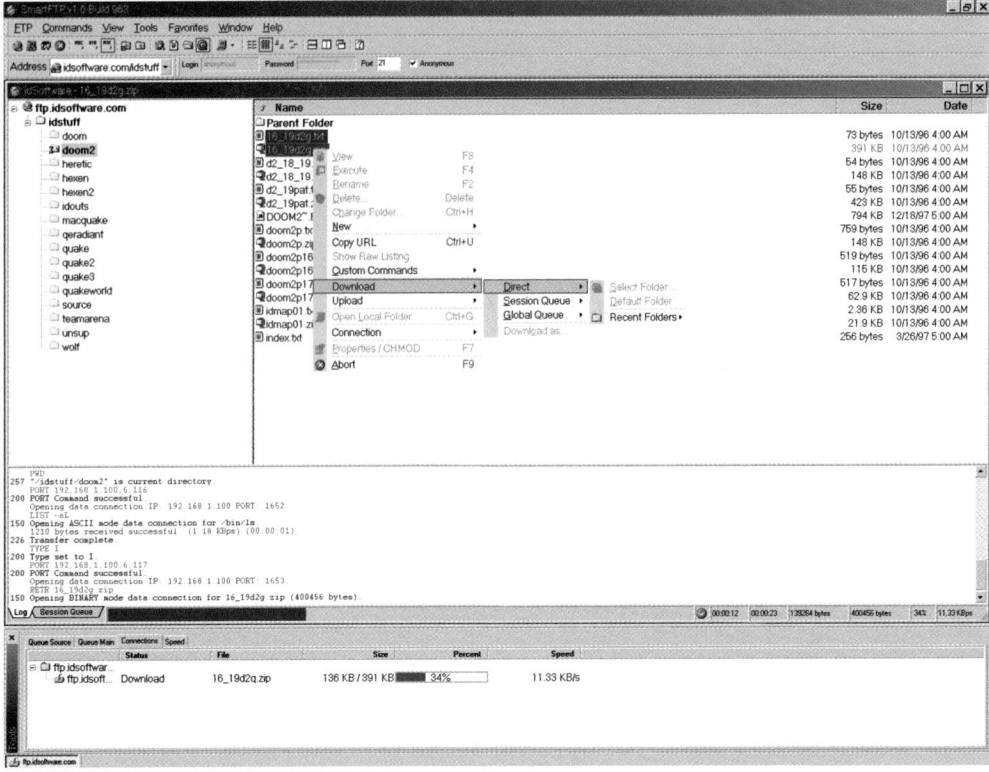

Many of the programs provide different interfaces, but one thing should remain relatively constant. The files on your computer will appear on one screen or window and the computer hosting your site will appear on the other (see Figure 13.24). After connecting to the Internet and opening your FTP program, you will need to identify the server to which you wish to connect and usually provide both a user name and password. After you have signed in, you will need to find the directory on the server to which you want to upload your files, or create one. Make sure this directory is selected before uploading your files.

In the window containing the files on your computer, navigate to the directory holding your website files. Select the files you wish to transfer and click on the arrow pointing to the host computer. This will transfer the selected files. However, there is one catch. While most current FTP programs will attempt to do this automatically, it is important to transfer HTML files in ASCII mode and image files (including sound and video) in binary mode. There will be a checkbox in the program to allow you to set either binary or ASCII mode. Once the file transfer has been accomplished, your site should be active and on the Web.

CONCLUSION

This brief introduction to preparing for entry on the Web has only touched on the highlights and basic items necessary to get started. You will find thick books in most bookstores with detailed HTML code, Java, JavaScript, VRML, and much more to help you get the most out of your Web-developing experience. But remember, all the code in the world cannot take the place of a good design and a well-planned and organized page.

Only a handful of visionaries were able to see the usefulness of the Web for communicating information, although none could foresee its impact. In the last few decades we have seen incredible changes in digital technologies and the tools available to those in the arts. Artists are now beginning to design artwork exclusively for the Web. In some cases the pages they design carry a message for a client or product. In other cases the Web experience they design is not a representation of a client's product, but an actual work of art in and of itself. Each individual artist has the potential to represent an experience on the Web. It is an exciting time to be working. Driven forward by creative and innovative technology in the hands of artists determined to redefine the Web experience, the Internet seems determined to reinvent itself once again.

Projects: Designing for the Web

1 BASIC WEB PAGE

Create a basic introductory Web page (index page) about yourself or your family, including three links to two other pages and a website. Make the background a color.

2A MAKING JPEGs AND ICONS (*NOTE:* PROJECT 2 IS A THREE-PART PROJECT)

Make JPEGs of six individual images you have scanned. For this project, be sure they are no larger than 400 × 550 pixels in size. Try to keep their file size under 50K. In addition, create icons for each of the images no larger than 120 pixels in their longest dimension.

2B IMAGE PAGES

Create six individual Web pages featuring one of the JPEG images you created. Save them with simple names (i.e., image1.htm, image2.htm, and so on). Make sure you have a color background and center the image on the page.

2C ICONS AND LINKS PAGE: INTRO TO TABLES

Create a Web page with an introduction to your images and a table having two rows of three cells each. Have an icon in each cell with a link to the page holding the larger image it represents.

3 BASIC FRAMES

Create a page with a set of three frames. The top frame should contain your name, created using the text tools in your image-editing program. The left frame should be narrow—perhaps 200 pixels—and contain a column of the icons you created for Project 2. The right frame will be the content frame and display the larger image when the icon in the left column is clicked on.

PART 4

Epilogue

14

The Digital Studio: Artist Portfolios
Introduction

As we have seen, there are clearly many new avenues of creative expression artists may follow. Of equal interest to those who are beginning their exploration of the new media are the many career opportunities for digital artists. There is a great need for creative people who are experienced with computer technology. Some of today's digital careers are ones that have existed for a long time, like sculpture, illustration, and set design. The artists in those professions are simply utilizing new, if impressive, tools. Others, like Web design and creating 3-D mattes for computer games, are truly new. The professional lives of the six artists profiled in this chapter are just a sampling of the various careers in digital media. A comprehensive review would require an entire book, if not a series.

While their career paths have been different, the following artists share a common excitement and delight in absorbing new techniques. All began their careers working in traditional media and then discovered new ways to achieve their goals. Like every digital artist, they have also experienced the frustrations of computers crashing and had hours of work lost when their data became "corrupted." However, they also have what every successful digital artist needs—the discipline and dedication necessary to overcome setbacks and complete a body of work.

Maggie Taylor is a fine artist who offers the viewer a glimpse into a mystical reality where everyday objects are combined to create new and powerful relationships and associations. Her images evoke a world of fantasy and mythic connections that we are invited to unravel. Boyd Ostroff is a set designer who also works with creating new realities, but with a major difference. His digital images are destined to be made into real space that can be entered both visually and physically on the stage of the Opera Company of Philadelphia.

Simon Bosch is a professional illustrator whose signature "pumped up" style creates an unusual space in which everything is crushed into shallow, almost sculptural relief while maintaining a distinct sense of spatial clarity. John Crane's cutaway views of futuristic machines or carefully rendered models might also be considered illustrations but inhabit a very different world—the deep virtual space of three dimensions.

Peter Baustaedter's production paintings have been used in a variety of computer games and motion pictures. His carefully constructed visions of strange, new worlds combine fantasy with believable attention to detail. Robert Lazzarini creates digital distortions of 3-D objects that are then rendered as 3-D models using the original materials of the distorted object. These sculptures create a feeling akin to vertigo in the viewer as he or she struggles to find a view that might bring the distortions into some semblance of the reality in which he or she has been conditioned to believe.

All of these artists have made the computer part of their creative process rather than simply a mechanical aid. They are pioneers of a true revolution in the visual arts searching for a language of its own.

Maggie Taylor

1987 MFA in Photography, University of Florida
1983 BA in Philosophy, Yale University

Background

Maggie Taylor studied both photography and photo history while an undergraduate at Yale in the early 1980s, although her primary area of study was philosophy. However, by the time she graduated in 1983, she knew that she wanted to attend graduate school for photography.

In 1985 she started working on her Master of Fine Arts in photography at the University of Florida. Except for a few basic drawing and printmaking classes, her background in traditional media was limited to photography. In 1987 she received an MFA in photography from the University of Florida, where she studied with Jerry Uelsmann and Evon Streetman. During that time her work evolved from black-and-white suburban landscapes into much more personal and narrative color still-life imagery. Using an old 4″ × 5″ view camera and natural light, she photographed bits and pieces of everyday life—old toys, broken bottles, and animals from her garden. Frequently these images included text, either handwritten or typed, which both enhanced and complicated the narrative intentions of the work. Since 1987 her still-life photographs have been exhibited in more than seventy one-person exhibitions throughout the United States.

In September of 1996 Taylor received a one-year, Florida Individual Artist's Fellowship in Visual Arts. This grant enabled her to further explore the still-life image by experimenting with a computer, using a flatbed scanner in place of a camera. By placing objects directly on the glass of the scanner, she was able to create a unique type of digital image that still maintained photographic qualities.

Working Methods

In 1996, when Taylor finally got a computer containing enough memory to work on an image using PhotoShop, she was primarily interested in using the computer to retouch her color photographs. She soon saw all kinds of other possibilities, particularly with the flatbed scanner. "Over the years I have collected a lot of little objects and background materials that I used in set-up scenes to photograph. These same little things were just the right size to try putting directly on the glass top of the flatbed scanner—so I began experimenting." At first many of the images consisted of only two or three scans (for example, one background drawing and two small objects scanned separately). Gradually, as she learned more about PhotoShop's layers and blend modes, she began to create more complex composites.

When creating her still-life images, Taylor usually begins with an object (such as a doll or an old tintype portrait), which she scans. The image is then retouched and the tone and color are adjusted as necessary. She works slowly in this initial phase, believing it helps her contemplate what she might want to do with the image. "In my studio I have all kinds of things—old dolls, insects, string, fabric, rocks—and I often go through drawers and boxes to find just the right element to try in an image." Many times she finds that she has added too many different objects to one image, and then spends time eliminating some, paring down and simplifying. Along the way she usually makes a number of small inkjet prints of the image as she works on it. She then sets these prints out on her desk, which frees her to move on and work with another image. She likes to work on three to six images as a group, bouncing back and forth between them. "Sometimes something that isn't quite right in one image works well in another. I enjoy looking at my little proof prints . . . and letting the images gestate a little, before making any further corrections or additions." The whole process of working on an image can take anywhere from two days to two months before it is ready to be sent off for an IRIS proof.

From the beginning, Taylor knew that she wanted to have IRIS prints made of her images, which requires collaboration with a printer. When an image is finished, she copies it to a CD and sends it off to be proofed. She usually views a series of trial proofs, providing feedback to the printer on each one, until she is ready to approve a final print.

When she first encountered digital art, Taylor felt that the computer offered so many options for the visual artist that it became a kind of stumbling block creatively. "It is difficult to make decisions sometimes, and even more difficult to let go of an image and decide that I am finished working on it." She finds herself constantly trying to find a balance between exploring technical options and being overwhelmed by them. She has made a consistent effort to devise simple strategies that allow her to use the software to explore but not overwhelm the image.

Professional Application

Taylor began entering juried shows and sent out slides of her work to galleries soon after completing graduate school. At first, her goal was to be included in group shows and occasionally have a solo show at a university gallery or an art department. She initially received a positive response about ten percent of the time. Soon, however, galleries began to respond more positively to her work, enabling her to become more selective about where her work was shown. "But really, promoting the work can be very time-consuming and frustrating. It is important not to let this task overwhelm your creative time."

Today, Taylor's work is primarily exhibited in galleries and sold to individuals, collectors, and institutions. A small percentage of what she does is commercial (i.e., book covers, CD covers, or other commercial applications). Her work has also been published in numerous magazines and photographic texts. "Working on a very regular basis certainly has helped me. I don't have a strict schedule, and at times I may go weeks or even a month without making a new image that I am satisfied with. But I am constantly planning, doing the preliminary work, collecting, and thinking about the images. It has been helpful to have secretarial skills as well—to send out letters, slides, to monitor my own website, and so on."

Currently, Taylor is developing a series of images of women that are scheduled to appear in a collaborative book of poetry. She has also been collecting images of landscapes with her 35mm point-and-shoot camera and a small digital camera. She intends to work on a series of digital landscapes that will use this material as a point of departure (see Figures 14.1 through 14.6).

■ **Figure 14.1**

Maggie Taylor, *Just Looking*, 1999.

Figure 14.2
Maggie Taylor, *Late*, 2000.

"Before color management was a part of my workflow, I found it difficult to get accurate prints of the images as I saw them on my monitor. Now I am careful to profile my monitor and input devices, and use the color management features of PhotoShop."

Figure 14.3
Maggie Taylor, *Messenger*, 2000.

"I am constantly influenced by all kinds of art and non-art things that I encounter. I love folk art in particular, and I am a collector of all kinds of old objects at flea markets."

■ **Figure 14.4**
Maggie Taylor, *Night Garden*, 2000.

■ **Figure 14.5**
Maggie Taylor, *The Loomer*, 2000.

> Don't spend all your time learning technical things like how to use a particular type of software, or how to put together a web page. These things can be very frustrating and time-consuming, and in the end the software will probably be changed and you will need to learn another program. I am not saying ignore the technical aspects—in fact, it is helpful if you enjoy them. But try to find a balance. Read books and find enrichment from a variety of sources.

Boyd Ostroff

Currently Director of Design & Technology at the Opera Company of Philadelphia

1993 MFA in Scenery and Lighting Design, Carnegie-Mellon University (CMU)

1971 BA in Theater, University of Virginia

Background

Boyd Ostroff's father was an aerospace design engineer. During a vacation from college in 1968, Ostroff visited his father's office where he was shown their new state-of-the-art CAD/CAM system, supported by a computer center full of mainframes—one of the most sophisticated in the world at that time (see Chapter 2). He watched in awe as an engineer displayed drawings of airplanes in orthographic, isometric, and perspective views. The workstations had big vector-graphic CRT displays and used light pens. He remembers, "leaving the building feeling overwhelmed by the power of such a system. At the same time I was also sad, thinking that technology as expensive as this would probably never be in reach of us theater people."

After that experience, he resolved to learn everything he could about computers. He took courses and wrote programs on punch cards, taught himself FORTRAN (an early computer language), and then BASIC. He read everything he could find about the relatively new field of computer graphics.

However, it wasn't until 1976 that he was able to apply any of this to art or design. His wife, Shima, was completing her BFA degree in costume design at CMU. He learned that all CMU students were entitled to a certain amount of time on the university's time-sharing computer system, so his wife obtained an account, which he then proceeded to use in the evenings. Armed with a teletype terminal connected to CMU's IBM system 360 mainframe and a small HP plotter, he was finally able to get graphic output from the computer. He spent hours writing a small program that would read a file of x-y-z coordinates, translate and rotate them as desired, and then feed them to the plotter. The result was a crude wireframe drawing. He kept working until one spring day when he logged onto the computer and was told that he had not only exhausted the time allotted to his wife's account, but, the entire drama department as well—and he wasn't even a student! It turned out that no one in the drama department had ever even gone into the computer science building, much less opened an account.

Working Methods

Ostroff currently uses a Power Macintosh G4/733 with 768MB of RAM and an Apple 21″ Studio Display. All 3-D modeling is completed with Strata 3-D Pro V3.5. His technique has been dictated by his background in scene design. "In traditional scene design it is common to use 2-D cut-out set pieces and painted backdrops. This technique translates very well to simple 3-D models. It's very easy to make virtual 'cardboard cutouts' of 2-D objects and insert them in your 3-D model. Using this simple technique, I can often approximate the appearance of complex objects that would be very difficult to truly model in three dimensions."

Ostroff also incorporates photos taken with his Nikon 990 digital camera as well as scanned images. A piece of hardware he considers indispensable is a small Wacom pressure-sensitive graphics tablet (see Chapter 8) that he uses to sketch and edit his images. In addition to Strata, he uses Adobe PhotoShop LE exclusively for all 2-D work, appreciating its simplicity. Also, he works with Bryce 4 to create skies and terrain for backdrops. For drafting he uses VectorWorks, a CAD program that makes stage design easier. Recently, he began working with digital video using a Sony VX-2000 digital handycam.

Sometimes Ostroff begins with a photo he has taken. Other times, he just digs right in and starts modeling 3-D objects, or a 2-D backdrop and some atmospheric lighting. But regardless of how he starts, it's usually a long road to the end result. "The real strength of working digitally is that you can explore lots of options. With traditional media I tended to stick with what I had and not take so many chances for fear of 'messing up' hours of work. On the computer you can just save the file as a new version and change anything you like. Sometimes I think this is too much freedom, and you don't commit enough to a design since you know it's easy to change later. Sooner or later, I just have to pronounce it done."

Professional Application

When Ostroff started working at the Opera Company of Philadelphia, he bought a Macintosh laptop and was ready to begin his transition to digital media. He set aside his drawing board and began to design on the computer. Floor plans for the *Magic Flute* were among his first efforts. By 1995 most of the drafting for the operas he designed was done on the computer. At this time he used the computer like a drawing board without taking advantage of 3-D modeling software. Beginning with the design for the backdrop, he then completed line drawings for the foreground elements. He printed the sketches and painted over them with watercolor, resorting to traditional materials to present his digital designs.

With the help of a $10,000 grant, the Opera Company of Philadelphia received a Power Macintosh 8100 system, complete with 3-D modeling software and video-editing capabilities. Finally, Ostroff could employ digital techniques from concept through final renderings—and his personal transition was complete.

During the winter of 1998 Ostroff modeled the entire set for a production in three weeks. He learned how to do tricks with texture maps, simulate scrims, and create dramatic lighting effects. He continued to build on this foundation, with each succeeding stage design depending more and more on his growing digital skills.

Of course, in theater this is really just the beginning. After completing the design, Ostroff must figure out how to actually build the design and stay on budget. He must prepare all the drafting schematics for the carpenters and paint elevations for the scenic artists. All these are completed on the computer and printed as color elevations. The recent advances in affordable high-quality color printing have helped make it practical for him to go completely digital with his stage design work (see Figures 14.7 through 14.12).

> “ I think one of the problems in using the computer is that the direction your designs take are strongly influenced by your ‘bag of tricks.’ I find it a constant challenge to look at a project objectively and resist the temptation to use all the familiar tricks. It’s a constant learning process which can be quite frustrating at times. ”

■ **Figure 14.7**
Boyd Ostroff, preliminary design for *I Capuleti e I Montecchi*, Opera Company of Philadelphia, 2001.

■ **Figure 14.8**

Boyd Ostroff, design for Act 2 of *Werther*, Opera Company of Philadelphia, 2001.

■ **Figure 14.9**

Boyd Ostroff, design for Act 4 of *The Marriage of Figaro*, Opera Company of Philadelphia, 1999.

■ **Figure 14.10**

Boyd Ostroff, design for Act 1 of *Tosca*, Opera Company of Philadelphia, 2000.

■ **Figure 14.11**

Boyd Ostroff, design for *Norma*, Opera Company of Philadelphia, 1998.

❝ Get a computer and whatever software you can afford, then see what you can do with it. The Internet offers a fantastic opportunity for you to show the world what you are capable of. ❞

❝ You should have some idea of what you want to say and accomplish, but don't be afraid to take some chances. Stick to your ideals—follow your star—but also be willing to listen to advice and learn from criticism. ❞

Simon Bosch

1984 Griffith University (Queensland College of Art)

Background

Simon Bosch studied illustration as part of a visual communication curriculum at Griffith University in Australia, with most of the courses taught within a fine arts context—lots of drawing and painting electives, as well as design and typography. For someone who drew whenever possible from the time he was old enough to hold a pencil, getting into an art college was the best move of his life. "It legitimized my need to be creative and to be able to find a profession. Art college was an absolutely fantastic experience, as it opened my eyes to so much that I'd never seen before. I didn't really even know what an illustrator was up to that point. Wow, drawing pictures for a living!"

Immediately after finishing college, Bosch worked at factory jobs to supplement his new freelance illustration career. "I desperately wanted to become an editorial illustrator. It was pretty tough early on and I had to rework my entire portfolio of college work for over a year before I got much work." He was eventually commissioned for a few illustrations in some of the larger newspapers in Australia; illustrations for magazines soon followed.

In 1994 Bosch began to notice digitally executed illustrations and graphics appearing in various publications. Originally, he didn't think that much of it looked very good and wondered whether the technology or the artists were to blame. He now realizes that, "the software back then was a bit limited for illustrators. . . . I mean, they didn't even have layers in PhotoShop. Imagine a world without layers!" At this time he was completely computer illiterate, but he started to talk to graphic designer friends about the sort of hardware and software they were using. One of them sat him down at a Mac with an early version of PhotoShop. As he became more and more interested, Bosch decided to try to create some illustrations digitally. Jumping in with both feet, he took out a huge loan, bought a Mac, drawing tablet, and "a wonderful bit of software called Painter (version2!)," and hasn't stopped trying to learn new tricks since.

On a technical level, Bosch believes that artists should try to think things out before turning on the computer. "That glowing screen can suck you in and keep you amused for hours without any real forward progress aesthetically. And remember that basic drawing skills will always be critical to your career as an artist, so never stop drawing!"

Working Methods

Bosch's work begins once a *brief* of a project is e-mailed or faxed to him. He responds by drawing a rough sketch which he faxes or e-mails back to the client (sometimes newspaper work has a two-to-three hour turnaround time). Once approved, he scans his original drawing into PhotoShop. He then opens the image in Painter, using vector tools to trace most of the image into smaller sections. Sometimes this involves many hundreds of bits, more layers in fact than PhotoShop can handle. Volume is then added using special filters within the program as well as plug-in filters from vendors like KPT. Many of the layers then need to be grouped and collapsed, being careful not to collapse layers which contain colors that may shift badly when converted to CMYK. "I try to avoid these colors in Painter, especially really bright reds, which never convert successfully as they are outside the gamut of printable colors." The layered image is then opened in PhotoShop, converted to CMYK, and the colors are adjusted. The final image is flattened, often with a clipping path for the convenience of the designer, saved as a JPEG, and e-mailed to the client. "Six months later they send me a check."

Professional Application

Bosch worked as a freelance illustrator for almost ten years before "going digital." Now that he has "seen the light," he has branched out to do a much wider variety of work for a broader range of clients. "The computer has kept me on my toes and helped me to avoid ever getting pinned down to one style and getting bored with what I do."

Through a combination of luck and determination, the "pumped up" style he has evolved is now technically easy to achieve in PhotoShop using a number of plug-ins, but it evolved from an early version of Painter and took a lot of effort. Today he concentrates more on composition and less on technique. He actually learned how to use Painter before PhotoShop and in the long run feels this has worked to his advantage as an illustrator.

Bosch feels that prospective artists need to be positive and not linger on minor setbacks. "Be prepared to listen to what experienced artists have to say to you. You are not obliged to agree with them or walk in their footsteps, but armed with a bit of knowledge, you may avoid some of the pitfalls." He is also quick to point out that to become an illustrator you need to have ambitions to become more than a page decorator. "It helps to keep up with current affairs. Whenever you get a text to illustrate that you don't understand, don't be afraid to ask to talk to the writer for an explanation. And be aware that style doesn't mean substance. You need to offer a client more than just a 'style.' " An illustrator needs to conceptualize and solve problems (see Figures 14.13 through 14.18). "They give you a text to illustrate (the problem)—you create an image based on that text (the solution)."

> " I am inspired by originality—not just in the arts but wherever it pops up its head. I get very angry when I see lazy 'copyists' making a living out of other people's styles. This is so easy to do with a computer. I, too, am influenced by other people's originality. I want to be just like them (i.e., original) without being them (i.e., a copyist). "

Figure 14.13
Simon Bosch, *Space Disco*, 2001.

Figure 14.14
Simon Bosch, *Bug Patcher*, 2001.

Figure 14.15

Simon Bosch, *Creepy Crawlies*, 2001.

" The computer is only my chosen tool and does not in itself guarantee successful pictures. The conceptual side of my work is usually far more important to me than how the end result is achieved. The training I got at Art college, even though non-digital, really set the groundwork for what has followed. Illustration is about problem solving. So is rebooting a frozen Mac, I guess. . . . "

Figure 14.16

Simon Bosch, *Runaway Chicken*, 2000.

Simon Bosch, *Software Pirate*, 2001.

■ **Figure 14.18**
Simon Bosch, *First Day, New School*, 2000.

John Crane

1984 BFA in Graphic Design, Colorado State University

Background

Involved with art from an early age, John Crane started his career with drawing lessons at a local art league and continued his studies throughout high school and college, where he earned a Bachelor of Fine Arts degree in graphic design/illustration. It was this experience in traditional media that established a foundation for Crane as he began to experiment with digital art media.

Although his family was immersed in the world of engineering, they supported and fostered John's interest in the arts and encouraged him to become involved in art activities in the local community and at school. "Inertia and a series of logical decisions kept me heading in that direction." He would find himself sitting for hours in front of a still life, focusing on obscure elements of the composition rather than the obvious—textures of a corn stalk, for example.

Moving to the computer in the late 1980s was a huge step for Crane because prior to that he had barely been able to turn one on. As his father purchased newer Macintosh computers, John would get the "hand-me-downs," which he would nurse along until he developed a bigger appetite. It took patience and many long-distance phone calls to his father, but Crane eventually passed through his creative impediment to see the computer as a creative enabler. In retrospect, he feels it was a fascinating exercise in logic, patience, and shifting from one side of the brain to another. "It was one of the most deeply focused times of my career and my life and I must say I enjoyed it immensely."

Various sources influenced Crane's life. Bill Allen at *3D Artist* magazine was instrumental in helping Crane "lose the training wheels" when it came to 3-D illustration and animation and jump into the big leagues, opening doors to worlds Crane never would have known existed. When offering advice to artists just starting out, Crane acknowledges that most artists are impatient by nature and want to see tangible progress fast. He cautions patience and notes that there are many good schools and educational options that simply weren't available for the study of computer art in the 1980s. "But really there are no short cuts to sitting down, powering up your machine, and getting to it. Have patience, pay attention to what you're doing, and keep saving."

Crane never developed into the airbrush illustrator he wanted to be. Something about the process stifled his creativity, and he found himself drifting into the role of technician rather than artist. The spontaneity of airbrush illustration just wasn't there for him, and the process left him wanting something more. It wasn't until 1992 that he actually sat down with software to create a piece of "art." It was a simple project using CorelDraw 2.0 to draw a machine bolt with vector art lines and gradations. It turned out better than he had anticipated. Three years later, he and his wife were walking through a book/software store in Albuquerque, New Mexico, looking at software. He picked up a box and saw stunning color illustrations. He looked at the price—$200. He looked at the minimum system requirements and realized his current computer would barely run the software. He discussed this "major" purchase with his wife and went home with the software. "I loaded it on my antiquated machine and immediately began banging my head on the table. Shortly after I awoke I ordered a new computer, an 80MHz Power Macintosh Power PC with 32MB of RAM. This is the machine *Ant Acid* was born on."

Working Methods

To begin a project, Crane often sits down and creates a sketch with pencil and paper. After working out some of the more obvious trouble spots, he moves to the computer to resolve the image. "I love to model and have a great appreciation for well-designed things, so I try to take my time and build something as well as possible rather than cutting as many corners as possible to do it fast. I then take great care in surfacing my models. This is what separates the novice from someone who is accomplished." Crane will spend hours getting the right procedural formula, texture map, or surfacing attribute. He will surface a model, test render, then surface again. "Anyone who does 3-D will tell you it's the textures (surfaces) that make the piece." Crane treats light and composition with great care and always renders at a higher resolution than he thinks he needs in order to avoid up-sampling and image degradation. All of these steps add up and extend the process far beyond that of a typical "down and dirty" production approach. For this reason, he is careful about the nature of the projects he accepts. "If it's worth doing, it's worth doing right, and I've turned down projects to honor this philosophy."

Crane recognizes that the computer by itself can be a technical challenge, depending upon how your brain works. Rare is the mind that can function optimally in both an artistically creative-abstract realm and a precise, method/process-oriented, logical realm. "Everything about the nature of art on the computer is technical. Learning to see through this technology and beyond, into the aesthetic world it's capable of helping you create, is the real challenge."

Professional Application

Crane originally conceived *Ant Acid* in college and executed it as a 2-D technical drawing for a class project. After photographing heavy earth-moving machines, Crane assembled hand-drawn components, such as backhoe assemblies for arms, into a coherent whole. Ten years later, when he first started working with 3-D modeling on the computer (using Ray Dream Designer 3), he decided that reworking this project would be a good way to learn the software. He submitted the finished work to an international art competition called Modern Masters of 3-D, sponsored by Fractal Design Corporation. *Ant Acid* won first place in the "Characters of Your Imagination" category and was published in many of the international computer graphics magazines, including the *New York Society of Illustrators*—a breakthrough for the young designer.

The spectrometer was a dream project for Crane. The client had spent four years developing this unit for release. Unfortunately, it had been modeled in Unigraphics, a high-end CAD application, and was trapped in a flat-shaded world—thereby unusable by marketing people. The technical challenge Crane faced was translating a mass of trim curves and CAD equations into polygons that could be surfaced, animated, and rendered. When asked by someone from John Deere "how much of this is artist license," he replied, "all of it." Without that, only a mass of flat gray shapes with no meaning except to engineers and manufacturing machines would be visible.

Windows 2000 magazine commissioned the Ramscape project, which depicted a high-tech traffic-copter hovering over a circuit board city monitoring the flow of activity. Using his own model library (Crane never purchases stock wireframe models, preferring to model everything from scratch), he was able to complete the piece quickly and successfully.

With his sketchbook giving birth to new ideas every day and more software to learn (see Figures 14.19 through 14.24), Crane's fear is not living long enough to see them all materialize.

66 "I've always gravitated toward close study of things, trying to capture a detailed essence and unique perspective of what I thought I saw. 99

66 "I've studied art theory, art history and just about everything else there is to study about it, but mostly I just love to create things. 99

66 I've consciously avoided emulating anyone else in art. I've tried to keep my products clean of obvious external influence and just let it unfold. I work hard at letting the project and the process decide the look of the finished piece. 99

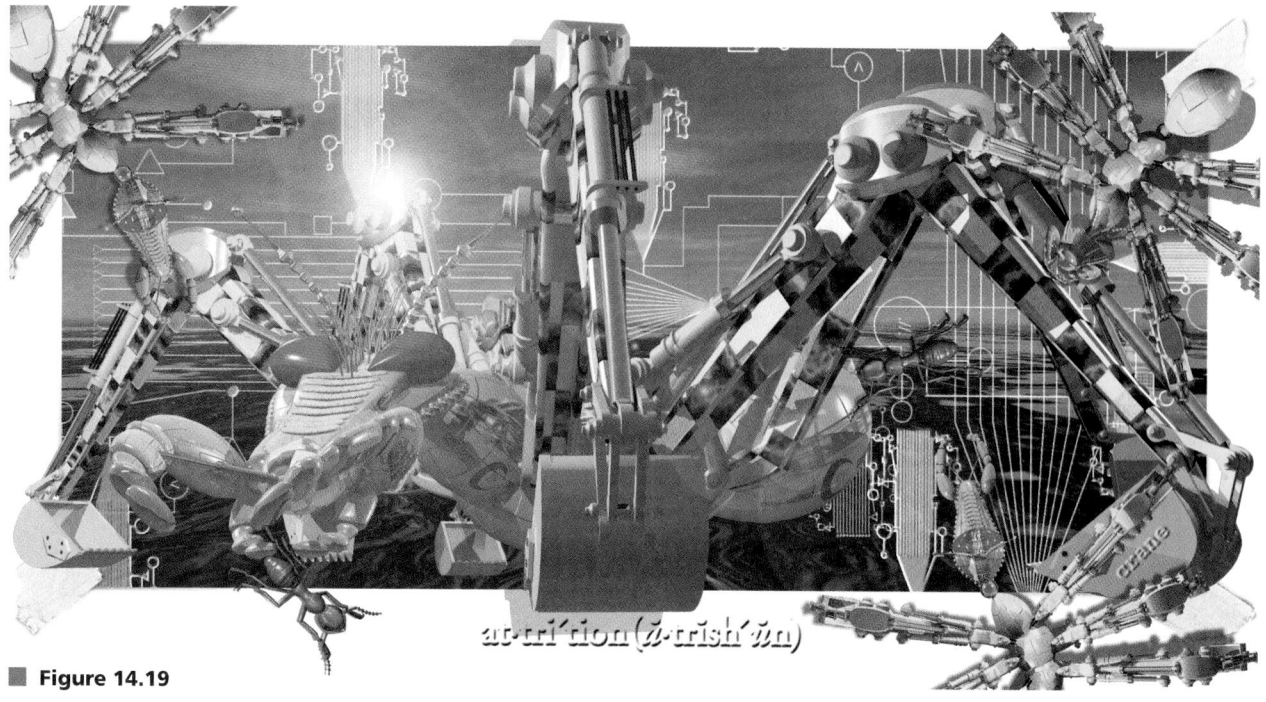

■ **Figure 14.19**

John Crane, *Ant Acid*, 1996.

66 Study art. After you've laid a good foundation of understanding the core principles of art (color theory, composition, lighting, etc.), then pick a software package and learn it inside and out. Become an expert. A guru. Know everything about your software and learn what other kinds of software can enhance your niche. Learn those just as well. 99

■ **Figure 14.20**

John Crane, *Circuit City*, 2001.

Artist rendering of
DNA double helix molecule

■ **Figure 14.21**
John Crane, *Artist's Representation of DNA Strand*, 1998.

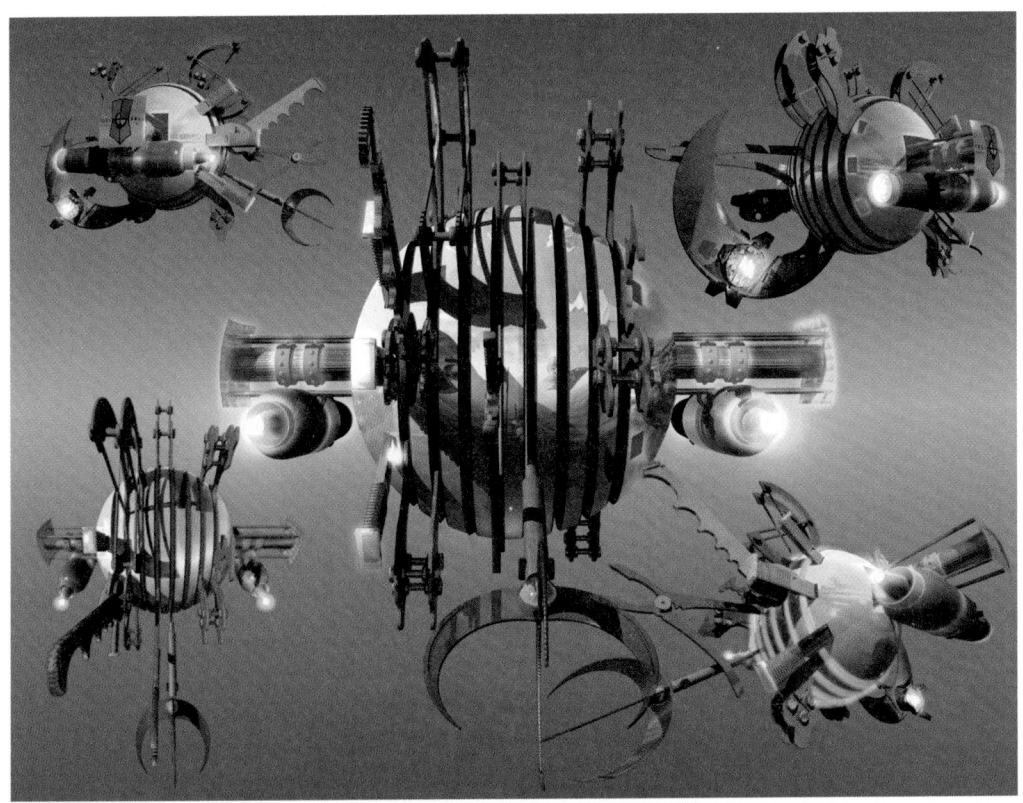

■ **Figure 14.22**
John Crane, *Toolball*, 2000.

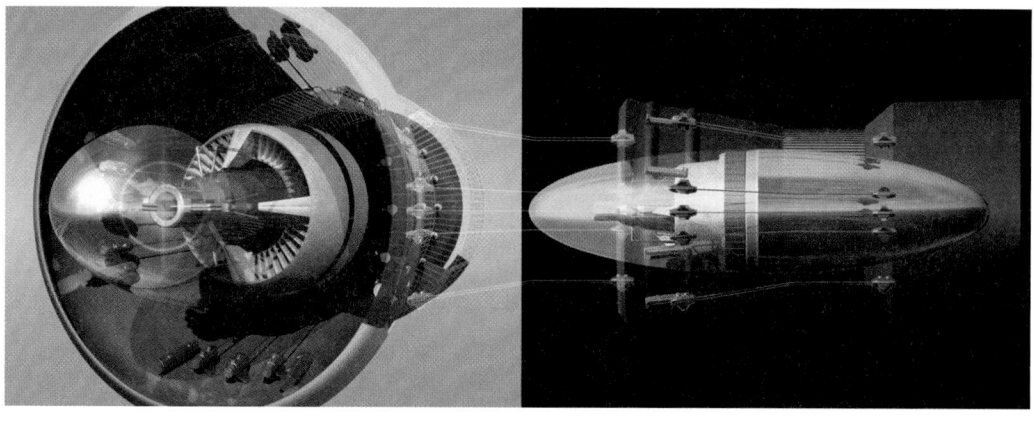

❝ Once you have the ability to create your own computer-generated reality, the learning and experimenting never, ever, ever ends. That's why I love it so much. ❞

Peter Baustaedter

1991 Ortwein Schule (Ortwein School), Graz, Austria

Background

Austrian Peter Baustaedter was fourteen years old when he got his first computer, and painted his first digital image when he was fifteen—a four-color work at a resolution of 160 × 200 pixels. He had always drawn a lot before trying computer graphics, but the computer offered him an image that was perfect. Since he was "a very messy and uncoordinated artist with traditional media," this seemed very attractive to him.

Instead of going to college, Baustaedter attended an art school for five years and began to work as soon as school ended. While at art school, he studied the field of film, photography, and video, and had a rather limited background in traditional art media like painting and drawing. As Baustaedter currently works for the film industry, where a knowledge of cameras, lenses, and all that comes with it is quite beneficial, his early training

■ **Figure 14.24**
John Crane, *Flying Under the Radar*, 1999.

was appropriate. When he began to work with computer graphics there was no opportunity to study its creative side—only the technical—which he was not interested in. As a result, he is largely self-taught. He remembers people looking at him strangely when he told them he was "painting on the computer." While his persistence has paid off, he feels that a more traditional education would have been beneficial and is occasionally sorely missed.

Initially, Baustaedter worked in the prepress business and produced graphics for computer games. After he moved to the United States in the beginning of 1995, he worked exclusively in the visual effects field. After getting his green card, he was also able to branch out in the neighboring fields of production illustration and computer games.

Baustaedter draws inspiration from a variety of sources, including the books he reads, movies he sees—even something he might encounter when free-diving (holding your breath while diving to great depths) or creating electronic music in a little studio he has assembled.

Working Methods

Usually, Baustaedter's work starts with an extensive conversation with the client. During this first meeting he tries to get all the information necessary for his project and clarify as exactly as possible what the client wants. This helps in avoiding changes late in the design process—which can and still does happen.

Once the basic parameters of the design are established, Baustaedter then proceeds to make a *production painting*. This quick, throwaway painting is used to further establish the look and feel of the final production piece. After client approval, work begins on the real thing. While the work is in progress, he usually delivers temporary versions to the client for continued approval, as well as to place his image in context to see if everything is correct and working the way it should.

Technical challenges are plentiful. Often Baustaedter must match perspective in an anamorphic plate without lens information, deal with the images of others hired to work on the same project, and even produce print versions of work in programs that don't always run the way they should.

Baustaedter doesn't limit himself to pure paint work. He utilizes 3-D graphics to save time and add realism to his painting, particularly 3-D graphics in scenes with a lot of architecture, rather than drafting out complex perspective scenes. This is very helpful at the beginning of a project, since the client can be shown different angles and other variations quickly and easily. In addition, a carefully lit 3-D scene speeds up the painting process and allows more time for "crafting" an image. Baustaedter's main focus is always on creating images with whatever technique is necessary to achieve his goal. "If a potato print works best, well, then I'll carve potatoes!"

Professional Application

Baustaedter started creating images for computer games—an interest he developed while spending his teen years in front of a Commodore Amiga. Together with two friends, he co-founded a computer game software company and took part in creating a number of games while he was there. (The company still exists today, and is very successful in the European market.)

As the computer games industry developed through the early 1990s, Baustaedter began to work with digital image manipulation for the first time. When he was twenty-two years old, he joined a studio called Vienna Paint and worked on what was then a state-of-the-art compositing and retouching program called Quantel Graphic Paintbox in order to create images for magazine ads and billboards. After an eight-month tour of duty with the Austrian Armed Forces, Baustaedter decided to apply to the visual effects segment of Digital Domain, where he began work on the movie *Apollo 13*, his first feature film project. After working on movies like *Dante's Peak* (where he had the role of a 3-D art director), *The Fifth Element, Titanic,* and *Terminator 2/3D* (a theme park ride), he left Digital Domain to spend two years in Hawaii as a digital matte and production painter working on *Final Fantasy,* the fully CG-animated

■ **Figure 14.25**

Peter Baustaedter, *Princess' Palace*, 1999.

■ **Figure 14.26**

Peter Baustaedter, *Oil City*, 2000.

Figure 14.27

Figure 14.27

Peter Baustaedter, *The Tunnel*,
2001.

feature from Squaresoft. Baustaedter now works as a freelance digital matte artist (see Figures 14.25 through 14.30) and conceptual artist for various film productions like *Swordfish*, *The Time Machine*, and *Lord of the Rings*.

66 "Important to me is being fulfilled in my work and always having the opportunity to create—be it painting or making music. These things keep my life in balance. 99

Figure 14.29

Peter Baustaedter,
Kaina Point, 1999.

" A good artistic training is having the upper hand over intricate technical knowledge. The process of digital creation will change as time goes on—what will always stay more or less the same is the creative process of conception and production. If you put your time there, the technical side will come by itself if the interest is there. "

" Do not give up. If you want to do it, do it. Work, work, work and don't let anyone discourage you—don't discourage yourself either. "

" Images I do for fun usually try to take the viewer to another world in a fairly realistic manner—very typical for fantasy paintings. But that has foremost been my motivation and I never seem to get tired of it. You could say 'Blowing up three dimensional bubbles into "no-space" and creating a little world of your own inside'—to be really corny. "

■ **Figure 14.28**
Peter Baustaedter, *World of Canyons*, 2000.

■ **Figure 14.30**
Peter Baustaedter, *Squeed*, 2001.

Robert Lazzarini

1990 BFA, School of Visual Arts, New York
1985 Parsons School of Design

Background

Robert Lazzarini's grandfather was an art teacher for many years and kept him inspired with art history books and well stocked with art supplies since he was seven years old. Lazzarini's formal training started in his junior year in college and centered primarily around contemporary artforms and the materials and techniques of traditional sculpture. This early training is still the basis for the work he does now. The transition between being a student of art and being a professional artist was very difficult for him. "It took a lot of time to develop a vocabulary that connected my ideas and their forms with the viewer's interpretation of them. I was moving between works on paper and sculptural forms for a number of years."

Lazzarini started showing his works on paper. It was about that time that he started to work with compound distortions of 3-D objects. He moved to digital media in 1995, realizing that it was the best way to solve some of the formal issues in his work. He soon became interested in creating derivatives of specific objects. "I knew that working with CAD/CAM technology would give me an unprecedented control over their geometries." Although he was familiar with PhotoShop at that time, he had no knowledge whatsoever of 3-D programs. It took him a while to teach himself the programs he needed to use and to create working dialogues with both 3-D modelers and rapid prototyping service bureaus. Some pieces he designed at that time couldn't be made until four or five years later.

Working Methods

Lazzarini's vertigo-inducing sculptures are created from the digitization of actual objects, which are then manipulated and distorted in a 3-D modeling program. The compound distortions create a strange, almost surrealistic juxtaposition of 2- and 3-D realities.

There are three main stages to the process Lazzarini uses to create his work. He starts with a design created in a 3-D modeling program, makes a model for review using relatively new rapid prototyping (computer-generated model making) hardware, and then produces the final sculpture—often using the same materials found in the original object. Once he picks an object or a group of objects, Lazzarini will use a photograph of them to create an initial 2-D sketch in PhotoShop. "Although I'm not working with the full geometry of the object at this point, I am able to approach the nature of the distortion. Also, I'm addressing the object as image—which is an extremely important issue in my work."

By reverse drafting the object or laser scanning its surface, Lazzarini creates a virtual version of the object. Working with a combination of animation and industrial design programs, he addresses the distortion in three dimensions and formats it for physical output as a rapid prototype model. Lazzarini will often create a half-dozen lower resolution models until he arrives at a final modification of the object's geometry. He considers these to be 3-D sketches.

Once he chooses the best 3-D sketch, it serves as his final model. The geometry and the material used to create the sculpture determines the resolution that he will need to create the final piece. For example, each skull had two final models. The first was a rapid prototype wax pattern, which he then manually modified. From that wax model a mold was made and a production model was cast from the mold in rigid plastic. This production model was further modified by hand to create a production mold. A small edition of the final sculpture was then cast from the production mold.

The final production of each piece varies in complexity based on the materials of the final object. Parts range from cast plastic to cast stainless steel, carved wood to cast rubber. Once the distorted geometry is in its final material, Lazzarini needs to address it again as an image. He is interested in his sculptures having a visual fidelity to the wear and tear of the original object. All of the sculptures are based on found objects, so their surface condition or *patina* is very important to how they read as an image.

Professional Application

Robert Lazzarini received a New York State Foundation for the Arts grant in 1985 and 1986. In 1995, at the age of twenty-nine, Lazzarini's first one-person show of works on paper opened in New York. By his second solo show he was able to further develop some of the ideas dealing with distortions of 3-D objects in his work. Since then, he has exhibited his work in a number of group and solo shows and is now represented by Pierogi Gallery in New York City. Perhaps most notable was the inclusion of his work in two exhibitions at the Whitney Museum in New York, Bitstreams (2001) and the 2000 Whitney Biennial, in which his work was singled out for critical acclaim.

As he works with his notion of the impossible object and the spatial paradox in the fluctuation between 2-D and 3-D space, it is not uncommon for Lazzarini to work a fourteen- to seventeen-hour day. Nevertheless, his primary concern is always the past, present, and future of the object as well as its physical, psychological, and emotive response (see Figures 14.31 through 14.37).

> "Many times before an important show, I will work straight through 3 or 4 days with no sleep. The only boundaries around my work are the ones that I accept."

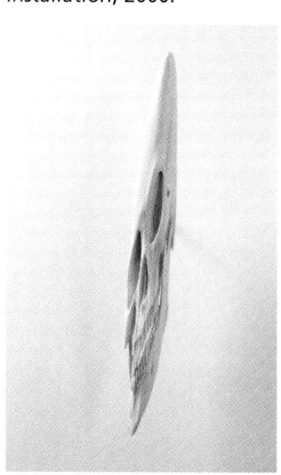

■ **Figure 14.31**
Robert Lazzarini, skull from *Skulls Installation*, 2000.

■ **Figure 14.32**
Robert Lazzarini, skull from *Skulls Installation*, 2000.

❝ When someone views a work of art, it is immediately clear how deep the investigation of the artist is. It's like a conversation. I hope to speak in a way that is both genuine and meaningful. ❞

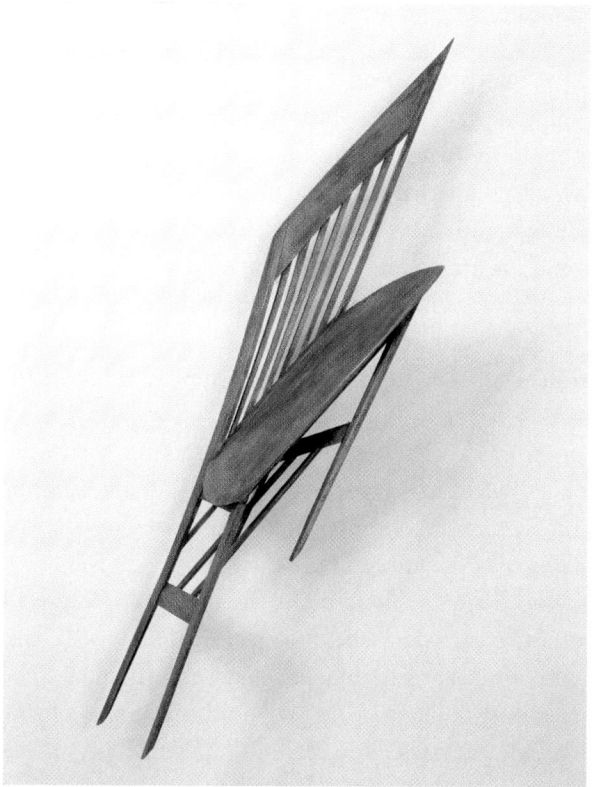

■ **Figure 14.35**
Robert Lazzarini, *Chair*, 2000.

■ **Figure 14.36**
Robert Lazzarini, *Payphone*, 2002.

■ **Figure 14.37**
Robert Lazzarini, *Skulls Installation*, 2000.

CONCLUSION

The story of the digital revolution in art is just beginning to unfold. From the early days of imaginative engineers working on huge mainframes to artists sketching on today's lightweight digitizing tablets with built-in screens, there have been extraordinary changes and many new ways to create art. Every new year seems to offer additional programs along with updated versions of current software. The list of techniques and capabilities keeps increasing so fast that no one person can ever truly keep abreast of them. However, as exciting as the digital media are, in the end, they simply provide a new set of tools for bringing the artist's imagination to reality.

With all the different programs available there is the temptation to continually experiment and never resolve a single work. The artists discussed in this chapter are well aware of the danger of constant and enthusiastic exploration. From time to time, they may have even succumbed to its allure but in the end have risen above it and developed a compelling body of work.

In the years ahead, we can be sure that we will be astounded by what has been put in the hands of artists by scientists, engineers, and programmers. The opportunities for exhibiting and collaborating will only increase, as fast broadband networking becomes universal. However, the challenge for you, as for every artist, remains what it has always been: To use the medium you have chosen to make works that reveal your emotions and ideas, to find a way to represent your vision, and to tap into the timeless power of imagination.

Glossary

Abacus The first calculator. This calculating system, invented between 3 and 5 thousand years ago by travelling traders in ancient China and Babylonia, has beads that slide along several strings in a frame. Each string represent ones, tens, hundreds, and so on.

ADC (analog to digital converter) Converts analog information to either a one or a zero (binary code).

Additive color model See *RGB mode*.

Adobe Gamma control panel Monitor calibration system that makes it easy to adjust gray values on a monitor in order to eliminate color casts that might affect the color balance of your work.

Advanced Research Projects Agency (ARPA) Organization founded in 1957 to re-establish America's lead in the military development of science and technology particularly after Russian scientists succeeded in putting a satellite into orbit before the United States.

AGP bus The AGP bus is dedicated specifically to video cards, and provides a faster and more direct interface between the video card and memory. This works especially well for 3-D graphics and video.

Alpha channel A stored selection or mask.

Ambient lighting Light spread across an entire scene without a focus, which illuminates all objects equally.

Amplitude The height of a sound as seen in a *sound wavegraph*. Technically, how much change in pressure a sound creates. The taller a wavegraph's amplitude, the louder the sound.

Analytical Engine Early computing machine designed by Charles Babbage in the early 1800s, controlled by a set of punch cards that interacted with pins on metal wheels. Although never completed, it was an important forerunner of modern computers. This machine was larger than his earlier *Difference Engine*.

Anchor Tag that starts and ends links in an HTML document.

Animated symbol In digital animation, a short sequence, like a cycle, that can repeat several times to form a longer action. It can be saved with the file and reused again in different places in the animation without increasing the overall file size. Also known as a *sprite*.

Anime (pronounced "annie-may") The Japanese style of animation. Compared to cartoons in the United States, anime has much greater variety in subject matter and is enjoyed by all age groups.

Anti-aliasing Process that smooths the edge of a selection but will not soften it as extensively as *feathering* has the capability of doing. Curved selections will benefit the most from anti-aliasing.

Aperture grill mask Used instead of a shadow mask, this type of cathode ray tube uses hundreds of fine metal strips running vertically from the top of the screen surface to the bottom in order to define the image area to be illuminated. Pixels are separated vertically by the scan lines used to compose the image.

AppleTalk A network protocol that allowed Macintosh computers to communicate with one another and share printers and disk resources.

ARPANET The first wide area network, created by the U.S. Defense Advanced Research Project Agency (ARPA) in 1969 in order to link universities and research centers. This precursor to the Internet was originally created by linking computers at UCLA, Stanford Research Institute, the University of Utah, and the University of California at Santa Barbara.

ASCII (American Standard Code for Information Interchange) Standard, universal text set of 96 characters.

AT (attention command) Invented by the Hayes Corporation during the late 1970s to begin each modem command.

Attributes In 3-D animation, an object's characteristics, such as its rigidity and weight.

Authoring software A program that integrates graphics, text, animations, video, and sounds, usually for presentations or publishing CD-ROMs.

Backface elimination In 3-D modeling, a method to save processing power and time in the final rendering of an image by including only the sides of the model visible in the viewing plane.

Baseline shifting Allows you to select and then move individual letters above or below their *baselines*, the imaginary line upon which all letters would normally sit.

BASIC (Beginners All-purpose Symbolic Instruction Code) A relatively easy-to-use programming language of the 1960s and 1970s.

Beveling A simple and very common variation of *extrusion* that pushes forward a flat shape and adds angled edges along its sides, so the original shape becomes the front face of the new 3-D object. Sometimes called *face extrusion*.

Bézier curve Another name for a vector curve, which is typically created with the pen or *Bézier* tool.

Bézier tool Another name for the pen tool used for creating vector graphics.

Bicubic A relatively sophisticated method of interpolation that samples all existing pixels in the area in which new information must be created. New pixels are then added based on an averaging together of that information.

Bilinear interpolation Averages the pixels to either side of the area in which new information must be created.

Binary code Basic computer code composed entirely of zeros and ones.

Bit The smallest unit of data in computing, with a value of either zero or one.

Bit depth The maximum number of colors or shades in each pixel. The greater the bit depth, the more subtle and realistic color and grayscale images will appear.

Bitmap Images created by a series of dots. Bitmap type can lose quality as it is enlarged.

Bitmap painting software Programs that create digital pictures that have the look and range of traditional painting, as well as other artist materials. Also called *natural media* software.

Bleed In a digital layout and design program, a bleed is an element such as an illustration, solid, or rule that extends beyond the trimmed edge of a printed page. Full-bleed proofs show what a print would look like if an image went right to the edge of the paper.

Bookmark Saved website to be revisited.

Boolean intersection In 3-D modeling, a *Boolean operation* where only the overlapping parts of the two shapes are preserved and every other part is eliminated.

Boolean operation In 3-D modeling, a method of creating more complex solid forms by overlapping solid shapes and combining them in a variety of ways by adding or subtracting an object from another. Examples are *Boolean union, subtraction,* and *intersection.*

Boolean subtraction In 3-D modeling, where one form is cut away from the other.

Boolean union In 3-D modeling, where the outer forms of two volumes are added together and whatever intersects internally is eliminated.

Boot The loading of the operating system into a computer and starting of initial processes.

Bounding box In 3-D programs, a quick-rendering viewing mode where only a simple box, large enough to contain the object, is seen rather than its wire mesh.

Broadband Internet access at speeds in the range of 1MHz or more is considered broadband access; for example, ISDN and cable modem access.

Browsers A software program that allows users to navigate through a network in order to access information.

Brushes Tools that imitate *natural media tools,* like chalk or pencils.

Bump maps In 3-D modeling, an advanced form of *texture mapping.* This technique simulates how a textured surface would reflect light naturally, without actually changing the geometry of the model. The illusion of the texture's depth is based on the contrast between the bright and dark parts of the image.

Bus A data pathway that connects a processor to memory and to other "peripheral" buses like SCSI, PCI, and AGP.

Byte Eight *bits* of data.

Cable modem A device that connects a computer to the coaxial cable provided by a cable television (CATV) network. Cable modems are always online and are capable of multimegabit data transfer.

CAD (computer-aided design) A special kind of vector-based 3-D modeling used by industrial and fashion designers, engineers, and architects to create models for manufacturing and architecture. Sometimes called a *drafting* program.

Camera dolly In 3-D animation, a camera that follows subjects as they move, based on a moving platform attached to a track in a traditional film studio.

Camera target In 3-D modeling, a marker on the wireframe drawing that shows where the camera is focused.

Camera-ready art Mechanical, photograph, or other art prepared to be photographed in order to create a plate for printing on an offset lithography press. See *Paste up* and *Mechanical.*

Canvas The work area in digital painting software where the new image will be created.

CCD (charged coupled device) Converts light into analog electrical current. Flatbed scanners use linear arrays of CCDs.

CD-R (compact disc recordable) Instead of creating pits and lands in a disc, the CD-R heats (burns) special chemicals on the disc, causing them to reflect less light than areas not burned. The burned areas reflecting less light work in a similar fashion as a "pit" on a conventional CD-ROM, with unburned, more highly reflective areas becoming the land. Due to the chemical composition of their coating, CD-R discs can be written only once.

Cel animation In traditional animation, a series of drawings made on sheets of clear acetate or *cels*. Registration is ensured by placing cels on a fixed platform with pegs that match punched holes in the cels. In digital animation, the drawings are made on a series of transparent keyframes. Also known as *keyframe animation*.

Centered Centers text between the left and right edges of a text block.

CERN (Conseil Européen pour la Recherche Nucleaire) Located in Geneva, Switzerland, this is the founding organization of the World Wide Web. One of the world's oldest and largest scientific laboratories, it is dedicated to research in the field of particle physics.

Channels Separate eight-bit images that the computer mixes together to create a full-color, 24-bit image. Each of these independent 8-bit images represents the tonal values for red, green, and blue in RGB and cyan, yellow, magenta, and black in CMYK.

Chipset Microcircuits that control the flow of information from one part of the computer to another and determine the way in which the processor will access memory, the way it will communicate with peripheral devices, the type of RAM memory that can be used, and so on.

Clipping path Defines the area of an image that will be visible when placed in a digital layout and design program.

Clock tick The speed with which the CPU can execute instructions.

Clones Computers that utilize functionally identical computing systems. Generally, these are IBM-compatible computers.

Cloning A method of painting with part of another picture or another location of the current picture.

Closed path In vector illustration, a path that begins and ends at the same point and describes a shape. A rectangle and circle are both examples of closed paths.

CMYK color model Format for images designed for printing on a press. Cyan, magenta, yellow, and black inks are printed one after the other to create full-color images. Unlike *RGB*, CMYK utilizes a subtractive model based on the reflected light of inks rather than projected light. As light strikes the ink, a portion of that light is absorbed.

COBOL (Common Business Oriented Language) A hardware-independent programming language for government and business use developed by Grace Hopper in 1959. Unlike *FORTRAN*, it uses words rather than numbers.

Color separation A method to transform color artwork into cyan, magenta, yellow, and black components,

from which most colors can be reproduced. See also *CMYK color model*.

Compound path In vector illustration programs, this is a complex shape made from two or more overlapping shapes. Shapes can be combined or *united* and become one form sharing the same overall outline, or made where the forms *intersect* only, eliminating all other parts. *Exclude* eliminates only the areas where the shapes overlap. *Merge* combines only the overlapping shapes that share the same fill color. *Crop* removes any parts below the top shape. *Punch* or *Minus front* cuts away the topmost shape from the group. *Divide* increases the number of sections by splitting the shapes into smaller ones wherever they overlap.

Computer Graphics Research Group (CGRG) Group founded at Ohio State University in 1969 by Charles Csuri to advance research in computer animation. In 1987, the group was renamed the Advanced Computing Center for Arts and Design (ACCAD).

Constraining Forcing a rectangle to become a square or an ellipse to be a circle by holding down a special key while drawing.

Constraints In 3-D animation, a restriction added to a linked motion in order to limit the range of movement and make it appear more natural.

Contone Abbreviation for continuous tone.

Cooperative multitasking An early form of task switching that allowed the user to change from one program to another.

Copyfitting The adjustment of type to fit into a given space or number of pages.

Corner point In vector illustration, a kind of anchor point made with the pen tool that changes the direction of a curve (for example, from upward to downward), as in a collection of waves versus rolling hills.

CPU (central processing unit) The computer's brain, it processes and executes operations after taking requests from applications.

CRT (cathode ray tube) Although usually used as another name for a computer monitor, it is technically the tube of a monitor in which electron rays are beamed onto a phosphorescent screen to produce images.

CSS (cascading style sheets) A method for assigning properties to various elements of a Web page, which helps provide a consistent look to websites of many pages. For example, style sheets can be used to control font size, color, style, weight, and line spacing.

Curves A control in most image-editing programs that allows you to selectively raise or lower values in specific areas of an image.

Cycles A time-saver for animators, cycles are short sequences that can be repeated over and over again, like a character walking. In digital animation, they can be saved with the file and be reused again in different places. Also known as a *sprite* or *animated symbol*.

Daisy wheel An impact printing system that uses a spoked wheel with type characters positioned at the end of each spoke. A print hammer strikes the key and pushes it into an inked ribbon, which then strikes the paper to create a text character.

Dataglove Glove designed to allow users to appear to touch and manipulate objects in a virtual environment.

Deformation Modification of a simple 3-D model, such as stretching, squashing, bending, twisting, or skewing it in one direction.

Depth of field The amount of visual information that appears to be in focus. In 3-D software, how far back from the camera objects can be seen in focus.

Descreen Removing or minimizing halftone dot patterns from printed material.

Desktop publishing system Term from the mid-1980s for the first software and hardware used for graphic design, providing control over fonts and layout, and permitting printing directly from a personal computer.

Difference Engine Early computing machine designed by Charles Babbage in the early 1800s. Although never completed, it was an important forerunner of modern computers, as it was designed to do calculations for mathematical tables mechanically and to print automatically.

Digital cameras Cameras that use an array of *CCD* sensors to capture light and convert it to digital data.

Digital layout and design software The primary tool of graphic designers for laying out text and pictures in ads, magazines, newspapers, and books; once known as "desktop publishing."

Digital media The artforms created with computer technology.

Digitize Convert analog data to digital data.

Digitizing tablet A flat, pressure-sensitive input device. A pen-shaped stylus is used to draw directly on the tablet.

DIMM (dual inline memory module) A type of pre-assembled RAM module supporting a wider data path than SIMMs, which allows faster memory access.

Direct selection A special selection tool for vector forms (usually displayed as a white arrow); designed for making precise modifications to parts of a path and individual anchor points.

Direction lines Lines used to reshape a curve's height and slope in vector illustration. They are connected to the anchor points of a curve and are made visible after clicking on a curve with the *direct selection* tool.

Directory A folder or group of folders that can contain files as well as other folders.

Direct-point (or surface) modeling In 3-D modeling, dragging and stretching individual vertices in the wireframe mesh to reshape the surface of a form.

Disc Optical storage media like CD-R, CD-ROM, DVD, and so on, as opposed to magnetic storage systems.

Disk Magnetic storage media like floppy disks, zip disks, and hard disks as opposed to optical storage systems.

Display Another name for the monitor.

Dissolve In film and animation, where one scene fades in as the other fades out. This implies a logical connection between the two scenes.

Dithering The approximation of an unavailable color by using a mixture of available colors.

Dmax The maximum density within an image as measured by a densitometer.

Dmin The minimum density within an image as measured by a densitometer.

DNS (Domain Name System) The standard method for assigning website addresses. Domain names are organized in a categorical hierarchy based on the type of group that is the host; for example, commercial sites (.com), educational sites (.edu), government sites (.gov), military sites (.mil), and general organizations (.org).

DOD (drop on demand) Printing technology in which small drops of ink, triggered by heat and controlled by a printer's software, squirt onto the paper.

Dollying In 3-D animation, moving the camera toward or away from objects to zoom in or out on subjects. In traditional film, a camera on a wheeled platform.

Dot gain The spreading of ink dots as they print on paper. Ink dots are affected by the absorptive qualities of the paper and the size and shape of the halftone screen dot. Uncorrected dot gain can make images appear too dark and shift color values.

Dot-matrix printers Printers that use a matrix of small hammers, instead of actual type letters, to push pins against an ink-coated ribbon, which in turn transfers ink dots onto the paper to form letters.

Dot pitch Measurement of the distance between similarly colored phosphors on the inner surface of the CRT. The closer together the phosphors are, the smaller the dot pitch and the finer the screen image will be.

Download Information transferred from an *ISP* to a personal computer.

Downsample Resampling approach that deletes information from an image.

Dpi (dots per inch) A method of calculating printer resolution, which describes the number of dots per linear inch.

Drag and drop An action performed using a mouse to move icons, text, images, etc. on the computer screen.

Drivers Software developed by individual hardware manufacturers to implement the devices they manufacture.

Drum scanner High-resolution professional scanner that uses PMTs (photo multiplier tubes) which have a much higher sensitivity to light and lower noise levels than *CCDs* found in flatbed scanners.

DSL (Digital Subscriber Line) High-speed Internet access via installed copper telephone wires which provides speeds up to twenty times faster than conventional 56K *POTS* modems.

DVD (digital versatile disc) Similar in appearance to CD-ROM discs, high-capacity optical discs able to store up to 4.7GB of data on a single side. Used for computer applications and full-length movies. Double-sided DVDs can store from 8.5 to 17GB of information.

Dye-sublimation printers Printers designed to produce prints by vaporizing inks. They turn solid colors into a gas which then solidifies or *sublimates* on the paper, thus producing prints indistinguishable from those produced in a conventional photographic darkroom.

Dynamic IP address A temporary Internet address that changes each time you log on. Its use makes it difficult for someone to track your actions or illegally enter your system.

Dynamic range Measure of a scanner's ability to differentiate differences in tones from light to dark.

E.A.T. (Experiments in Art and Technology) Organization founded in 1966 by the artist Robert Rauschenberg and the Bell Laboratory scientist Billy Kluver to bring together artists, choreographers, musicians, scientists, and engineers to imagine new forms of art.

EDVAC (Electronic Discrete Variable Automatic Computer) The successor to *ENIAC,* this was the first computing machine with a central processing unit (*CPU*) that coordinated all operations. Also, it was the first machine with true computer memory for storing programs and data.

EEPROM (Electrically Erasable Programmable ROM) The type of *ROM* most often used in motherboards today. It allows the user to "flash" or upgrade the BIOS to take advantage of processor improvements or bugs found in earlier releases of the BIOS ROM.

Electro-photography First introduced in 1948 as a means of copying documents, it eventually evolved to *xerography* (Greek for "dry writing").

ENIAC (Electronic Numerical Integrator and Computer) Completed in 1945 at the University of Pennsylvania, ENIAC was the fastest calculating machine of its time; one thousand times faster than the previous *Mark 1.*

EPS (Encapsulated PostScript) A *PostScript* language format that can contain both vector and bitmap graphics and is supported by all page-layout programs.

Establishing shot In film, an introduction to a scene, where new subjects are seen first at a distance. Typically, the camera then slowly moves in closer.

Expansion cards Printed circuit boards that connect to *expansion slots* to add to a computer's functions; also known as expansion boards.

Expansion slots Allow the attachments of different kinds of *expansion cards* to the computer.

Exposure sheet A very detailed chart used by teams of animators, which describes every frame of the film in terms of the general, detail of action, special effects, and sounds; also known as a *work schedule.*

Extrusion In 3-D modeling, giving a 2-D shape depth by pulling it out into 3-D space (sometimes called *lofting*). For example, by extruding a circle vertically upward, you can make a column.

Face In 3-D modeling, one of the geometric planes that describes a form. For example, a cube has six interconnected square faces.

Fair use Use of copyrighted material for educational purposes. Other fair use applications apply to small sections of an original work used for news reporting, reviews, criticism, and parody.

Feathering The selection of a certain number of pixels with which to soften the edge of a selection or mask. This is helpful when selected areas need to be blended in with their surroundings at some point in the editing process.

Field of view In 3-D software, the size of the area seen by the viewer.

Fill In vector illustration, a color, gradient, or pattern applied to the open area inside a *closed path.*

Fill lighting (sometimes called *omnidirectional*) Light spread from one general direction, without strong cast shadows or highlights. It can also be used to fill in dark areas in shadow.

Filters Can be applied to an entire image or limited to selections or masks in order to create a special effect or modification (i.e., unsharp masking).

Firewall Enforces an access control policy between two networks, preventing unauthorized access to your computer.

Flat shading In 3-D modeling, a simple type of shading that applies one tone and color to each facet or polygon on the surface of the model without smoothing them.

Flatbed scanner A computer peripheral designed to *digitize* flat images, like photographs, prints, and drawings. The most common form of scanner, it uses linear arrays of *CCDs* to convert analog images to digital signals.

Flowchart In Web designing, a schematic plan for a website outlining how information is to be connected.

Flush left Aligns text with the left side of a text block.

Flush right Aligns text with the right side of a text block.

FM (frequency modulation) A mathematical sound synthesis approach to recreating the sound of an instrument.

Forced justification Aligns all text, including the last line (which may be shorter), with the left and right edges of a text block.

Format Method to organize a hard or floppy disk into individual storage locations called *tracks* and *sectors.*

FORTRAN (formula translation) The first hardware-independent programming language, created by a team led by John Backus in 1957.

Forward kinematics In 3-D animation, a kind of linked motion where one part initiates the movement of all other linked parts, as compared to inverse kinematics.

Fractals Unusual geometric shapes whose smallest part resembles the larger shape. Because their structure resembles the organizing principle behind natural forms, fractals are used to create digital landscapes of extraordinary realism. They are also used for image compression applications.

Frames A method of displaying more than one HTML document in the same browser window, with each frame capable of displaying information independently of the others.

Frameset Document used when creating *frames*, which contains instructions defining the size and orientation of each frame and which HTML document should be displayed in those frames.

Free-form modeling In 3-D modeling, shifting and pulling the polygons that make up the wireframe mesh that covers all 3-D objects.

FTP (File Transfer Protocol) Software that allows you to transfer files between your computer and a remote server. FTP can resume transfer, even if interrupted, from the point at which the interruption took place.

Galleys Sheets of printed type.

Gamma Refers to the midrange values in an image between black and white.

Gamut Describes the range of colors that can be displayed on a monitor or printed. The *RGB* gamut contains the colors that can be accurately viewed on a color monitor. The *CMYK* gamut represents colors that can be printed with cyan, magenta, yellow, and black process inks. The L*A*B* color model has the largest gamut of all containing the colors in both the RGB and CMYK color models.

GIF (Graphics Interchange Format) An image compression format, limited to 256 colors, commonly used in Web pages. Created by CompuServe in 1987 so images could be shared easily.

GIF 89A See *GIF animation*.

GIF animation (also known as the GIF 89A format) On Web pages, several bitmapped pictures with very small file sizes linked together and appearing animated as they play sequentially.

Gigabyte One thousand megabytes.

Gigahertz One gigahertz (GHz) equals 1,000 megahertz, or one billion *clock ticks* per second.

Gopher The earliest of the systems available for organizing and displaying files on the World Wide Web.

Gouraud shading In 3-D modeling, a shading method that results in much smoother tonal blends than *flat shad-*

ing by mathematically interpolating a series of lines and, hence, smoothing the edges of the polygons. Conceived by Henri Gouraud at the University of Utah in 1971. Also known as smooth shading.

Gradient meshes In vector illustration, smooth multicolored gradients that create a 3-D look for forms. When revealed, they appear as a net of lines and points criss-crossing over an object, that can be modified to reshape a form.

Gradients A gradual blend of a range of colors, which is a common way to apply multiple colors in digital media software. Gradients can be linear or radial, and in some programs, spiral or circular.

Graphical User Interface (GUI– pronounced "gooey") Computer software that is graphical, or picture based, rather than text based. It utilizes icons to represent programs and folders for storing files. First created by Alan Kay at *Xerox PARC*.

Graphics accelerator A video card with a dedicated processor to boost performance.

Grayscale 256 shades of gray used to represent a black-and-white image. Pixels in a grayscale image have a value ranging from black (0) to white (255).

Gutter The space formed by the inner margins of two facing printed pages.

Halftone cels Groups of dots positioned closer together or further apart to create what appears to be a continuous tone.

HDCD (high-definition CD) A type of compact disc that utilizes a higher frequency to read bit patterns from a disc, resulting in better detail and resolution of the master recording.

Hexadecimal In Web design, a numbering system used to designate colors.

Hidden line mode In 3-D programs, a viewing mode for wireframes that hides any facets that would normally be blocked from view if fully rendered.

Hi-fi color A color system with additional colors to supplement the four CMYK process colors. For example, Pantone's Hexachrome inks use six printing inks instead of the traditional four. The result is more lifelike and natural color.

High resolution A monitor or video card that can display fine detail and millions of colors.

Histogram A visual representation of the tonal and color range of an image.

Hollerith Electric Tabulating System An early computing machine designed by Hans Hollerith in the late 1800s, for the U.S. Census, it utilized a punch card system that could be tabulated mechanically. The punch cards stored eighty variables about an individual on a single card.

Hot swappable The ability to plug and unplug devices from a port without first having to turn off the computer.

HSB The color system whose variables are hue, saturation, and brightness.

HTML *(hypertext markup language)* The code or programming language of Web pages, *hypertext* is used to create links in the text to other words, images, or documents and offers the reader a new, nonlinear way to seek information.

Hue The name of the basic color, as in "red" or "blue."

Hypermedia Audio, video, image, or text files that are "linked," or connected, with other files of this nature through hypertext markup language.

Hypertext A nonlinear approach to writing, allowing the reader to make choices about which threads of information are going to be followed in Web pages.

Hypertext Editing System (HES) Developed by Nelson and van Dam, this system allowed for on-screen editing, links within documents that led to other parts of the same document, or even links to other documents. HES eventually concentrated on printout and formatting, becoming one of the prototypes of today's word processing systems.

I/O (input/output) Refers to any operation in which data is transferred in or out of the computer.

ICC (International Color Consortium) Used in color-managed applications that support the Kodak Color Management System.

ICM profiles Used in color-managed applications that support the Kodak Color Management System; Windows version of *ICC*.

Illustration software Another name for vector illustration software.

Image compositing The combination of separate images to create a greater imaginative whole.

Imagesetter A machine capable of printing text at high resolution to film or on long sheets of photographic paper to ensure smooth crisp typography.

Indexed color Uses a maximum of 256 colors to represent a full-color image.

Inkjet printer A type of printer that sprays ink from nozzles as the nozzles pass over the paper to create full-color images from overlapping dots of color.

Input The information a user sends to the computer; for example, utilizing a keyboard and mouse.

Integrated circuit A circuit whose every part is made of silicon, not just the transistor itself; it makes possible mass-produced circuit boards and the miniaturization of the embedded transistors.

Intensity The chromatic purity of a color.

Interface message processors Communication equipment that manages network traffic flow. These were initially the minicomputers that connected nodes on the ARPANET to the network. They are known today as *routers*.

Interlaced CRTs *(cathode ray tube)* CRTs that scan in two passes, first scanning the even lines and then the odd lines, to create a single scan. They are typically used in home television sets.

Interlaced GIFs This option allows a low-resolution version of an image to appear in web browser while a higher resolution image is downloading. While interlacing increases file size, it can make downloading time seen shorter because an initial image appears quickly.

Interpolated resolution Additional pixels created by a scanner's software beyond the optical resolution the scanner can deliver.

Interpolation Creating new pixels by comparing existing pixels. See *Resampling*.

Inverse kinematics In 3-D animation, a sophisticated kind of linked motion where a chain of actions can be initiated at either end of a chain of links.

IrDA (Infrared Data Association) Port for wireless infrared devices such as keyboards, mice, and printers.

IRIS printers Extremely sophisticated inkjet printers capable of producing fine art prints on any smooth material up to 35 × 47 inches.

ISA (Industry Standard Architecture) Type of bus developed by IBM for their first PCs with an eight-bit transfer rate.

ISDN (Integrated Services Digital Networking) Service that has the ability to deliver two simultaneous connections that allow voice, data, and video to be transmitted digitally through a single conventional phone line.

ITU (International Telecommunications Union) Organization created by the United Nations to coordinate and standardize international telecommunications.

Jacquard loom Weaving machine invented in the early 1800s by Joseph-Marie Jacquard that was a forerunner of punch-card computing systems. Patterns were mechanically controlled by a set of boards with punched holes.

JANET (Joint Academic Network) Organization formed in 1984 to serve the entire academic community with Internet connections and not just selected scholars.

Java A powerful programming language with the ability to create actual applications or applets for insertion into a Web page as well as stand-alone applications. It can also run the programs it creates on PC, Mac, and Unix computers.

JavaScript A programming language that can be embedded in an HTML document to open a range of possible interactive features. It allows you to embed special effects, open new message windows, perform calculations, write interactive games, and more.

JPEG (Joint Photographic Experts Group) An image compression format introduced in 1991 to compress 24-bit images/photographs. A lossy compression scheme with high compression capabilities, it is commonly used to prepare photographic images for Web use.

Justified Aligns text with the left and right sides of a text block.

Kerning Adjusts the amount of space between two type characters.

Keyframe animation See *Cel animation*.

Keyframes In animation, moments of important changes in action.

Kilobyte 1,024 bytes.

L*A*B* color An international standard for color measurement, renamed *CIE L*A*B** in 1976. Designed to be device independent, L*A*B* color has a lightness component (L), and two chromatic A and B channels. The A channel controls the color from green to red and the B channel controls the color from blue to yellow. *CIE L*A*B** is often the internal color model used to convert images from one color model to another.

Lathing In 3-D modeling, a simple shape is spun around its center to create a new object with volume. For example, a swept right triangle would create a cone. Also called *sweeping*.

Layers Separate levels where elements of an image can be placed. Each layer is independent of other layers and can be modified separately.

LCD (liquid crystal display) A monitor that utilizes liquid crystal cells and polarizing filters instead of electron beams and phosphors to create an image.

Leading (pronounced "ledding") Refers to the space between lines of type. In a word processing program, a simple form of leading might be to choose between single or double spacing.

Line scans Crisp, one-bit black and white images with no gray values.

Linear Usually refers to an image-editing program's brightness and contrast controls which adjust highlight, midtone, and shadow values at the same time. Linear controls have the potential to remove information in shadows or highlights that cannot be recovered.

Linear–array digital camera back A digital photographic attachment for traditional cameras, which contains a single row of sensors that work much like a flatbed scanner and record directly into the computer.

Line-mode browser Text-based World Wide Web browser.

Local bus A bus connecting a processor to memory, usually on the same circuit board, in order to speed up transfer of information. *PCI* is one current example of a local bus.

Lossless compression Refers to an image that is compressed and can be opened with no loss of any of the information it originally had. Traditional GIF files are an example of a lossless compression scheme.

Lossy compression Discards or loses information as the file is compressed. When the file is opened from its com-

pressed state, that information cannot be regained. A JPEG file is an example of a format using lossy compression.

Lpi (Lines per inch) The unit in which halftone frequency is measured for reproducing continuous-tone images.

Machine cycle The four steps that the CPU carries out for each instruction: fetch, decode, execute, and store.

Mapping In 3-D modeling, adding a surface or skin to a wireframe model. This can include the addition of colors, patterns, materials, and textures, as well as properties like shininess and transparency. Also known as assigning material attributes to an object.

Mark 1 The Automatic Sequence Controlled Calculator developed at Harvard with the assistance of IBM engineers in 1943. The first truly automatic computing machine, it was fifty-one-feet long, eight-feet tall, and weighed five tons. Information was fed into it with rolls of paper tape.

Mask When you make a selection within an image, the area of the image that is not selected is protected (masked) from whatever changes are about to be made to the image. Selections are often saved as masks in a new alpha channel or even converted to paths and stored for future use.

Mechanical In traditional graphic design, camera-ready paste-up of type, graphics, and other elements.

Megabyte 1,024 kilobytes, or approximately one million bytes.

Megahertz One megahertz (MHz) is equal to 1,000,000 clock ticks (cycles) per second.

Megapixel One million pixels.

Microprocessor A computer chip that has combined on it all the arithmetic and logic circuits necessary to do calculations. The first was originally designed for calculators by Intel engineer Ted Hoff in 1971. Also known as an integrated circuit.

MIDI (Musical Instrument Digital Interface) A type of sound file that uses prerecorded instrumental sounds that are resident in the memory of a sound card. It encodes data for recording and playing musical instruments digitally. In addition, it is a port for attaching a digital musical instrument, such as a piano keyboard, to the computer.

MILNET Internet system for military use only.

Mixing Layering sounds on top of one another.

Model sheet A guide to a character created by the lead animator for the other animators. Each character is drawn at various angles. Colors and costumes are carefully detailed.

Modem A device for communication over telephone or cable lines which modulates or alternates between two different tones to represent the zeroes and ones of computer language.

Modules In 3-D software, add-on packages that handle complex tasks, such as light in fog, or provide special tools. Also known as *plug-ins*.

Moiré patterns A pattern of visible "waves" caused by reproducing superimposed halftones or halftones with improperly aligned screen angles.

Monospace text A font in which all characters occupy the same amount of space.

Moore's Law A graph drawn in 1965 by Gordon Moore, one of the founders of Intel, that showed that the capacity of memory chips would double roughly every eighteen months while the cost of producing them would be cut by half.

Morphing Tweens where one image progressively changes smoothly into another.

Mosaic The first true Web browser, which transformed the Internet from a text-based environment to one with colors and images. It was created in 1993 by a group of computer science students at the University of Illinois, led by Marc Andreessen.

Motherboard Primary circuit board where many of the most critical elements of a computer are located. It is the nerve center of the computer, connecting to the power supply and distributing electricity to all the other parts of the computer.

Motion path In animation, a line drawn to guide an object, light, or camera's movement.

Motion capturing In 3-D animation, recording live-action movement digitally and then translating it into an animated sequence with computer software.

Multiplane camera An animation camera that creates a more convincing sense of depth by varying the focus on different layers of a scene as it zooms in and out. This was first used by Disney Studios.

Multisession A CD writing system capable of writing additional data to a disk at a later time.

Natural media software A program designed to recreate traditional drawing and painting tools, like pencils, chalk, crayons, watercolor, and oil paints; another name for digital painting software.

Nearest neighbor Interpolation method that samples a single pixel and then duplicates it.

Nodes Network processing locations. For example, the University of California at Los Angeles, Stanford Research Institute (SRI), the University of California at Santa Barbara, and the University of Utah were the first nodes on the ARPANET. Each of the nodes had a unique address that would identify it to other computers.

Noninterlaced A kind of display that paints every line on the screen in sequence as it scans from top to bottom. The faster the scan rate, the less flicker will be apparent.

NSFNET Network developed by the National Science Foundation (NSF) to replace *ARPANET* as the main government network linking universities and research facilities.

NUBUS Bus developed by Apple for their Macintosh II.

NURBS Non-uniform rational b-splines. In 3-D modeling, a special kind of *spline* designed for modeling organic forms. NURBS splines have adjustable weights attached to each control point so you can increase or reduce the impact of any change by individual control points.

Object-oriented software Another name for *vector illustration* programs.

OEM Original equipment manufacturers.

Onion skin In traditional animation, semi-transparent pages which allow one to see earlier drawings on other frames. In animation software, ghosts of images in previous frames.

Opacity The degree of transparency of a color or image.

Open architecture A computing system whose specifications are made public. It allows computer makers to utilize components purchased from other manufacturers.

Open path In vector illustration, a line with endpoints that are not connected.

Operating system Software that runs the programs and controls all the components of a computer. For PC users, it will be either Microsoft Windows or Linux. Macintosh owners use one of the versions of Mac OS.

Ordered list In Web design, a numbered list.

Orphan Word or short line of text at the end of a paragraph carried to the top of a page or column.

Out of gamut Colors that can be approximated on a computer screen but not printed accurately using the CMYK color ink set. Part of preparing an image for print is the process of "correcting" out-of-gamut colors, usually by reducing their intensity or contrast.

Packet switching A method of dividing data into packets or pieces before they are sent across a network to another computer. Separate packets, each with part of a complete message, can be transmitted individually, even following different routes before arriving at their final destination. They are reassembled back into a complete message at their destination.

Panning A slow movement across a wide scene by a camera, usually used at a distance from the main subjects.

Pantone A professional standard color library with specific CMYK mixtures used for choosing *spot colors*.

Papyrus A reed found in Egypt, which was slit, then peeled and soaked in water. The flattened reeds were bonded under pressure to form a writing surface.

Parallel ports An interface typically found on the back of a computer used for printers and external storage devices such as Zip drives and scanners.

Parallel processing Processors that work simultaneously rather than sequentially. A method to speed computer processing.

Parent-child relationships In 3-D animation, a kind of linked motion where moving one part causes a second to move.

Particle systems In 3-D software, a kind of *procedural modeling* (either as a special feature or *plug-in*) which generates realistic special effects like smoke, fire, fog, clouds, and explosions. These systems eliminate the need to individually animate countless elements.

Pascaline Wheel calculator invented around 1640 by Blaise Pascal. Calculations are made by rotating eight metal dials linked together by gears in a box.

Paste-up In traditional graphic design, where text and images used in a design are cut up and pasted down on a piece of white mounting board.

Path (1) In vector illustration, a straight line that connects between points, creating forms that are always sharp and clear. All forms are built with *paths* composed of anchor points and the lines between them. There are two kinds of paths: *open* and *closed*. This is also known as a *stroke*. (2) In a digital layout and design program, the accumulation of line segments or curves to be filled or overwritten with text.

PCI (Peripheral Component Interconnect) A computer bus common to both PC and Macintosh computers. The PCI bus can transfer data at speeds of up to 132MB per second and have the ability to perform certain tasks independently of the CPU.

PCL A printer control language developed by Hewlett-Packard to support various printing tasks, including graphics, scalable fonts, vector printing descriptions, and bidirectional printing.

PDF (portable document format) A *PostScript* file that has saved an entire design, including typography, fonts, layout information, graphics, and photographs.

PDL (page description language) Controls the formatting and layout of a printed page.

Persistence of vision A visual phenomenon on which the illusion of animation depends. Because we see images for a split-second longer than they are actually in front of us, a series of pictures drawn in sequence appear to be one continuous picture in motion.

Phong shading In 3-D modeling, a complex form of shading conceived by Phong Bui Toung at the University of Utah in 1974 that smoothes the polygons of a wireframe pixel by pixel and creates realistic highlights on shaded objects. It is also known as *specular shading*.

Picture boxes Shapes that act as placeholders for photographs or other art.

Piezo-electric A printing technology that uses a piezo crystal (a thin section of a crystal which oscillates when voltage is applied) behind the ink reservoir. When electrical current is applied to the piezo crystal, it flexes, forcing ink out of the nozzle.

Pits and lands The method of storage used in compact discs. A land represents a one and a pit represents a zero. A laser reads a CD by distinguishing a pit and a land by the shift in position of the reflected laser light that occurs when the beam hits the surface.

Pixels Picture elements; an individual point of light on the computer's monitor.

Platen A kind of pressure plate in early printing presses used to make firm and even contact between the paper and type.

Platform independent Software that runs on any computing system.

Plotters Large-format printers with moving pens that make linear images on rolls of paper.

Plug and play An automated installation process used to connect peripherals to a computer so each new component runs more or less effortlessly when plugged in.

Plug-ins Add-on packages that increase a software package's capabilities. They usually handle complex tasks, such as light in fog in 3-D software, or provide special tools. They are also known as *modules*.

PMT (photomultiplier tube) Used in *drum scanners*, these extremely sensitive tubes are capable of sensing very low levels of light and are able to amplify them into electronic signals that can be converted to digital information.

Polygon mesh In 3-D modeling, a series of connected polygons with which objects are constructed.

Ports Sockets that permit external devices to be attached to the computer.

PostScript A page description language developed by Adobe Systems, Inc. to describe the appearance of text, graphics, and images in a device-independent way.

POTS Abbreviation for Plain Old Telephone Service, a term used to describe a connection to an Internet Service Provider through a telephone modem.

PPI (pixels per inch) A method to describe screen resolution, which also refers to image size in pixels.

Primitives In 3-D modeling, basic 3-D geometrical shapes supplied by the animation program; for example, cubes, spheres, cylinders, and cones.

Print to file A *PostScript* description of a designed page created as a file. It contains all color, font description, image and layout information needed to print an accurate representation of your document.

Procedural modeling In 3-D modeling, software that utilizes formulas that take into account the randomness of natural phenomena; for example, fractal geometry.

Process colors Another name for cyan, yellow, magenta, and black.

Progressive JPEGs An interlaced or progressive image that appears on a Web page as a series of images. It starts with a very low-resolution, blocky image that appears quickly, then successively as more defined images, until the image appears in full resolution.

Proofing Reviewing a document or design for errors before it is actually printed.

Proportionally spaced text Text where the space each letter occupies is different and can be adjusted for maximum readability.

Protocol Formal set of rules determining the way in which data can be transmitted across networks.

PUSH technology Technology that broadcasts or pushes information to you on your computer screen; for example, stock market tickers that pop up.

RAM (Random Access Memory) Fast, short-term memory used by the computer for holding data and programs as you work. It sends information to the computer's CPU at high speed so there is a minimum amount of time the processor must wait for it. Unlike *ROM*, RAM can be read and written to.

Raster Bitmap images that use a grid of small squares known as pixels to represent images.

Ray tracing In 3-D modeling, a complex form of shading that recreates the reflections of light and color that we use to see objects in the real world. A line of light is traced from the light source to every pixel of an object and then bounced to the camera as a light ray.

Refresh rate Determines how many times each second a scan occurs on a monitor.

Remap Shifting values within an image to correct for poor contrast, or an image that is too light or dark.

Removable hard disks Disk storage systems with removable media that have much larger capacities than a standard floppy disk.

Renderfarm A room full of networked workstations, that share the chore of rendering the complicated models, scenes, and action of 3-D animation.

Rendering The final stage in 3-D modeling and animation—the computer generation of a finished scene from the viewer's point of view. In 3-D software, a bitmapped image or animated sequence created from the wireframe forms, the mapped colors and textures, as well as the lights, shadows, reflections, and any special effects.

RenderMan A photorealistic digital rendering software system created by Pixar Studios.

Resampling An approach to interpolating new data. Resampling occurs when you make an image larger or smaller by adding or deleting pixels. This changes the file size accordingly.

Resizing Allows you to move pixels further apart or closer together in order to make an image larger or smaller. This will change the effective size and dpi of an image but will not create or eliminate pixels like resampling does.

Resolution-independent graphics Another name for vector graphics. No matter how much or how many times vector images are resized, their edges will remain smooth and distinct because the change is made mathematically.

Reversed text Creates white text on whatever color background you are using.

RGB (red, green, and blue) The primary colors of a computer monitor; also known as additive colors.

RGB mode The default color model in most image-editing programs. In RGB mode, the visual spectrum is created by projected light, mixing the three visual primary colors to create white.

ROM (Read-Only Memory) Relatively slow, permanent memory that can only be read, not written to (changed).

Rotoscope An animation aid invented by the Fleischer brothers, which transfers live action on film to drawn ones for animation.

Rubber stamp tool Designed for duplicating portions of an image from one location to another. Information from a sample point is copied to a destination point, and thus, *cloned.*

SAGE (Semi-Automatic Ground Environment) Air defense system of the mid-1950s designed to visually track Soviet aircraft near U.S. airspace. The first interactive computer system with vector graphics.

Sampled sound Sound made with digital recording equipment; for example, speaking into a microphone connected to a sound card. Among the standard sampling file formats are WAV (PCs), AIF (Macintosh), AU (Sun), and MP3.

Sampling (1) Selecting a color already in an image by clicking on it with the eyedropper tool. (2) Selecting a portion of a sound file.

Satellite modems Satellite network systems that communicate with computers via connections of coaxial cable attached to a satellite dish mounted outside the home.

Saturation The intensity or degree of a color's purity.

Scalable architecture A concept where a family of computers all share accessories and use the same language, increasing the capacity of a company's computers without replacing the whole system.

Scaling Resizing.

Script (1) In animation, the outline of the basic story from beginning to end, along with a description of the characters; also known as a *treatment.* (2) In programming, a command in a computer language.

SCSI (Small Computer Systems Interface) (pronounced "**scuzzy**") A fast bus standard used to connect peripheral devices, including hard drives, to computers.

Secondary storage A storage method that holds information even after the power to the computer has been turned off.

Sectors On a hard or floppy disk, segments of the *tracks*. Each sector can hold 512 bytes of data.

Selection A determined limited area that is isolated from the rest of the image, either to limit work to that area; to protect (or *mask* it); or to choose it for cutting, copying, or moving.

Semiconductor A material that conducts electricity only under special conditions; for example, silicon used in manufacturing *transistors*.

Shade A hue plus the addition of black to lower both value and intensity.

Shading In 3-D modeling, applying surfaces with color and tone to a wireframe model.

Shadow mask A perforated metal screen (typically made of Invar, an alloy that resists expansion and distortion as the shadow mask gets hot) that lies just inside the monitor tube and in front of the phosphor layer to ensure that the three electron beams only strike the correct phosphor dots.

SIMM (single inline memory module) A preassembled unit of RAM chips on a circuit board that must be installed in pairs.

Sketchpad A drawing system created in 1962 by Ivan Sutherland, which utilized vector software and a light pen for drawing on a monitor. Conceptually, it was the foundation for all future vector-drawing programs. Often called the beginning of computer graphics because for the first time images were created by hand rather than by mathematical programs.

Skewing Shifting a form at an angle.

Slide scanners Digitizers that provide quality scans from transparent film materials.

Smooth point In vector illustration, a kind of anchor point made with the pen tool. It is used for drawing continuous curves, as in rolling hills versus a collection of waves.

Smooth textured In 3-D programs, a viewing mode that shows each sculptural form in color as well as how it is lit.

Solid-state A kind of electrical device with all solid working parts.

Sound cards Special cards that convert audio input in two ways. First, they can convert input from the computer itself or from other sources into the analog format utilized by speakers. Second, they can digitize analog input, for example, from a microphone, so the sound can be edited in the computer.

Sound processing Editing sounds with filters; for example, adding echoes or changing the pitch.

Sound wavegraph In sound-editing software, how each recorded sound is pictured. The graph shows the wave itself, the length of the sound over time, and the wave's *amplitude*.

Specify type Communicating to the typesetter all of the type characteristics for a specific printing job. This is also known as "spec'ing" type.

Spi (samples per inch) A measure of scan resolution based upon the number of samples taken in the scanning process.

Spline-based modeling In 3-D modeling, individually editing the curved *splines* in a wireframe.

Splines Vector-based curves in 3-D modeling; for example, *Bézier*, B-splines, and *NURBS*.

Spot colors Special premixed solid colors used in addition to the process colors or independently to emphasize or create a point of interest on the page.

Spot lighting A very focused light, emitted from one point and directed at another, usually as a cone of light. Spotlights create strong shadows and very concentrated lit areas. They are also known as key lighting.

Sprite See *Animated symbol*.

Static IP addresses A permanent network address.

Stenciling A special mask that allows drawing only inside a selection.

Stored-program concept A method to speed computer processing. Instead of computers depending on instructions fed in with tapes or punch cards, programs are stored in the computer itself and only the data is fed in.

Storyboard In film, video, and animation, a storyboard shows the key moments of an animation in a series of small boxes with written notes below. Each major change of action is illustrated.

Stripe pitch The distance between stripes of the same color on an aperture grill monitor.

Stripping film In traditional printing, positioning and assembling negatives from a copy camera or typesetter in their proper placement, orientation, and registration.

Stroke In vector illustration, the linear portion of the path and its characteristics. In an *open path*, it is the line itself. In a *closed path*, it is the outline around a shape. A line or outline's width, color, and style are all part of its stroke.

Superscalar The ability of a CPU to run two or even more pipelines that rapidly process many instructions at the same time.

Swatch A small rectangle of color, usually part of a collection found in the swatches panel in digital media programs.

Sweeping In 3-D modeling, a simple shape is spun around its center to create a new object with volume. For example, a swept right triangle would create a cone. This is also called *lathing*.

Sympathetic movement One of the laws of animated action, where a fast moving object will change its form by stretching to accentuate its path.

Synching Methods of integrating soundtracks with animated action.

Synthesized sound Sound that is computer generated from formulas. The most common format is MIDI. Like another mathematical format, vector graphics, synthesized music results in small file sizes.

System clock See *clock tick*.

T1 lines Fast Internet connection capable of handling 1.5 *Mbps* (megabytes per second).

T3 lines Very fast Internet connection capable of handling 45Mbps. These lines are typically leased at a high monthly rate and serve many individual users.

Tables Method in *HTML* of organizing the design of a Web page using rows and columns.

TCP/IP (Transmission Control Protocol/Internet Protocol) The protocol the military adopted as a "defense standard" in 1980 for transferring information over their network. Ultimately, this helped made the Internet possible.

Telnet Type of terminal emulation program for communicating with other computers connected to the Internet. The protocol also allows for interactive text between computers.

Text block A space (typically rectangular) drawn by the user in which text can be entered.

Texture mapping In 3-D modeling, a time-saving form of mapping where a bitmap image is wrapped around a wireframe form. For example, wrapping an image of tree bark around a column to make a tree trunk.

Thaumatrope A nineteenth-century toy that created animated effects by utilizing the *persistence of vision*. It was a round disk with different pictures on each side and a string threaded through it. A child would hold both ends of the string and spin the disk quickly. The pictures on both sides would appear together.

Thermal wax transfer Printing technology that uses small heating elements to melt dots of cyan, magenta, yellow, and black wax-based ink onto paper or transparency film to create an image.

Three-dimensional animation The movement in virtual space of 3-D models.

Three-dimensional modeling The construction of digital objects that can be viewed at any angle.

TIFF (tagged image file format) A file format for high-resolution bitmapped images.

Tile Small image with a small file size used to create a Web page's background. Web browsers automatically repeat a tile to form a seamless background for the whole page, eliminating the need to download a page-sized image.

Timeline In animation and some authoring software, a panel where one works with frames and layers. Frames are numbered and represented in time sequence, layers in the order of their stacking. The timeline is also where soundtracks are synchronized with images, with each track appearing as a separate layer.

Tints A hue plus the addition of white to raise (lighten) the value of the color. This can also diminish its intensity.

Tracing In some software, a pale version of an image on a separate bottom layer, which appears as if it is below a sheet of tracing paper. The pale image is only for tracing; it is not part of the final image.

Trackball Input device that is, essentially, an upside-down mouse with a larger ball, which is rolled between your fingers or under your palm.

Tracking (1) In layout and design, tracking adjusts the amount of space between letters and words. (2) In 3-D animation, keeping the camera dolly at a set distance from an object as it moves along a scene.

Tracks On a hard or floppy disk, tracks are thin concentric bands forming a full circle. They contain the *sectors*, each of which can hold 512 bytes of data.

Transistors Devices that control the flow of electricity. They require very little electricity to operate, create much less heat, and are much smaller and longer lasting than the vacuum tubes they replaced. Invented by John Bardeen, Walter Brittain, and William Schockley at Bell Telephone Laboratories in 1947.

Trapping Safeguards against the common, small degree of misregistration in the printing process by slightly overlapping adjacent colors.

Treatment See *Script*.

Tri-color cartridge A single-print cartridge holding separate cyan, yellow, and magenta inks.

Tweener In traditional animation studios, the role of creating the in-between frames for the keyframes created by lead animators.

Tweening Drawing the in-between frames between keyframes. In digital animation, software automates this time-consuming process.

Type color The overall tone of the text on the page. The size and style of the typeface, the amount of space around the characters, and the space between the lines all affect typographic color.

Type founding The mechanical production of cast type, which made the printing of books possible.

UNIVAC (Universal Automatic Computer) Manufactured by Remington-Rand in the early 1950s, the most technologically advanced computer of its time and the first commercially successful mainframe. For the first time, data was stored on magnetic, rather than paper, tape.

Unordered list In Web design, a nonnumbered list with bullets.

Upload Information that is sent from a personal computer to an *ISP* (Internet Service Provider).

USB (Universal Serial Bus) *Bus* used primarily for installing devices outside the computer. External devices such as keyboards, CD-ROMs, scanners, printers, and other peripherals can be plugged directly into a USB port on the computer.

Value The lightness or darkness of a color.

Vector animation A method of creating animations, which utilizes vector forms rather than bitmapped ones. Often used for Web pages because vector graphics result in much smaller files than bitmapped images.

Vector illustration Image-making that is geometry based, rather than pixel based. Images are made up of geometric descriptions of points, lines, and shapes and their relative positions. Because a vector file is composed with mathematical equations, much less information is stored compared to a bitmap image. Images and fonts can also be resized without loss of quality.

Vectorscope Early computer monitor attached to a mainframe computer.

Viewing plane In 3-D programs, a rectangular field that shows what the audience will ultimately see in the frame.

Viewports In 3-D programs, the windows for creating and editing forms with views of the object at different angles. There are usually four, with views from the front, top, bottom, and either left or right side.

VRML (Virtual Reality Modeling Language) A Web browser programming language for creating interactive 3-D experiences on Web pages. Special plug-ins are usually required for Web browsers.

WAIS (Wide Area Information System) Method of supported document retrieval from Internet databases through full-text search. WAIS also supported listings of directories of servers, which could then be searched for a particular source by name or topic.

Wavetable synthesis Sound synthesis method that uses samples of actual instruments and sounds to create the music dictated by the application.

Web-safe colors 216 specific colors which can be used safely for all Web applications without fear of the colors changing from one application to another.

Widow Word or short line of text sitting alone at the end of a paragraph.

Wipe In film and animation, where one scene is cleared off the screen at an angle by the next scene.

Wireframe mode In 3-D programs, a viewing mode where objects are displayed like a mesh sculpture wrapped in netting. Each line and vertice is represented and the overall form can be seen.

Work schedule See *Exposure sheet.*

WORM (Write Once, Read Many) Compact disc system with a chemical coating that allows areas of that coating to be rendered either reflective or nonreflective by a laser, mimicking the lands and pits of commercial CD discs.

WYSIWYG (pronounced "wizzy-wig") "What you see is what you get." Refers to programs where what one sees on the screen is quite close to the printed or final document.

Xerox PARC Xerox Corporation's Palo Alto Research Center, founded in 1970. Its research scientists pioneered many of the foundations of personal computing today. Their slogan was "The easiest way to predict the future is to invent it."

Zoetrope A nineteenth-century toy that created animated effects by utilizing the *persistence of vision*. The toy was an open metal cylinder with evenly spaced slits, resting on a pedestal. A strip of paper with drawings was placed inside and the cylinder was spun rapidly. By looking through the slits as they rotated, a child could see the drawings move in sequence.

Credits

71 (top) Reprinted as a courtesy of Xerox Corporation

(bottom) Reprinted as a courtesy of Xerox Corporation

72 Handbook of Advertising Art Production by Sclemmer, ©. Reprinted by permission of Pearson Education, Inc., Upper Saddle River, NJ.

74 Reprinted as a courtesy of Xerox Corporation

77 Reprinted with permission from Creo, Inc. (www.creo.com)

78 (top) Reprinted as a courtesy of Xerox Corporation

(bottom) Reprinted as a courtesy of Xerox Corporation

79 Reprinted as a courtesy of Xerox Corporation

82 AT&T Archives

92 (top) Research Library, The Getty Research Institute, Los Angeles (940003)

(bottom) Research Library, The Getty Research Institute, Los Angeles (940003)

93 (top) Reprinted with permission from Computer History Museum

(middle) Reprinted with permission from Boeing Company

94 (top) Reprinted with permission from Ken Knowlton

(middle) Reprinted with permission from A. Michael Knoll

(bottom) Reprinted with permission of MIT Lincoln Laboratory, Lexington, Massachusetts

95 Used with permission from SRI International and Special Collections, Standford University Libraries

96 (left) Reprinted with permission from Andrew Burbanks

(right) Reprinted with permission from Andrew Burbanks

98 (top) "Mona/Leo," Lillian F. Schwartz. Copyright © 1986, Computer Creations Corp. Reprinted with permission. (www.lillian.com)

(middle) Reprinted with permission from Myron Krueger

(bottom) Yalkut, Jud. "The Electronic Super Highway: Nam June Paik in the Nineties." 1995. Courtesy Eletronic Arts Intermix (EAI), New York

99 (bottom) Courtesy Experimental Television Center

101 Courtesy of the Palo Alto Research Center (PARC)

102 © Apple Computer, Inc. Use with permission. All rights reserved. Apple and the Apple logo are registered trademarks of Apple Computer, Inc.

103 © Apple Computer, Inc. Use with permission. All rights reserved. Apple and the Apple logo are registered trademarks of Apple Computer, Inc.

105 (left) Transjovian Pipeline, 1979. Reprinted with permission from David Em. Photograph by James Seligman

(right) Photograph by James Seligman. Reprinted with permission from David Em

106 Reprinted with permission from James F. Blinn

109 Reprinted with permission from Infogrames Interactive, Inc, All rights reserved

110 All Myst, Riven and D'ni images and text © Cyan Worlds, Inc. All rights reserved Myst ® Riven ® and D'ni ® Cyan Worlds, Inc.

111 Courtesy of the National Center for Supercomputing Applications (NCSA) and the Board of Trustees of the University of Illinois

112 (top) © Peter Menzel

(bottom) Reprinted with permission from Fakespace Systems (www.fakespacesystems.com)

116 (bottom) Bodleian Library

117 (top) Reprinted with permission from Dartmouth College Library

(middle) Bible, Old Testament, Book of Ester (Hebrew). 8th Century, A.D. Melbert B. Cary, Jr. Graphic Arts Collection, Rochester Institute of Technology.

(bottom) Reprinted with permission from Staatliche Museen zu Berlin—Preussischer, Kulturbesitz, Antikensammlung

120 (bottom) Getty Images Inc.—Hulton Archive Photos

121 (top) Handbook of Advertising Art Production by Sclemmer, ©. Reprinted by permission of Pearson Education, Inc., Upper Saddle River, NJ

(bottom, left) Encyclopedia of Graphic Communications by Romano©. Reprinted by permission of Pearson Education, Inc., Upper Saddle River, NJ

180 Reprinted with permission Corel Corporation 2002

181 Reprinted with permission from Chet Phillips (www.chetart.com)

182 (top) Reprinted with permission Corel Corporation 2002

(bottom) Reprinted with permission Corel Corporation 2002

185 Reprinted with permission Corel Corporation 2002

186 Reprinted with permission Corel Corporation 2002

194 Adobe product screen shot reprinted with permission from Adobe Systems Incorporated

197 Designed by Leslie Cabarga, (www.flashfonts.com)

206 Reprinted with permission from Infogrames, Inc. All rights reserved

208 (top) Library of Congress

(bottom) Reprinted with permission from The North Carolina School of Science and Mathematics

209 (top) Inkwell Images

(bottom) The John Canemaker Animation Collection: Fales Library & Special Collection, New York University

210 Inkwell Images/Fleischer Studios

212 Photo courtesy of Don Bluth Films ©2002

214 (top) Reprinted with permission of Deneger Japanese Fine Prints

(bottom) Used with permission from Tezuka Productions Co., Ltd.

215 © Pixar Animation Studios

223 (top) Reprinted with permission from Photo-Sonics, Inc.

226 Created by Joe Shields, reprinted with permission from Joe Cartoon (www.joecartoon,com)

230 (top) Reprinted with permission from Daniel Cerasale

(bottom) Images are taken from GETTING STARTED WITH 3D. © 1998 by Janet Ashford and John Odam. # and published by Peachpit Press. Reprinted by permission of Pearson Education, Inc.

231 (top) Images are taken from GETTING STARTED WITH 3D. © 1998 by Janet Ashford and John Odam. # and published by Peachpit Press. Reprinted by permission of Pearson Education, Inc.

232 (left) Images are taken from GETTING STARTED WITH 3D. ©1998 by Janet Ashford and John Odam. # and published by Peachpit Press. Reprinted by permission of Pearson Education, Inc.

(right) Images are taken from GETTING STARTED WITH 3D. © 1998 by Janet Ashford and John Odam. # and published by Peachpit Press. Reprinted by permission of Pearson Education, Inc.

(bottom) Images are taken from GETTING STARTED WITH 3D. © 1998 by Janet Ashford and John Odam. # and published by Peachpit Press. Reprinted by permission of Pearson Education, Inc.

233 (top) Images are taken from GETTING STARTED WITH 3D. © 1998 by Janet Ashford and John Odam. # and published by Peachpit Press. Reprinted by permission of Pearson Education, Inc.

(bottom) Images are taken from GETTING STARTED WITH 3D. © 1998 by Janet Ashford and John Odam. # and published by Peachpit Press. Reprinted by permission of Pearson Education, Inc.

234 (top) Created by Daniel Cerasale, used with permission

(middle) Images are taken from GETTING STARTED WITH 3D. © 1998 by Janet Ashford and John Odam. # and published by Peachpit Press. Reprinted by permission of Pearson Education, Inc.

(bottom) Images are taken from GETTING STARTED WITH 3D. © 1998 by Janet Ashford and John Odam. # and published by Peachpit Press. Reprinted by permission of Pearson Education, Inc.

235 Reprinted with permission from Richard F. Voss

236 (top) Reprinted with permission from Autodesk, Inc.

(bottom) ©TAMCB Guggenheim Bilbao Museoa. Photographer: All Rights Reserved. Total or partial preproduction is prohibited

237 (top) Viewpoint model reprinted with permission from Digimation (www.digimation.com)

(bottom) Images are taken from GETTING STARTED WITH 3D. © 1998 by Janet Ashford and John Odam. # and published by Peachpit Press. Reprinted by permission of Pearson Education, Inc.

238 Images are taken from GETTING STARTED WITH 3D. © 1998 by Janet Ashford and John Odam. # and published by Peachpit Press. Reprinted by permission of Pearson Education, Inc.

239 Images on are taken from GETTING STARTED WITH 3D. © 1998 by Janet Ashford and John Odam. # and published by Peachpit Press. Reprinted by permission of Pearson Education, Inc.

240 Images are taken from GETTING STARTED WITH 3D. © 1998 by Janet Ashford and John Odam. # and published by Peachpit Press. Reprinted by permission of Pearson Education, Inc.

242 Images are taken from GETTING STARTED WITH 3D. © 1998 by Janet Ashford and John Odam. # and published by Peachpit Press. Reprinted by permission of Pearson Education, Inc.

243 (top) Images are taken from GETTING STARTED WITH 3D. © 1998 by Janet Ashford and John Odam. # and published by Peachpit Press. Reprinted by permission of Pearson Education, Inc.

(bottom) Reprinted with permission from the archives of R/GA (www.rga.com)

244 Images are taken from GETTING STARTED WITH 3D. © 1998 by Janet Ashford and John Odam. # and published by Peachpit Press. Reprinted by permission of Pearson Education, Inc.

245 (left) Reprinted with permission from Northwest Research Associates, Inc. and Michael J. Gourley.

(right) Reprinted with permission from Northwest Research Associates, Inc. and Michael J. Gourley.

246 (top) Images are taken from GETTING STARTED WITH 3D. © 1998 by Janet Ashford and John Odam. # and published by Peachpit Press. Reprinted by permission of Pearson Education, Inc.

(bottom) Reprinted with permission from Autodesk, Inc.

247 (top) Reprinted with permission from Paul Kaiser (www.kaiserworks.com)

(bottom) Reprinted with permission from Paul Kaiser (www.kaiserworks.com)

249 Project by DigitalSpace Corporation. Designers: Stuart Gold/Jeremy Smith. Modelers: DM3D Studios

252 Burch/Cheswick map courtesy Lumeta Corp.

255 (bottom) Reprinted with permission from Ivan E. Suterland, Sun Microsystems, Inc.

257 (top) Reprinted with permission from BBN Technologies. Inc.

259 Handbook of Digital Publishing Vol II by Kleper, Michael L.,©. Reprinted by permission of Pearson Education, Inc. Upper Saddle River, NJ

261 Reprinted with permission from Andries van Dam

284 CERN/European Organization for Nuclear Research

Every effort was made to credit all images. Use of images without proper credit is unintentional.

Index

1973 Robert Meetcalfe creates Ethernet to link minicomputers at PARC

Westworld is first major film to utilize computer animation (2-D)

1974 Toshiba introduces the first 5.25 floppy disk drive

Dick Shoup and Alvy Ray Smith create SuperPaint, a prototype for all bitmap color paint systems

Doctoral candidate Ed Catmull writes his thesis on texture mapping

BYTE magazine is published

1975 Benoit Mandelbrot of France publishes A Theory of Fractal Sets after twenty years of research

Bui Toung Phong creates Phong shading, creating highlights on shaded objects

Bill Gates and Paul Allen found Microsoft and license BASIC to their first customer

Altair releases its first computer

1976 Steve Jobs and Steve Wozniak found the Apple Computer Company

Microprocessors are used to control still cameras

IBM announces ink-jet printing and the first laser printer

1979 Software Arts releases VisiCalc

Apple Computer engineers examine Xerox Palo GUI

Atari introduces coin-operated version of Asteroids

Turner Whitted develops ray-tracing for animation; renders take 24 hours per frame

George Lucas hires Edwin Catmull and Alvy Ray Smith to start Lucasfilm's special effects development division, later to become Pixar

Hayes markets its first modem

Cellular phones are tested in Japan and Chicago

1980 Nicholas Negroponte establishes the MIT Media Lab

The United States uses more than 1 million computers

Apple Computer introduces the Apple III

Radio Shack introduces its TRS-80 Color Computer

IBM hires Microsoft to develop an operating system (OS) for its personal computer (PC)

Phototypesetting can be done by laser

1981 BITNET is established to serve academic institutions

Japanese invent a camera with electronic storage

Sony announces the Compact Disc

1983 Autodesk introduces AutoCAD for the PC

Bill Reeves creates particle systems

The personal computer is Time's Man of the Year

Microsoft introduces Word 1.0

Total computers in the United States exceed 10 million

Jim Clark founds Silicon Graphics

Microsoft introduces the Microsoft Mouse

IBM releases its Personal Computer XT

1984 Dell Computer is founded in Austin, Texas

Apple introduces the Macintosh in a commercial during the Super Bowl

Sony and Phillips introduce the CD-ROM

Microtek introduces the first desktop halftone scanner

IBM introduces the PC AT

Hewlett-Packard introduces a desktop laser printer

The 3.5-inch diskette is introduced

Bill Kovacs releases Wavefront, 3-D animation for the workstation

1975

1980

1985

1977 Radio Shack announces the TRS-80

Doctoral candidate Jim Blinn creates bump mapping

Apple Computer introduces the Apple II

1978 Total computers in the United States exceed .5 million units

First major microcomputer bulletin board appears

5.25-inch floppy disk becomes the industry standard

Epson introduces its MX-80 dot matrix printer

450,000 transistors fit on a 1/4-inch square silicon chip

Hayes introduces the Smartmodem 300 with standard AT command set and releases a modem that transfers data at 1,200 bps

Xerox introduces a graphical Star workstation with the first GUI

Automobile manufacturers begin to install computer chips in cars

IBM introduces a PC with a Microsoft-developed OS

1982 Lotus Development is founded and introduces Lotus 1-2-3

Sun Microsystems is founded

PC Magazine publishes its first issue

Autodesk is founded

John Warnock of the University of Utah and Charles Geshchke found Adobe

Star Trek II: The Wrath of Khan's Genesis effect draws worldwide attention to 3D computer graphics

Disney's Tron has 235 scenes with computer animation

Hayes releases a 2,400 bps modem

1985 Adobe introduces PostScript printer language; WYSIWYG on the screen is what prints

Commodore Amiga 1000 introduces multimedia (graphics, sound, and video)

Aldus releases PageMaker

Gateway 2000 is founded in Sioux City, Iowa

CD-ROM can put 270,000 pages of text on a disc

Cellular telephones go into cars

Digital image processing is used for editing stills

Apple introduces the LaserWriter

1986 Number of computers in the United States exceeds 30 million

Aldus introduces the TIFF

Steve Jobs buys Pixar from Lucasfilm

1987 Hayes demonstrates the ISDN modem

Compuserve introduces the GIF format

Aldus introduces PageMaker for the PC

Microsoft releases Windows 2.0 and Works

1988 The United States uses 45 million PCs

Lucasfilm introduces morphing in *Willow*

Pixar patents RenderMan

1989 Computers in the United States exceed 50M units

More than 100 million computers are in use worldwide

Microsoft introduces Word for Windows

Pixar creates *Tin Toy*

PC manufacturers introduce the first 80486-based computers

Creative Labs introduces SoundBlaster

1990 Motorola introduces the 68040 microprocessor

Amiga releases Video Toaster for its computers

Autodesk introduces 3-D Studio for the PC

Adobe introduces Photoshop for the Mac

Microsoft releases Windows 3.0

The term Graphical User Interface (GUI) is used for the first time

1991 Sony, Philips, and Microsoft introduce CD-ROM-extended architecture

Most PC vendors introduce Notebook PCs

IBM releases OS/2 2.1

The World Wide Web is born

Number of host computers on Internet passes 1 million mark

Apple introduces Quicktime

Apple Computer launches the Newton MessagePad

Motorola begins shipping its PowerPC 601 processors

1993 NCSA develops the Mosaic browser at the University of Illinois

Broderbund releases the computer game Myst

Adobe makes Photoshop available for Windows

Wired magazine is launched

Gateway 2000 sells its millionth computer

50 World Wide Web (www) servers exist as of January

Pentium-based systems start shipping

1994 Apple Computer introduces Power Macintosh 6100/60

SGI and Nintendo create the Nintendo 64

Kodak releases its DC 40 Digital camera

Iomega introduces the Zip Drive

1996 DVD disks are introduced

33.6 kbps modems are introduced

CD-ReWritable (CD-RW) discs are introduced

Microsoft releases Windows NT 4.0

Bill Gates becomes the richest man in the United States

Intel introduces its 200 MHz Pentium processor

Deep Blue beats chess master Gary Kasparov in two chess matches

1997 Advanced Micro Devices (AMD) introduces the K6 processor with MMX instructions

Apple releases Mac OS 8.0

1998 Intel introduces the Celeron processor

Intel introduces the Slot 1 Pentium II

Motorola introduces the G4 processor

Microsoft releases Windows 98

America Online buys Netscape

1999 *Star Wars: Episode One* uses over 60 digital characters

Apple releases Mac OS 9

Intel introduces the Pentium III processor

AMD introduces the Athlon processor

1990

Logitech ships its 10 millionth mouse

Industrial Light and Magic creates special effects for *Terminator 2;* its computer morphing astonishes moviegoers

Linus Torvalds develops Linux

Apple develops QuickTime video compression

JPEG (Joint Photographic Experts Group) compression format is developed

Tim Berners-Lee at CERN develops the Web as a research tool

University of Minnesota develops Gopher

A cartoon, *Beauty and the Beast,* receives an Oscar nomination for best picture

1992 Microsoft ships Windows 3.1

Bill Gates is now the second richest man in the United States

Intel introduces PCI local-bus

1995

Industrial Light and Magic creates special effects for *Jurassic Park*

ID Software releases the computer game Doom

Aldus and Adobe merge

Apple ships Macintoshes using the PowerPC

Netscape Navigator browser software is released

1995 Intel introduces the Pentium Pro microprocessor

Sony introduces its Playstation

John Lasseter and Pixar release *Toy Story*, the first full-length computer generated feature film

Major U.S. dailies create national online newspaper network

Microsoft releases Windows 95

2000 – present

2000 AMD introduces its 1.1 GHz processor

Intel introduces its Pentium 4 1.5 GHz processor

Microsoft releases Windows 2000

2001 AMD introduces the XP, MP, 1.4 GHz Thunderbird processors

Intel introduces the 1.7-2.2 GHz Pentium 4 processor

2002 Lucasfilm releases the entirely digitally filmed *Star Wars: Episode Two*